Presentations with Persuasion

Kate Hatsy Thompson
Keith J. Thompson

Brady

New York   London   Toronto   Sydney   Tokyo   Singapore

Brady

Simon & Schuster, Inc.
15 Columbus Circle
New York, NY 10023

Manufactured in the United States of America

10 9 8 7 6 5 4 3 2 1

Library of Congress Cataloging-in-Publication Data

Thompson, Kate Hatsy.
    Presentations with Persuasion/Kate Hatsy Thompson and Keith Thompson.
        p.   cm.
    Includes index.
    1. Aldus Persuasion (Computer program)   2. Business presentations—
computer programs.   I. Thompson, Keith.   II. Title.
    HF5718.22.T46   1990
    808.5'1'02855369—dc20
    ISBN 0-13-106782-6   90-45597
                                            CIP

Acknowledgments

We have many people to thank for their contributions and support during the gestation and birth of this book. Susan Hunt, our editor at Brady Books, contributed her unerring critical judgment and patience throughout the project. Peter Polash, the father of Persuasion, read the manuscript and helped keep us honest. Mary Batterson and Laury Bryant of Aldus Public Relations provided beta software and support. Paul Parisi reviewed Chapters 17-19 and drew the technical illustrations that grace those chapters. Our families and friends reassured us during our darkest hours. Without all their help, our book would never have made it to press!

Dedication

For K.C. and H.A.T.—K.J.T.

Disclaimer

The authors and publisher of this book make no representations or warranties with respect to the accuracy or completeness of the contents hereof and specifically disclaim any implied warranties of merchantability or fitness for any particular purpose.

Trademarks

Contents

Introduction

Let's face it. Most of us would rather die than speak to a group. In fact, public speaking ranks first among human fears, above bankruptcy, bugs, heights, deep water, sickness, and death, according to some experts. Using effective visuals—whether slides, overheads, flip charts, or computer-based slide shows—to back up your presentation can help you overcome this nearly universal fear.

Fortifying your presentation with visuals won't just make you *feel* better. Studies have shown that visuals can make you appear better prepared, more professional, more credible, more influential, and more persuasive. Not only that, your audience is more likely to understand, remember, and agree with what you say.

In the "old days" (say, five years ago), preparing slides and overheads was daunting enough to discourage all but the most seasoned presenters from using them. For quick-and-dirty overheads, you could use a typewriter to create simple text slides, which you could then photostat onto clear acetate. But the results—text all in the same size (tiny) and same typeface (basic) and no graphics at all—were hardly impressive. Or you could take your notes and sketches to your art department (if you had one) and ask them to translate your ideas into visuals using "real" type and graphics. Or you could hire a professional slide service bureau to produce lavish color slides and charge you through the teeth for them.

As it has so many things, the personal computer has revolutionized the business of making presentation visuals. At first, people used word processors to create simple text slides and spreadsheet programs to produce graphs and charts. Next, page layout programs like Aldus PageMaker were pressed into service for their sophisticated typesetting capabilities. Most recently, a new breed of software—presentation programs—has refined and simplified the art of creating powerful visual aids.

Aldus Persuasion represents the state of the art of presentation software. With tools for building outlines that flow automatically into preformatted slides, for producing speaker notes and audience handouts, and for creating electronic slide shows on your computer screen or overhead projector, Persuasion lets you move from concept to finished presentation quickly, economically, and without sacrificing control over the creative process.

Paradoxically, Persuasion is both simple and complex—a key virture of well-designed software. This means you can use the program at different levels, depending on your needs and your skill. If you're new to Persuasion, you can take it out of the box and produce a basic presentation in an hour or so. But even if you've been using Persuasion for awhile, you're probably still discovering new features and techniques—especially if you've just upgraded to Persuasion 2.0 In fact, much of Persuasion's subtlety and power can elude even the seasoned user. We wrote this book because we think Persuasion is an excellent product and we wanted to help people—both newcomers and pros—use it even better.

What's In This Book

Unlike a novel, you don't have to read this book through from beginning to end in order to get the full experience. Instead, you can browse according to your needs and tastes. The book is divided into four parts, each focussing on a different aspect of producing presentations with Persuasion.

For basics, consult Part I, *Getting Started*. You'll find everything you need to get up and running fast—including a tutorial to guide you through creating and producing your first presentation. If you're new to Persuasion, begin here. If you've been working with Persuasion for awhile, or if you're upgrading to version 2.0, skim this section for new tidbits of information, then go on to Section II.

For in-depth information on all of Persuasion's many features, refer to Part II, *Working with Persuasion*. Tips, tricks, and caveats are woven throughout the fully-illustrated discussions of how to do everything from building an outline to preparing audience handouts.

Mastering the science of Persuasion is one thing; mastering the art of persuasive presentations is quite another. No matter how adept you become using Persuasion's rich array of tools, you'll need a thorough understanding of type, layout, and color in order to make your slides communicate effectively. Part III, *Behind the Scenes*, addresses key design issues ranging from selecting a legible typeface to choosing harmonious colors. A chapter on planning and delivering a presentation offers tips on everything from extension cords to room layout. Part III is recommended reading for everyone except design professionals.

And then, of course, there's producing your presentation. Part IV, *The Big Production*, includes chapters on overheads, slides, and on-screen slide shows, covering questions such as, What is PostScript and why is it important? Why don't the colors on my monitor match the colors on my overheads? How can I use my Macintosh SE for an on-screen slide show? Reading Part IV will suggest new production techniques, help you avoid disappointing and expensive misunderstandings, and ensure that what you see on your screen is what you get on your slides.

Part I ◆ Getting Started

Chapter 1

Installing Persuasion

Let's start at the very beginning. Before you can learn to use Persuasion 2.0 to create your first presentation, you'll need to set up your hardware equipment and software tools. To help you do that, this chapter is divided into two parts. The first part describes the hardware you'll need to run Persuasion, and the second part explains how to install Persuasion onto your computer's hard disk. If you're already all set up and ready to go, skim this chapter for tidbits of information you may have missed, and then go on to Chapter 2, *A Guided Tour*.

Set Up Your Equipment

With Persuasion, you can produce presentations ranging from simple black and white to complex color. There are two key questions you need to consider when choosing hardware:

- How much memory do you need?

- How much computing power do you need?

The answers to these questions depend on the kind of presentations you'll be producing. The following discussion of equipment is intended to help you build an optimum hardware setup for your particular presentation requirements.

If most of your presentations are relatively short—say 25 or fewer slides— the computing power of a Macintosh Plus or SE combined with 1 megabyte (MB) of memory will meet your needs. You'll still be able to produce longer presentations of up to 70 slides, but you may notice that your computer slows down as the number of slides increases.

If you routinely create presentations longer than 25 slides or with lots of charts, or if you want to run Persuasion under MultiFinder, we recommend increasing memory to 2 MB.

Tip: Consider dividing a longer presentation into two shorter presentations to optimize your computer's performance without upgrading your equipment.

When it comes to producing color presentations, you have a choice. You can use a black-and-white monitor to assign colors to slides; even though they won't display in color on your monitor, they will print in color on a color output device. Or, you can use a gray-scale or color monitor to see the shades or colors you're working with. A color or gray-scale monitor requires more computing power and memory than black and white because each pixel on the screen must hold much more information. A Macintosh SE/30 or a Macintosh II with a minimum of 2 MB of memory will provide that extra computing power. If you intend to produce long, lavish, color presentations with lots of charts, you'll be most comfortable with 4 MB of memory.

Table 1.1 summarizes our recommendations for minimum hardware configurations. For more information about monitors and output devices, see Part IV, *The Big Production*.

Table 1.1

Type of presentation	Minimum hardware configuration
Short presentations (25 slides or fewer) using a black-and-white monitor	Macintosh Plus or SE with 1 MB of memory
Longer presentations using a black-and-white monitor (or, to run Persuasion with MultiFinder)	Macintosh Plus or SE with 2 MB of memory
Short presentations using a color or gray-scale monitor	Macintosh SE/30 or II with 2 MB of memory
Long, complex presentations using a color or gray-scale monitor	Macintosh SE/30 or II with 4 MB of memory

Additionally, to run Persuasion, you'll need to check for the following:

- **Apple System file Version 4.2 (or later) and Finder file Version 6.0 (or later).** Be sure to use the most recent versions of Apple's System, Finder and other System documents on your Macintosh. And, make sure you have only one System folder, containing only one copy of the System and Finder file on your hard disk.

- **At least one output device driver.** When you get to the point of actually producing a presentation, you'll need an output driver for whatever output device you intend to use (laser printer, film recorder, or slide service bureau). The output driver is a file that tells Persuasion how to communicate with your output device.

  But, before that, just to run Persuasion, you'll need at least one driver —any driver—located in your System folder. Without it, you'll get an error message. (Since the Persuasion 2.0 Installer automatically installs a driver for the Autographix slide service, this shouldn't be a problem.)

Prepare for Installation

Check your Persuasion package. In addition to the manuals, you should have five disks labeled Disk 1 through Disk 5. For those of you who are curious, Table 1.2 shows what is on them.

Table 1.2

Disk	File or folder name	What it is
Disk 1	Aldus Installer/Utility	The application that automatically installs Persuasion 2.0
	COMPresenting Persuasion 2.0	A compressed presentation demonstrating Persuasion 2.0
	TeachText	An application that allows you to read various text files
	ReadMe	A text file containing news newer than the manuals
	Control File	A file that manages the installation process

(continued)

Disk 2	COMPersuasion 2.0	The compressed Persuasion 2.0 application
	COMAutographix	A compressed driver for the slide service Autographix
	COMAGXit!	A compressed utility for transmitting presentation files to the slide service Autographix
Disk 3	Presentation fonts	Helvetica, Times, and Symbol screen fonts
	Persuasion dictionaries	Dictionaries for Persuasion's spell checker, and Persuasion's Help file
Disk 4	AutoTemplates	The 36 Persuasion 2.0 AutoTemplates
Disk 5	Art of Persuasion	A collection of clip art

Before you make backup copies of your original disks, protect them by pushing the write-protect tab in the upper right corner of the disks into the locked position. Aldus recommends that you use the "disk-to-disk" method for making backup disks. (Consult your Macintosh documentation if you're not sure how to do this.) Make sure the name of each backup disk exactly matches the name on the original, space for space, capital letter for capital letter. If the copies don't perfectly match the originals, you won't be able to install Persuasion from the backup disks.

Persuasion 2.0 comes with its own automatic installation program, *Persuasion 2.0 Installer*. To conserve disk space, some of the Persuasion 2.0 files are compressed. Persuasion 2.0 Installer decompresses them and copies all the Persuasion files to your hard disk. All you have to do during installation is sit back, answer a few questions, and insert and remove disks when prompted. On-screen help is available at every step along the way. The entire installation should take about 10 minutes.

During installation, you are asked to choose which, if any, of Persuasion's 36 AutoTemplates you want to install. Each AutoTemplate consists of six slide masters that you can use to format your presentation automatically. You are also invited to select one of the AutoTemplates as the default presentation, the presentation that will open automatically every time you choose *New* from the File menu. The AutoTemplate you choose will be saved as *Persuasion Prefs*. We suggest you review the templates before you start so you can make an informed decision. Consult the sample slides from each template reproduced in the Persuasion *Desktop Reference* guide. The entire template collection requires about 1.5 MB of hard disk space; each template averages 40 to 50K.

Finally, you are given the choice of installing the Art of Persuasion, the clip art library that comes with Persuasion 2.0. Take a look at *The Art of Persuasion* brochure to see if any of the art strikes your fancy. The complete library requires about 500K of hard disk space.

Make sure you're running under the Finder only, not under MultiFinder. Persuasion 2.0 Installer does not work with MultiFinder. To switch from MultiFinder to Finder temporarily (for this work session), press the Command key while choosing *Restart* from the Special menu on the Apple desktop.

> *Note:* If Persuasion 1.0 is already installed on your hard disk, you needn't trash it before you install Persuasion 2.0. But if you've been using Persuasion 1.0 AutoTemplates, you're better off replacing them with the new Persuasion 2.0 set. Not only are there 12 additional Auto-Templates, the templates have been altered so that you can see a thumbnail preview in the Open presentation dialog box. They've also been modified to make use of background masters and other Persuasion 2.0 features.

> When you install Persuasion 2.0, the Persuasion 2.0 Installer will create a folder called Aldus folder within your System folder and place your new Persuasion Prefs file (containing your default presentation specifications) in that folder. If you wish to use an old Persuasion Prefs file, drag it into the new Aldus folder and click *OK* when the Finder asks you if you want to replace the existing version.

Install Persuasion 2.0

Insert Disk 1 in the floppy disk drive on your Macintosh and double-click the Aldus Installer/Utility icon. You'll get a brief glimpse of Aldus Corporation's logo, a portrait engraving of Aldus Manutius, the fifteenth-century Italian printer immortalized by his work with typography and illustration.

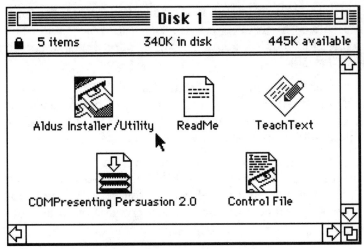

Figure 1.1.   Double-click the Aldus Installer/Utility icon to begin installing Persuasion.

Then, you'll see the Aldus Installer Main Window. At the top of the screen, a dialog box asks you to select what you want installed. All four options are already checked, so you must deselect any option you don't want installed by clicking the selection box to its left. Here are your options:

- **Aldus Persuasion 2.0** installs the Persuasion 2.0 application, along with spelling dictionaries, online help files, demo presentation, screen fonts, Autographix driver, and the installer itself.

- **Aldus Persuasion AutoTemplates** allows you to choose one or more of the 36 AutoTemplates to install on your disk. If you leave this option selected, you'll be asked to choose which AutoTemplates to install.

- **Learning Persuasion files** installs the sample files for the tutorials contained in Persuasion's user manual.

- **Art of Persuasion** installs files containing Persuasion's electronic clip art library.

Three windows fill the remainder of the screen. Clicking any window's title bar brings that window to the front, where you can read its contents:

- **ReadMe** contains the latest information about Persuasion 2.0, too new to have made it into the printed documentation. Take a minute to skim it before you proceed with the installation.

- **Aldus Installer Diagnostics** will be empty now. If you run any of the diagnostics utilities described a little later, the results will be displayed here.

- **Aldus Installer History** also begins as a blank slate. As you proceed, it chronicles the progress of the installation. You can watch it list each file that's decompressed and copied, and print or review it later if any problems arise.

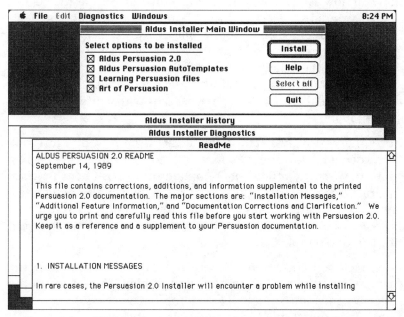

Figure 1.2.   The Installer Main window lets you select what you want installed and provides you with information about the installation process.

All three files are TeachText files. To read or print a TeachText file once the installation is complete, double-click its icon to run the TeachText application and open the file. Choose *Print* from the File menu if you want a printed copy.

When you've made sure the options you want installed are checked and you've reviewed the ReadMe file, click *Install* (or press the Return key) to begin the installation.

Every window you'll see during the installation process has a Help button that you can click if you're in doubt about what to do. You can stop the installation at any time by clicking *Quit* (in the Aldus Installer dialog box) or *Cancel* in subsequent dialog boxes.

If you selected the option *Aldus Persuasion AutoTemplates*, you'll be asked which AutoTemplates to install. To install all 36, click *Select all*. To install a single template, just click its name. To select a few templates, click the first one, then press the Shift key and click another until you've selected all you want. (If you're installing all but a few, it's quicker to click *Select all* to select them all, and then press the Shift key and click to deselect those you don't want.) When you're finished selecting AutoTemplates, click *OK*.

Persuasion will now ask you to designate an AutoTemplate as the default presentation. (If you didn't select any AutoTemplates to install, you'll see only one template, *Basic Template [AutoTemplate A]*, listed in this dialog box). Whenever you open a new presentation, you'll get a copy of the Auto-Template you select as the default, so you should choose the AutoTemplate you'll use most often. AutoTemplate A is the "default default." It consists of slide masters for simple, black-and-white overheads with centered text and a single horizontal line.

Don't worry that every presentation you create from now on must look exactly like the default AutoTemplate. As you'll see, you can always begin a new presentation with any other AutoTemplate simply by choosing *Open* from the File menu and selecting an alternative. You can also designate a new AutoTemplate or custom presentation as the default at any time by saving it as *Persuasion Prefs*. Finally, you can create a new presentation from scratch using no AutoTemplate at all.

When you've selected a default AutoTemplate, click *OK*. At this point, the Installer checks your system configuration and displays the results in the Aldus Installer Diagnostics window. Depending on what equipment you have, yours will look something like the one shown below.

Now you will be asked to personalize your copy of Persuasion 2.0. Type your name, company name, and serial number. Use the Tab key (or click an insertion point with the mouse) to move from field to field within this dialog box. You must type something in each box, and your serial number must be entered correctly, number for number, including the hyphens. Your serial number appears conveniently in four locations: on Disk 2 (or the Program disk if you upgraded from Persuasion 1.0), inside the front cover of the user manual, on the registration card, and on the bottom of the Persuasion box.

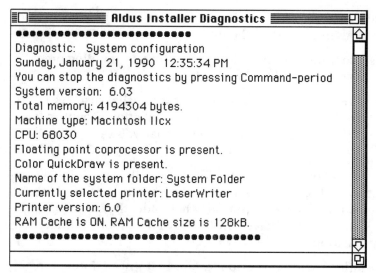

Figure 1.3.   The Installer Diagnostics window tells you about your
system configuration.

When you've finished entering this information, click *OK*. You'll be given a chance to change or verify what you've just typed. Click *OK* to accept it or *Change* to make corrections.

The Installer will then ask you where you want to install Persuasion 2.0. Use the scroll box to designate the desired drive, disk, and folder, and then click *Install*. (The default folder name is *Aldus Persuasion 2.0*.)

The Installer scans the disk you designate to make sure there's enough space to accommodate the options you've chosen. If all's well, you'll see the message, "You can install on this disk," displayed below the scroll box. If space is too short, you'll see a warning message, "Not enough disk space available." Click *Cancel* to return to the Installer start-up screen. Now you have two options. You can either select fewer options to install or you can click *Quit* to stop the installation, clean some of the underbrush off your hard disk, and start the installation again.

If all goes smoothly (and it almost always does), the Persuasion Installer will do the rest of the work, prompting you to insert the disks required by your selections. In between disk insertions, the Installer History window comes forward so you can monitor the progress of the installation. When it's all over, click *Quit* or wait five seconds and the dialog box will vanish by itself.

If you chose to install all of the Persuasion 2.0 files, here's what you should see in the Aldus Persuasion 2.0 folder:

- **AGXit!** is a communications utility that automates sending presentation files to an Autographix slide service.

- **Aldus Installer Diagnostics** is a TeachText file that displays the results of diagnostic tests performed during installation. Double-click its icon to run the TeachText application so that you can read or print this file.

- **Aldus Installer History** is another TeachText file containing a complete history of the installation, including when it took place, the names of the files that were installed, what folder they were placed in, what disk they were installed from, and any problems that arose during installation.

- **Aldus Installer/Utility** is the application that just performed the installation. You can double-click it at any time to run diagnostic tests or install additional options.

- **Art of Persuasion** is a folder containing a clip art collection grouped according to subject.

- **AutoTemplates** is a folder containing the AutoTemplates you selected for installation.

- **Learning Persuasion** is a folder containing tutorial files.

- **Persuasion 2.0** is the Persuasion application.

- **Presentation fonts** is a folder containing screen fonts for Times, Helvetica, and Symbol.

- **Presenting Persuasion 2.0** is a sample presentation that takes Persuasion 2.0 through its paces.

- **ReadMe** is a TeachText file containing information hot off the presses, as well as additions and corrections to the Persuasion documentation.

- **TeachText** is the application that allows you to read the TeachText files *Aldus Installer Diagnostics*, *Aldus Installer History*, and *ReadMe*.

During installation, Persuasion tucks a few more files and folders in your System folder. There, you'll find the following:

- **Autographix** is the slide service driver that you can select from the Chooser.

- **Aldus folder** contains two items:
  —**Persuasion Dictionaries** is a folder that holds the spelling dictionaries and the Persuasion Help file.
  —**Persuasion Prefs** is the default AutoTemplate for new presentations.

If you like to keep your System folder uncluttered, you can move the Aldus folder to the Persuasion 2.0 folder. Persuasion 2.0 looks for the Dictionaries, Help, and Prefs files as follows: First it looks for an Aldus folder in the System folder, then it looks in the System folder at large, and then finally it looks in the Persuasion 2.0 folder. Although keeping the Persuasion Dictionaries folder in the Persuasion 2.0 folder makes it easy to do regular backups of your supplementary dictionary, you can, in fact, put it anywhere on your hard disk. If it's not in the System or Persuasion 2.0 folder, however, you'll be prompted to specify its location when you use Help or run the spelling checker.

Install Presentation Fonts

During installation, the Persuasion 2.0 Installer copies suitcases containing screen fonts to the Presentation fonts folder in your hard disk. Included are fonts for Times, Helvetica, and Symbol in 12-, 14-, 18-, 24-, 36-, 40-, 48-, 56-, and 72-point sizes.

Do you need to use these fonts or not? Unfortunately, this is not a simple question. Let's back up and ask a simpler question—what is a screen font, anyway, and why is it important?

A screen font tells your Macintosh exactly how to display a particular typeface, style, and size most accurately. Using the right screen fonts dramatically increases the quality of on-screen typographic display as well as the output quality of QuickDraw devices (that is, most non-PostScript printers). Figure 1.4 shows the difference between 72-point Times Roman with and without its associated screen font. In general, if you don't have the screen font for a particular size, your Macintosh will mathematically calculate a description of that size from another size or substitute another font altogether. The Mac's extrapolations and substitutions are never as good as the real McCoy.

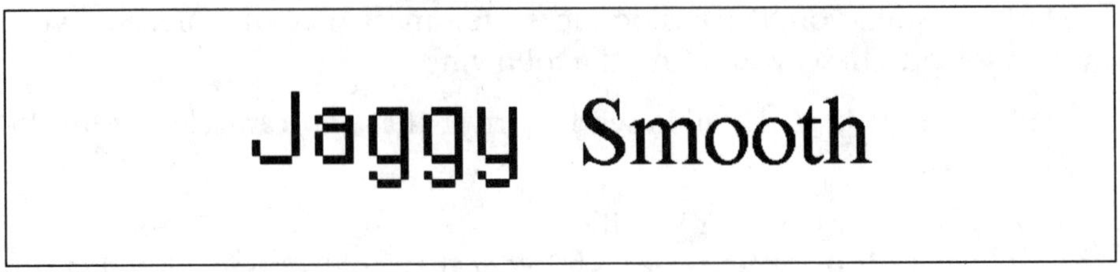

Jaggy Smooth

Figure 1.4.   For the best display of type on screen, install screen fonts for the typefaces and sizes you intend to use most often.

So, what can you do to make sure your Mac has the information it needs to optimize the appearance of fonts? Basically, there are three strategies. The first two strategies require you to use Persuasion's presentation screen fonts and limit you to certain point sizes for the best screen display. The sizes for which you install screen fonts appear in outline type in Persuasion's Size submenu to remind you that only they will look smooth on your screen. The third strategy lets you jettison the presentation fonts and gives you smooth outlines at all sizes.

Note: These are all strategies to ensure that type looks good on the screen. Printing type is another issue, one that's covered in great detail in the chapters on producing presentations.

Strategy 1: Copy the Fonts

Copy the presentation fonts from their suitcases into your System file, where they'll be accessible to all applications, including Persuasion 2.0. This is the least sophisticated and least flexible method of handling presentation fonts. The more fonts you install in your System file, the larger and slower it becomes. However, if you're running System 6.X and you're not using a font management utility, this is your only choice.

To install the presentation fonts, you must use Apple's Font/DA Mover to copy them into your System file. Here's how it works.

First of all, make sure you're running under the Finder only, not under MultiFinder. To switch temporarily from MultiFinder to Finder, choose *Set Startup* from the Special menu while pressing the Command key.

Open the Persuasion fonts folder on your hard disk. You should see the icons of the three font "suitcase" files—Helvetica, Symbol, and Times—contained in the folder.

Place First Class
Postage Here
Post Office
Will Not Deliver
Without Postage

Brady Books
15 Columbus Circle
New York, NY 10023

ATT: J. Padlad

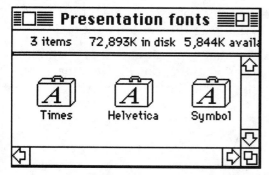

Figure 1.5. The Presentations fonts folder contains three font suitcases.

Double-click on any of the suitcase files to run the Font/DA Mover application and open that file. On the left side of the Font/DA Mover dialog box, you'll see a list of font sizes contained in that file.

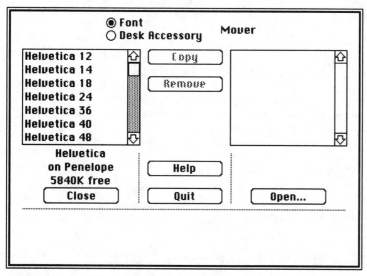

Figure 1.6. The contents of the Helvetica suitcase are displayed on the left side of the Font/DA Mover dialog box.

Click the *Open* button below the list box on the right side of the dialog box. Locate the System folder on your hard disk. A list of the fonts currently installed in your System file appears in the list box on the right. Click to select the Persuasion font sizes that you want to install from the list on the left. If you select just one size, you'll see a sample of it displayed at the bottom of the list box. To select more than one size, click on the first one, then press the Shift key and select another size. To deselect a size you've already selected, press the Shift key and click the size you want to deselect.

When you've selected the sizes you want to install, click the *Copy* button. Notice the arrows indicating the direction of the copying, from the Presentation fonts folder (on the left) to the System file (on the right).

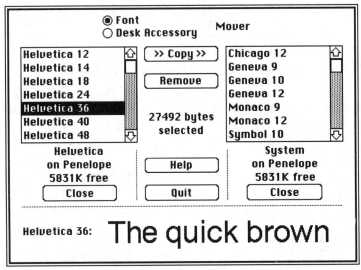

Figure 1.7.   The selected fonts will be copied from the Helvetica fonts suitcase on the left to the System file on the right.

When you've finished installing all the desired sizes of a font, click the *Close* button below the list box on the right. To install additional fonts, click on a new font name and repeat the copying process. When you've installed all the sizes of all the fonts you want, click *Quit* to close the Font/DA Mover.

Strategy 2: Use a Font Management Utility

Use a font management utility, such as Suitcase II or Master Juggler, to open and close the presentation font suitcases as needed. Font management utilities save you from having to install fonts directly into your System file. There are two advantages of a font management utility: 1) you can store font suitcases anywhere on your hard disk, opening or closing them as needed to keep font menus short and uncluttered; and 2) you avoid increasing the size of your System file and hence the amount of memory and storage it requires.

If you're using a font utility, you may want to pack a custom suitcase with all the presentation fonts. Then, you'll only have to open and close one instead of three suitcases when you want to use Times, Helvetica, and Symbol.

To pack your own font suitcase, find and double-click the icon for the Font/DA Mover application. Then click the *Close* button below the list box on the left to close the System file. Click *Open*, then click *New* to create a new font file. Name the suitcase something like *Presentation Fonts*, and make sure it's in your System folder (you should see the open System folder icon above the list box). Then copy the fonts you want from the Presentation fonts folder into your newly-created Presentation Fonts suitcase.

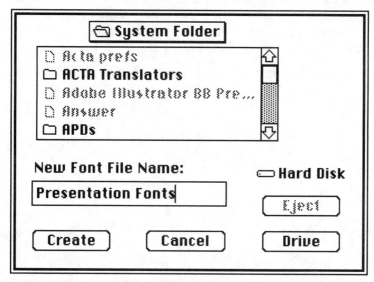

Figure 1.8.   Pack your own presentations fonts suitcase using the Font/DA Mover.

Remember, for optimum screen display, be sure to use only the outlined sizes from Persuasion's Size submenu.

Strategy 3: Use Adobe Type Manager or Apple's System 7.0

A third font management strategy requires either Adobe Type Manager or Apple's System 7.0. With Adobe Type Manager (ATM), you need to install only one font size in order for all sizes to be rendered smoothly on screen.

Although ATM is hard to beat for the quality of its type display, it's not without a hitch or two. First of all, you must have the corresponding printer font, since ATM reads the information contained in the printer font to display the font on screen. Secondly, not all output devices support ATM. Check with your slide service bureau, if you intend to use one, or with the dealer who sold you your printer or film recorder before you commit yourself to using ATM. Thirdly, you may notice slower screen redrawing and should aim to get more memory. (As of this writing, Apple's System 7.0 promises similar benefits and similar drawbacks.)

If you're using ATM, as long as you have one size of Times, Helvetica, and Symbol installed in your System file or in an open suitcase and the corresponding printer fonts in your System folder or in the same folder with the open suitcase, you can drag Persuasion's Presentation fonts folder directly into the trash. (For more information on setting up your screen and printer fonts to work with ATM, consult your ATM manual.)

Now that you're up and running, let's celebrate with a grand tour of Persuasion.

Chapter 2

A Guided Tour

The Best Tools for the Job

Let's begin with a provocative question: why bother to use Persuasion to create presentations in the first place? Why not just use the word processing, page layout, or drawing program you already have?

The answer is quite simple. Persuasion is designed for one purpose only—to streamline the process of creating presentations. A Persuasion presentation doesn't consist only of slides or overheads; it includes speaker notes (a script for the speaker) and audience handouts. Persuasion combines word processing, page layout, drawing, and charting features all rolled into one; yet it contains only those features that you need for creating presentations. For example, for word processing, it offers a spelling checker and a find/change feature. But how often does a presentation call for a table of contents, an index, or footnotes? For page layout, it provides a simple "snap to" grid and rulers for positioning elements, but dispenses with tools for flowing columns of text around irregular-shaped graphics.

Dedicated word processing, page layout, and drawing programs can actually be quite cumbersome for creating presentations. For example, how do you get text from an outline onto individual slides? Lots and lots of repetitive cutting and pasting? Persuasion features a dynamic link between outline and slides that automates slide layout. If you're using a drawing program, how do you check spelling? By reading the screen or hard copy and leaving it to your own eye? If you're using a word processor, how do you prepare a chart? Open a spreadsheet program, create a chart there, then cut and paste it into the presentation? What happens if the numbers change? Back to the spreadsheet....

19

Persuasion is a specialty program that assembles under one roof all the various tools required to create all possible components of a presentation. It's also pretty easy to use, once you understand its overall structure and how its various components are linked to each other. Basically, Persuasion allows you to produce four main physical elements:

- **Outline.** Most presentations begin with an outline—organized thought in skeleton form. Persuasion's outliner gives you the advantage of being able to work exclusively with the text in your presentation: you can tinker with and refine your thoughts until they flow smoothly and logically. Then you can tackle typography and design.

- **Slides.** Slides are the heart of a presentation, the translation of ideas into visual form. A dynamic link between Persuasion's outline and slide modes automates the transformation of words onto slides. Whatever you type in the outline automatically "flows" into position on a slide. (Like the Persuasion documentation and program, we use the term "slides" generically to mean the visual part of a presentation, whether it's 35-mm slides, overhead transparencies, or flipcharts.)

- **Speaker notes.** Speaker notes contain a slide miniature and whatever notes or script you need to deliver an effective presentation. A dynamic link between the outline and notes view lets you type notes directly into the outline, and then pours those notes onto individual speaker notes pages.

- **Audience handouts.** Audience handouts consist of between one and six slide miniatures per page, to help your audience retain the information in your presentation.

These four elements are dynamically linked. They are the products of a streamlined, automated process for creating, editing, and producing a presentation.

Here's a typical scenario for building a presentation with Persuasion. First, you type in your outline and speaker notes, rearranging the sequence and hierarchy of your thoughts, and editing the wording. When you're satisfied with your outline, you move from outline to slide mode. There, you'll see all the headings and subheadings you typed in the outline automatically arranged and formatted on individual slides, depending on their position in the outline. Next, you move to speaker notes mode, where you'll find the speaker notes you typed in the outline automatically placed below a miniature image of the slide—an instant script for your presentation! Finally, you switch to the audience handouts mode, where you determine how many slide miniatures appear per page.

When you're finished preparing the presentation, you print the various components to an appropriate output device, your slides to a film recorder, for example, or your outline, speaker notes, and audience handouts to a laser printer. Of course, you don't have to produce all four elements. If you don't need speaker notes or audience handouts, just don't print them! At every step in the production process, you can exercise as much control as you want over the appearance of your outline, slides, speaker notes, and audience handouts—or, if you prefer, you can let Persuasion do the work for you. Persuasion's flexible array of tools can accommodate a range of working styles. Let's take a closer look at the inner workings of a Persuasion presentation.

AutoTemplates, Slide Masters, and Background Masters

The key to Persuasion's ease of use is the **AutoTemplate**. An AutoTemplate is simply a presentation that includes built-in settings for layout, color, type, and other visual elements, and a complete set of **slide masters**.

A slide master is like a page layout template or "dummy". It contain elements that you want repeated on each slide, such as background color and pattern, or your company logo, or a rectangular border. A slide master also includes **placeholders**, containers for the slide title, subtitle, and slide text, as well as for charts, graphs, and tables. A placeholder has formatting instructions built into it: font, size, style, and color for text placeholders, and chart format, color, line weight, and fill patterns for chart placeholders. If you change a placeholder on a slide master, all slides based on that master will automatically change as well.

Usually, you'll need one slide master for each type of layout required by the material in your presentation. For example, some of your slides may consist of a title and a few lines of text, others may call for many lines of text, and still others may require charts or tables. Each of these various slide layouts requires a different treatment for its elements. All of the AutoTemplates that come with Persuasion include a slide master for several types of layouts—one for a title slide, one for a bulleted list, one for an organizational chart, and so on. As you prepare each slide for a presentation, you choose and apply the slide master that best fits its particular selection of elements. Using slide masters saves you from having to format each slide individually.

A dynamic link allows information to pass back and forth between placeholders and Persuasion's outliner, data sheet, and speaker notes.

When you type into the outliner, for example, Persuasion pours the text onto a slide into a title, subtitle, or text placeholder and formats it according to the placeholder's specs. If you edit text that's flowed from the outliner into a placeholder on a slide, the outliner will be updated; if you edit the outline, text on the slide will also change.

With a chart placeholder, data that you import or type into a worksheet automatically builds the type of chart you want. There's a placeholder for tables that lets you determine how many rows and columns the table will contain. And there's even a placeholder for organizational charts that lets you select the number of organizational levels and boxes within each level.

Figure 2.1 shows the six slide masters that compose Persuasion's Auto-Template F. As you can see, there's a slide master containing just the title of the presentation, two slide masters for differing amounts of text, two slide masters for different chart layouts, and one slide master for an organizational chart. Despite their differences, however, these slide masters are unified by common elements: the horizontal row of squares along the top of the slide and the centered square above and below the text or chart. In addition, the same typeface, Times, has been applied all the slide masters. Persuasion's AutoTemplate/slide master combination provides you both flexibility and consistency to ensure a high-quality presentation.

In addition to slide masters, Persuasion also uses background masters. A background master is an optional background that can contain color, pattern, graphics, and text. You can apply different background masters to slide masters.

How does this all work? Think of a slide as consisting of three main images placed on top of one another—the background master on the bottom, the slide master in the middle, and individual slide elements on top. You can have one background master assigned to many slide masters, and you can have one slide master assigned to many slides. You can also mix and match background masters and slide masters. For example, let's say you have two background masters: *Background 1* is blue and *Background 2* is green. And let's say you have two slide masters: *Title Master* for a title slide and *Chart Master* for a bar chart. You can apply *Background 1* to *Title Master* for a blue title slide; *Background 2* to *Title Master* for a green title slide; *Background 1* to *Chart Master* for a bar chart with a blue background; and *Background 2* to *Chart Master* for a bar chart with a green background. Mixing and matching background and slide masters gives you lots of possibilities without forcing you to sacrifice consistency or set up the same format over and over again. Remember, too, that background masters are optional. You can do very well without them.

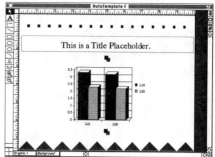

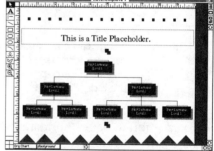

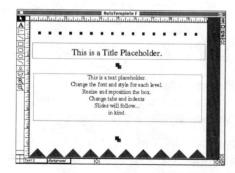
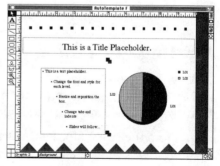

Figure 2.1.   Persuasion's AutoTemplate F consists of six slide masters for
different types of layouts.

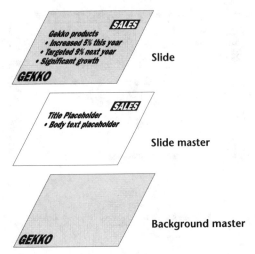

Slide

Slide master

Background master

Figure 2.2.   A slide can consist of up to three layers. You can use a
background master to carry color and pattern, a slide
master to carry placeholders and graphic elements, and
the individual slide to carry text from the outline.

In addition to background and slide masters, AutoTemplates can contain
a color palette and a selection of text formats similar to the style sheets used
in desktop publishing applications. We'll come back to each of these Auto-
Template elements for a much closer look later on.

So much for theory. Let's launch Persuasion and get down to work.

Starting Persuasion

As with any other Macintosh application, there are two ways to start Persuasion: You can run the program from the Finder and then open the document you want or open the document directly from the Finder.

1. From the Finder, locate the Persuasion 2.0 folder, double-click to open
   it, then double-click the Persuasion icon to start Persuasion. You'll see
   Persuasion's desktop and the Persuasion start-up screen. Choose *Open*
   from the File menu to open an AutoTemplate or an existing presentation.

2. From the Finder, open an AutoTemplate or an existing presentation
   directly. Just double-click an AutoTemplate icon or the icon of the
   presentation you want to open. This starts Persuasion and places you
   directly in either an untitled copy of an AutoTemplate or an existing
   presentation, depending on what you selected.

Notice that there are two kinds of Persuasion documents: presentations and AutoTemplates. Usually you build new presentations from an Auto-Template or from an existing presentation. Sometimes, however, you'll build a new presentation from the ground up and create your own Auto-Template from scratch.

AutoTemplate A

Presenting Persuasion 2.0

Figure 2.3. There are two kinds of Persuasion documents, AutoTemplates and presentations.

Persuasion's Views

Persuasion allows you to look at your presentation in seven different views. The view you choose will depend on what part of the presentation you're working on.

When you open a new presentation, you'll usually be placed in Persuasion's **Outline view**. (All of Persuasion's AutoTemplates were saved in Outline view.) Typically, you'll begin your presentation with the outline, working with words and ideas. In the Outline view, you can type and rearrange the words and ideas in your presentation, arrange the order of slides, and assign slide masters and transition effects to slides. You can also create speaker notes to help guide your delivery during the presentation.

Along the top of the screen, you'll see the upper Menu bar consisting of the six pull-down menus available in Outline view. Just below it, the Title bar shows the title of your presentation.

The column along the left side of the presentation window indicates slide numbers. A Persuasion outline is divided into distinct units called headings and subheads, whose function is identified by different icons. A holder of slides, indicated by a hollow round bullet, is a heading that appears only in Outline view. You can use a holder of slides to organize your presentation. For example, you might insert a holder of slides to group slides according to subject matter. A slide title, identified by a miniature slide icon, will appear on a slide as a title. Subheads, marked by a short, horizontal bar, appear as body text on slides.

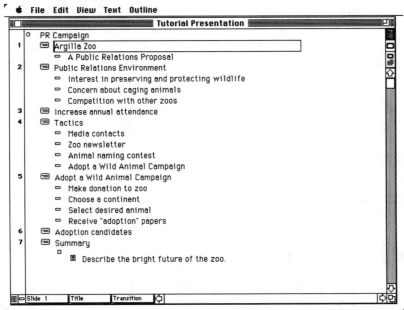

Figure 2.4.   You'll begin most presentations in Outline view, where you'll hone your ideas.

On the top right edge of the window, three View icons let you navigate among Persuasion's views. Along the bottom of the window, another Menu bar contains three pop-up menus. We'll explore the View icons and the menus a little later.

Note: If you're taking this tour with Persuasion running on the screen in front of you, use the View menu to move among the views described below.

When the outline is perfected, you can move to **Slide view**, where you can see and modify the slides that have automatically been created from the outline text. In Slide view, you construct and edit individual slides, adding and formatting text, drawing graphics, and plotting and editing charts and tables. (If outlines make you queasy, you can avoid an outline altogether by working directly on slides in Slide view.)

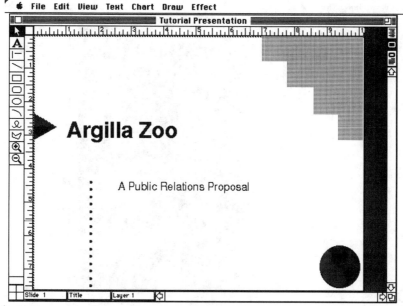

Figure 2.5.   You'll do much of your work in Slide view, building and editing individual slides.

Slide view contains its own set of menus in the upper Menu bar, some of which are the same as in Outline view, and some of which are different. The View icons and the lower Menu bar are similar to those in Outline view. Along the left side of the window, Persuasion's toolbox contains tools for creating text and graphics, and for enlarging and reducing your view of slides. In the bottom left corner, the Tool default displays information about Persuasion's drawing tools. The Toolbox and the Tool default displays are described in detail below.

When you're finished creating slides, you'll turn your attention to speaker notes and audience handouts. For each slide in a presentation, **Notes view** displays a slide miniature and the slide title and speaker notes you entered in the outline. The Notes pop-up menu appears in the bottom left corner.

To rearrange the sequence of slides in a presentation, you'll go to **Slide sorter view**. There, you'll see miniatures of all your presentation's slides in one window. You can select one or more slides, and then delete them or move them to another location within the presentation. You can also assign background masters and slide masters to individual slides. The changes you make in Slide sorter view will automatically update the outline.

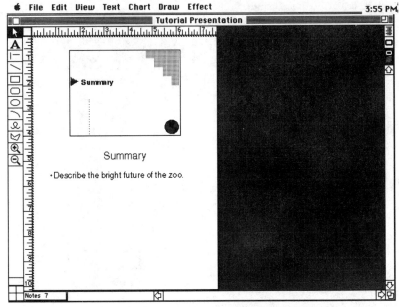

Figure 2.6.   In Notes view, you set up a format for speaker notes.

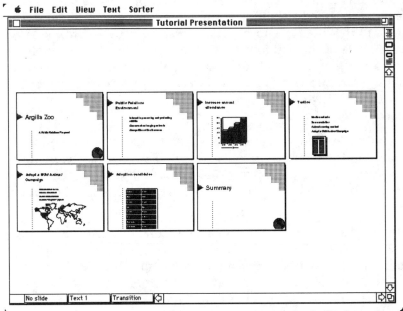

Figure 2.7.   In Slide sorter view, you can review and edit the flow of your presentation.

In addition to the four general views we've just described, Persuasion includes three master views. The master views let you set up the overall structure and appearance of slides, notes, and audience handouts.

In **Slide master view**, you create slide masters containing background color and pattern, placeholders for text and charts, and static graphic and text elements. You can also set up background masters in this view.

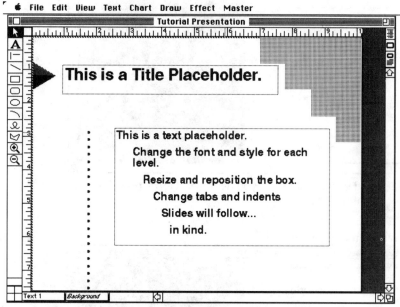

Figure 2.8.   In Slide master view, you add containers called placeholders into which text and data flow.

In **Notes master view**, you design and format speaker notes. You can determine the size and placement of the slide miniature, spec the slide title and speaker note text, and add a page number placeholder.

In **Handouts master view**, you position up to six slide miniatures and add headers or footers or other information appropriate for audience handouts.

Depending on the task at hand—whether it's looking at the overall sequence of a presentation or removing a semicolon from a chart legend—you'll find that one or more of Persuasion's seven views will meet your needs.

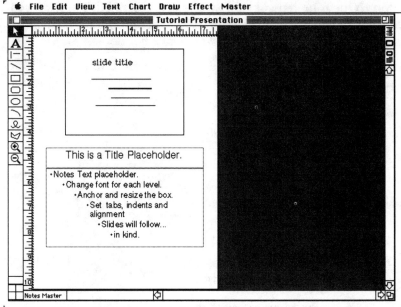

Figure 2.9.　In Notes master view, you design and format speaker notes.

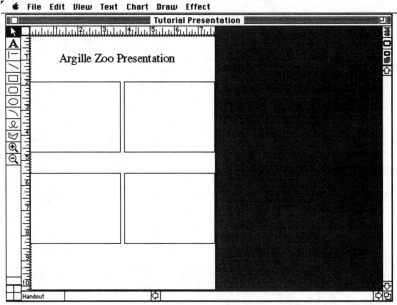

Figure 2.10.　In Handouts master view, you prepare audience handouts.

Persuasion's Menus

Across the top of the screen, you'll see the main Menu bar. Just below it is the Title bar, showing the title of the open presentation (if it's a new presentation or an AutoTemplate, it will read "Untitled" until you first save it).

Persuasion uses two types of menus, pull-down menus in the main Menu bar, and pop-up menus in the lower Menu bar along the bottom of the window. Some of the pop-up menus also serve as status indicators; that is, they tell you something about the current slide or master. The selection of available menus depends on what view you're in.

Let's take a quick tour of the menus to give you a peek into each one and to acquaint you with Persuasion's many tools. We'll cover how to use each menu in detail in subsequent chapters. Let's begin with the pull-down menus in the main Menu bar.

Pull-down Menus in the Main Menu Bar

The **Apple menu** functions the same way in Persuasion as it does in any other Macintosh application. It gives you access to any desk accessories you may have installed, and, if you're running MultiFinder, it allows you to switch between applications. In addition, Persuasion's online Help feature can be found here, along with a pull-down windows submenu that lets you move between open presentations.

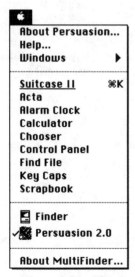

Figure 2.11. The Apple menu offers access to Help and to other open presentations.

Persuasion provides you with a context-sensitive, on-line Help feature, so assistance is never more than a mouse click or two away. There are two ways to call for help:

1. **Using the Apple menu.** Choose *Help* from the Apple menu. (Pressing the Help key—if you have one—on the keyboard will also produce the Help dialog box.) You will be given three options: You can get help on how to get help by clicking *Using Help*, you can choose *Commands*, or you can choose *Topics*. *Commands* displays an alphabetized list of Persuasion commands, while *Topics* displays a list of common topics, such as *Opening a presentation* or *Using the spell checker*. Click to select the command or topic you want explained and then click *Select* (or just double-click the topic). If the help text continues beyond the first screen, use the scroll bars to see the rest. Click the *More Help* pop-up menu in the bottom right corner of the dialog box to take you to related subjects. (If there are no related subjects, clicking on this menu accomplishes nothing.) Click *Commands* or *Topics* again to research another command or topic, or click *Quit Help* to close the Help dialog box.

2. **Using context-sensitive Help.** Hold down the Command key and type a question mark. If you're in a dialog box, you'll get the help screen that pertains to that dialog box. If you're not in a dialog box, the cursor turns into a large, black question mark. Choose a command from a menu, or click the area of the window that catches your interest. If you click at the center of the current window, for example, you can get help about the options available to you in whatever view you're in. (You may need to hunt to figure out which areas of the screen will respond. Individual tools in the toolbox, pop-up menus along the bottom of the screen, and icons along the upper right corner are good candidates.)

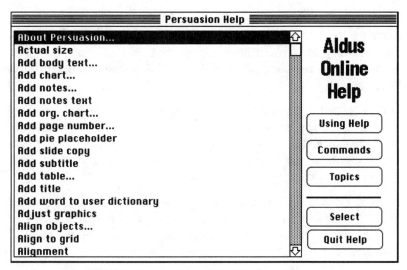

Figure 2.12. Click *Commands* to research a Persuasion command.

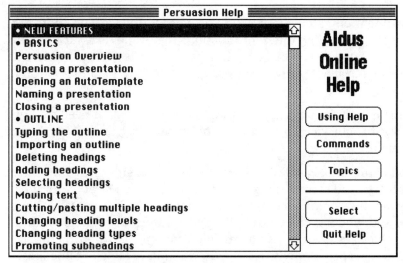

Figure 2.13. Click *Topics* if you want information on a Persuasion concept or procedure.

The **File menu** is Persuasion's gatekeeper and production department. Use the File menu to open new or existing presentations, to save presentations, to import and export presentation elements, to create or import chart data, and to print or set up a slide show. You'll find the all-important *Quit* command here as well.

The **Edit menu** contains commands for modifying elements, including tasks such as cutting, copying, pasting, duplicating, finding and changing text, and spell checking. The *Undo* command, always a blessing when you have second thoughts about something you've just done, is at the top of this menu; its keyboard shortcut is *Command+Z*.

The **View menu** is Persuasion's navigator. It allows you to move between the three main Persuasion views, Outline, Slide, and Notes, as well as to other specialized views, including Slide sorter, Slide master, Notes master, and Handout master.

The **Text menu** is Persuasion's typesetting department. Here, you'll find commands for formatting text, including font, size, style, and color, for both slide and outline text.

The **Outline menu** allows you to add new heads or add or promote subheads. You can also assign different functions to outline text, such as title, subtitle, body text, and you can control what outline levels are visible. The Outline menu is available only when you're working on the presentation in Outline view.

If you're taking this tour while running Persuasion, you'll need to move from Outline to Slide view to see the rest of the menus. Choose *Slide 1* from the View menu.

The **Chart menu** is Persuasion's graphics department. Here, you select the type of chart and control its finer features, such as whether or not it will have a legend, how many increments will show on the horizontal and vertical axes, and whether the chart will have a frame. Persuasion's built-in spreadsheet or data sheet is also accessible through the Chart menu. The Chart menu is available only when you're working in Slide or Slide master view. When you're not working on a chart, its contents will be dimmed.

File	
New	⌘N
Open...	⌘O
Close	
Data sheet	▶
Save	⌘S
Save as...	
Revert	
Import...	
AutoTemplates...	
Export...	
Page setup...	
Print...	⌘P
Slide show...	
Preferences...	
Quit	⌘Q

Figure 2.14. The File menu is Persuasion's gatekeeper.

Edit	
Undo text	⌘Z
Cut	⌘H
Copy	⌘C
Paste	⌘V
Clear	
Select all	⌘A
Duplicate	⌘D
Find/Change...	⌘5
Find again	⌘6
Change	⌘7
Change then find	⌘8
Spelling...	⌘9
Insert	⌘I
Delete	⌘K

Figure 2.15. The Edit menu contains commands for
            modifying elements.

Figure 2.16. The View menu is Persuasion's navigator.

Figure 2.17. The Text menu is Persuasion's typesetting department.

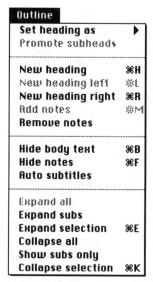

Figure 2.18. The Outline menu contains tools for organizing your thoughts.

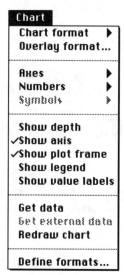

Figure 2.19. The Chart menu is Persuasion's graphics department.

The **Draw menu** controls the behavior of objects such as lines and circles that you draw, as well as Persuasion's text and chart placeholders. Here, you find commands for grouping and ungrouping objects, aligning objects to each other or to Persuasion's grid, for sending objects in front of and behind one another, and for flipping and rotating objects. The Draw menu is always available except when you're working on the outline. When no drawing tool or drawn object is selected, most of the Draw commands will be dimmed.

The **Effect menu** allows you to choose how objects will look: the style and pattern of lines, the fill pattern and color of rectangles and circles, whether they'll have a shadow, and so forth. In addition, the Effect menu contains commands for setting up and modifying Persuasion's color palette. Like the Draw menu, the Effect menu is always available in graphics editing views—that is, when you're working on slides or notes, and never when you're working on an outline.

Two more menus—the Master menu and the Sorter menu—each require a special view to see them. First, go to the Master view by choosing *Slide master* from the View menu and then choose *Current* (or *Background*) from the pull-down submenu.

The **Master menu** contains tools for building slide, background, and notes masters. It includes commands for creating several types of placeholders, as well as slide background fills. You can also construct special effects involving Persuasion's layer feature. You'll see the Master menu only when you're setting up a Slide or Notes master in one of Persuasion's master views.

The **Sorter menu** controls the size of the slide miniatures in Slide sorter view. It's available only when you go to Slide sorter view for a overview of your presentation.

Before we move on, a few quick words about the finer points of Persuasion's menu conventions. Although these conventions are pretty standard in the Macintosh world, they're both very useful and easily overlooked.

Menus contain more than just the names of options and commands. Keyboard equivalents of commands are listed along the right edge of the menu. ⌘ followed by a character means press the Command key (also known as the Apple key), and then type the character. For example, in the File menu, you'll see that the keyboard shortcut for *Save* is *Command+S*, and for *Open* is *Command+O*. After you've worked with Persuasion awhile, encourage yourself to pay attention to these keyboard shortcuts—focus on the right edge of a menu when you open it—to help yourself gently but surely learn the shortcuts, and wean yourself from the mouse to the more efficient keyboard. Throughout this book, we list the keyboard equivalent of a menu command, in parentheses, the first time it's mentioned.

Some commands are followed by ellipses (three periods...). The ellipses warn you that you'll be asked to make additional selections from a dialog box before that command takes effect. Menu commands without ellipses take effect immediately. For example, when you choose the *Open* command from the File menu, you'll see the Open presentation dialog box, which asks you to select a presentation. By contrast, the *Close* command simply closes the current presentation without asking any questions.

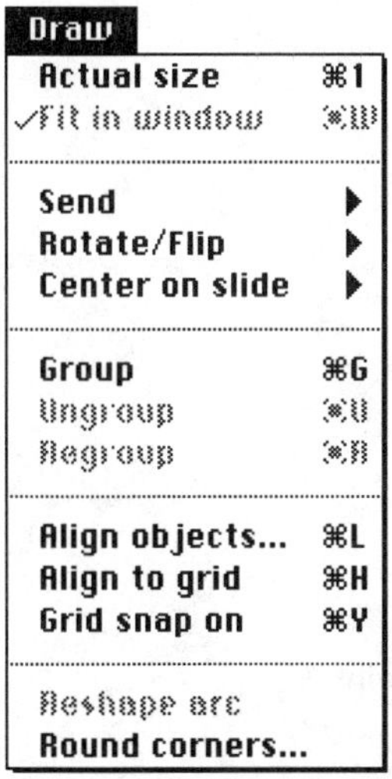

Draw	
Actual size	⌘1
✓Fit in window	⌘W
Send	▶
Rotate/Flip	▶
Center on slide	▶
Group	⌘G
Ungroup	⌘U
Regroup	⌘R
Align objects...	⌘L
Align to grid	⌘H
Grid snap on	⌘Y
Reshape arc	
Round corners...	

Figure 2.20. The Draw menu contains tools for manipulating objects.

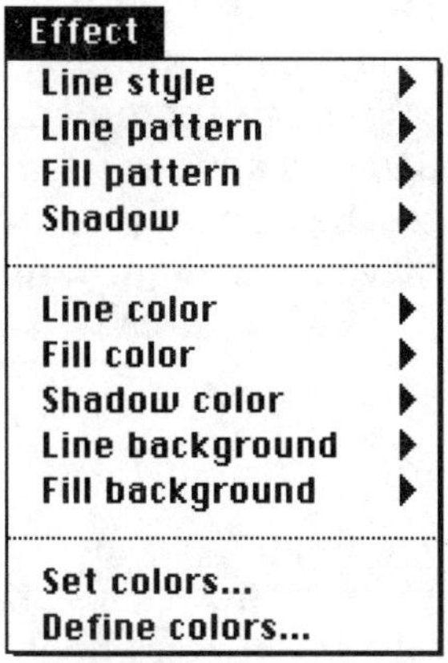

Effect	
Line style	▶
Line pattern	▶
Fill pattern	▶
Shadow	▶
Line color	▶
Fill color	▶
Shadow color	▶
Line background	▶
Fill background	▶
Set colors...	
Define colors...	

Figure 2.21. The Effect menu controls the style, fill, and color objects.

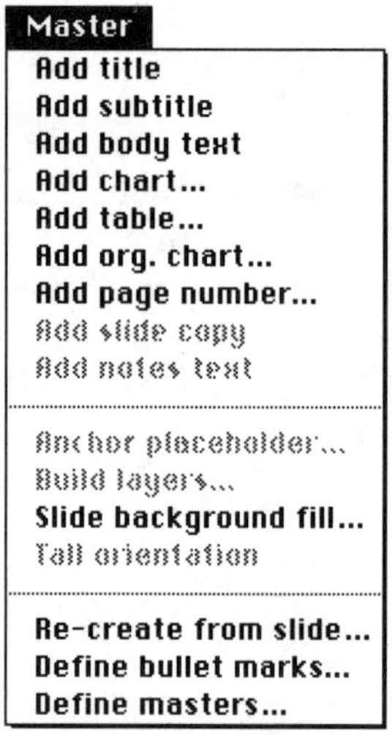

```
┌─────────────────────────────────┐
│ Master                          │
├─────────────────────────────────┤
│ Add title                       │
│ Add subtitle                    │
│ Add body text                   │
│ Add chart...                    │
│ Add table...                    │
│ Add org. chart...               │
│ Add page number...              │
│ Add slide copy                  │
│ Add notes text                  │
│ ·······························  │
│ Anchor placeholder...           │
│ Build layers...                 │
│ Slide background fill...        │
│ Tall orientation                │
│ ·······························  │
│ Re-create from slide...         │
│ Define bullet marks...          │
│ Define masters...               │
└─────────────────────────────────┘
```

Figure 2.22. The Master menu contains commands for building
masters of various kinds.

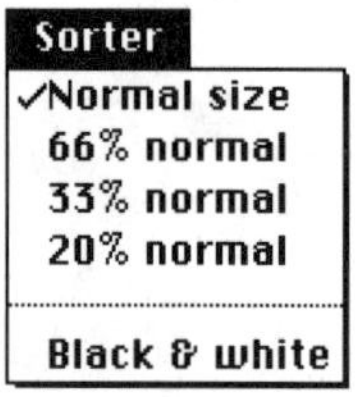

```
┌──────────────────────┐
│ Sorter               │
├──────────────────────┤
│ ✓Normal size         │
│  66% normal          │
│  33% normal          │
│  20% normal          │
│ ···················· │
│ Black & white        │
└──────────────────────┘
```

Figure 2.23. The Sorter menu controls the size of the slide miniatures in
the slide sorter.

Commands in menus are grouped according to function, with dotted gray lines grouping related commands. An arrowhead to the left or the right of a command indicates an associated pull-down submenu and the direction you must move the mouse to open it. A check mark next to a command or an option indicates that it's currently selected. A diamond appears when you have more than one object selected, and indicates the current presentation default (what Persuasion assumes you want if you don't give any special instructions).

Pop-up Menus in the Lower Menu Bar

As with the pull-down menus in the main Menu bar, the pop-up menus you'll see in the lower Menu bar depend on what view you're in. We'll start with the menus in Outline view, so if you're not already there, choose *Outline* from the View menu.

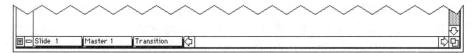

Figure 2.24. The lower Menu bar contains pop-up menus that also
serve as status indicators.

Pop-up menus serve two functions. As status indicators, they tell you things such as what slide you're looking at or what slide master has been applied to the current slide. They also let you move between views and assign slide masters, background masters, transitional effects, and drawing layers. When you click on a pop-up menu, the menu title will be replaced by a brief description of what the menu does or what you can do with it. When you first use Persuasion, be sure to read that message to help keep track of what you're doing.

The left-most menu is always a *Go to* menu. (If you are on a slide, it is a *Go to slide* menu; if you are on a master, it is a *Go to master* menu). The middle and right menus are always *assignment* menus. (If you are on a slide, the middle menu is an *Assign master to slide* menu; if you are on a master, it is an *Assign background to master* menu.)

The **Slide** pop-up menu (on the left) tells you what slide is currently selected. When you click on it, you'll see the words *Go to slide*. To move to another slide, select a number from the pop-up menu. To create a new slide, select *New*. (You'll learn other ways to create a new slide later on.) The Slide pop-up menu is available when you're working with the outline or with slides (but not when you're setting up masters).

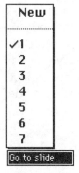

Figure 2.25. The Slide pop-up menu tells you what slide is currently
selected and lets you move between slides.

The **Assign Master to Slide** pop-up menu in the middle tells you what slide master is assigned to the slide that's currently selected. To assign a new background or slide master to the current slide, choose a background or slide master name from the pop-up menu. To preview the current slide formatted with different slide masters, choose *Gallery*.

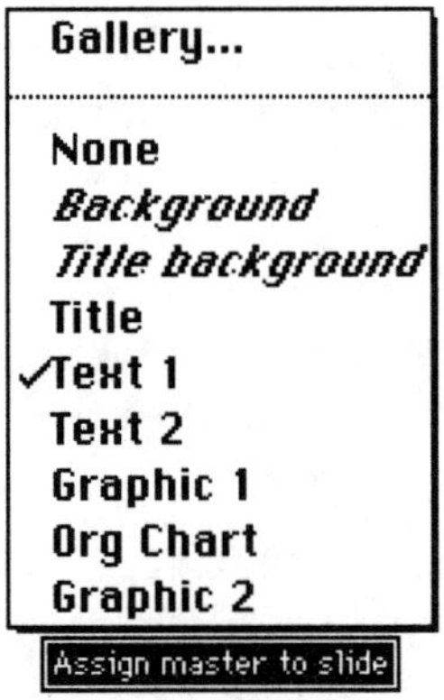

```
Gallery...
..........................................
None
Background
Title background
Title
✓Text 1
Text 2
Graphic 1
Org Chart
Graphic 2
```
Assign master to slide

Figure 2.26. The Assign Master to Slide pop-up menu lets you assign
slide masters to slides.

The **Transition** pop-up menu (on the right in Outline and Slide sorter views) tells you what effect will be used during the transition from the current slide to the one following it. You can assign a different transition effect by choosing the effect you want from the menu. You can also assign different effects to slide layers by choosing *Layers*. The Transition menu is available when you're working on the outline, or when you're using the Slide sorter to edit the presentation as a whole.

When you're working on slides in Slide view, the Transition pop-up menu on the right is replaced by the **Layer** pop-up menu, which indicates the current drawing layer. The number to the right tells you the layer of any selected object. To set the default drawing layer or to assign selected objects to a new layer, choose a layer from the pop-up menu. *Set* allows you to determine which layers will be active and visible.

Figure 2.27. The Transition pop-up menu lets you assign transition effects to slides.

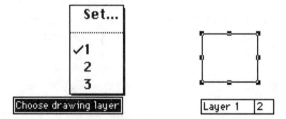

Figure 2.28. The Layer pop-up menu (*left*) indicates the current drawing layer. The number to the right of the pop-up menu tells you the layer of any selected object.

When you're setting up a slide master in Slide master view, the **Go to Master** pop-up menu tells you what slide master is currently selected. Choosing a slide or background master name from the pop-up menu takes you to that master. Background master names are italicized, to distinguish them from slide masters. Choosing *New* or *New background* creates a new slide or background master.

In Slide master view, the **Background** pop-up menu tells you what background master is assigned to the current slide master. You can select another background or remove it entirely by selecting *None*.

Figure 2.29. The Go to Master pop-up menu lets you move among slide and background masters.

Figure 2.30. The Background pop-up menu tells you the current slide's background master.

Note: The relationship between slide and background masters and their respective views can be a bit confusing at first. In the Slide master view proper, you see two pop-up menus side-by side. On the left is the Go to master menu (a go-to menu—"Go to slide master"); on the right is the Background menu (an assignment menu—"Assign background master to slide master"). Choosing *Go to master* gives you several options:

- Go to a different slide master;
- Create a new slide master;
- Go to a different background master; and
- Create a new background master.

If you go to a background master, whether existing or new, you'll see only one menu: since you can't assign anything to a background master, the Background menu ("Assign background master to slide master") disappears, leaving only the Go to master menu.

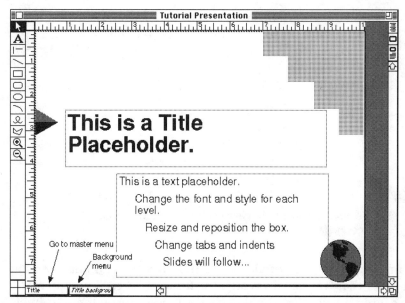

Figure 2.31. In Slide master view, the Go to master and Background menus appear side-by-side.

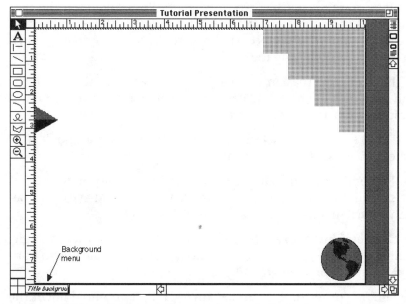

Figure 2.32. In Background master view, only the Background menu appears.

The **Notes** pop-up menu indicates the currently selected note. To move to a different note, choose its number from the pop-up menu.

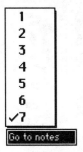

Figure 2.33. The Notes pop-up menu lets you move among speaker
notes pages.

If you find this rich array of views and menus a bit intimidating right now, remember that you can always tell the function of each pop-up menu by clicking on it and reading the descriptive message. You'll get to know them each very well later on in this book.

The Toolbox

The Toolbox, always available except when you're working on the outline, contains all the equipment you need for building slides, notes, and handouts. In addition to all-purpose and text tools, there are eight graphic drawing tools and two viewing tools:

- The **Pointer** is Persuasion's general, all-purpose tool, the electronic equivalent of your hand. The Pointer lets you select, move, and resize graphic objects and text blocks.

- With the **Text tool**, you select, edit, and enter text in placeholders, or create text blocks directly on slides.

- The **Perpendicular-line drawing tool** allows you to draw straight vertical and horizontal lines, no matter how little hand-eye coordination you may have.

- The **Diagonal-line tool** allows you to draw straight lines at any angle. Holding down the Shift key while drawing constrains the line to horizontal, vertical, or 45-degree angles.

- The **Square-corner tool** draws rectangles and, if you hold down the Shift key while drawing, the tool draws perfect squares.

- The **Round corner tool** produces rectangles and squares with rounded corners. You can modify the shape of the corners by choosing *Round corners* from the Draw menu.

- The **Ellipse tool** draws ellipses and, if you hold down the Shift key while drawing, perfect circles.

- The **Arc tool** draws curved lines, which you can edit by choosing *Reshape arc* from the Draw menu. Holding down the Shift key while drawing an arc produces a quarter circle.

- The **Freeform tool** draws freeform shapes.

- The **Polygon tool** draws many-sided open and closed shapes. Polygons can be edited after they're drawn by choosing *Reshape poly* from the Draw menu.

- The **Magnifying glass icon** enlarges the view in the window. Select the magnifying glass icon, then click the location you want centered in the enlarged view. Continue clicking until you've reached the view you want. When you get to 400%, the icon will change from a plus sign to solid white.

- The **Reduction glass icon** reduces the view in the window. Its minus sign will vanish when you reach 25%, the opposite end of the scale. Pressing the Option key while using either the magnifying or reduction glass icon will do the opposite.

Text tool
Perpendicular-line tool
Diagonal-line tool
Square-corner tool
Round-corner tool
Ellipse tool
Arc tool
Freeform tool
Polygon tool
Magnifying glass icon
Reduction glass icon

Figure 2.34. The Toolbox contains all the tools you'll need for building a presentation.

The last two tools are viewing icons that control the size at which slides, notes, and handouts are displayed in the presentation window. You can choose from a range of magnification including 400% or 200% of the current view, 100% (actual size), fit in window, and 50% and 25% of the current view. When you want precision control in a close-up view, zoom in to 200% or 400%. When you want to see things as they really are, choose 100% or fit in window. And when you want a bird's eye view or need to work simultaneously on two presentations in side-by-side windows, zoom out to 50% or 25%.

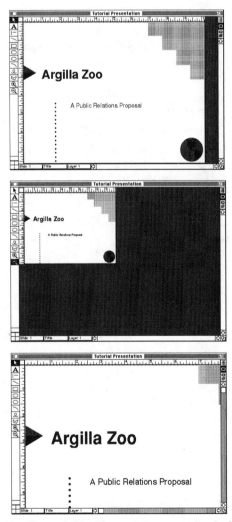

Figure 2.35. The same presentation in fit in window, 50%, and 200% views.

Persuasion also provides you with keyboard shortcuts for the two most commonly used views, as shown in Table 2.1.

Table 2.1

View	Keyboard shortcut
Fit in window	Command+W
Actual size (100%)	Command+1

Tip: For the most accurate display of type and graphics, use Actual size view. Other views may introduce slight and not-so-slight distortions.

Tip: To force the display to odd sizes, for example roughly 75% or 125%, use the size box in the bottom right corner of the window to resize the window. Then, when you use the keyboard shortcut for Fit in window (Command+W), the slide, note, or handout master will fit itself to the current size of the window.

In the bottom left corner of the presentation window, you'll see the **Presentation tool default display**. Once you learn to read it, you'll discover there's lots of information packed into this little display.

When the Pointer is selected, the display indicates the current default settings for the drawing tools. In other words, if you choose any of the drawing tools and begin to draw, you'll get what you see in the default display. The horizontal rectangle along the top shows a sample of the default fill pattern, fill color, and fill background. The square at the bottom shows a sample of the default horizontal and vertical line style, pattern, color, and background. In the figure below, the display indicates that the current defaults are a checkered fill pattern, a thick vertical black line with small white dots, and a thin horizontal line.

When you actually select a drawing tool, a second display appears above the first one. This is the **Current tool default display**. At first, it will look exactly like the Presentation tool default display. But if you change any settings in the Effect menu *with* a drawing tool selected, the Current tool default display will reflect this. The Current tool default display reflects the settings for the tool that's currently selected, rather than for all drawing tools for the presentation as a whole. In Figure 2.36 below, for example, when we selected the square-corner tool, its defaults were a thin vertical line, thick gray horizontal line, and solid black fill pattern.

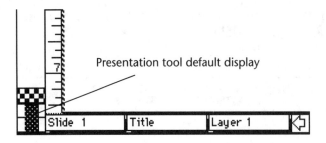

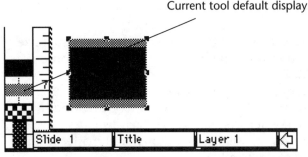

Figure 2.36. The Presentation tool default display (*top*) tells you what you'll get if you choose a tool and draw with it. The Current tool default display caption appears above it when you choose a drawing tool and change the settings in the Effect menu.

Persuasion really tries to take the guesswork out of drawing. You'll find that whenever you select a drawing tool, even the cursor shows you what to expect: its shape, color, and fill pattern change to reflect the current defaults.

Navigating Persuasion

Persuasion offers many routes between views and slides. As you accumulate experience, you'll develop a feel for the shortest path to your destination. Here are various alternatives.

The View Menu

As we saw earlier during our menu tour, the View menu allows you to move among Persuasion's seven views. In addition, you can use the View menu to move to a particular slide or slide master. In short, the View menu will take you wherever you want to go. Regardless of what view you're currently in, choosing:

- *Outline* takes you to the Outline view of your presentation.

- *Slide #* takes you to the Slide view of the currently selected slide.

- *Notes #* takes you the Notes view of the currently selected slide.

- *Slide sorter* takes you to the slide sorter view, where you'll see miniatures of all slides in the presentation.

The next three commands allow you to move quickly between Persuasion's three master views:

- *Slide master* takes you to the master of the currently selected slide.

- *Notes master* takes you to the notes master of your presentation.

- *Handout master* takes you to the handout master of your presentation.

Finally, the last two commands allow you to move to other slides in the presentation:

- *Go to slide* gives you a pull-down menu listing all the slides in the presentation. You'll move to the slide whose number you choose. The *New* option on this menu allows you to create a brand-new slide in slide view.

- *Go to master* gives you a list of all slide and background masters. The names of background masters appear in italic type to distinguish them from the slide masters. The *New* and *New background* options allow you to create new slide and background masters.

View Icons

In addition to the View menu, you can use the View icons to navigate between the three main Persuasion views. Click on the first icon, which looks like a miniature outline, to go to Outline view. Clicking on the second icon, a miniature slide, takes you to Slide view. The third, showing an even more miniature slide and some text below it, takes you to Notes view.

Combining the view icons with keyboard commands increases your navigational possibilities. Pressing the Option key while clicking the Outline icon will place you in Slide sorter view. Combining the Option key and Slide icon moves you to Slide master view. The Option and Command keys plus the Slide icon will take you even deeper, to the Background master view. And pressing the Option key while clicking the Notes icon sets you down in Notes master view.

Figure 2.37. The View icons let you move quickly between views.

That's not all. To move between the Outline, Slide, and Notes view of a particular slide, use the Command key in combination with the left or right arrow key. The Command key plus the up or down arrow key moves you between individual slides, notes, or masters in Slide view, Notes view or Slide master view.

Pop-up Menus

You can also use some of the pop-up menus you've already encountered to get where you want to go. When you're working on the outline or are in the Slide sorter, the Slide pop-up menu in the lower menu bar will take you directly to the Slide view of whatever slide you select. When you're working with slides or masters, the pop-up menu lets you move between individual slides.

Figure 2.38. Use the Slide pop-up menu to navigate between slides.

Slide Numbers in Outline View

Finally, clicking on any slide number in the left column in Outline view will take you to the Slide view of that slide. And pressing Option and clicking a slide number will take you to the Notes view of that slide.

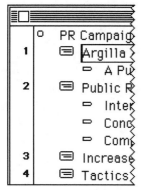

Figure 2.39. Click on a slide number to go from Outline view to the
Slide view of that slide.

Table 2.2 summarizes the keystroke navigation techniques.

Table 2.2

To move to	Press
Outline view	Click Outline icon
Slide view	Click Slide icon
Notes view	Click Notes icon
Slide sorter view	Option+click Outline icon
Slide master view	Option+click Slide icon
Background master view	Option+Command+click Slide icon
Notes master view	Option+click Notes icon
To move among views of a selected slide (Outline, Slide, and Notes views)	Command+left or right arrow
To move between individual slides, notes, or masters (depending on the current view)	Command+up or down arrow
In Outline view, to move to the Slide view of a slide	Click slide number in left column
In Outline view, to move to the Notes view of a slide	Option+click slide number in left column

Spend some time practicing these moves before you read on. The more at home you can make yourself with Persuasion, the more efficient your presentation work will be.

Now that you understand the overall structure of Persuasion and are familiar with some of its landmarks, let's roll up our sleeves and get down to work.

Chapter 3

Quick Start Tutorial

This tutorial is designed to get you up and running fast, and to give you a taste of how easy and fun it is to work with Persuasion.

To add a touch of excitement and urgency to the learning process, let's assume that you've just been hired as Director of Public Relations for the Argilla Zoo, a declining institution whose board of directors has recently decided to resurrect it. In exactly two hours, you have to make a presentation on how a public relations strategy can bring the Zoo around. If you succeed, fame and fortune will be yours. If you fail, you lose your job.

Without Persuasion, you'd be in an impossible pinch. With Persuasion, though, fate is on your side. First, you'll open a Persuasion AutoTemplate. This alone will save you several hours of work, since the template already includes many high-quality presentation ingredients, from effective slide layouts to sound typographic specifications. You'll type in your outline, apply a few master slides, add a couple of graphics and a chart or two, and you'll be ready to appear before the board with scarcely a hair out of place.

To stop this tutorial at any time, choose *Quit* from the File menu. If you're asked whether you want to save changes to the presentation, click *Yes* or *No*, depending on your inclination. If you change your mind about quitting, click *Cancel* to return to the presentation.

Note: During this tutorial, we'll import a couple of graphics from Persuasion's clip art collection, the Art of Persuasion. If you haven't installed it, take a minute to do it now before you begin. Pop Disk 5 into your floppy disk drive, then drag the Art of Persuasion folder into the Persuasion 2.0 folder on your hard disk.

If you're using a font management utility such as Suitcase II or Font/ DA Juggler, make sure the suitcases containing the larger-size fonts of Helvetica and Times are open.

Opening an AutoTemplate

To open an AutoTemplate, perform the following steps:

1. Locate the Persuasion 2.0 folder and double-click to open it.

2. Double-click to open the AutoTemplates folder.

3. Find AutoTemplate Q (use the scroll bars to make it visible), then double-click to run Persuasion and open the template. Persuasion's desktop appears, displaying the copyright screen. In a second or two, you'll find yourself in Outline view of an untitled copy (not the original) of AutoTemplate Q.

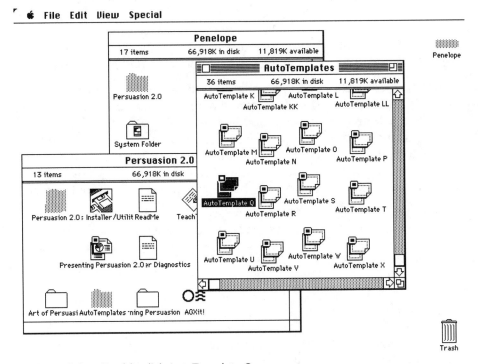

Figure 3.1.   Double-click AutoTemplate Q.

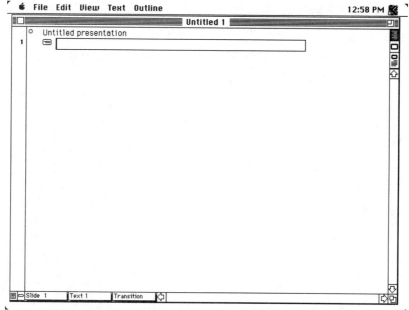

Figure 3.2.   Outline view of an untitled copy of AutoTemplate Q.

Let's take a minute to get our bearings. First of all, notice that the Outline view icon along the upper right corner of the presentation window is high-lighted to remind you you're in Outline view. Clicking the Slide view or Notes view icons below it switches you to Slide or Notes view (don't try it yet—there's plenty of time to experiment later).

In the bottom left corner of the window you'll discover the *Slide* pop-up menu, which tells you you're looking at Slide 1 and lets you move from slide to slide. Just to its right is the *Slide master* pop-up menu, which indicates that the slide master assigned to Slide 1 is Text 1. Finally, the *Transition* pop-up menu allows you to assign transition effects that will appear between slides in a slide show.

In the outline itself, you'll see the words "Untitled presentation" and an empty outline heading below it. In a minute, we'll begin typing the outline there. But first, let's name and save this untitled copy of AutoTemplate Q as a presentation.

Saving a New Presentation

In the title bar across the top of the screen, notice that the title of this presentation is "Untitled 1." Let's give it a more meaningful name:

1. Choose *Save as* or *Save* from the File menu.

Figure 3.3.   Choose *Save as* from the File menu.

2. In the *Save presentation as* dialog box, place the pointer on *Auto-Templates*, and then drag down to select the Persuasion 2.0 folder. Your new presentation will be saved in the Persuasion 2.0 folder. If you'd prefer to put it somewhere else, drag to open the folder you want it stored in.

3. Type *Argilla Zoo Presentation* to replace the highlighted text "Untitled 1." Just below the text box, you're given the option of saving as a presentation or an AutoTemplate. If you intended to construct your own AutoTemplate now, here's where you'd begin. We're going to create just one simple presentation, though, so leave *Presentation* checked.

4. Click *OK*. The title bar of your outline now displays the presentation's new name.

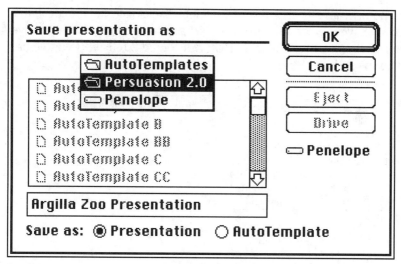

Figure 3.4.   Save your presentation as *Argilla Zoo Presentation* in the Persuasion 2.0 folder.

Typing an Outline

We'll begin this presentation in the usual way, by typing, editing, and reorganizing an outline:

1. Drag to highlight "Untitled presentation." Type *PR Campaign* in its place. The first line of every outline is a **slide holder**, a nonprinting label that identifies and "contains" the presentation's slides. It won't ever appear on a slide.

2. Press the down arrow to move the cursor to the beginning of the next line. Type *Argilla Zoo*. The slide icon indicates that this is a **slide title**. Notice the **slide number** in the column to the left. Clicking on a slide number is the quickest way to move to Slide view of that slide. It's also very easy to do by mistake. (If you do it, just click the Outline view icon to return to Outline view.)

3. Press Return, and then press Tab. Type *A Public Relations Proposal*. Pressing Return creates a new line at the same level in the outline hierarchy. Pressing Tab indents the entire topic one level to the right when the insertion point is at the beginning of a line. The bullet indicates that what you type will appear as body text on the slide. (You could have achieved the same effect by using the mouse to drag the topic's icon to the right, or by using the *Move right* command in the Text menu.)

4. Press Return, and then press the Delete/Backspace key. Type *Public Relations Environment*. Pressing Delete/Backspace moves you one level higher in the outline. The slide icon numbered 2 tells you you've created a new slide.

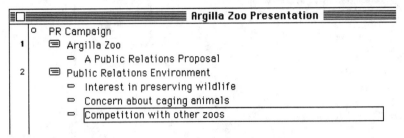

Figure 3.5. To move one level higher in the outline, press the Delete/Backspace key.

5. Press Return, then press Tab. Type *Interest in preserving wildlife*.

6. Press Return. Type *Concern about caging animals*.

7. Press Return, then type *Competition with other zoos*.

8. Press Return and Delete/Backspace to create a new slide title.

9. Continue typing the rest of the outline as it appears in Figure 3.6. Remember, to start a new line at the same level, press Return. To start a new line at a lower level, press Return then Tab. To start a new line at a higher level, press Return then Delete/Backspace. *Don't* press Return after the last heading.

```
3  ▤ Increase annual zoo attendance
4  ▤ Summary
5  ▤ Adopt a Wild Animal Campaign
      ▭ Receive "adoption" papers
      ▭ Choose a compliment
      ▭ Select desired animal
6  ▤ Adoption candidates
7  ▤ Tactics
      ▭ Media contacts
      ▭ Zoo newsletter
      ▭ Animal naming contest
      ▭ Adopt a Wild Animal campaign
```

Figure 3.6. Type the remainder of the outline as it appears above.

Finished typing? Well, it would be a shame to lose all that work! Choose *Save* from the File menu to save a copy of all you've done so far. (From now on, we'll leave it to you to save. Use the keyboard shortcut *Command+S* to make frequent saving as painless as possible.)

Editing an Outline

Well, if you followed orders perfectly, you made a few mistakes in the outline and left a few things in need of rearranging. Let's clean them up.

Adding Text to the Outline

On slide 2, click after the word "preserving", then type *and protecting*. When you click in a heading, a blinking vertical line (the insertion point) appears. What you type is entered to the left of the insertion point.

Changing a Word

On slide 5, double-click on the word "compliment" to highlight it, then type *continent*. What you type replaces whatever text was highlighted.

Adding a Subhead

On slide 5, click the bullet to the left of the subhead "Receive "adoption" papers" to select it. A solid frame appears around the subhead to let you know it's active.

Press Return to start a new line at the same level, and type *Make donation to zoo*. If you click an insertion point within a slide title or subhead then press Return, you'll simply start a new line within the same subhead, instead of inserting a new subhead below it.

Rearranging Subheads

On slide 5, move the subhead "Receive "adoption" papers" below "Select desired animal." Click the bullet to the left of the subhead you want to move, then drag it to its new location. As you begin to drag, you'll see a few changes: the pointer turns into a pointing hand, the solid frame around the subhead becomes a dotted frame, and a solid horizontal bar indicates where the subhead will go when you release the mouse button. Subheads can be moved up, down, left, and right using this clicking and dragging technique.

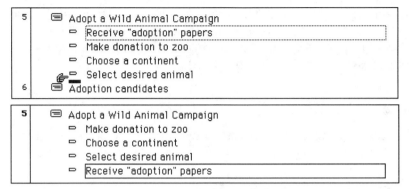

Figure 3.7.   Drag the subhead to its new location.

Rearranging Slides

Move slide 7, "Tactics," before slide 5, "Adopt a Wild Animal Campaign." Click the slide icon for slide 7, and then drag it to its new location above slide 5. As you begin to drag, you'll notice some of the same changes you saw when moving subheads: the pointer turns into a pointing hand, the solid frame around the slide title turns into a dotted line, and the horizontal bar indicates the slide's new position. All slides affected by the move are automatically renumbered in their new positions.

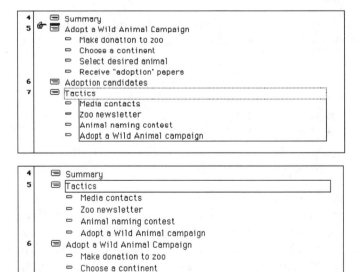

Figure 3.8.   Drag the slide icon for slide 7 to its new location above slide 5.

Notice that when you move a slide title, its subordinate headings move with it. In fact, any time you move an item with subordinate levels, they travel along too.

So much for the outline, for the time being. Let's move to Slide view and see the fruits of our labors.

Working in Slide View

Click on the slide number in the column to the left of slide 1. The pointer turns into a slide icon to warn you that you're about to be catapulted in Slide view. (Another way to move to Slide view, of course, is to click the Slide view icon in the upper right corner of the window while the outline text for slide 1 is selected. You could also choose *Slide #* from the View menu or the *Go to slide* pop-up menu at the lower left of the window. You could even press Command plus the right arrow key.)

Here we are in Slide view at Fit in window size. (Fit in window size may be larger or smaller than the actual size of the slide, depending on whether your monitor is large or small.) Slide 1 appears with the words you typed in the outline transformed into a slide title and subtitle, following the specifications of the placeholder on the master slide.

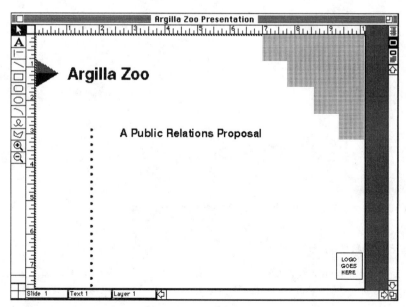

Figure 3.9.   Slide 1 at Fit in window size in Slide view.

In the lower menu bar, the *Slide* pop-up menu tells you what you already know, namely that you're looking at slide 1. The *Slide master* pop-up menu shows that the slide master assigned to this slide is Text 1. And the *Layer* pop-up menu indicates that you're seeing Layer 1, the slide's basic drawing layer.

After the initial thrill of seeing your outline magically turned into slides, your critical eye should tell you that the type is really too small for the title slide of your presentation. No problem: we'll reformat the slide by applying a more appropriate slide master.

Applying a New Slide Master

The 36 AutoTemplates that come with Persuasion use the slide master Text 1 as the default, so initially every slide in your presentation will be formatted as Text 1. For some slides, Text 1 will provide the best layout. For others, you'll want to reassign a more appropriate slide master.

Choose *Title* from the *Slide master* pop-up menu. With the new Slide master, both slide title and subtitle are larger and better placed. For example, the title changes from 36 to 48 point type and is centered vertically on the slide. The *Slide master* pop-up menu now reads *Title*.

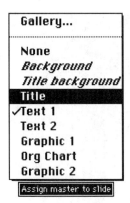

Figure 3.10. Choose *Title* from the *Slide master* pop-up menu.

Editing a Slide Master

The Title slide master provides a logo placeholder of sorts (the square containing the words "LOGO GOES HERE"). We need to replace it with the Zoo's logo.

You may remember from our guided tour that a slide can really have two masters, a slide master, such as Text 1 or Title, and a background master. Which of these masters contains the logo placeholder? Let's find out. To go to the slide master for the current slide, press Option and click the Slide view icon.

Figure 3.11. Press Option and click the Slide view icon to go to the
slide master for the current slide.

Since this is our first peek at the inner workings of a slide master, let's pause and look around. First of all, the slide master contains two placeholders, one for the slide title and one for text. Each placeholder includes formatting for the kind of text entrusted to its care. The title placeholder, for example, is set in 48 point Helvetica bold. If you change the formatting of a slide master's placeholder, the text on any slide assigned that master will automatically reflect the formatting changes.

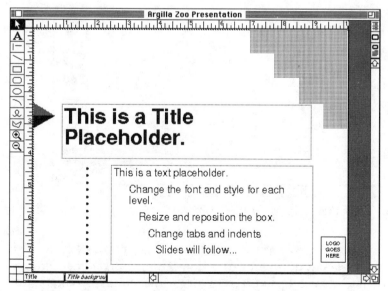

Figure 3.12. The slide master *Title* in Slide master view.

The *Slide master* pop-up menu tells us we're on the Title slide master, and the *Background master* pop-up menu lets us know that the background master *Title background* is applied to this slide master.

However, the logo placeholder isn't on this slide master, after all. It's on the background master. (To prove this to yourself, click on the logo place-holder. The fact that you can't select it tells you it's on the background master.) So we need to go one level deeper, to the background master.

Editing a Background Master

To go to the Background master, choose *Slide master* from the View menu, and then choose *Background* from the submenu (or press the Command and Option keys while clicking on the Slide view icon). What does a background master look like? This one contains several background elements: the stairstep graphic in the upper right corner, the triangular graphics along the left side, the dotted rule, and the logo placeholder.

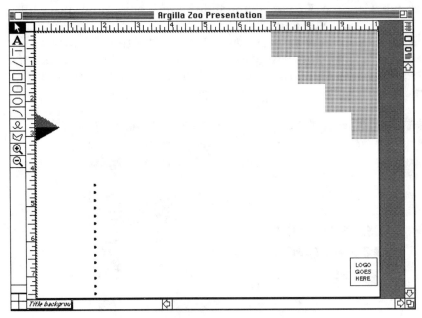

Figure 3.13. The background master *Title background*.

Any master slide assigned this background will automatically take on all these elements. As we saw during the tour, combining different background and slide masters gives you lots of possibilities without making you do lots of work.

Click to select the logo placeholder, then press the Delete/Backspace key to remove it. The logo placeholder is removed from the slide. Where will we find the Zoo logo? We'll have to import it.

Figure 3.14. Delete the logo placeholder.

Importing and Customizing a Graphic

Persuasion allows you to import both text and graphics from many other applications. In this case, we'll import a graphic from Persuasion's own clip art library, the Art of Persuasion.

Importing a Graphic

Perform the following steps to import a graphic:

1. Choose *Import* from the File menu.

2. In the Import dialog box, double-click to open the Art of Persuasion folder, then double-click the Maps folder, and then double click *Globe*. The graphic appears in the center of your screen.

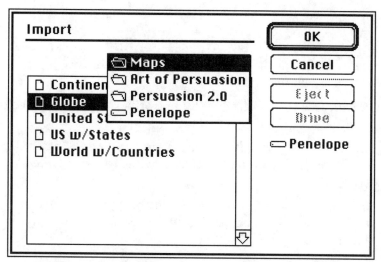

Figure 3.15. Open the file called *Globe* in the Maps folder in the Art of Persuasion clip art collection.

3. Point to the center of the graphic and drag it to the bottom right corner of the slide.

Now that the graphic is in position, let's customize it. We'll make the continents black and the oceans gray. But first let's enlarge the globe to get a better view of it.

Enlarging the View

Choose the magnifying glass icon from the toolbox and then click twice on the globe. This changes the display from Fit in window size to 100%, then to 200%. Whatever slide element you click will appear centered (more or less) in the window in the enlarged view.

Customizing a Graphic

The globe is a PICT graphic composed of elements that can be ungrouped and modified individually. Here's how:

1. Make sure the graphic is selected.

2. Select *Ungroup* from the Draw menu. To modify any imported PICT image, you must ungroup it at least once. This breaks the image into its component parts, so that you can edit them individually.

3. Select *Ungroup* a second time. This time, two sets of selection handles appear, one for the continents and one for the oceans.

4. Click away from the globe to deselect it.

5. Click North or South America to select the continents.

6. Choose *Fill pattern* from the Effect menu, then choose a solid black fill. The Americas will turn black.

7. Click the Pacific Ocean way off the coast of North America to deselect the continents and select the oceans.

8. Choose *Fill pattern* from the Effect menu, then choose a 50% gray fill. Since the fill color that's currently selected is white, you won't see any changes yet.

9. Choose *Fill color* from the Effect menu, and then choose black. The oceans will turn gray (because you've combined a 50% fill pattern with the color black).

Figure 3.16. When you ungroup the globe, two sets of selection
handles appear.

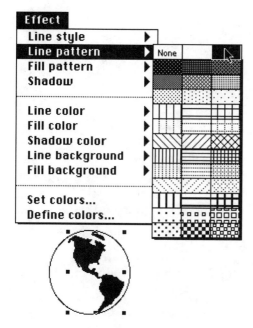

Figure 3.17. Apply a solid black fill pattern to the continents.

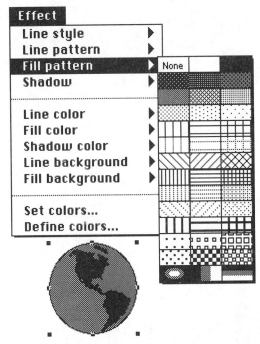

Figure 3.18. Apply a 50% black fill pattern to the oceans.

10. Choose *Regroup* from the Draw menu. When you ungroup a PICT image, Persuasion remembers all levels of grouping. The Regroup command reassembles a graphic's component parts in the opposite order from which they were taken apart.

11. Press *Command* plus *W* to return to Fit in window view. You could select the Reduction glass icon from the toolbox and click twice, but *Command+W* is much quicker.

Now that we've modified the background master by adding the customized globe, any slide master assigned this background master will contain the globe as well.

12. Click the Slide view icon to return to the Slide view of slide 1. Congratulations on completing your first slide! It should look like the one in Figure 3.19.

Now we'll go to slide 2. Slide 2 will be relatively easy. The default slide master, Text 1, suits it perfectly. However, we want to remove the logo placeholder from all but the first and last slides in our presentation. All we need to do is remove the logo placeholder from the other background master used in this presentation.

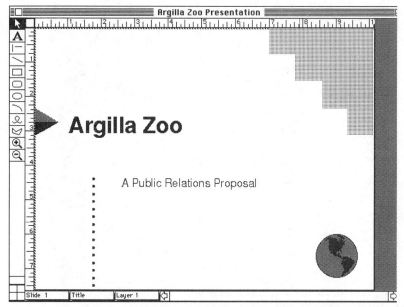

Figure 3.19. The completed slide 1.

Editing Another Background Master

Select Slide 2 from the *Slide* pop-up menu (or use the keyboard shortcut Command plus the down arrow key). The *Slide master* pop-up menu shows that slide 2's slide master is *Text 1* and background master is *Background*. Although the overall layout of this slide is fine as is, we must remove the logo placeholder from the background master.

Pressing Command and the up or down arrow key moves you from slide to slide, or from master to master, or from notes page to notes page, depending on which view you're in. Press the Command and Option keys while clicking the Slide view icon to go to the background master assigned to slide 2.

Pressing the Command and Option keys while clicking the Slide view icon is the fastest way to go to the current slide's background master. As you can see from the *Background* pop-up menu, the current background master is named, conveniently enough, "*Background*."

Click to select the logo placeholder, and then press the Delete/Backspace key to delete it. Click the Slide view icon to return to slide 2. Your completed slide 2 should look like the one shown in Figure 3.20.

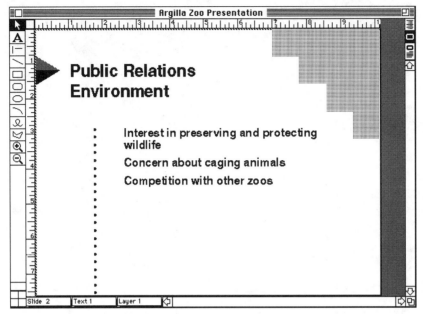

Figure 3.20. The completed slide 2.

Next, we'll work on slide 3. Our mission is to create a chart showing projected zoo attendance over the next 3 years.

Using the Gallery Feature to Preview Slide Masters

Let's begin by seeing which slide master would be most appropriate for our attendance slide. We'll need a layout that calls for a minimum amount of text and leaves lots of room for the chart. The Gallery feature allows you to preview how a slide will look with different slide and background masters applied to it:

1. Press Command and the down arrow to move to slide 3.

2. Choose *Gallery* from the *Slide master* pop-up menu. You'll see a miniature of the slide with the current slide master, Text 1, applied to it.

3. Choose Graphic 1 from the pop-up menu. The resulting slide miniature shows the slide title and below it a stacked bar chart. Although we're going to build a different kind of chart for our attendance data, the positioning of elements seems suitable: the slide title is high enough to leave room for a good-sized chart.

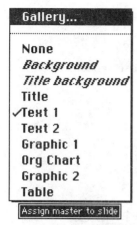

Figure 3.21. Choose *Gallery* from the Slide master pop-up menu.

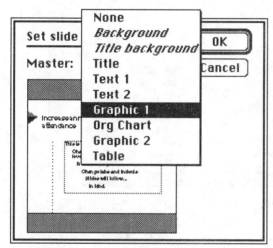

Figure 3.22. Choose *Graphic 1* from the pop-up menu to see a
miniature of how Slide 3 will look with that slide master
applied to it.

4. Click *OK* to close the dialog box and apply the new master to the slide.

Creating a Chart

Creating a chart involves typing or importing data into Persuasion's
spreadsheet (called the data sheet), selecting an appropriate chart or table
format, and plotting the data. Once you've created a chart, you can tinker
with and refine many aspects of its appearance.

Using Persuasion's Data Sheet

Set up a data sheet by performing the following steps:

1. Choose *Data sheet* from the File menu, then choose *Work area* to open Persuasion's own data sheet.

2. Place the pointer on the upper left cell and drag diagonally down to select an area two columns wide by five rows deep. If you make a mistake as you select, click anywhere in the data sheet to deselect what's selected, then start again.

3. Type the data as it appears in table 3.1

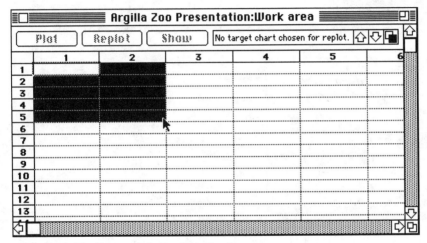

Figure 3.23. Drag to select a 2-by-5 cell area.

Table 3.1.

Year	Attendance
1989	125
1990	150
1991	200
1992	275

Leave the top left cell blank. To enter the data by columns, press Return. To enter the data by rows, press Tab.

Each time you press the Tab or Return key to move to a new cell, the cell will turn white to indicate it's active. Highlighting an area of the data sheet before you start typing confines the cursor to that area.

Make sure the cells are still highlighted when you finish entering data. (If not, use the pointer to drag and reselect them.) Your data sheet should look like the one shown below.

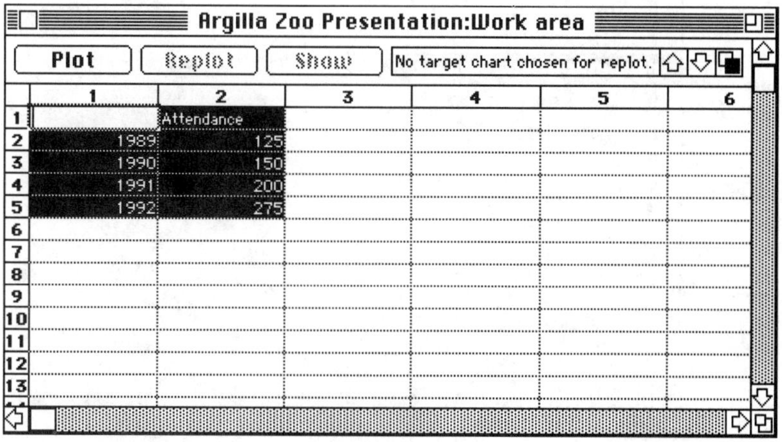

Figure 3.24. The completed data sheet.

Choosing a Chart Format

Now we need to tell Persuasion how we want this data displayed:

1. Choose *Chart format* from the Chart menu. Notice the check mark next to Graphic 1. This is the default chart format for the slide master we're using, Graphic 1. As you'll see later on, you can set up other chart formats and build them into the definition of your slide masters. Now, however, we want to display our data in column format.

2. Choose *Column* from the submenu of chart formats.

3. Click the *Plot* button at the top of the data sheet. Persuasion will plot the data in a column chart, laying it out and formatting it according to the chart placeholder on the slide master. (If the slide master assigned to the current slide had no chart placeholder, the default chart format for the presentation would be used instead.)

When the data is plotted, you'll see a message above the data sheet telling you what kind of chart was plotted, and where, in this case, "Column chart on slide 3 (Top)."

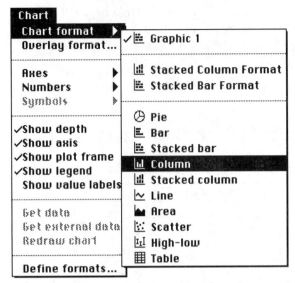

Figure 3.25. Choose *Column* from the submenu of chart formats.

4. Click the close box in the upper left corner of the data sheet to close it. The data sheet closes, revealing the column chart shown below.

5. Point to the center of the column chart and drag it into place. The top of the chart should align, more or less, with the top dot in the vertical dotted line.

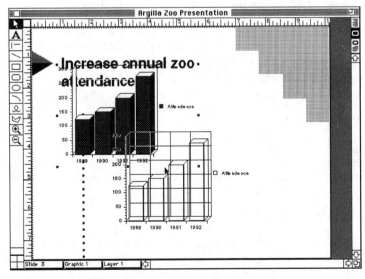

Figure 3.26. Drag the chart into place.

Although the chart looks pretty good for a first pass, the legend doesn't add much information. Let's replace it with a more meaningful caption.

Fine-Tuning the Chart

1. Make sure the chart is still selected, then choose *Show legend* from the Chart menu to hide the legend. The legend will disappear and the menu item *Show legend* will no longer be checked.

Now we'll create a caption below the chart, explaining that the numbers along the vertical axis represent projected attendance in thousands.

2. Select the text tool and click below the chart, in line with the left edge of the frame. An empty text block appears, along with a flashing in-sertion point ready to receive what you type. The text ruler above it shows you the position of tabs and indent markers.

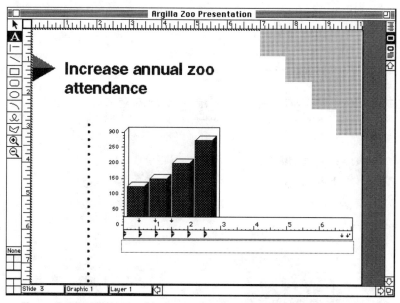

Figure 3.27. Clicking with the text tool creates an empty text block for the caption.

3. From the Text menu, open the Size submenu, and then choose *14*. Any selections you make in the Text menu when the insertion point is active will be reflected in whatever you type.

4. Type *Attendance in thousands (projected)*.

5. Choose the pointer to hide the text ruler. Your slide 3 should look pretty much like the one shown below. Use Command plus the down arrow or the *Slide* pop-up menu to move to Slide 4.

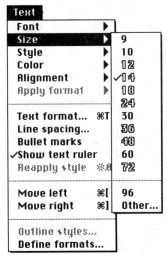

Figure 3.28. Choose 14 points from the Size submenu.

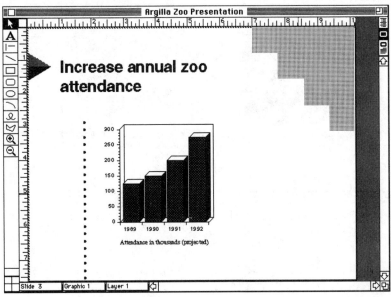

Figure 3.29. The completed slide 3.

Wait a minute, what's the Summary doing here in the middle of the presentation? Shouldn't it be at the end? Let's use the Slide sorter to fix things up.

Using the Slide Sorter

The Slide sorter displays miniatures of all the slides in your presentation. You can use it to check the overall flow and sequence of slides, to rearrange them, and to assign slide and background masters.

Choose *Slide sorter* from the View menu. You'll see all seven slides in your presentation. The number of slides in each row will vary depending on the size of your monitor, so what you see may be different than what's shown in Figure 3.30.

The Sorter menu lets you change the size of the slide miniatures so that more of them can be seen at once. Now they're displayed at the largest size, *Normal*.

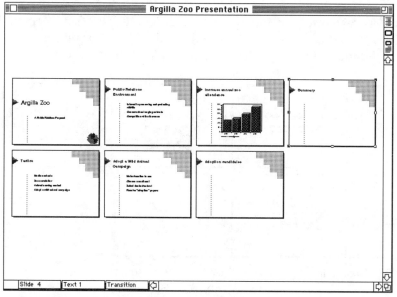

Figure 3.30. The Slide sorter view gives you an overview of your presentation.

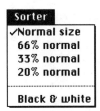

Figure 3.31. The Sorter menu lets you see slide miniatures at various sizes.

In the lower menu bar, the Slide pop-up menu tells you which slide is currently selected. Using the Slide master and Transition pop-up menus, you can apply masters and transition effects. Along the upper right edge of the Slide sorter window, the familiar view icons let you move to Outline, Slide, and Notes views.

Click slide 4, Summary. You'll see selection handles appear on slide 4 and the Slide pop-up menu display change from *No slide* to *Slide 4*.

Let's move slide 4 to the end of the presentation, where it belongs.

Drag slide 4 down into position after the last slide. As you drag, a rectangular outline marks the current position of the slide. A solid vertical bar tells you where the slide will end up when you release the mouse button.

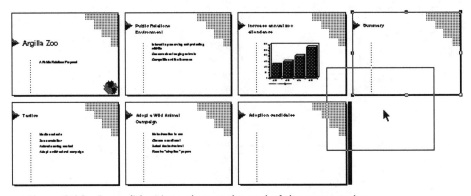

Figure 3.32. Drag slide 4 into place at the end of the presentation.

When you release the mouse button, the Summary slide you moved will still be selected. The Slide pop-up menu tells you it's now slide 7. And all the slides after the one you moved have automatically been renumbered.

By the way, any changes you make in the presentation sequence in Slide sorter view will be reflected in all other views—another one of Persuasion's powerful dynamic links!

While we're still here in Slide sorter view, let's change the slide master applied to the Summary slide, now slide 7.

Changing the Slide Master in Slide Sorter View

Choose Title from the Slide master pop-up menu. With the Title slide master applied, the word "Summary" grows and drops lower on the slide, and the globe logo appears (because it's on the background master assigned to the Title slide master, remember?).

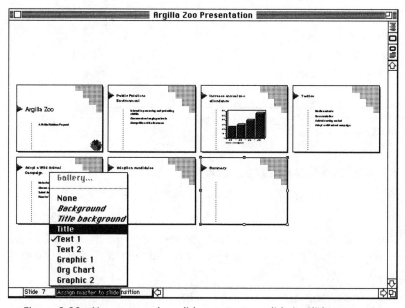

Figure 3.33. You can apply a slide master to a slide in Slide sorter view.

As you can see in the bird's eye view afforded by Slide sorter view, now both the first and the last slide in the presentation include the logo.

Double-click slide 7 to leave Slide sorter view and return to Slide view. Double-clicking a slide in Slide sorter view is the fastest way to go to the Slide view of that slide. With any luck, your completed slide 7 should look like the one shown below!

Now, let's backtrack to the new slide 4. Choose *Slide 4* from the Slide pop-up menu. Slide 4 will be a challenge to your artistic skills. We'll use Persuasion's drawing tools to create a simple graphic of a newsletter. Then we'll reformat one of the subheads to make it stand out.

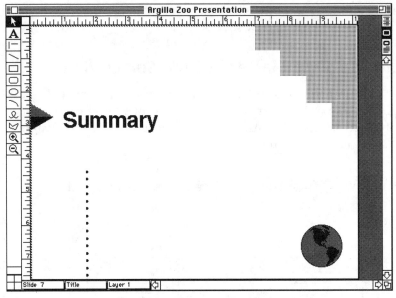

Figure 3.34. The completed slide 7.

Working with Drawing Tools

Before we launch into this operation, let's zoom in for a closer look at the operating field.

1. Click the magnifying glass icon in the toolbox, and then click once below the text. This enlarges the view of the area you clicked to 100% (actual size).

2. Select the square-corner tool from toolbox.

3. Using the rulers as a guide, position the crossbar at 3 inches on the horizontal ruler and 5 inches on the vertical ruler. When you move the drawing tool into the presentation window, it changes into a crossbar. The fine dotted lines in the rulers reflect its current position.

4. Drag diagonally down and to the right, creating a rectangle 1 1/2 inches wide and 2 inches tall (at 4 1/2 inches on the horizontal ruler and 7 inches on the vertical ruler).

5. Now, let's use a shadow to make our newsletter really stand off the page. Choose *Shadow* from the Effects menu, and then choose a solid black shadow from the pop-down menu.

6. Next, we'll draw the newsletter's nameplate and simulate two columns of text. Choose the perpendicular line tool from toolbox.

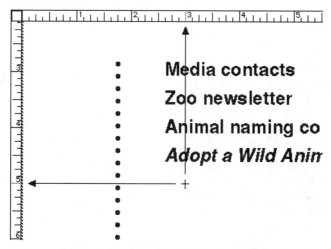

Figure 3.35. Using the rulers as a guide, position the crossbar where
you want the upper left corner of the graphic.

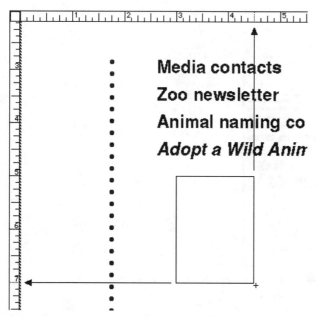

Figure 3.36. Drag to draw a rectangle.

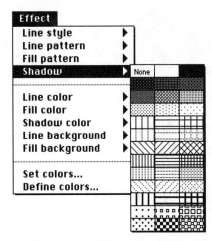

Figure 3.37. Choose a solid black shadow to make the newsletter stand off the page.

7. Choose *Line style* from the Effects menu, then choose a heavy horizontal rule.

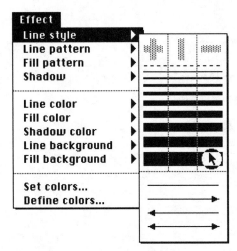

Figure 3.38. Choose a heavy horizontal line style to simulate the newsletter's nameplate.

8. Draw a horizontal rule as shown in Figure 3.39. Notice that the shape of the drawing tool reflects the line style settings you just selected.

Figure 3.39. The shape of the drawing tool reflects the line style
settings you selected.

9.   Choose the square-corner tool.

10. Choose *Fill pattern* from the Effects menu, then select a medium gray
fill pattern.

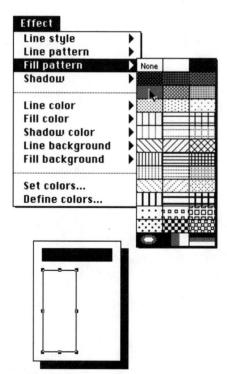

Figure 3.40. Choose a medium gray fill pattern, then draw a rectangle
to simulate a column of text.

11. Draw a rectangle as shown in Figure 3.40. When you release the mouse button, the rectangle shows its fill pattern.

12. Choose *Duplicate* from the Edit menu to copy the rectangle. Although you could copy and paste the rectangle, the *Duplicate* command is the fastest way to make a copy of an element.

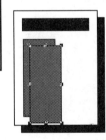

Figure 3.41. The *Duplicate* command is the fastest way to copy an element.

13. Choose the pointer, then drag the duplicate rectangle into place beside the original.

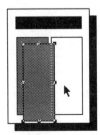

Figure 3.42. Drag the second rectangle into place alongside the first to simulate two text columns.

Congratulations! You've just drawn your very first newsletter. Now let's group all the separate elements you've created into a single whole, so that we can move them all at once.

Grouping Objects

To group objects, begin by dragging a selection box around the newsletter graphic. When you release the mouse button, all elements within the selection box will be selected.

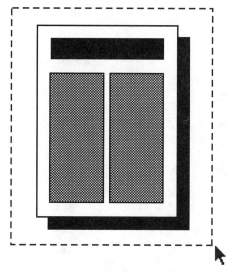

Figure 3.43. Drag a selection box around the newsletter elements to select all of them.

Then, choose *Group* from the Draw menu. Instead of one set of selection handles for each element, you'll see just one set for the grouped newsletter graphic. You can always ungroup a grouped graphic so as to modify its component parts.

Next, let's move the completed graphic into place.

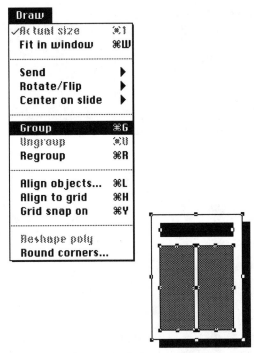

Figure 3.44. With all the newsletter elements selected, choose *Group* to make one object from many.

Aligning Objects

Persuasion offers several alignment commands that save you from having to rely on your eye. Let's use one to align the newsletter graphic with the body text block. But first, we'll return to the view we were in before we began to draw.

1. Return to Fit in window view by pressing *Command+W*.

2. Click on the newsletter graphic to select it, and then hold down the Shift key and click on the body text block.

3. Choose *Align objects* from the Draw menu.

4. From the Align objects dialog box, after the Left/Right option, click *Left*. Using combinations of these options, you can align objects vertically, horizontally, or both, using any of their edges. Determining what objects move and where in order to line up depends upon the object that's farthest out; that is, the topmost, leftmost, rightmost, or lowest object.

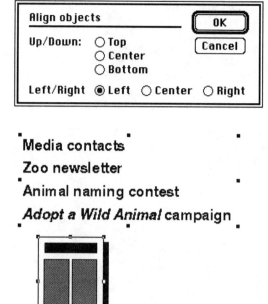

Figure 3.45. Align the text block and newsletter graphic along their left
sides.

5. Click *OK*. The text block and the graphic will be aligned to the left-most point of the leftmost object.

One final modification and we're finished with slide 4. Let's italicize the words *Adopt a Wild Animal* to make clear it's the name of a special campaign.

Formatting Text on a Slide

In general, the fastest, most effective way of formatting slide text is by formatting the corresponding placeholders on the slide master. But you can balance the global control that placeholders provide with local precision. You can always go to an individual slide and format its text, overriding its placeholder's formatting. Let's do it now:

1. Select the text tool.

2. Click on the body text block to select it. The text block "opens" and the text ruler appears above it.

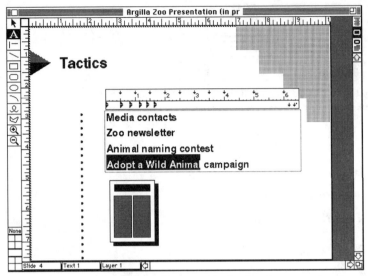

Figure 3.46. Selected text in a text block with the text ruler showing above it.

3. Drag to highlight the words *Adopt a Wild Animal*.

4. Choose *Style* from the Text menu, then choose *Italic*.

5. Select the pointer tool to hide the text ruler. Your completed slide 4 should look the one in Figure 3.47.

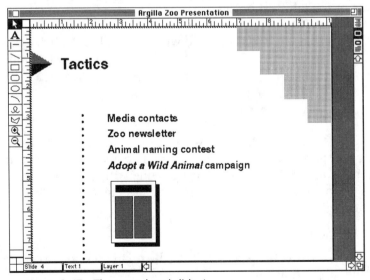

Figure 3.47. The completed slide 4.

Your Turn to Practice

In this brief time you've already acquired quite a selection of presentation skills. We'll let you practice some of them on slide 5.

Slide 5 requires you to perform three steps. The first two you've done before. The third has a few new twists, which we'll explain as you go along.

Press Command plus the down arrow to move to slide 5.

1. Select and italicize *Adopt a Wild Animal*. Refer to the instructions for slide 4 if you're not sure how to proceed.

2. Apply slide master Text 2 to make room for a graphic. If necessary, refer to the instructions for slide 2.

The body text placeholder on slide master Text 2 is formatted with smaller text than the one on Text 1, to make room for larger amounts of text or a graphic.

3. Import the graphic *World w/Countries* from the Maps folder in the Art of Persuasion folder. If your memory needs refreshing, consult the directions for slide 1.

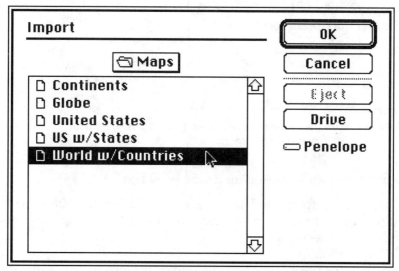

Figure 3.48. Import the *World w/Countries* graphic from the Maps folder.

Once you've imported the graphic, you'll need to resize and customize it. Here's how.

Resizing a Graphic

To resize a graphic, perform the following steps:

1. Select the graphic with the mouse, drag one of the selection handles, and press on the Shift key to maintain the graphic's aspect ratio. The Shift key forces proportional resizing. It prevents you from distorting a graphic as you resize it (in this case, flattening the world into a pancake). Make sure to release the mouse *before* you let go of the Shift key. Otherwise, the graphic may end up being distorted after all.

Note that you can also hold down the Command and Shift key, and then click the upper right corner of the graphic and drag diagonally down to the left. When you hold down the Command key, the pointer turns into a four way arrow, the resizing tool. With it, you can click anywhere on a graphic to select it, not just on one of its selection handles.

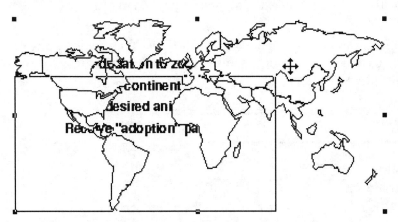

Figure 3.49. To resize the graphic proportionately, hold down the Shift key while dragging a corner.

2. Drag the world into position under the body text.

3. Choose *Ungroup* from the Draw menu. As you learned before, you must ungroup any PICT image before you can edit it using the commands in the Effects menu.

When we modified the globe logo, we ungrouped a second time to divide the earth into land and water. This time, instead of ungrouping the world again, we'll use a different technique called subselecting.

4. Double-click to select the country or continent of your choice. (Try a large one, like the United States or Africa.) Subselecting allows you to select individual elements within a graphic by double-clicking, while the graphic can still be moved as a single unit.

Figure 3.50. Double-click the country or continent of your choice.

5. Apply a fill pattern and/or fill color from the Effect menu to make your chosen country or continent stand out from all the rest.

6. Regroup the world.

Your completed slide should look like the one shown below, depending on what continent or country you selected, and how you filled it.

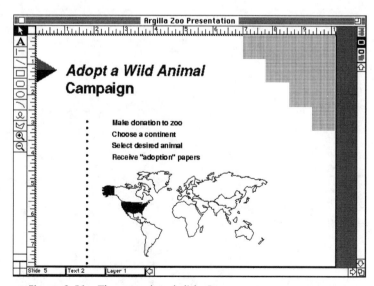

Figure 3.51. The completed slide 5.

Okay, we're in the home stretch—only one more slide to go (since we've already taken care of slide 7, the summary).

But slide 6 is not easy. We're going to build our own slide master, especially suited for a table. We'll create a new slide master, and then add and format a table placeholder. Then we'll enter data in the data sheet. When we plot it, it will be formatted according to the table placeholder.

(We could do this more easily by choosing *Table* from Chart menu. But we want to give you a taste of how to create your very own slide master from scratch.)

Creating a New Slide Master

Perform the following steps to create a new slide master:

1. Press Command and down arrow to move to slide 6. Notice that the current Slide master is Text 1.

2. Press Option and click on the Slide view icon. This takes you to Slide master view. You should be looking at the Slide master Text 1 with its title and text placeholders. Note that when you move from Slide view to Slide master view, the pop-up menus along the lower title bar change. Instead of the *Slide, Assign master to slide,* and *Layer* menus, you see the *Master* and *Background* menus.

3. Choose *New* from the *Slide master* pop-up menu.

Figure 3.52. To create a new slide master, choose *New* from the Slide
              master pop-up menu.

4. In the New slide master dialog box, type *Table 1* as the Master name, and then click *OK*.

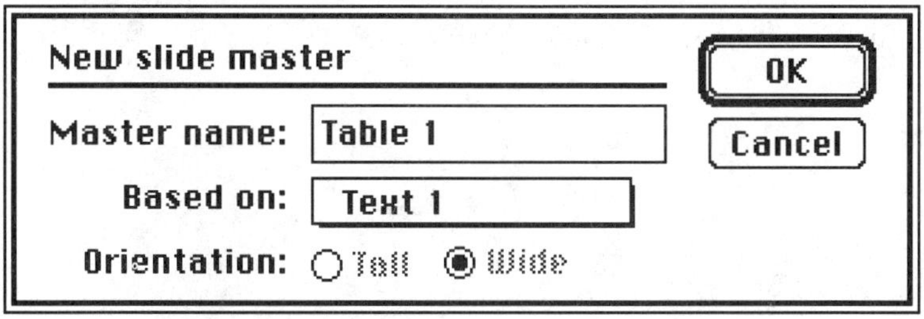

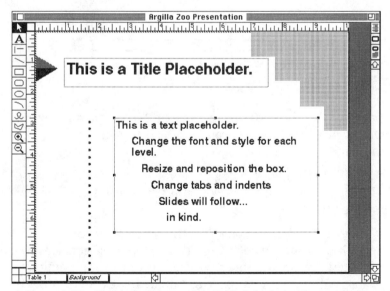

Figure 3.53. Type the name of the new slide master in the New slide master dialog box.

The new slide master will be based on the existing slide master Text 1. Basing one master on another is a shortcut that relieves you from having to construct each new master from scratch. As you can see from the figure below, our new slide master already contains all the same elements as Text 1 —the background graphics, the title placeholder, and the body text placeholder.

Figure 3.54. The new slide master, *Table 1*, includes the same elements as the *Text 1* slide master on which it's based.

Since there won't be any body text on a slide containing a table, we'll delete the body text placeholder and add a table placeholder.

5. Click the body text placeholder, and then select *Clear* from the Edit menu to remove it from the slide master.

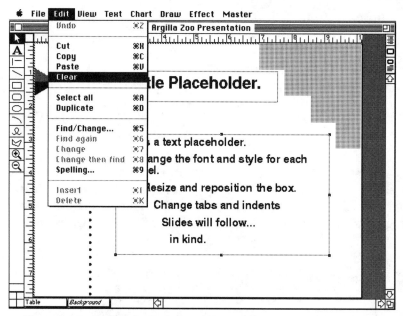

Figure 3.55.   Delete the body text placeholder by choosing *Clear* from the Edit menu.

6. Select *Add table* from the Master menu. The Master menu contains nine types of placeholders that can be added to slide, background, notes, and handout masters.

7. In the Add table placeholder dialog box, type *8* for default number of rows and *2* for default number of columns. Use the Tab key to move between typing fields in a dialog box.

8. Click *OK*. A table placeholder appears in the center of the master slide, reflecting both the row and column settings you just selected, as well as the fill pattern, color, and line style defaults of this AutoTemplate. Drag it into position, with its top edge aligned with the top of the vertical dotted line.

Master
Add title
Add subtitle
Add body text
Add chart...
Add table...
Add org. chart...
Add page number...
Add slide copy
Add notes text

Anchor placeholder...
Build layers...
Slide background fill...
Tall orientation

Re-create from slide...
Define bullet marks...
Define masters...

Figure 3.56. Use the Master menu to add a table placeholder.

	L10
L01	1.1
L02	1.2
L03	1.3
L04	1.4
L05	1.5
L06	1.6
L07	1.7

Figure 3.57. The table placeholder with two columns and eight rows.

Customizing a Placeholder

Let's customize the table placeholder. Make sure it's selected, and then practice your formatting skills as follows:

1. From the Effect menu, make the following selections:
   - Fill pattern: solid
   - Line color: white

Since the fill pattern is solid black and the type on top of it is also black, of course you can't see the text. Let's fix that.

2. From the Text menu, make the following selections:
   - Color: white
   - Size: 14

3. From the Chart menu, choose *Show depth*. When you're finished, the table placeholder should look like the one shown below. From now on, whenever you apply this Slide master to a slide, its table will take on the attributes of this table placeholder.

	L10
L01	1.1
L02	1.2
L03	1.3
L04	1.4
L05	1.5
L06	1.6
L07	1.7

Figure 3.58. The formatted table placeholder.

4. Click the Slide view icon to return to Slide view of slide 6.

5. Choose *Table* from the *Master* pop-up menu to apply the slide master *Table* we just created to slide 6. You won't see any visible difference until we actually build the table itself.

Setting Up a Table

Now we'll enter data in Persuasion's data sheet the same way we did for the attendance chart on slide 3.

1. Choose *Data sheet* from the File menu, and then choose *Work area*. The data sheet appears with the data from the previous chart still visible. Like a spreadsheet program, Persuasion allows you to use different areas of the same data sheet to plot data. Use the scroll bars or the resize box in the bottom right corner of the data sheet window to make room for new data.

2. Leave a blank row or two below the existing data, and then drag to highlight an area two columns wide by eight rows deep.

3. Type the data as it appears in Table 3.2 below.

Table 3.2.

Continent	Animal
Africa	Giraffe
Antarctica	Penguin
Asia	Tiger
Australia	Kangaroo
Europe	Reindeer
North America	Moose
South America	Peccary

Remember, to enter data by columns, press Return; to enter data by rows, press Tab. When you finish entering the data, make sure it's still highlighted. Your completed data sheet should look like the one shown below.

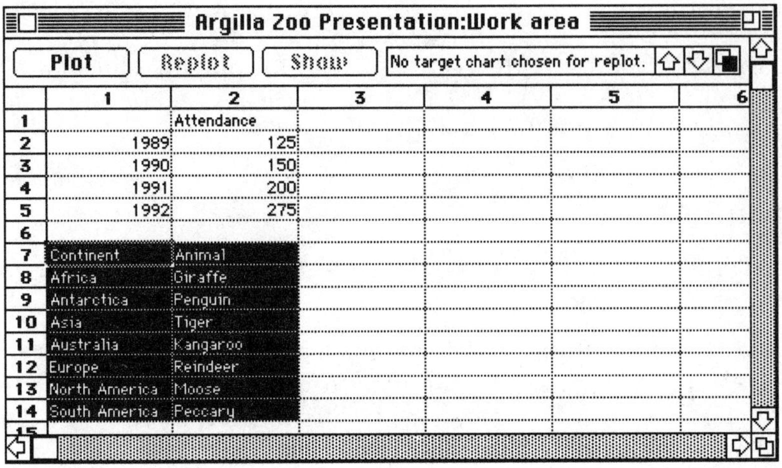

Figure 3.59. The completed data sheet.

4 Click *Plot*. The message along the top of the data sheets tell you, "Table chart on slide 6 (Top)."

5. Click in the close box to close the data sheet. There's your table! To make it even better, let's narrow the columns so the type doesn't float in them. With the same subselection technique we used to highlight a country on slide 5, we can select and modify individual table elements without ungrouping the table.

6. Double-click the white vertical line along the right edge of the table, and then drag it left until it's just to the right of the longest word in the right column.

The table is redrawn with the new column width.

7. Double-click the line separating the two columns, and then drag it left until the columns are roughly equal width.

Does your slide 6 look like the one shown in Figure 3.61? Good work!

From a graphic designer's point of view, slide 7 is fine as it is. But what about from a speaker's point of view? While all the other slides are pretty self-explanatory, what prompt will the contents of slide 7, Summary, give you when you're standing up there in front of the dour-faced Board members? Perhaps you'd like some notes to remind you what to summarize....

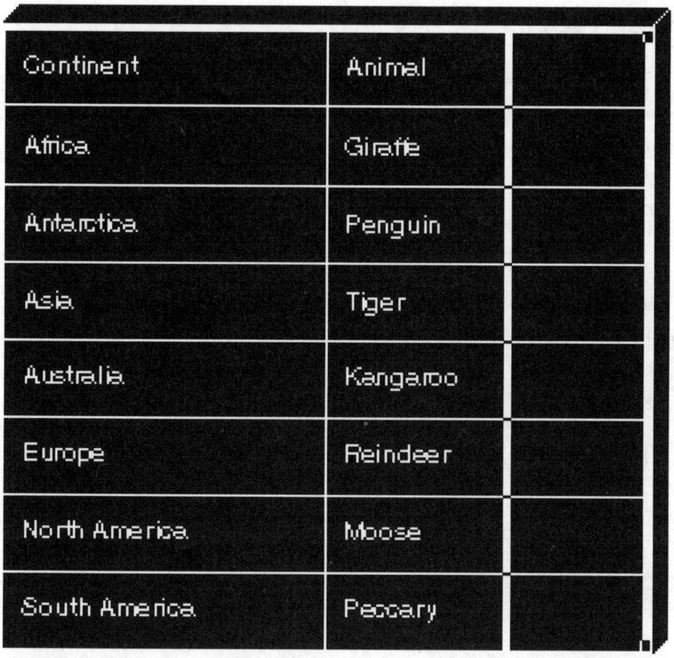

Continent
Animal
Africa
Giraffe
Antarctica
Penguin
Asia
Tiger
Australia
Kangaroo
Europe
Reindeer
North America
Moose
South America
Peccary

Figure 3.60. To change the width of a column, and drag one of its sides.

Argilla Zoo Presentation
Adoption candidates
Continent
Animal
Africa
Giraffe
Antarctica
Penguin
Asia
Tiger
Australia
Kangaroo
Europe
Reindeer
North America
Moose
South America
Peccary
Slide 6
Table
Layer 1

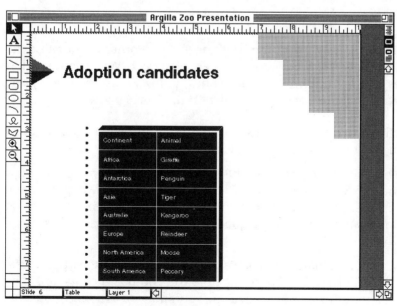

Figure 3.61. The completed slide 6.

Creating Speaker Notes

Persuasion allows you to create special outline headings specifically for speaker's notes. Like slide text, notes text is dynamically linked from the outline to a notes placeholder on the speaker notes master. Here's how it all works.

1. Click the Outline view icon to return to Outline view.

2. Click on the slide icon for slide 7. Remember, if you accidentally click the slide number in the column to the left instead of the slide icon, you'll suddenly find yourself in Slide view.

3. From the Outline menu, choose *Add notes*. Persuasion adds a main notes icon (the hollow square), followed by an empty notes text icon (the miniature notes page) just waiting for you to type your notes.

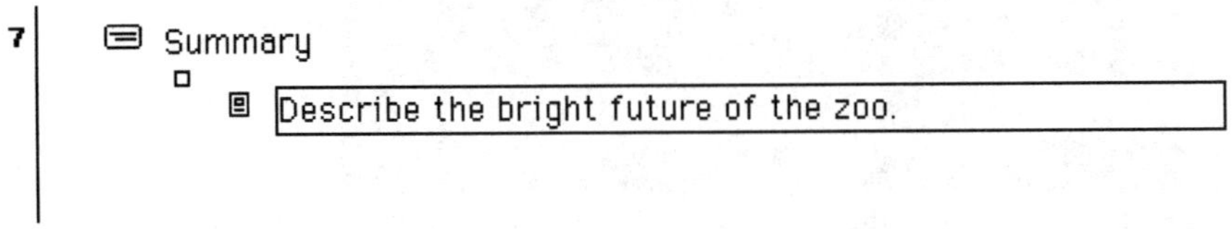

7   🖻 Summary

      □

          🔲 | Describe the bright future of the zoo.

Figure 3.62. Type speaker notes into the outline after the notes text icon.

4. Type *Describe the bright future of the zoo.*

5. Click the Notes view icon in the upper right corner of the presentation window to go to the Notes view of slide 7. What you typed as notes text in Outline view automatically flows onto the notes page, formatted by the notes placeholder on the Notes master.

To see the Notes master with its title and notes placeholder, hold down the Option key and click again on the Notes view icon.

Let's go back to the beginning of the presentation. Click on the Slide view icon to return to Slide view of slide 7, and then use the *Slide* pop-up menu to move to slide 1. Even though you've been saving your presentation at regular intervals (right?), now is a good time to do a final save. Press *Command +S.*

Our hearty congratulations. You've put together an excellent presentation, and you still have half an hour before the Zoo Board convenes! Why not take a few minutes for a dry run, using your monitor as a slide projector? Better to have any ugly surprises in the privacy of your office than in front of twelve surly Board members!

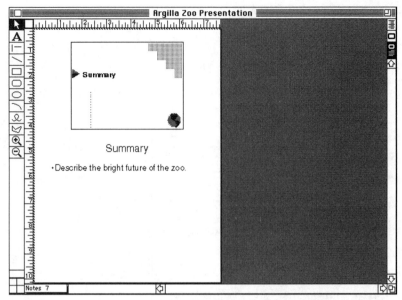

Figure 3.63. The completed speaker notes page for slide 7.

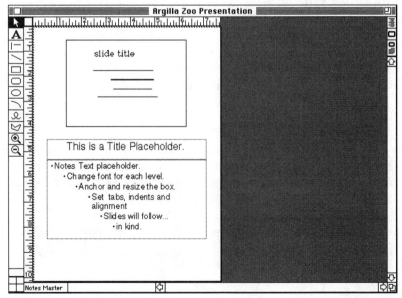

Figure 3.64. The speaker notes master.

Running a Slide Show

To run a slide show, perform the following steps:

1. From the File menu, choose *Slide show*.

2. In the Slide show dialog box, click to check *Full screen*, and click to uncheck *Continuous cycle*.

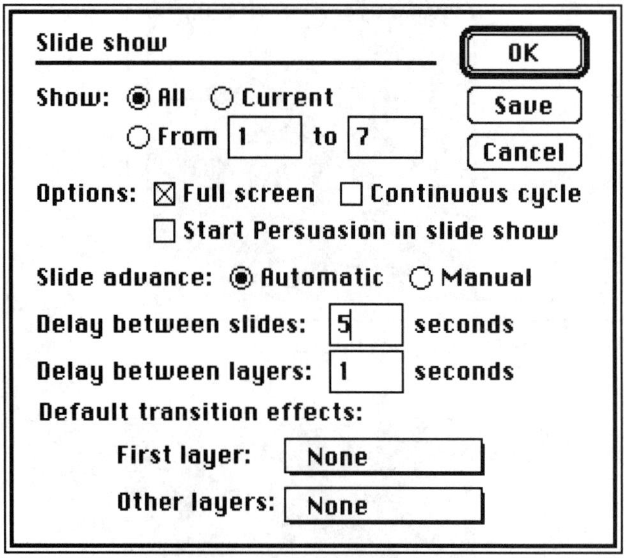

```
┌─────────────────────────────────────────────────┐
│  Slide show                            ╭────────╮ │
│  ─────────────────────────────────     │   OK   │ │
│  Show: ⦿ All  ○ Current                ╰────────╯ │
│         ○ From [1    ] to [7    ]        ( Save )  │
│                                                    │
│  Options: ⊠ Full screen  □ Continuous cycle       │
│           □ Start Persuasion in slide show  (Cancel)│
│                                                    │
│  Slide advance: ⦿ Automatic  ○ Manual             │
│  Delay between slides:  [5    ] seconds            │
│  Delay between layers:  [1    ] seconds            │
│  Default transition effects:                       │
│      First layer:  [ None            ]             │
│      Other layers: [ None            ]             │
└─────────────────────────────────────────────────┘
```

Figure 3.65. Make your selections in the Slide show dialog box.

3. Type in a 5-second delay between slides.

4. Click *OK*. The seven slides in your presentation will be displayed consecutively with each one remaining on your screen for 5 seconds. When the slide show is finished, you'll be returned to Slide view of slide 1 (where you began).

You can stop the slide show at any time by pressing *Command+*. (period).

Do you like what you see? Good! Let's commit it to print.

Printing a Presentation

Perform the following steps to print a presentation:

1. Choose *Print* from the File menu.

2. Click to uncheck *Builds*. You can print any combination of slides, outline, notes, and handouts. Unless you're pressed for time or paper, why not print all of them, just to see what they look like?

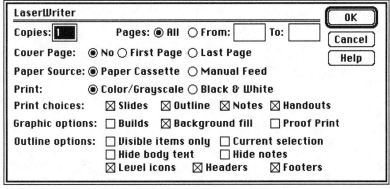

Figure 3.66. Choose the printing options you want from the Print dialog box.

3. Click *OK* to print.

4. When you're finished printing, choose *Quit* from the File menu. Persuasion may ask you if you want to save changes made to your presentation. Click *Yes* or *No*, depending on your mood. Persuasion will close the presentation, and then close itself.

Remove the pages from your printer, turn off your Macintosh, take a few minutes to congratulate yourself and collect your thoughts, and then head off to the Zoo Board meeting and your future brilliant career!

Okay, now that you're a veteran Persuasion user, you're ready to dig deeper into the power and complexity of Persuasion's features.

Part II ◆ Working with Persuasion

Chapter 4

Setting Up a Presentation

Now that you've whetted your appetite with the Argilla Zoo presentation, how do you actually use all these views and menus and tools to assemble an effective presentation on your own? In this chapter, we'll take a look at some of the most basic—and important—decisions you'll make as you set up your first presentation:

Persuasion offers you four ways to start a new presentation:

1. Open an AutoTemplate.

2. Start a new presentation based on the default AutoTemplate you selected when you installed Persuasion.

3. Open an existing presentation and modify it.

4. Start a brand new presentation from scratch.

Until you've been working with Persuasion for a while, you'll probably want to play it safe and start with an AutoTemplate—either the default AutoTemplate or some other—so we'll focus on the first two options in this chapter. As you work your way through this book, you'll gradually acquire all the skills you'll need for the third option, modifying an existing presentation. The fourth option, starting from scratch, requires a little more expertise, so we've devoted an entire chapter to it later on.

Decisions, Decisions, Decisions

Before you even set finger to keyboard or hand to mouse, you have to make a couple of crucial decisions.

First of all, you must choose a presentation medium. What will best convey your message—slides, overhead transparencies, or an on-screen presentation of some kind? What kind of facilities and equipment do you have to work with? Your answers to these questions will determine which Auto-Template you select.

Secondly, you must select an output device. Why is this such an important step? An output device "driver" or file contains information Persuasion needs to translate your presentation into a format that a particular printer or film recorder or plotter will understand. Most importantly from your point of view, selecting an output device tells Persuasion what dimensions and proportions to use when formatting your presentation.

If you're preparing an on-screen presentation instead of slides or overheads, you might think you won't need an output device. But Persuasion requires that you choose one anyway; since you'll probably want to print notes or handouts, select a laser printer. You'll get a chance later on to explain to Persuasion that you want the presentation composed for the dimensions of the screen you're using.

To select an output device, open the Chooser in the Apple menu. The icons you'll see in the Chooser depend on what driver files you have in your System folder. At the very least, you should see the Autographix driver that comes with Persuasion. Click on the icon for the output device you intend to use.

You may get a message saying, "Be sure to choose Page Setup and confirm the settings so that the application can format documents correctly for LaserWriter" (or whatever output device you've chosen). This is just a reminder to do what you'll shortly learn how to do, namely, specify the presentation setup.

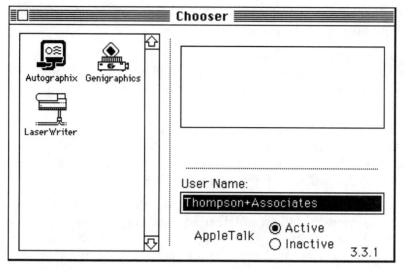

Figure 4.1   Select an output device in the Chooser.

Opening an AutoTemplate

Review the AutoTemplates in the *Desktop Reference* to find one you want to use. (To get your bearings quickly in the two-sided manual, open it from the side labeled AutoTemplates.) AutoTemplates labeled A through R and AA through FF are for black-and-white overheads. AutoTemplates labeled S through X and GG through LL are for color slides. All but three AutoTemplates (GG through II) have both black-and-white and color equivalents.

Although you can modify a slide template to produce overheads and vice versa, you're much better off starting with a template designed for your intended medium. If you're preparing an on-screen presentation, you have more freedom: your choice of a template will depend primarily on whether it's black and white or color.

You can begin a presentation with an AutoTemplate in any of the following three ways:

1. Open the AutoTemplates folder and double-click the icon of the Auto-Template you want to use. This is the fastest technique. It launches Persuasion and places you in Outline view of the AutoTemplate you select.

2. Open the Persuasion 2.0 folder, double-click the Persuasion icon to launch Persuasion, and then select *New* from the File menu. This opens a copy of the AutoTemplate you specified as the default when

you installed Persuasion (the black-and-white overhead AutoTemplate A, unless you chose another one).

3. Open the Persuasion 2.0 folder and double-click the Persuasion icon. This launches Persuasion and displays the Persuasion desktop, along with the copyright screen featuring Aldus Manutius and your "personalization" data.

Select *Open* from the File menu. In the Open presentation dialog box, double-click to open the AutoTemplates folder. There, you'll see a list of AutoTemplates. To open one, double-click its name. Use the scroll bars to see the templates hiding below the list box.

Persuasion includes a preview feature that allows you to review a thumbnail version of the template right there in the dialog box. Make sure the *Show thumbnail* option is selected, and then click the template you're considering. Persuasion displays a miniature of the template in the window in the bottom right corner of the dialog box (in color, if it's a color template). Usually what you'll see is the slide title master, with dotted lines indicating the position of placeholders. To scroll and preview the templates one by one, press the down or up arrow key.

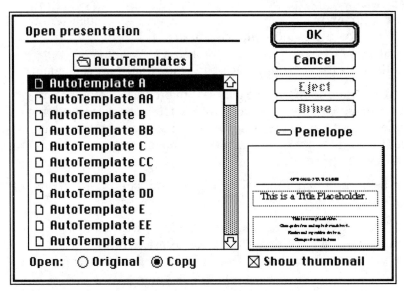

Figure 4.2.   The Open presentation dialog box shows you a thumbnail sketch of the selected presentation.

Note: Whenever you save a presentation, Persuasion automatically creates and saves an accompanying thumbnail version for display in this dialog box. If you're working on a large presentation while running several applications under MultiFinder on a computer without much memory—in other words, if available memory is low when you save the presentation—Persuasion may not be able to save a thumbnail version. However, Persuasion will try again the next time you open and save the presentation.

Persuasion 1.0 didn't include the thumbnail feature. To create a thumbnail for a Persuasion 1.0 presentation, open the presentation, and then use the *Save as* command to save it again with the same name.

Specifying the Presentation Setup

Now you must tell Persuasion how you want to set up your presentation, including what "slide" shape you want to use. ("Slide" in this case, and throughout Persuasion's menus and dialog boxes, refers to whatever is being projected during the presentation, whether it's overheads, 35-mm slides, or an on-screen presentation.) Choosing the right slide shape before you begin will make your life much simpler. Not only are the dimensions of each medium different, so are their proportions. The ratio of width to height (or "aspect ratio") of overheads and many monitors (such as the 13-inch Apple color monitor) is 4:3, and that of slides is 3:2. If you construct a presentation for overheads, and then decide to produce 35-mm slides, you must readjust all the slide elements so they fit within the new aspect ratio. Although Persuasion includes an automatic resize/reformat feature for unavoidable format changes, you're still better off starting in the right direction instead of changing course in midstream.

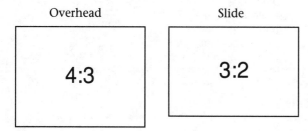

Figure 4.3.   The aspect ratio of overheads is 4:3 and of slides 3:2.

Choosing a Page Setup for Your Output Device

Choose *Page setup* from the File menu. You'll see two dialog boxes, one on top of the other. The top dialog box will ask you to specify various options to set up your output device (the one you just selected from the Chooser).

Printing to a Laser Printer

If you selected a LaserWriter or another laser printer, you'll see the Laser-Writer Page Setup dialog box or your printer's equivalent.

Select the correct paper size. If you wish to reduce or enlarge what you're printing (for example, for flip charts or actual-size slide proofs), type in the percentage you want.

Select one of the two options for orientation, vertical (portrait) or horizontal (landscape). Note that the orientation option you select here governs the entire presentation rather than individual slides or note pages. *Orientation* affects only whether your outline and handouts will print in landscape or portrait format. As you'll see later on, you control the orientation of slides and notes by setting up and assigning vertical or horizontal slide or notes masters.

We'll explore printing effects in detail in Part IV, *The Big Production*. You'll probably also have to refer to your printer's manual to see how these options affect your particular printer. For now, when you've made the basic selections you want, click *OK*.

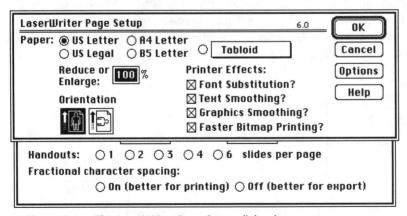

Figure 4.4.   The LaserWriter Page Setup dialog box.

Printing to a Slide Service Bureau

If you selected Autographix, you'll see the dialog box shown below. The *Orientation* option has no effect on slides created in Persuasion. Just click *OK* to continue.

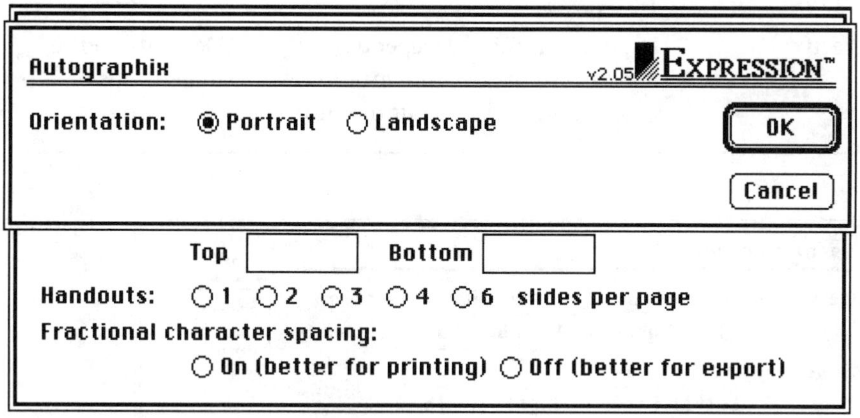

| Autographix | v2.05 **EXPRESSION**™ |

Orientation: ● Portrait   ○ Landscape   OK   Cancel

Top [   ]   Bottom [   ]
Handouts: ○1 ○2 ○3 ○4 ○6 slides per page
Fractional character spacing:
○ On (better for printing) ○ Off (better for export)

Figure 4.5.   The Autographix dialog box.

Printing to Other Output Devices

If you're printing to an output device other than the LaserWriter or Autographix, such as a color printer, plotter, or film recorder, consult its manual for special instructions.

Specify a Presentation Setup

When you close the top output device dialog box, you'll see Persuasion's own Presentation setup dialog box. The following text describes what you should do.

Slide Shape

Select a slide shape—*Overhead, 35-mm Slide, Screen,* or *Custom*—for your presentation. If you select *Overhead* or *35-mm Slide*, the dimensions of the working area in the presentation window will be determined by the output device you specified in the Chooser. If you select *Screen*, Persuasion will automatically read and display the dimensions of your monitor (for example, 8.89 inches by 6.67 inches for a 13-inch AppleColor monitor). Table 3.1 below shows you how the dimensions of the working area vary depending on what slide shape and output device you're working with.

Table 3.1

Slide Shape	LaserWriter	Autographix	Genigraphics
Overhead	10.14" × 7.6"	12.28" × 9.21"	7.94" × 5.96"
35-mm	10.14" × 6.75"	13.81" × 9.21"	8.89" × 5.92"
Screen	Depends on the dimensions of your monitor	Depends on the dimensions of your monitor	Depends on the dimensions of your monitor

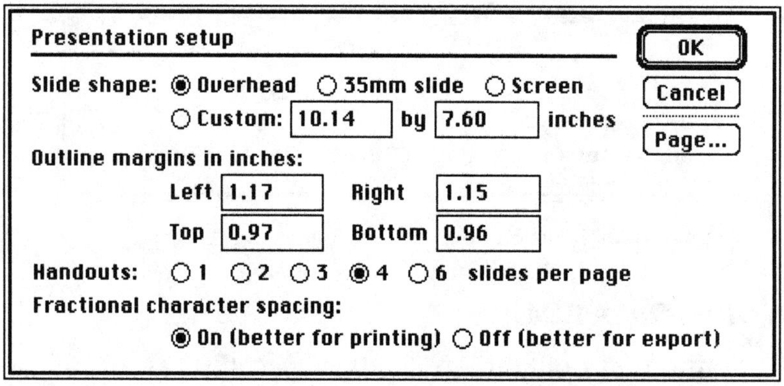

Figure 4.6.   Choose a slide shape in the Presentation setup dialog box.

Tip: In many cases, you'll have more than one output device. For example, you may want to print slides to a film recorder or slide service bureau, and then print notes and overheads to a laser printer. Always choose the output device you intend to use for the slides themselves. Then, when you're finished composing and printing slides, you can go back and choose the output device on which you want to produce notes and handouts.

Outline Margins

Persuasion calculates margins so that text will fit within the width of your screen in Outline view. To change the line length of the outline, type a new number after *Right*. (To widen the outline, type a smaller number; to narrow it, type a larger number.)

Tip: If you shrink a window (for example, to work on two outlines simultaneously in side-by-side windows), you'll need to adjust the right margin so that text will wrap to the window's new dimensions and still be visible.

If you switch monitors, you may need to adjust the outline margins. The dimensions of the monitor on which a presentation is composed are saved with the presentation; they won't change automatically to adjust to a new monitor.

Although the margin settings in an AutoTemplate are initially set for optimum screen display, they also determine the printed margins of an outline. When the outline is printed, the other three margin settings, *Left, Top, and Bottom*, also come into play.

Handouts

Handouts controls how many miniature slide images will appear on each page of your audience handouts. Once you've chosen the number of miniatures per page, you can adjust their size and position on the Handout master.

Fractional Character Spacing

This is one of those options that you'll rarely need to worry about, but when you do you'll be glad it's there. In general, most output devices support fractional character spacing. But if lines of text are longer when printed than they appear on screen, this may be a sign that your output device is one of the few that do not: turn *Fractional character spacing* off and see if the problem improves.

On the other hand, most applications that import PICT files *don't* support fractional character spacing. If you intend to import your presentation into another application, turn *Fractional character spacing* off.

To save the changes you've made and close the dialog box, click *OK*. To cancel the changes, click *Cancel*. To return to the dialog box for the output device, click *Page*.

Adjusting Graphics After Changing Slide Shape

What happens if, despite our warnings, you must select a slide shape different from the one for which an AutoTemplate was created? For example, say you want to use one of Persuasion's overhead AutoTemplates as the basis for a slide show presentation on your AppleColor monitor. You open the AutoTemplate and select *Screen* as the presentation setup. Now what?

Here's the problem. The dimensions of the AutoTemplate overhead are 10.14 × 7.6 inches. But your screen measures 8.89 × 6.67 inches. How does Persuasion handle slide elements with size discrepancies like this? For example, what happens to a 9-inch horizontal rule along the top of each slide?

The answer is, Persuasion turns to you for help. Whenever you choose a slide shape different from the one for which the AutoTemplate was created and click *OK* to complete the page setup changes, you'll see the Adjust graphics dialog box warning you that the page size of various elements has changed, and asking whether and how to modify the elements so they'll fit.

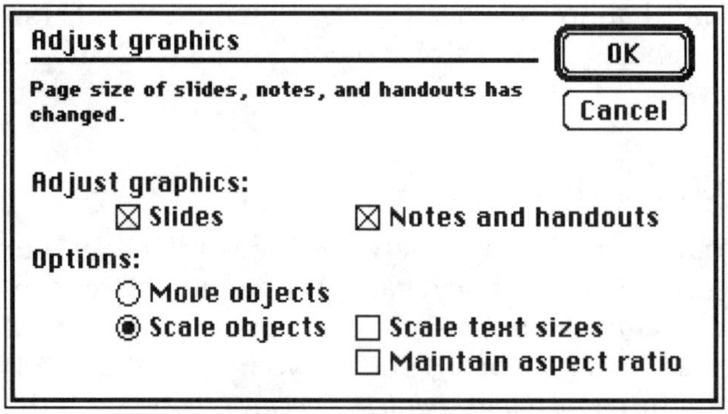

Figure 4.7. Whenever you change the slide shape, the Adjust graphics dialog box asks you how to modify presentation elements.

Not all presentation elements will be affected by a slide shape change. Persuasion will tell you what needs adjusting—slides or notes and handouts, or all three. Elements unaffected by the change will be dimmed. Click the options—*Slides* or *Notes and handouts*, or both—that you want to adjust.

Note: Slides will almost always be affected by changes in slide shape. Notes and handouts are generally only affected by changes in output device. (For more information on what graphics to adjust when, see Chapter 14, *Importing and Exporting*.)

How should you adjust the presentation elements for the different size? You have a couple of options.

The *Move objects* option centers all elements on the slide as a group. If the new slide shape is larger than the original, the background fill will be extended to fill the gap. If the new slide shape is smaller, however, slide elements that extend beyond the new dimensions will be cut off; in this case, you will want to choose the next option, *Scale objects*.

Scale objects enlarges or reduces slide elements to fit the new dimensions. Once again, and there are a couple of ways this can be done.

Scale text sizes scales text at the same percentage as the slide, and then converts the result to the nearest size available in the Size submenu of the Font menu. Practically speaking, this rarely results in visible changes. For example, if you switch from an overhead to a slide, the slide height will shrink by about 10%. 72-point type would be scaled 10% to about 62 point, and then converted to the nearest submenu size, which just happens to be 72 point. This option works best when the difference between old and new slide shapes is large.

Maintain aspect ratio scales all elements, including text boxes, to the new size, while keeping their original proportions. What does this mean exactly? Without *Maintain aspect ratio*, the height and the width of each object change—independently of each other—in proportion to the changes in the height and width of the slide. Height may change 10% while width changes 5%. This may distort some objects; for example, a square may become a rectangle, and a circle may turn into an ellipse.

With *Maintain aspect ratio* selected, both the height and width of each element change in the same proportion. The bottom line? If your Auto-Template contains elements such as squares and circles that you don't want distorted, click *Maintain aspect ratio*.

A word of encouragement: don't worry if the issues of scaling and maintaining aspect ratios seem a bit much to absorb right now. Most of the time, you won't need to adjust graphics at all. And, if you must, there's lots more information in Chapter 14, *Importing and Exporting*.

Now that we've successfully opened and set up a presentation, let's explore Persuasion's powerful and versatile outliner.

Figure 4.8. When enlarging slide shape with *Move objects* selected, background fill is extended to fill the gap (*center*). Objects are centered as a group but aren't resized to fit the new dimensions. When reducing slide shape with *Move objects* selected, objects may extend beyond the edge of the slide (*bottom*).

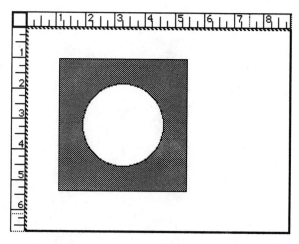

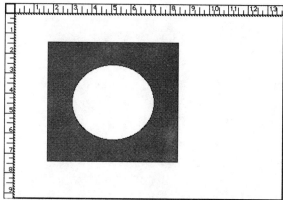

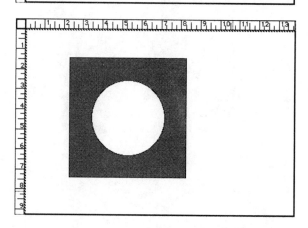

Figure 4.9   Changing from screen to slide shape. Without *Maintain aspect ratio* selected, square and circle are distorted (*center*). With *Maintain aspect ratio*, no distortion occurs (*bottom*).

Chapter 5

Beginning with Ideas

Whether you are putting together your first presentation or your one hundredth, getting started can be intimidating. The journey from idea to finished production can be a long one. One way to make it with less trepidation is to divide the presentation project into discrete parts. Then, step by step, you finally reach your goal of a finished production.

The first step in the process is to organize your presentation information in the form of an outline. Persuasion is the first presentation product to offer both an industrial-strength outliner and production tools under one roof, so to speak. Earlier electronic presentation software concentrated exclusively on producing rather than organizing a presentation and users had to create their outline elsewhere. Given the importance of word choice and organization to an effective presentation, Persuasion's built-in outliner is a compelling advantage.

The Persuasion Outline

It is possible to do an end-run around Persuasion's outliner and create text for your slides directly in the slide view. You can always simply choose the *New* option on the Go to slide pop-up menu to create new slides. However, unless you are just putting together a few ad hoc slides you will miss many of the inherent advantages that the outliner brings to the process of creating a presentation. Using the framework of Persuasion's outliner you can exert far more control over your text. You can make sure that the flow of text is strictly logical, and you can automatically move slide headings, subheadings, and body text without having to edit each individual slide.

Whether you enter text in the outliner or on individual slides, the fact remains that the best way to organize a presentation is as an outline. Based upon that outline, Persuasion creates slides and speaker notes. Figure 5.1 *A* shows a sample outline entry, with each type and level of outline heading; 5.1 *B* shows how that outline determines the positioning of text elements on a slide; the corresponding master slide for Figure 5.1 *B* is shown in 5.1 *C*. By working with the master slide you can control the placement and format for each type of heading.

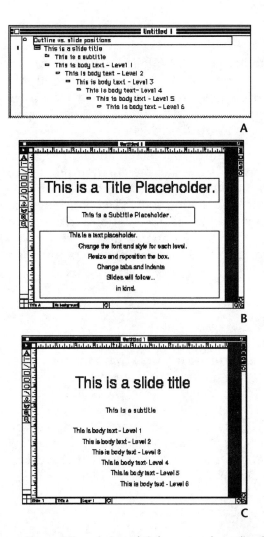

Figure 5.1.　　*A*, *B*, and *C* show sample outline headings, positioning of text on a slide, and corresponding master slide.

Bear in mind this relationship between outline and slide as you work with your outline; as you compose heading labels, remember that you are designating text as slide title, subtitle, and body text. Then, when it comes time to view the outline as a sequence of slides, Persuasion will not surprise you. If you change your mind about your slide layouts, you only have to edit your master slides and Persuasion will rearrange the labeled headings accordingly.

Anatomy of an Outline

The way the outliner functions is simple. You type in a line of text for each topic, or heading, and then, using various levels of indentation, you designate that topic as a holder of slides, a slide title, a subtitle, body text, or a note. Note that you can always reassign a different function to a heading with the *Set heading as...* option on the Outline menu. Each topic will appear in a reserved space on the final slide depending on how you have defined the slide master. You can see in Figure 5.2 what each of the five types of outline entries looks like, along with their respective symbols.

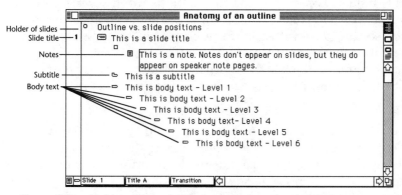

Figure 5.2. Holder, title, subtitle, body text, and note labels.

Before we start to build an outline, let's take a moment to look at all of its pieces.

Slide Holder

Every new Persuasion outline begins with a line of text that categorizes the list of slides that follows. This text entry at the very top of the outline window is called a slide holder, or "Holder of slides" in Persuasion parlance (see in Figure 5.2). You can identify a slide holder by a small circle displayed to the left of the slide holder text. Slide holder text does not appear on slides. It only appears in the outline view. Let's take a look at how you can use the slide holder.

Think of the slide holder as an organizer, sort of an electronic manila folder. In this folder you keep slides that share something in common. One way you might categorize a presentation, for example, would be to place a slide holder at each major division in the presentation. You could set a slide holder for the introduction, another for the sales pitch, and another for the closing comments. The slide holder not only helps you visualize each discrete part of your presentation, it is also a perfect place to jot notes about the slides that follow since slide holders cannot appear on slides, only in an outline.

Tip: Slide holders come in handy in situations when several people work on separate parts of the same outline. Using slide holders to separate each section makes it easier for each person to concentrate on their own section of the presentation. Another use for slide holders is for making comments about the slides that follow, such as "Jim used these charts last month—be sure to update the charts before you use them again."

If you want slide holder text to appear on a slide, you can convert the slide holder into another type of label by selecting the slide holder. Don't forget that you can always convert a slide holder into a slide title by clicking on the slide holder and choosing *Slide title* from the *Set heading as...* command in the Outline menu.

The Slide Title

The focal point of every slide is its title. Like a movie marquis, the title proclaims in large letters what the slide is all about. Sometimes a slide title is the only text element on a slide; at other times, the title is supported with a subtitle and body text.

Persuasion creates a slide for every slide title in your outline. You can identify a title by the slide title symbol at the left of the title text (see Figure 5.2) along with a slide number next to the symbol. Sometimes the slide number will be bold, which is a visual cue that Persuasion has already created a slide from the outline item. Whether the slide number is bold or not doesn't actually matter, since Persuasion will automatically update the slides for any outline items you add or edit.

Note: Although every slide requires a title label in the outline, you can always leave the title label blank if you don't want a title on the slide.

By default, all first level headings are automatically assigned as slide titles. However, there are circumstances when you will want indented headings to appear as separate slides. For example, let's say you create a slide listing several topics that you want to discuss in greater detail. You can use the first level heading for the introductory slide. So far, this is the default. But you need to assign slide titles to some of the indented headings as well. To convert a heading to a slide title (thus giving it its own slide) select the heading, and choose *Set heading as Slide title* from the Outline menu. If you change your mind and want to reassign the heading as body text, click on the heading and choose *Set heading as Body text* from the Outline menu. This features gives you considerable latitude over how you can structure the slides in your presentation.

The Subtitle

The subtitle outline heading label is a new addition in Persuasion 2.0. The definition of a subtitle is somewhere between a slide title and body text: it's purpose is to allow you to add a few words to amplify the main slide title which is usually just a word or so long. You can also format it and position it independently of the slide title and body text. A subtitle is normally set in large type, but smaller than the title itself. You can see the label icon for a subtitle heading in Figure 5.2.

Body Text

The third type of outline label you can use to have text appear on a slide is a body text label. Where a slide title shouts to get attention, body text explains more calmly what the slide is all about. Body text headings are commonly used to provide support for the slide title in the form of bulleted lists. Body text customarily appears on the slide in smaller text than either the title or subtitle. Body text is represented on an outline by a hollow bar symbol next to the body text (see Figure 5.2). An outline can have only one title and one subtitle per slide, but it can have a practically unlimited number of body text lines. As you will see in a moment, you can indent body text lines in the outline.

By default, all headings below and to the right of the title are assigned as body text. You can define each level of indentation with a different format on the slide.

Notes Headings

The slide title, subtitle, and body text can all appear on slides. There is a fourth type of topic heading you can include in an outline, the note. The most important thing to know about a note is that text for note text appears on the speaker's note page only and never on a slide. Note headings are used to include additional information that can be extremely useful for the speaker. The notes only appear on his or her copy of the presentation; yet the viewers never see them on the slide. You could use notes to fully script a presentation, if you wanted to.

Notes are formatted on the notes page according by using the notes placeholder in the notes master page view. Figure 5.2 illustrates what a note symbol looks like in an outline.

Starting a New Presentation

In Chapter Three, the Quick Start Tutorial, we created a simple outline that only scratched the surface of the power and convenience of Persuasion's outliner. In this section we'll go beyond the basics and look at alternative ways of entering, editing, and manipulating outline entries. Once you get the hang of it, you'll be able to capture your presentation in an outline in no time at all.

There are two ways to create a Persuasion outline. You can type your text directly into Persuasion, or you can import text from another application such as a word processor or spreadsheet. In this chapter we will discuss techniques for creating an outline in Persuasion; later, in Chapter 14, *Importing and Exporting*, we will detail the ways you can import text directly into a Persuasion outline.

An important thought to keep in the back of your mind as you work with an outline is the direct relationship that the outline has with slides. Each outline label and line indentation level has its own unique formatting on a slide.

The Outline

Creating an outline from scratch in Persuasion is not difficult. Once you familiarize yourself with the terminology and with Persuasion's conventions for identifying the different elements of an outline, you can roll up your sleeves and turn out your first presentation.

Whenever you are in the outline view, the Outline menu appears on the right of the menu bar. Within this menu are most of the commands you will use to create and finesse an outline.

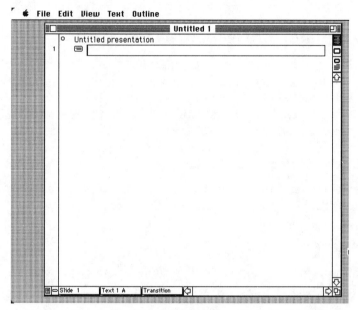

Figure 5.3.   An outline window along with its Outline menu.

Assume that you have just chosen *New* from the File menu; the new file opens in outline view with the slide holder line labeled "Untitled Presentation." The first heading in every new outline window is a holder of slides; the second line is an empty text box next to the first slide title label and a slide number "1" in the left margin. Double-click or drag over the words "Untitled Presentation" and replace them with something more pertinent. The top slide holder is a perfect place to type information like the creation and editing dates and your name so that someone else opening the presentation will be able to identify it. You can add other slide holders throughout your presentation to add other annotations. Since comments in slide holders only appear in the outline view, you don't have to be concerned about what (if anything) you type in this space.

The Slide Title

When you start a new presentation, the insertion point appears at the slide title for the first slide. Type in the title, press Return, and Persuasion will create a new outline heading for the second slide title. Type the slide title heading for your second slide and press Return again.

If your presentation consisted of nothing more than headlines on slides, you could type your entire presentation following the two steps above. However, most presentations are comprised of slides that include subtitles and body text along with a title.

Removing Slides and/or Headings

To remove a title heading or any other heading, click the insertion point in the heading you want to remove and choose *Cut* or *Clear* from the Edit menu. This action will remove that heading and all of its subordinates. If your heading is a slide title, clearing that title will delete the entire slide. Persuasion will ask you to confirm your delete command before it actually deletes the heading. If you accidentally delete a heading, you can restore it if you immediately choose *Undo* from the Edit menu.

You can also delete several headings at once by selecting the headings using the multiple selection techniques later in this chapter.

Adding a Subtitle

Subtitles play an important role on a slide. A subtitle acts as a transition between the title and other information on the slide. Consider these two examples:

Census Statistics (title)
An Overview (subtitle)

Banks in Change (title)
Boom or Bust? (subtitle)

In both examples, the title introduces the topic and the subtitle prepares the viewer for the message itself as shown in body text or graphics. A subtitle eases the viewer into the focal point of the slide.

There are two ways to make an outline heading a subtitle, manually and automatically. Which method you choose depends on whether you use subtitles as a rule or only by exception.

Manual Subtitles

If you only occasionally want subtitles use the manual method. Position the cursor in the first heading directly below the slide title. Then, on the Outline menu choose *Set headings as* and then *Subtitle*, or you can bypass the menu command by simply pressing *Command+2* (see Figure 5.4). The icon label will change accordingly.

Note: You can only position a subtitle immediately after a slide title. If you attempt to specify any other heading as a subtitle, you will find the Subtitle command on the submenu dimmed.

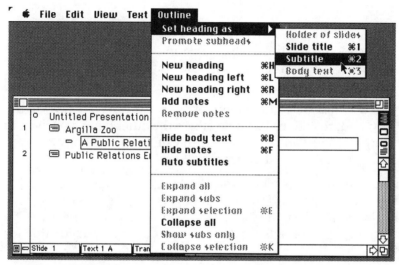

Figure 5.4.   The Subtitle command in the Outline menu.

Automatic Subtitles

If you plan to use a subtitle on the majority of your slides, you can set Persuasion to create the subtitle heading automatically after you type each slide title.

Before you set Persuasion to create subtitles automatically, you have to check to make sure that your master slide includes a subtitle placeholder. Check on this by clicking on the slide view icon and choosing the *Slide master—Current* from the View menu. Look at the master slide. You should see a placeholder that says "This is a Subtitle Placeholder." If you don't see this, choose *Add subtitle* from the Master menu. Don't worry about the subtitle placeholder's position on the master slide right now. The main thing is simply to have the subtitle placeholder on the master slide.

Now return to the outline view (select *Outline* from the View menu or click on the outline view icon). Choose *Auto subtitles* from the Outline menu.

Note: When you choose *Auto subtitle* from the Outline menu and Persuasion does not add a subtitle when you press return at the end of a slide title text entry, the master slide assigned to the outline heading doesn't have a subtitle placeholder. To add a subtitle either switch master slides to one that has a subtitle placeholder, or add one to the master slide.

Let's move on to adding body text to the outline.

Body Text

The slide title's job is to shout to get attention; the body text's job is to maintain the viewer's attention with additional information supporting the title.

Coming up with just the right amount of body text can be tricky. On the one hand, you want to add sufficient detail; on the other hand, you need to keep your body text short and concise. The rule of thumb for body text is to limit it to three or four bulleted points per slide.

But what about instances when you absolutely need more points? For example, if you are presenting "twelve steps to better sales," you don't have much choice but to list the points on a slide. The answer is to divide the list into three or four separate slides and use a copy of the same slide title for each.

However, in most cases, too many body text points indicates that you have not broken your message down into small enough pieces. Rather than just continue a list of bullet points from slide to slide, it would be better for you to reexamine your list of points, subdivide the list and create slides with unique titles.

Body text headings are more flexible than other types of outline headings. For one thing, body text can appear anywhere in the outline (unlike a subtitle that must be positioned directly under the slide title). You can also indent body text so that some body text headings are at different indentation levels than others. This allows you to indent items that depend on other items. Later, when it is time to format your slides you can format each outline heading separately using the body text placeholder. Figure 5.5 shows the relationship between different levels of body text and different level headings appear on a slide depending on how you format your body text placeholder.

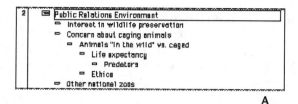

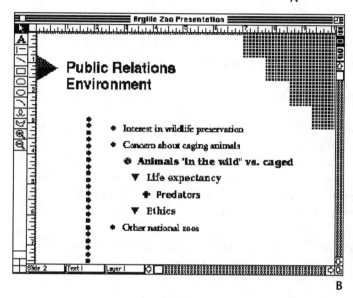

Figure 5.5. *A* and *B* show how you can format each level of body text using the body text placeholder.

To insert a body text heading into an outline, click on the heading in the outline just above where the new heading should appear. Then, follow one of these steps (depending on what level you want the new heading to be):

- *To create a new heading of the same level,* place the insertion point either at the very beginning or at the very end of the preceding heading and press Return. A new heading symbol will appear below the highlighted heading and the insertion point will be positioned ready for typing in another heading. Alternatively, you can choose *New heading* from the Outline menu or simply press *Command+H.*

- *To create a new heading one level lower* (indented to the right), place the insertion point either at the very beginning or at the very end of the preceding heading, press Return, and then the Tab key. You can also choose *"New heading right"* from the Outline menu or press *Command+R.*

- *To create a new heading one level higher (indented to the left),* place the insertion point either at the very beginning or at the very end of the preceding heading, press Return, and then press Shift-Tab. Persuasion will move position the new heading to the left one level. You can also choose *New heading left* from the Outline menu or press *Command+L.*

Why does Persuasion offer so many options for creating headings? Because Persuasion wants to make it as easy as possible for you to get your ideas down by choosing the method that feels most comfortable to you.

Speaker Notes

So far we have discussed how to create and assign slide titles, subtitles, and body text in an outline. The last type of outline entry is called a note. Notes do not appear on any slides. They are intended for the speaker's eyes only. When you print your presentation with the notes option checked Persuasion prints a set of speakers notes—one for each slide in the presentation. Notes will never print on the slide itself; they only print on speaker note pages. A speaker note page typically shows a miniature of the slide at the top of the page and whatever notes are attached to the slide in the outline view at the bottom of the page, as shown in Figure 5.6.

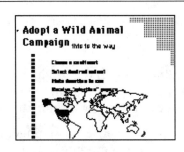

Figure 5.6.   The notes page is an invaluable help to the speaker. He or she can both see an image of the slide and read the script for the slide at once.

Many times notes are used to fully or partially script a presentation. Some presenters take advantage of notes to list the answers to commonly asked questions about the slide. In other instances, notes are a perfect place to record incidental footnotes about what's on a slide and where the information came from. To summarize, notes are perfect for any type of information that the speaker can use to make the presentation run more smoothly.

Adding Notes

Having explained how valuable notes are to a presentation, let's get on with how to add a note to an outline. Position the cursor in a slide title or in any of the slide's subheadings, and choose *Add Notes* from the Outline menu (or type *Command+M*). Persuasion places a new heading directly under the slide title heading, and the cursor moves to the new note heading. A small box also appears directly under the slide title when you place your first note. We'll explain its function in just a few moments.

Once you have created a new note, just start typing the note text. As your text nears the right margin Persuasion automatically starts a new line for the note. To create a second paragraph within the same note, you must press Shift-Return. If you don't hold the Shift key down when you press Return, Persuasion will start an entirely new note heading.

To create separate additional note entries; press Return when the cursor is in either the first or last position in an existing note heading. Creating separate notes permits you to reorganize notes within the notes section of a slide, just as you would rearrange other types of outline headings. In a sense, you can treat the notes section of a slide like a miniature outline. You can move note headings and subheadings until they are in the order you want. Like body text headings, you can format each note level separately using the notes placeholder in the notes master slide.

The rules for creating and reorganizing indented notes headings are the same as they are for body text. The only thing to keep in mind is that you have to keep notes headings together directly below the slide title. If you attempt to move a note heading to another location in the outline, Persuasion will automatically convert the note into body text. Remember this trick if you ever want to convert a note into body text. Likewise, you can convert any other type of outline heading to a note by moving the heading into the notes section.

Hiding Notes

Persuasion 2.0's outliner accommodates notes very conveniently. It is possible to keep pertinent notes about a slide together with the slide's outline entry. As you rearrange the order of your slides, you can be sure that the notes will stay with the slide.

However, sometimes you may want to work on your outline unfettered by extensive notes that can distract you from the contents of the slides. Persuasion's answer to this problem is its *Hide notes* command which places your notes just out of view. There are three ways to hide notes. The easiest is probably to just click on the notes icon in the lower left corner of the outline window. Or you can either press either *Command+F* or choose *Hide notes* in the Outline menu.

You can always tell that you have hidden all of your notes by glancing at the notes icon. If your notes are hidden, the notes icon will be half-obscured as you can see in Figure 5.7.

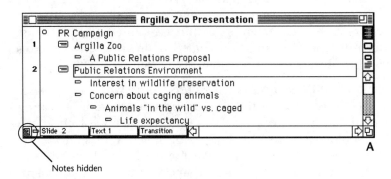

Notes hidden

A

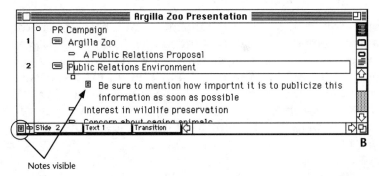

Notes visible

B

Figure 5.7.　Click on the hide notes icon (*A*) to hide temporarily all notes in your outline. Click on a half-obscured notes icon (*B*) to display notes immediately.

When you want to display all notes again, use any of the three *Hide notes* commands. Since the notes are already hidden Persuasion will know that you now want to display the notes again.

The *Hide notes* command is global: it hides all of an outline's notes at once. But sometimes you may want to hide just certain notes instead of all of them. Persuasion lets you do this, too. Remember the hollow square that appeared when you created your first note? This icon, called the main note icon, toggles the notes for that slide on and off. If you double-click on the icon the notes for that slide will be hidden; double-click on it again and the notes reappear.

Permanently Removing Notes

Persuasion gives you two ways to remove notes. If you want to remove all notes from a slide (and the notes icon), click on the slide title and choose *Remove notes* from the Outline menu. There is no keyboard shortcut for removing notes.

You can also remove an individual note by clicking on the note and choosing *Cut* from the Edit menu.

Tip: If you cut an entire note or a single note and then change your mind, use the Undo Clear command in the Edit menu to restore the note.

Reorganizing and Modifying an Outline

One of the most amazing things about an electronic outline is the ease with which you can reorganize your presentation outline. With a drag of the mouse, you can quickly move headings, change heading levels, and change heading types. For example, you can make a body text bullet point into a slide title simply by moving the body text to where you want it and then changing its type to *Slide title* in the Outline menu. The possibilities are almost limitless.

Moving Headings

The most basic alteration to an outline is to move a heading from one spot to another. After you have entered several items you may notice that some items more logically belong to another group. Using the mouse, you can easily rearrange every heading until you are totally satisfied with the way your outline is organized.

To a move heading from one location to another, point the mouse on a heading icon, and then hold down the mouse button. The pointer will change shape to a small pointing hand, and a selection box will appear around the entire subheading as seen in Figure 5.8. Note that if the selected heading has related subheadings, these will be automatically selected also.

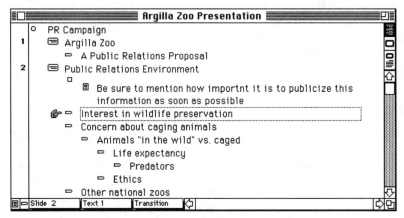

Figure 5.8.   When the small pointing hand and selection box appears around a subheading move the pointer to the new location for the subheading and release the mouse.

Drag the pointing hand up or down. As you drag you will see a small black bar appear at each possible insertion point in the outline as shown in Figure 5.9.

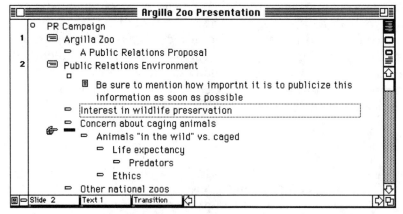

Figure 5.9.   The horizontal black bar that appears when you drag a headline indicates where the headline's new location will be when you release the mouse button.

When you release the mouse button, the heading and its related sub-headings (if any) immediately relocate to where the small black bar is. There is one main organizational rule about moving headings with Persuasion. You cannot insert a slide title in between another slide title and its sub-headings.

When you move a heading, all of its related subheadings normally get moved along with the heading itself. To move just a heading and leave its subordinates behind, hold down the Option key when you drag the heading. If, however, you move a heading by itself and leave its subheads behind without a new heading that is immediately superior, Persuasion will alert you with the dialog box in Figure 5.10. To complete the heading move, you must promote the subheads out at least one level. Do this by clicking the heading you want to move and then choosing *Promote subheads* from the Outline menu. Then you will be able to move the single head and take care of the subheadings you will leave behind.

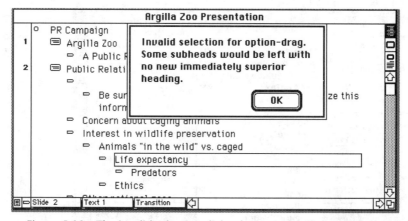

Figure 5.10. The invalid selection dialog box appears if you attempt to move a heading by itself and leave its subheads behind without a new heading that is immediately superior.

Changing a Heading Type

As you review your outline and make changes to its structure, you may decide that you want to change a heading type. You could decide, for example, to dedicate an entire slide to a particular heading that is labeled as body text, or visa versa. Or, you may want to make a holder of slides label to set aside a certain group of slides or headings.

To change a heading type, click anywhere in the heading to select it. Then, choose *Set heading as* from the Outline menu. Certain heading types may be dimmed in the submenu, which means that they are not available options for the selected heading.

Here's an example. Let's say that you want to make the body text, "Interest in Wildlife," into a subtitle. Click anywhere in the "Interest in Wildlife" heading. Next, choose the *Set heading* command in the Outline menu.

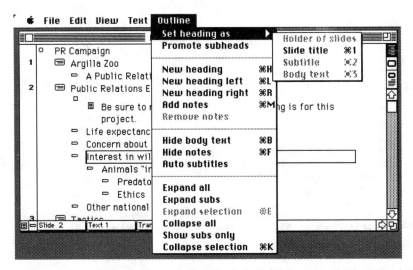

Figure 5.11. The subtitle command is unavailable because the heading has to be directly under the slide title heading to be defined as a subtitle.

As you can see in Figure 5.11, Persuasion will not let you convert the body text into a subtitle. Why? Remember, a subtitle must appear directly below a slide title. Once you move the heading directly below the slide title, Persuasion will allow you to convert it to a Subtitle via the *Set heading as* command in the Outline menu. Notice that in Figure 5.12 the Subtitle option is available. Select it and Persuasion will change the body text into a subtitle.

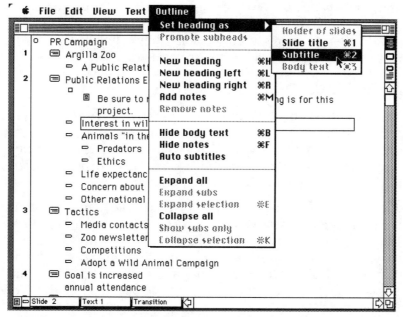

Figure 5.12. Moving the body text directly below the slide title positions the body text to be converted into a subtitle.

Changing Body Text Heading Levels

In general, a subordinate heading provides information at a further level of detail than its parent. Deeper level headings might be supportive points or examples that illustrate a larger idea.

You may often need to rearrange your body text headings to emphasize or isolate certain points and to play down others. With Persuasion, you can set the level of a heading either as you type it into an outline or, later, as you fine tune and reorganize your outline. We have already talked about how to set headings in different levels as you are typing them in. Now let's look at how you can move headings to different levels after you've finished your outline.

Changing the Level of an Individual Heading

Use the mouse to drag the heading's icon to the left or right. Or, click on the heading you want to change and choose *Move left* or *Move right* from the Text menu. Or, from the keyboard press *Command+[* or *Command+]*. If the cursor is at the very beginning of the line, you can press the Tab key to indent a level or press Shift-Tab to move out one indent level.

Note: When you change the level of a heading, all of its subordinate headings also shift a level in the same direction. To indent a heading without indenting its corresponding subheadings, hold down the Option key as you drag the heading to the new level.

Selecting Multiple Outline Headings

So far, we have limited our discussion of making changes to an outline to line-by-line changes. In some cases, however, you may need to perform the same command on several headings. You could work on each heading separately, or you can learn the commands to select and then manipulate several headings at once. That's what this section is about.

Persuasion 2.0 also allows you to make changes to more than one outline heading at a time. Let's say that you want to change a group of headings from bold to bold italic. Or, you want to change the font size of selected headings. If you need to perform the same operation on more than one heading, there are several ways to select multiple nonadjacent headings and then perform the operation just once and have the operation affect all of the selected headings.

All of these operations can be performed on multiple selected headings. Thinking ahead and selecting multiple headings can save you a lot of time when you are in the throes of a deadline. You can select multiple headings and then take these actions on the selected group as a whole:

- Drag;
- Clear;
- Assign a slide master;
- Select a transition effect;
- Remove notes using the *Remove notes* command;
- Cut, copy, and paste; and
- Set a heading using the *Set heading as...* command.

Selecting Multiple Headings Separately

Selecting multiple headings one-by-one follows the common Macintosh technique of shift-clicking. Here's how it works in Persuasion. Click on a heading to select it. Then, to add other headings to the same selection, hold down the Shift key, and click the individual heading's icons.

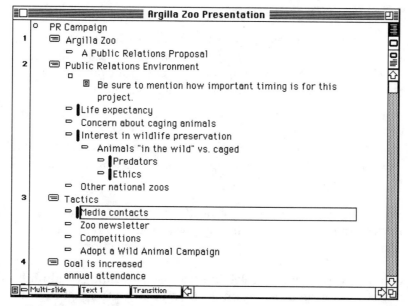

Figure 5.13. A short vertical bar indicates all headings that are selected.

Just as you add headings to the selection by shift-clicking, you can deselect individual headings by shift-clicking again on a selected headline. In effect, each time you shift-click on a heading you are selecting and deselecting the heading.

Selecting a Range of Adjacent Headings

Persuasion also provides a shortcut for selecting more than one adjacent heading. Click on the first heading in the group, hold down the Option-Shift keys and click on the last heading you want included in the selection. All headings in the range will be designated as selected, as noted by a vertical bar at the left.

Tip: You can easily select a range of adjacent headings with the mouse. Move the mouse just to the left of the heading until the pointer turns into a small rectangle. Position the rectangle in the upper left corner of the range of headings you want to select. Click and drag diagonally to surround the headings you want to select with a selection rectangle. When you release the mouse, all of the headings within the rectangle will be selected.

Other Selection Techniques

Persuasion offers other convenient ways to choose headings: you can choose them by a certain level all at once. This makes it possible for you to change the text formatting for headings at a set level, for example. Or, you may want to move a group of headings to another level all at once.

To select a range by level, click to select the first heading to anchor the range of headings you want to select, and then press Shift-Option-Command (all three keys at once) while you click on the last heading of the range you want to select. Persuasion will place a short vertical bar next to all headings of the same level.

Tip: After you have selected multiple headings you can always selectively deselect an individual heading by pressing the Shift key as you click the heading you don't want to include in the selection.

This technique works both for selecting same-level headings and multi-level headings within a range. For example, if you wanted to select all headings from the second level to the fourth level within a section of your outline, you would click on the first heading in the second level to anchor the range. Then you would hold down Shift-Option-Command and click on the last fourth-level heading in the end of the range. The result should look like Figure 5.14. Notice how Persuasion selects outline levels two, three, and four between the anchor heading and the end of the range.

To select the entire outline at once, use the Select all command in the Edit menu (or press *Command+A*). The *Select all* command actually has three types of responses, depending on how many successive times you invoke it. The first time you choose *Select all* Persuasion selects all the text in a single heading. If you choose *Select all* again, Persuasion selects all headings of the same level that share the same immediately superior heading. And, if you use *Select all* a third time, Persuasion selects every heading in the entire outline.

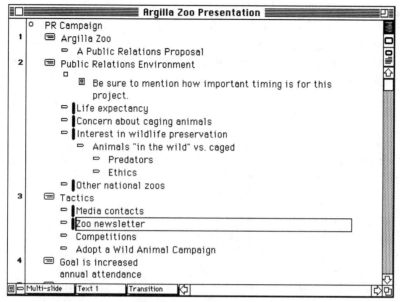

Figure 5.14. Clicking on an anchor heading and then pressing Shift-Option-Command selects all headings within the range between the two levels selected.

Dragging, Cutting, and Pasting a Multiple Selection

If you've selected multiple headings the entire selection reacts to changes as if it were a single outline. For example, if you drag a multiple selection to a new location in the outline, all of the headings move together. Likewise, if you choose the Cut command Persuasion will cut the entire selection. Mastering the various methods to select multiple headings can be a real time saver.

Expanding and Collapsing Headings

One of the most useful features in Persuasion's outliner is the ability to expand and collapse temporarily individual heading or groups of headlines (temporarily). When you want to focus your attention on the big picture; too many headings can sometimes be distracting. The solution is to hide some of the headings. Alternatively, when you want to flesh out part of the presentation with plenty of detail, you will need to have all of the subheads in that section in complete view.

When it comes to hiding and displaying individual headings, the best bet is to use the mouse. That way you can point to the headings you want to hide. In addition to duplicating the mouse's hide/display commands, the Outline menu has some commands that you can use to make more global changes to the outline.

Let's look at the techniques for hiding and displaying individual headings:

- To collapse a subheading using the mouse, move the mouse near the heading icon until the cursor shape turns into a pointer. Then double-click on the slide heading icon. All of the indented headings directly beneath disappear, and the heading icon turns black to signify that there are some headings hidden from view.

- To expand a subheading using the mouse, move the mouse near the blackened heading icon until the pointer appears. Then double-click on the icon just as you did to hide the heading. Or, instead of using the mouse, you can click on the heading you want to expand, and choose *Expand subheads* (or press *Command+E*) from the Outline menu.

Table 5.1 shows the other commands in the Outline menu that permit you to expand and collapse parts of an outline.

Table 5.1

Expand/collapse outline menu commands	Using the mouse	Result
Expand all	Option + double-click the topmost heading in the outline.	Displays all headings in the entire outline.
Collapse all	Command + double-click topmost heading in the outline.	Opposite of *Expand all*. Hides all subheadings in the outline leaving only slide titles displayed.
Expand subs	Option + double-click a heading icon.	Displays all subheads of the selected heading(s) at all subordinate levels in the outline.

(continued)

Expand selection (Command-E)	Double-click the outline level icon.	Displays the immediate subordinate(s) of the selected heading(s), leaving lower level subordinates open or closed as they were.
Show subs only	Command + double-click a heading icon.	Displays all headings immediately subordinate to the selected heading(s), but none below it. The command works whether or not selected heading(s) are collapsed or not.
Collapse selection (Command-K)	Double-click the outline level icon.	Hides all of the subheadings subordinate to the selected heading.

When you switch back and forth between viewing slide titles only and your full outline, don't overlook the hide body text icon in the lower left of the outline window. Click once on this icon to hide all subheadings in the outline (except the slide title). The body text icon will become half hidden. Click on the body text icon again and you will be back in full view of your outline.

Take advantage of Persuasion's many outline viewing options as you finetune your outline. As you can see, there are several commands to hide and display different sections. Depending on your workstyle and where you are in the presentation production process, you are able to hide headings that may distract you from the task at hand, and display those that you need to focus in on.

Formatting an Outline

Formatting does not transfer from outline view to slide view. The formatting you do in the outline remains with the outline. (Likewise, when you format slides, the formatting belongs just to the slide view.) So why bother taking the time to format an outline? For one thing, you may find it easier to work with an outline if you are using a font, size, and style that makes it easier for you to work in the outline view. This might be as simple as using an easily readable font, such as American Typewriter or Courier, as you edit an outline. Another reason to spend time formatting an outline is if you need to pass the outline around to others, perhaps to your boss or peers for review. You might even want to pass copies of the completed outline out to your audience along with Persuasion's audience handouts. Now let's get on with outline formatting.

Whenever you open a new outline, Persuasion sets the default fonts settings for 12-point Geneva plain for each of the outline's 15 possible levels. However, Persuasion also gives you complete control over the appearance of each letter in the outline just as you do in a standard word processor. You can control an individual letter's size, style, font, and even color if you want to.

Outlining with Style

There are two different methods of applying formatting to text in an outline. The first method is local applying new attributes to single letters or words; the second is global, changing the formatting of entire levels of headings within the outline.

First let's look at the commands available for localized formatting. You can change an individual letter or work's appearance by dragging over the letters you want to change and then choosing the new attribute from the Text menu.

Defining Formats

If you are changing more than one attribute, it will be easier for you to use the *Text format...* command, which is also in the Text menu. The difference between this command and the individual font, size, style, and color commands is that the Text format command allows you to select all of the attribute commands from one dialog box; it eliminates the need to keep going back to the menu—first to change the font, and then the size. The *Text format* command saves a lot of time and menu pulling.

Another shortcut to speedier, more consistent formatting is the *Define formats* command. This command lets you name and save formatting information that you can then reapply to new selected text by just choosing the format name. For example, if you want to highlight certain text in bold red, you could set up a format named (not surprisingly) "Bold Red." Once you have defined the format, whenever you want bold red again, all you have to do is choose bold red from the Apply format submenu in the Text menu.

To define a format, choose the *Define format* command from the bottom of the Text menu. A dialog box box appears like the one in Figure 5.15.

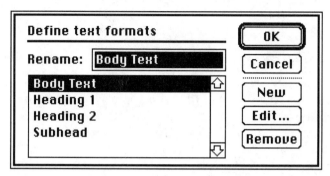

Figure 5.15. The Apply Format dialog box displays all of the formats you have already saved, giving you the option to edit, remove, or create a new named format.

To define a new format click the *New* button. The same text format dialog box appears that opens when you choose *Text Format* from the Text menu. Only this time, instead of setting new attributes for the selected text only, the options you select in this box become your format definition that you can use as many times as you want.

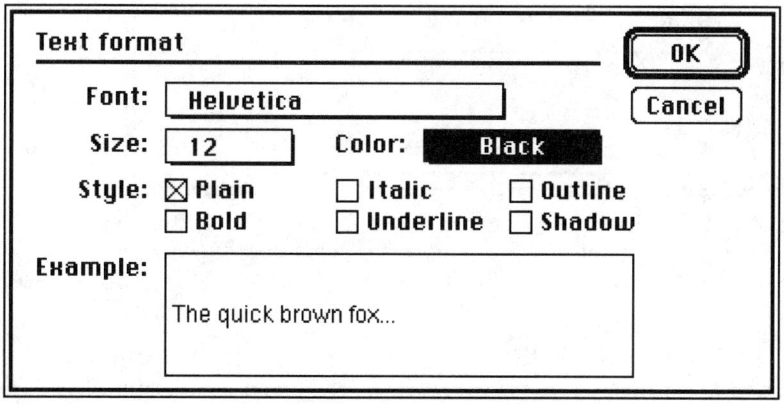

Text format ┌ OK ┐

Font: │ Helvetica │   Cancel

Size: │ 12 │   Color: │ Black │

Style: ☒ Plain   ☐ Italic   ☐ Outline
☐ Bold   ☐ Underline   ☐ Shadow

Example: │ The quick brown fox... │

Figure 5.16. You define a format from this text attributes dialog box.

You can set up an unlimited number of formats according to your needs. If you want to rename, edit, or remove a format from the format list, choose the *Define format* command again, and then click on the action you want to take.

Defining Outline Styles

At first glance, the difference between defining a text format and an outline style can be confusing. Just remember that you apply a format to individual characters or words, but you apply a style to an entire level of headings in an outline. For any outline level (or multiple levels, if you have selected more than one) you can set font, size, color, and style, as shown in the dialog box pictured in Figure 5.17. Notice that the options in this Outline styles dialog box are the same as those in the text format dialog box. In the Outline styles dialog box, however, you define text attributes for more global purposes; you define attributes for an entire heading level.

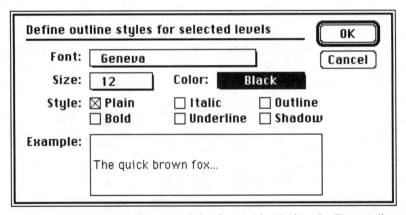

Figure 5.17. The Outline style dialog box is identical to the Text attributes
dialog box, but the changes you make in this dialog will
affect all selected heading levels in the entire outline.

To define an outline style, first select the heading in the outline at the level you want to change. If you want to apply the same new format to more than one level in the outline, use the shift-click technique to select more than one level of heading before you choose *Outline styles* in the the Text menu. Then, simply choose the text attributes from the Outline styles dialog box. These same attributes will take effect on the selected levels throughout the entire outline.

Note that there is a shortcut for defining styles for outline levels. For a given selection, instead of using the Outline styles command in the Text menu, you can select any given item in the text menu (e.g., font and style) and hold down the option key while making the selection.

Reapplying Styles

We have one more outline formatting command to cover, the *Reapply styles* command. This command applies the default style for each respective level to all selected text. The results of the *Reapply styles* command depend on exactly what text is selected at the time you choose the command:

- If you select more than one heading and then choose the *Reapply style* command, the default styles are applied to all selected headings.

- If you select a section of text within a single heading and then choose the *Reapply style* command, the text style for that particular heading level is reapplied to the selected text only.

Both of these commands are used to delete any localized highlighting that may have existed.

- If the selection is merely a single insertion point when you choose the *Reapply style* command, any new text you type will take on the style of the current heading level. This is particularly convenient when you are typing a paragraph that should appear mostly in the default format. For example, if you press *Command+Shift+B* to type in a phrase in bold, you need only press the shortcut combination *Command+0* (for *Reapply style*) to return to normal typing.

Printing an Outline

Persuasion 2.0 includes many special options for printing as you can see in the print dialog box (Figure 5.18).

In the figure, we have checked only the *Outline print* choice to show you the remaining choices that affect how your outline will look on a printed page.

The top part of the dialog box is the same as nearly every other Macintosh printing application, so let's focus on the outline-specific options:

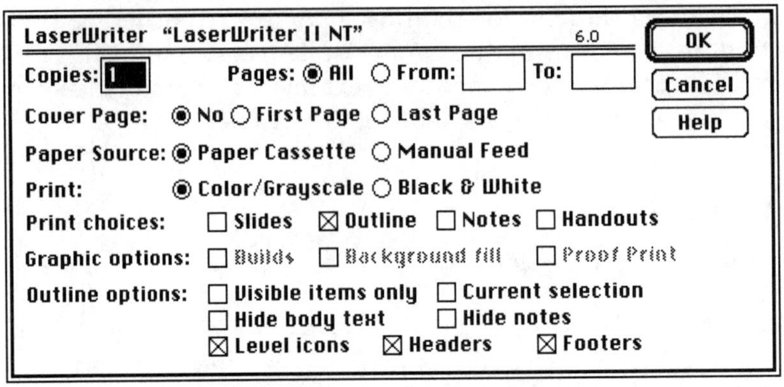

```
┌─────────────────────────────────────────────────────────────────┐
│ LaserWriter  "LaserWriter II NT"              6.0    ┌─────────┐  │
│                                                      │   OK    │  │
│ Copies:▐1▐      Pages: ◉ All  ○ From:▕   ▏ To:▕   ▏  └─────────┘  │
│                                                      ┌─────────┐  │
│ Cover Page:   ◉ No ○ First Page ○ Last Page         │ Cancel  │  │
│                                                      └─────────┘  │
│ Paper Source: ◉ Paper Cassette  ○ Manual Feed       ┌─────────┐  │
│                                                      │  Help   │  │
│ Print:        ◉ Color/Grayscale ○ Black & White     └─────────┘  │
│                                                                   │
│ Print choices:    □ Slides  ☒ Outline □ Notes □ Handouts          │
│                                                                   │
│ Graphic options: □ Builds  □ Background fill  □ Proof Print       │
│                                                                   │
│ Outline options: □ Visible items only □ Current selection         │
│                  □ Hide body text     □ Hide notes               │
│                  ☒ Level icons   ☒ Headers    ☒ Footers          │
└─────────────────────────────────────────────────────────────────┘
```

Figure 5.18. The print dialog box has many options for customizing your outline in print.

Table 5.3.

If checked	Printed result
Visible items only	Only items appearing in the outline view will print. Any text that is temporarily hidden will not print. For example, if you have some headings hidden and check this box, Persuasion will not print the hidden items. On the other hand, if you uncheck this box, Persuasion will print all levels of headings whether they are visible on the desktop or not.
Current selection	Only the selected heading and its subordinate headings will print. Check this box if you want printed copy of just a certain heading.
Hide body text/notes	Checking either or both of these choices will suppress printing of the corresponding body text or notes, respectively. These check boxes function like the hide text/notes icons in the outline window itself only in this case the check boxes pertain to what prints on the page.
Level icons	If this box is checked, the printed outline will include the respective icons for each heading topic. Left unchecked, the printer will not print any icons, but only text.

(continued)

Headers	Checking this box will automatically add the name of the presentation file to the top of every outline page. You cannot edit this header information except by editing the name of the file itself.
Footers	Checking this box will add cause Persuasion to automatically place a page number at the bottom of every outline printed page. You cannot edit a footer to print anything but a page number.

Putting It All Together

In this chapter, we have discussed the ins and outs of Persuasion's outliner. When we start a presentation, we use the outliner extensively to capture all of the information we think we want in our presentation. For example, if we were charged with preparing the Argilla tutorial presentation we would first sit down and enter all of the information we could think of for the presentation. Then, we would use the outliner to help us organize the information, choosing title slides, subtitles, and body text. If we had more than four or five points for any slide, we would break the slide into two slides so that we would not have too many ideas on a single slide.

After we finished with the outline, we would print it out and distribute it to others for review. Persuasion's outline formatting capability makes it easy for others to read the outline. When we receive the annotated printed outlines back from review, we return to Persuasion to make changes to the master outline before proceeding to design the presentation slides themselves.

You may find, as we did, that the more you use Persuasion's outliner the more you will come to rely on it as an important organizational tool for creating a presentation. The outliner is so helpful and intuitive that you may even decide to use it for organizing other projects besides presentations.

Chapter 6

Working with Objects

Now that we've threaded our way through the features and benefits of Persuasion's outliner, let's move on to topics and procedures for developing the visual part of a presentation. In this chapter, we'll cover the universal techniques you'll use for arranging and adjusting objects on slides, slide masters, speaker notes, and audience handouts. This is a nuts-and-bolts chapter. No bells and whistles here, just a collection of basic and not-so-basic tips and techniques that you can't get by without!

"Object" is one of those rarely defined, all-purpose words that you encounter repeatedly in computer manuals. By object, we mean any of the following:

- Text blocks;

- Graphics created with Persuasion's drawing tools;

- Imported graphics; or

- Charts and graphs.

What do these objects have in common? They all respond to the same techniques for:

- Selecting;

- Moving;

- Resizing; and

- Grouping, ungrouping, and regrouping.

Note: In Persuasion, as in many Macintosh applications, you work with text in two different modes, text-as-text and text-as-object. In the text-as-text mode, you use the text tool to type, edit, and format text. In the text-as-object mode, you use the pointer to manipulate the text's container; whether it's a placeholder on a slide master or a text block on a particular slide, you treat it exactly like a square or an imported graphic. Although this distinction between text-as-text and text-as-object may seem obvious and even trivial, it helps to have it clear in your mind. In this chapter, we're going to be talking about text-as-object. In the next chapter, we'll discuss text-as-text.

Selecting an Object

In Persuasion, as in all Macintosh applications, you must select an object before you can do anything to it. In fact, working is always a matter of making a selection and issuing a command.

To select an object, you must choose the pointer from the toolbox and click on the desired object. The object will sprout selection handles around its perimeter to let you know it's the chosen one. This is selection at its most basic.

To select more than one object, click the first one, then hold down the Shift key and click additional objects.

To select adjacent objects, drag a bounding box around them.

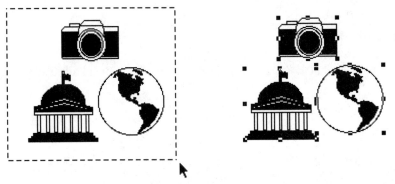

Figure 6.1.   To select adjacent objects, drag a bounding box around them.

Persuasion also features a *Select all* command *(Command+A)*. *Select all* functions differently depending on what tool is active and what objects are selected. Here's a summary.

Table 6.1

Active tool	*Select all* selects
Pointer	All objects on the slide
Drawing tool	All objects drawn with that tool
Text tool, with insertion point in a text block	All text in the text block

The first time you choose *Select all* with a tool other than the pointer active, objects created with that tool are selected. If you *Select all* a second time, the pointer becomes active and all objects on the slide are selected.

Once you've selected an object, what can you do with it? Here are some of the more common ways of treating objects.

Deleting an Object

Persuasion provides you with several ways to get rid of objects you don't want.

To delete an object permanently, choose *Clear* from the Edit menu (or press the Delete/Backspace key). This removes the object from the slide without moving it to the Clipboard, the Macintosh's temporary storage area. Use *Clear* when you're absolutely sure you'll never want to see the object again, or when there's something precious on the Clipboard that you don't want to bump. (Remember, the Clipboard handles only one item at a time.)

The *Clear* command is extreme, but it's not really permanent, as long as you change your mind right away. Persuasion offers an *Undo* command right at the top of the Edit menu, easily accessible in case of emergency. Its keyboard equivalent is one of those universal Macintosh shortcuts that ought to be indelibly impressed in your mind: *Command+Z*. The *Undo* command undoes whatever was done last: the last editing or formatting command. Although almost everything is undoable, including *Clear*, there's only one level of *Undo*. You cannot undo a whole series of steps one-by-one.

Cutting, Copying, or Pasting an Object

To copy or move objects between or within slides, use the *Copy* or *Cut* and *Paste* commands.

To copy an object, select it, and then choose *Copy* from the Edit menu (*Command+C*). A copy of the object will be placed in the Clipboard ready for pasting into a new location. The original remains untouched.

To cut an object, select it, and then choose *Cut* from the Edit menu (*Command+X*). The object is removed from the slide, and a copy is stored in the Clipboard.

To paste (or insert) an object from the Clipboard, move to the desired slide for the new location, then choose *Paste* from the Edit menu (*Command+V*). The contents of the Clipboard will be pasted into the center of the slide, ready for moving or resizing.

Caution: Whatever you cut or copy replaces the previous contents of the Clipboard. To be safe, if you intend to paste a cut or copied element, do so immediately after cutting or copying it. If you don't, you may forget it's there and inadvertently replace it in the Clipboard by cutting or copying another element.

If you cut or copy and paste multiple objects using the Shift key technique or the *Select all* command, the objects maintain their positions relative to each other throughout the ordeal.

Duplicating an Object

Another way to copy an object is to use the Duplicate command. *Duplicate* copies an object and pastes the copy slightly offset onto the slide. In fact, *Duplicate* does in one step what *Copy-and-Paste* does in two, with one important difference. *Duplicate* does not place a copy of the object in the Clipboard. *Duplicate* is the fastest way to make multiple copies of an object. It's also a good alternative to cutting and pasting when you want to preserve the contents of the Clipboard.

To duplicate an object, select it, and then choose *Duplicate* from the Edit menu (*Command+D*). The duplicate object can then be moved to its new location or edited.

Figure 6.2.   The *Duplicate* command is essentially a
one-step copy-and-paste operation.

The *Duplicate* command is best for simple graphics you create within Persuasion. Although you can duplicate any object, not all duplicates are perfect copies of the original: duplicated text blocks lose their link to the outline and duplicated charts and tables lose their link to the data sheet. If you want to copy a text block while preserving its link to the outline (for example, if you want the same text block to appear on two slides), you should copy the slide text in Outline view instead of duplicating it in Slide view. If you want the same chart to appear twice while staying linked to the data sheet, select and plot the data twice instead of using the *Duplicate* command.

Tip: You can use the *Duplicate* command to repeat any sequence of changes you made to a selected object since you last duplicated it. What does this mean? Let's say you select and duplicate a red rectangle, and then make these changes to the duplicate:

1. Change its fill color to white;

2. Apply a black shadow; and

3. Move it a half inch to the right and a quarter inch down.

Choosing *Duplicate* again not only copies the original duplicated red rectangle, it also repeats the subsequent three steps. The trick is to make sure you don't accidentally deselect the object in the middle of this procedure.

This aspect of the *Duplicate* command allows you to use it as a "step and repeat" feature to control the offset at which each duplicate copy is pasted onto the slide—select an object, duplicate it, move the duplicate into the right position relative to the original, and then choose *Duplicate* as many times as you like. This technique is most appropriate for creating borders or background patterns from simple objects.

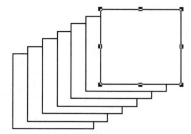

Figure 6.3. You can create a step-and-repeat effect by moving a duplicated object, and then duplicating it repeatedly.

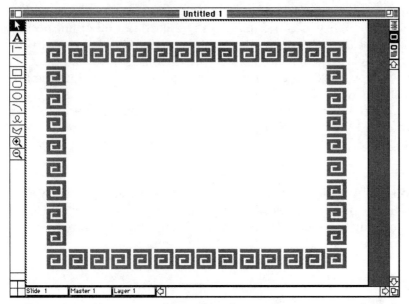

Figure 6.4. You can use the Duplicate feature to create step-and-repeat borders or background patterns.

Moving an Object

If you completed the Argilla Zoo tutorial, you're already a veteran object mover. But we'll summarize what you already know anyway, just for the record.

To move an object, select the pointer, click the object, and then drag it to its new location. An outline of the object travels with the pointer to tell you where it will end up when you release the mouse button.

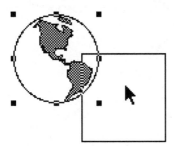

Figure 6.5. An outline of the moving object helps you track its progress.

For best results when moving an object, point to its center and avoid its selection handles. Selection handles are for resizing, not for moving. There's nothing more frustrating than setting out to move a graphic of a giraffe only to discover you've turned it into a dachshund by accidentally resizing it. If the object is hollow (has no fill), point to its outline instead of its center, but steer clear of its selection handles.

To move an object in only one direction, horizontal or vertical, hold down the Shift key while dragging. For example, let's say you're positioning a logo in the bottom left corner of a slide master. You like its current position relative to the bottom of the slide, but you want to nudge it a bit closer to the left edge. Hold down the Shift key to prevent accidentally moving the logo up or down as you drag it to the left. To retain the Shift key's constraining effect, be sure to release the mouse button before letting go of the Shift key.

Resizing an Object

To resize an object (or a selection of objects), select the object(s), click on any selection handle, and then drag to resize. (Unlike most other drawing programs, when Persuasion resizes multiple selected objects, it treats them as though they were grouped.) If you want to change both the width and height of an object, select a corner selection handle. A four-pointed arrow cursor tells you that you can move in all directions to resize both dimensions.

If you want to change only the width or the height, but not both, choose the selection handle on the side (or top or bottom) that you want to resize. A double-ended arrow indicates the directions in which you can move.

Tip: Persuasion's selection handles can be finicky. You have to get right on top of them before they'll respond. As a result, it's easy to find yourself accidentally moving an object you intended to resize. If this happens to you, use the *Undo* command (*Command+Z*) to undo the move, and then try again.

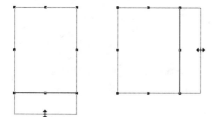

Figure 6.6.   Grab a side selection handle to resize in only one direction.

Variations on Resizing

To resize an object while maintaining its proportions, hold down the Shift key as you drag. The opposite selection handle will anchor the object, and the cursor will be constrained to proportional resizing. This technique is especially useful when you're resizing an imported graphic or a perfect square or circle and don't want to disturb its original proportions.

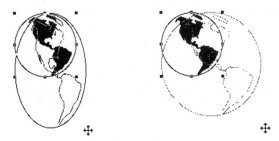

Figure 6.7.   Without the Shift key, it's easy to distort an object as you resize it.

To resize an object from its center, hold down the Option key as you drag. If you select a corner selection handle, the object can be resized from its center in all four directions. Selecting a side selection handle permits resizing in only two directions from the center. Use this resizing-from-the-center technique when the object's center is where you want it but the object's size needs adjusting (for example, if you've centered a rectangle horizontally and vertically on the slide, and then realize that you want the rectangle a bit smaller).

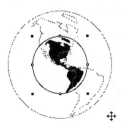

Figure 6.8.   Pressing the Option key resizes the object from its center.

To resize an object proportionately from its center, combine the Shift and Option keys. For example, if you're resizing a perfect square that's centered on the slide, holding down the Shift and Option keys will allow you to resize it while preserving its position and proportions.

To retain the Shift and Option keys' constraining effects, be sure to release the mouse button before letting go of either key.

Besides pointing to a particular selection handle, Persuasion offers you another approach to resizing. Make sure the object is selected, and then hold down the Command key and click anywhere near the selected object (not necessarily on a selection handle). Depending on where you click, a double-ended or a four-pointed arrow will tell you what your resizing options are. Drag to resize as you normally would. This Command-plus-click resizing technique can be faster than pointing to a selection handle (because the selection handles require a fine touch). In addition, it allows you to reduce or magnify the effects of the drag, depending on how close to the object you click: if you click quite close, the side(s) of the object you're dragging move right along with the cursor; the further away from the object you click, the more subtle the resizing effect will be. With practice, you'll develop a feel for the best way to perform a given resizing task.

Of course, all three modifier keys, Shift, Option, and Command, can be combined for advanced resizing. Here's a summary of resizing techniques.

Table 6.2

Desired effect	Action
To resize one dimension	Drag side selection handle
To resize two dimensions	Drag corner selection handle
To resize proportionately	Press Shift while dragging selection handle
To resize from center	Press Option while dragging selection handle
To resize proportionately from center	Press Shift+Option while dragging selection handle
To resize quickly	Press Command while clicking anywhere on the object, then drag

Note: The moving and resizing cursors in Persuasion can be confusing to seasoned PageMaker users. In Persuasion, a four-way arrow warns you that you're about to resize an object while, in PageMaker, the four-way arrow is used for moving. It just takes a bit of getting used to.

Using Persuasion's Rulers

Persuasion provides optional rulers along the top and left edges of the presentation window in all but Outline and Slide sorter views. As you move the cursor (whether you're using a drawing tool to draw an object or the pointer tool to move one), dashed lines in the ruler indicate its current position.

To turn the rulers on and off, choose *Preferences* from the File menu. In the Preferences dialog box, after *Drawing options,* check or uncheck *Show rulers.* (*Show ruler lines* displays a grid, which we'll look at in a minute.)

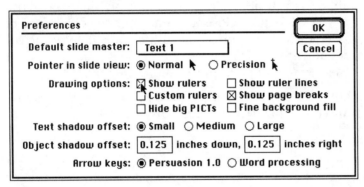

Figure 6.9.   You can turn Persuasion's rulers on and off in the Preferences dialog box.

Use the rulers to measure objects as you draw them. For example, let's say you want to draw a rectangle that's two inches wide by one inch tall. Position the square-corner tool at one inch on the horizontal and vertical rulers and draw until it's at three inches on the horizontal and two inches on the vertical. Now that it's the right size, you can move it into position on the slide.

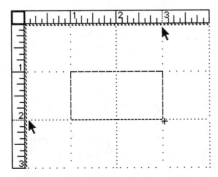

Figure 6.10. Persuasion's rulers let you measure objects as you create them.

Of course, you can always use a bit of simple math to calculate size and position at the same time. For example, to draw a three-by-four inch square two inches from the upper left corner of the slide, position the square-corner tool at two inches on the horizontal and vertical rulers, and then draw until the horizontal ruler reads five inches and the vertical ruler reads two inches. If you've ever worked with a drawing program, these tips will be familiar to you. If you're venturing into drawing for the first time, however, practice will perfect your technique.

Since Persuasion's rulers mark the location of the pointer tool rather than a selected object, they're less effective for positioning existing objects. Why? When positioning an object, especially one with a regular shape, you'll often want to use a side as a reference point. For example, you'll position the upper left corner of a square half an inch from the upper left corner of the slide or the right end point of a horizontal line one inch from the right edge of the slide. But when you go to move an object into position, you'll grab it by the middle rather than by a side (or else you'll resize it, remember?). In this case, all the rulers are telling you is the location of the pointer tool (somewhere in the middle of the object) not of the object's sides, and that's usually not good enough for precise positioning of the object you're moving. Use one of the techniques for aligning objects described below instead. To preview your slides without distraction, turn the rulers off.

Aligning Objects

Persuasion offers you several options for aligning objects with each other and with Persuasion's grid.

Aligning Objects with Each Other

Select two or more objects you want to align (use the Shift key to add to your selection). Choose *Align objects* from the Draw menu (*Command+L*).

In the Align objects dialog box, check the kind of alignment you want. There are three types of alignment:

- Vertical (*Up/Down*), aligning the tops, centers, or bottoms of objects;

- Horizontal (*Left/Right*), aligning the leftmost edges, centers, or rightmost edges of objects;

- Both vertical and horizontal, combining options from *Up/Down* and *Left/Right* (top left edges, bottom right edges, and so forth).

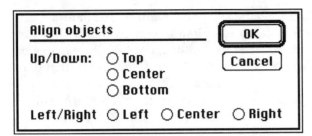

Figure 6.11. The Align objects dialog box lets you align objects
horizontally, vertically, or both.

Persuasion aligns two or more objects by "squaring off" the edges of the
imaginary rectangle formed by each object's selection handles.

Note: The *Align objects* command in the Draw menu allows you to align
objects, including text blocks, with each other. To align text within a
text block, however, you'll use the *Alignment* command in the Edit
menu, which is discussed in Chapter 7, *Working with Text*.

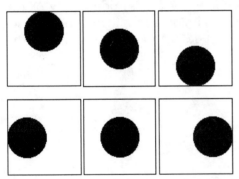

Figure 6.12. Here's an illustration of the alignment options. The top row
shows *Up/Down*: *Top*, *Center*, and *Bottom*. The bottom row
shows *Left/Right*: *Left*, *Center*, and *Right*.

Aligning Objects Using the Grid

To help with alignment tasks, you can have Persuasion display a grid in
the presentation window. You can determine several features of the grid:
whether it's visible, whether it exerts magnetic attraction on slide elements,
and what measurement units it uses. The grid can be visible but not magnetic, or magnetic but not visible. Here are some guidelines for using the
grid most effectively.

When you're setting up a slide or slide master and want maximum control over the position of elements as you create or place them, make the grid both visible and magnetic.

To make the grid visible, choose *Show ruler guides* from the Preferences dialog box in the File menu. Major grid divisions are indicated by numbers in the rulers across the top and left sides of the slide and by horizontal and vertical dotted lines on the slide. Minor grid divisions are indicated by tick marks in the rulers. Making the grid visible helps you decide where to place elements.

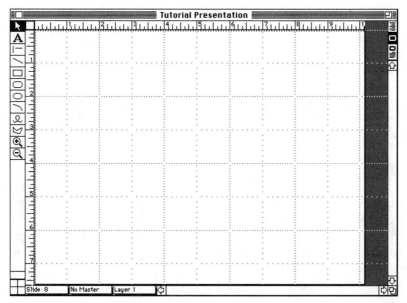

Figure 6.13. Numbers in the rulers and dashed ruler guides indicate major grid divisions; tick marks in the rulers indicate minor grid divisions.

To make the grid magnetic, choose *Grid snap on (Command+Y)* from the Effect menu. When you drag a drawing tool across the presentation window with grid snap turned on, the tool "hops" instead of travelling smoothly across the grid. This is because the grid's magnetic attraction forces the tool to align with the nearest grid division, either a major division indicated by a number in the rulers and a dotted line on the slide, or a minor division indicated by a tick mark in the rulers. Turning grid snap on helps you place elements automatically by forcing them into alignment with the grid. It's especially useful if you intend to draw several objects in a row, for example, if you're setting up a slide master with a series of short horizontal lines along the left edge of the slide.

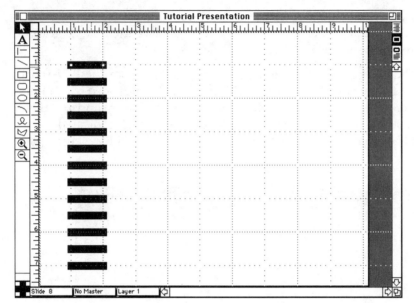

Figure 6.14. To align multiple objects with the grid as you draw them, turn *Grid snap* on.

You can make the grid visible but not magnetic. This is helpful when you want to arrange irregularly shaped elements visually. For example, if you want to align the "P" in the word "Pacific" with the Pacific coast, as shown in the figure below. Turning grid snap off but leaving the grid visible lets you guide the elements into place by hand using a grid line as a frame of reference. And, of course you can make the grid magnetic but not visible when you want snap-to power without the distractions of grid lines.

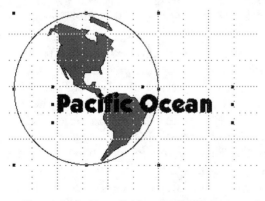

Figure 6.15. Turn *Grid snap* off when you want to align objects visually, such as the "P" in Pacific with the west coast of North America.

Caution: Grid snap may sometimes produce unexpected results with objects drawn with a thick line style. For example, let's say you want to draw a thick horizontal line beginning one inch from the left edge of the slide. You choose the line drawing tool, select a thick line style from the Effect menu, position the drawing tool at the one-inch mark on the horizontal ruler, and draw the line. When you finish, you see that the line really begins somewhat to the left of the one-inch mark. Why does this happen? Because Persuasion adds the actual thickness of the line you specified to the path of the line you traced with the drawing tool (see the figure below). If this is a problem, turn grid snap off and reposition the object visually.

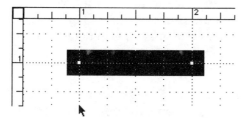

Figure 6.16. Persuasion aligns an object's selection handles, rather than it's edges, to the grid.

To align an object that's already on the slide, select it, then choose *Align to grid* (*Command+H*) from the Draw menu. Persuasion will align the boundaries of the object (as defined by its selection handles) to the nearest vertical and horizontal ruler guides. You can use this alignment technique on text blocks as well as graphics. Remember, in this chapter we're dealing with text-as-object rather than text-as-text. In a text block, the baseline of the first line of text will align with the nearest horizontal ruler guide.

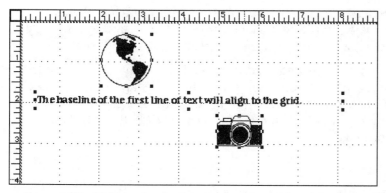

Figure 6.17. Objects align to the nearest ruler guide, while the baseline of the first line of text aligns to the nearest horizontal ruler.

Customizing Persuasion's Grid

Persuasion lets you customize several aspects of the grid. To customize the grid, choose *Preferences* from the File menu. In the Preferences dialog box, after *Drawing options*, click on *Custom rulers*. (If *Custom rulers* is already checked, you'll need to click twice, once to deselect it, and once to reselect it.) You'll see the Custom rulers dialog box as shown below.

Here are a couple of definitions before we investigate the possibilities for customizing the grid. As we saw above, major divisions are identified by numbers in the horizontal and vertical rulers, and by dotted grid lines. Minor divisions are identified only by tick marks between the major division numbers on the rulers. (This is true in Actual size and Fit in window views. In 200 and 400% views, some minor divisions may be indicated by lines; by contrast, in 50 and 25% views, some major division lines may disappear.) Both major and minor divisions exert magnetic attraction when grid snap is turned on, regardless of whether the grid is displayed.

Major division units specifies the unit of measure used on the rulers. Your choices are *inches*, *centimeters*, or *points/pixels*. Choose the option you prefer. (For most people, inches will be the increment of choice.)

Units per major division determines how many units of measure each major division will contain. For example, if you're working in inches and you specify 1 as the *Units per major division*, your grid will consist of major divisions each "containing" one inch (in other words, at one-inch intervals). If you're working in points and you specify 72 as the *Units per major division*, each major division will consist of 72 points. (Since there are 72 points to an inch, your grid will still show major divisions at one-inch intervals.) In general, you'll choose 1 if you're working in inches or centimeters, and 72 if you're working in points/pixels.

Increment numbers by specifies how major divisions are numbered. If you specify 1, the major divisions will be numbered 1, 2, 3, and so forth. If you specify 2, the major divisions will be numbered 2, 4, 6, and so on.

Minor divisions per major division determines how many subdivisions there will be within each major division. Minor divisions are indicated by tick marks on the ruler. The greater the number of minor divisions, the finer the grid, and the more snap-to options you'll have when the grid's magnetic attraction is turned on.

Centering Objects on a Slide

Not only can you align objects in relation to each other and to Persuasion's grid, you can automatically center objects vertically or horizontally on a slide. Select the object or objects you want to center, and then choose *Center on slide* from the Draw menu. Choose one of the two options, *Up/Down* or *Left/Right*, from the pop-down menu. (You can't center objects simultaneously in both dimensions; you have to open the Draw menu twice.)

If you select more than one object, Persuasion centers the selected objects as a group. The position of the objects relative to each other won't change. (To center the objects in relation to each other, of course, you'd use the *Align objects* feature described above.)

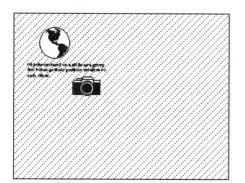 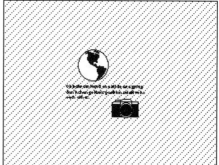

Figure 6.18. Three objects before and after being centered horizontally and vertically on the slide.

Rotating or Flipping an Object

Sometimes the only way to treat an object is to rotate or flip it. Flipping or rotating is most useful for customizing imported graphics. For example, in Figure 6.19 below we've customized samples of the Art of Persuasion clip art. We flipped the running woman so that she runs into instead of out of the slide, and we rotated the jet so that it flies west to east instead of taking off. In Persuasion, you can do this, rotating in 90-degree increments, or flipping vertically or horizontally.

Select the objects you want to manipulate, and then choose *Rotate/Flip* from the Draw menu. Choose one of the four options from the pop-down menu, *Rotate left*, *Rotate right*, *Flip horizontal*, or *Flip vertical*.

Figure 6.19. The Flip and Rotate commands let you customize clip art.

Figure 6.20. The Rotate command allows you to turn the world in 90-degree increments.

Figure 6.21. With the Flip command, you can flip the earth vertically or horizontally.

There are a few subtleties to flipping and rotating. All the *Flip/Rotate* options can be applied to any object created with Persuasion's drawing tools, as well as to organization charts. Other types of charts, such as bar and column charts, can only be flipped. Rotating these types of charts amounts to switching their axes; instead of *Rotate left* and *Rotate right*, you'll use the Switch axes command from the Chart menu. (See Chapter 10, *Working with Charts and Tables*).

Tables can be flipped horizontally or mirrored about a central axis so that left columns become right columns and vice versa. But you can't flip a table vertically so that top rows switch places with bottom rows. Nor can you rotate a table, changing rows into columns and columns into rows.

To flip a table horizontally, select it, and then drag one selection handle from one side of the table across to the opposite side. The columns will be mirrored across the center, although text will still read properly.

Imported PICT images can be flipped and rotated only after being ungrouped. To ungroup a PICT image, select it, and then choose *Ungroup* (*Command+U*) from the Draw menu.

Sorry, no rotating or flipping of imported EPS graphics is allowed.

Working with Overlapping Objects

As your Persuasion skills develop and you undertake more ambitious presentations, you'll encounter the problem of how to manage overlapping objects on a slide. For example, if you draw a rectangle, create a text block within it, then draw a rule, how do you control what's on top and what's underneath?

Persuasion offers you two strategies for managing objects on slides. You can either:

- Control how objects on the same layer overlap, as you would in a page layout program. You'd use this strategy for simple drawings.

- Assign objects to different layers, as you would in a drawing program. Choose this strategy for complex drawings, when you want to isolate and control different parts of the drawing as you work, and when you want to set up slide builds.

Let's look at each of these strategies in detail.

Managing Overlapping Objects on the Same Layer

When you draw overlapping objects, the newest object always goes in front. But once you've finished drawing, you can change the stacking order by selecting an object and moving it forward or back. For example, let's say you place your company's logo on a background master and realize it would stand out more if it were positioned on a solid field of color. You draw a box surrounding the logo. When you finish drawing, the box sits on top of and hides the logo. Simply select the box and choose the command *Backward* to send the box behind the logo.

Select the object you want to move, choose *Send* from the Draw menu, and then choose one of the four options from the submenu. Their effects are described in the table below, along with their keyboard shortcuts.

Table 6.3

To do this	Choose	Keyboard shortcut
Move an object in front of all other objects	*To front*	*Command+F*
Move an object forward one position	*Forward*	*Command+"="* (equals)
Move an object behind all other objects	*To back*	*Command+B*
Move an object backward one position	*Backward*	*Command+"-"* (minus)

If you're working with several overlapping objects, it may take some experimenting to figure out which object to send where. Keep tinkering, and you'll get the hang of it.

Tip: To select an object that's hidden by an object on top of it, hold down the Option key and click in the location of the hidden object. As you continue to click, Persuasion successively selects each layer, moving from front to back. Stop when you see the selection handles of the object you're aiming for.

Assigning Objects to Different Layers

The commands we've just explored allow you to change the stacking order of objects that are all on the same layer. This one-layer strategy works fine for slides containing only simple graphics, perhaps one imported graphic and a square or circle or two. But, if you intend to do complex drawing within Persuasion or if you want to construct slide "builds" that reveal each layer at intervals, you'll need a more sophisticated strategy involving multiple layers.

How would you use multiple layers for a slide build? Let's say you're preparing a bar chart showing projected zoo attendance figures for the next four years. To emphasize the zoo's very bright future, you want to build suspense by revealing the chart one bar at a time. You'd assign each bar to a different layer, and then choose *Builds* when printing slides or overheads, or assign a delay between layers when setting up an on-screen slide show. You can also create automatic builds on slide masters, as you'll see in Chapter 13, *Building an AutoTemplate*.

To assign an object to a drawing layer, select the object you want to work with. Then choose the appropriate layer from the Layer pop-up menu in the lower menu bar. Using our zoo attendance bar chart as an example, you'd select the bar representing 1990 attendance and assign it to layer 2, assign 1991 to layer 3, 1992 to layer 4, and so forth.

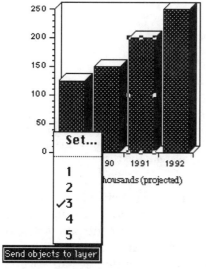

Figure 6.22. To assign an object to a drawing layer, select the object, and then select a layer from the Layer pop-up menu.

To see what layer an object's currently on, select the object and check the layer number in the small box on the right side of the Layer pop-up menu.

You can assign text as well as objects to layers. You could place each subhead within a text block or even each word of a slide title on a different layer. For example, you could build suspense by building word-by-word a slide title such as "Introducing...our...very...latest...model...." With the text tool, select the text you want to assign, and then choose a layer from the Layer pop-up menu.

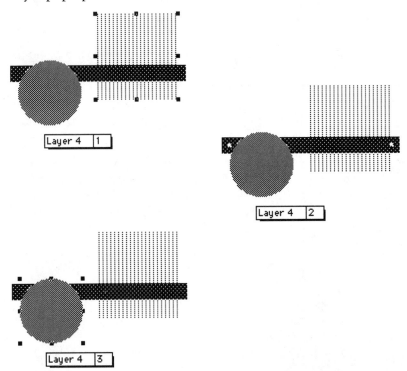

Figure 6.23. The Layer pop-up menu tells you what layer an object is assigned to. In the figures above, the square is on Layer 1, the horizontal line on Layer 2, and the circle on Layer 3. Layer 4 is the current drawing layer.

How would you use multiple layers when drawing? Let's say you're preparing a presentation on breeding scarlet tanagers, and you want to use Persuasion's drawing tools to draw a bird in a cage. By controlling which layers are visible and which layers are "active" (meaning you can draw and select objects on them), you can isolate and protect different parts of the drawing as you work. You starting by drawing the cage on layer 1. Then you make layer 2 the active layer, leaving layer 1 visible but inactive. With layer

1 still visible, you can draw the bird to fit the cage, but, with layer 1 now inactive, you'll avoid accidentally resizing a bar of the cage while drawing the bird's beak. When you've finished the bird's silhouette, you'll make layer 1 invisible so you can focus without distraction on the details of the bird's plumage.

To control what layers are visible and active, choose *Set* from the Layer pop-up menu to open the Set layer visibility dialog box. The current drawing layer is the layer on which anything you draw will be placed. To change the drawing layer, simply type in the number of the layer you want. Layer 1 is the default.

To make all layers active (so that you can select objects on all layers), choose *All* for *Active layers*. To avoid accidentally modifying objects on layers other than the drawing layer you're working on, select *Drawing layer only*. This makes all but the current drawing layer inactive. If you want to work on some but not all layers—for example, layers 2 and 3 but not layer 1—type in the range of layers after *From...to*.

To make all layers visible, select *All* for *Visible layers*. To make only the active layers visible, choose *Active layers only*.

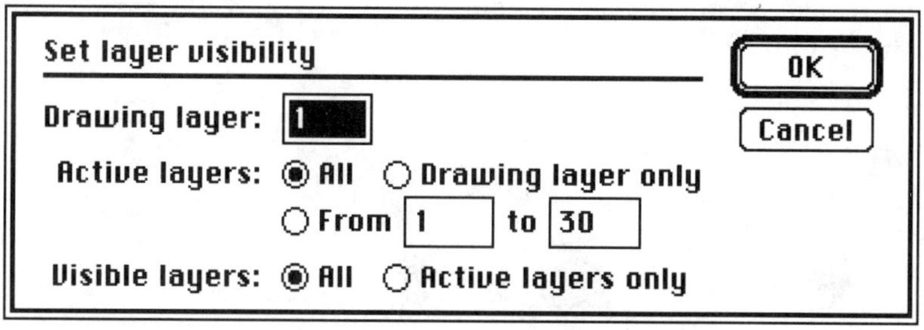

Figure 6.24. To control what layers are active and visible, choose *Set* from the Layer pop-up menu to open the Set layer visibility dialog box.

Let's return to our scarlet tanager example above. To draw the bird's plumage, you'd set the drawing layer to 2, and choose both *Active layers: Drawing layer only* and *Visible layers: Active layers only*. This leaves only layer 2 both active and visible, so you can focus on drawing the bird's plumage without worrying about bending a bar of the cage or being distracted by the pattern of the cage bars on layer 1.

Although visible layers can be active or inactive, an invisible layer will always be inactive (since you can't select what you can't see). When you first open a new presentation, each slide consists of three layers, with layer

1 as the default drawing layer. Persuasion makes sure there are always at least two unused layers, up to a maximum of 30. For example, when you first assign an object to layer 2, Persuasion adds layer 4; when you first assign an object to layer 3, Persuasion adds layer 5; and so forth.

Grouping, Ungrouping, and Regrouping Objects

Sometimes, you'll want to assemble several ingredients into a single composite object so that you can manipulate it more easily. For example, when we created the newsletter graphic in the Argilla Zoo tutorial, we began by drawing the overall shape of the newsletter, the nameplate, and the two columns of text. Then we grouped these elements so that we had one object instead of four. That allowed us to move the newsletter as a whole, instead of moving each element individually or selecting them all and moving them.

Grouping Objects

Select two or more objects to work with. Each object will sprout selection handles around its perimeter. Choose *Group* (*Command+G*) from the Draw menu. Now, instead of several sets of selection handles, you'll see one for the composite group.

Figure 6.25. After grouping, the composite object shows only one set
of selection handles.

Not only can grouped objects be moved and resized, they can also be cut, copied, pasted, rotated, and flipped. In short, you can do anything to a grouped object that you can do to a single object. Furthermore, you can group as many objects as you want. In fact, you can group grouped objects, thereby creating groups of groups.

Grouping is not a permanent condition. You can always use the *Ungroup* command to resize or delete just one of the elements of a group and then regroup. You might also group objects long enough to rotate them, for example, and then ungroup them so that you can resize one element separately.

Ungrouping Objects

To ungroup an object, select it, and then choose *Ungroup (Command+U)* from the Draw menu. In the same way that you can use the *Group* command repeatedly to group groups, you can use the *Ungroup* command to break a grouped group into its component groups. In other words, choosing *Ungroup* repeatedly will ungroup objects following the same pattern in which they were grouped.

By the way, you don't necessarily need to ungroup a grouped object to modify one of its parts. You can apply commands from the Effects menu to any element, and you can modify text elements simply by double-clicking the part you want to work with. This technique, called "subselecting," works for any component part, no matter how low in a hierarchy of groupings.

For example, if you want to format a text block that's part of a group, you wouldn't need to ungroup it. Just select the group of which the text block's a part, and then choose the options you want from the Text menu. In addition, you can always choose the text tool and click in the text block to edit, regardless of how deeply nested the text block is. You must, however, ungroup to resize a subelement other than text.

Regrouping Ungrouped Objects

Once you've ungrouped a grouped object, the easiest way to regroup it is to use the *Regroup* command. (You can, of course, select all the individual elements and then select *Group* again, but that's the hard way.)

Persuasion has a good memory for how objects were grouped, so much so that it will remember all successive groupings. In fact, you don't even need to have any of the objects selected. When you choose *Regroup* from the Draw menu, Persuasion reestablishes the most recently defined group, along with any changes you made to its ingredients. And each subsequent time you select *Regroup*, Persuasion will restore the latest grouping.

Not all objects can be grouped. Text blocks created with the text tool (that aren't linked to the outline), graphics drawn with Persuasion's tools, and imported text and graphics can be grouped. Charts and tables linked to the data sheet and text blocks linked to the outline cannot be grouped. However, duplicating any of the above creates objects that *can* be grouped and that are no longer linked to the data sheet or outline.

Grouping and ungrouping charts follows some special rules and procedures. We cover them in Chapter 10, *Working with Charts and Tables*.

So much for the nuts and bolts of working with objects on slides. Let's move on to the business of working with text.

Chapter 7

Working with Text

Words, both spoken and written, are the heart of a presentation. Although visuals such as charts and graphics are powerful tools for supporting your argument, your text—both what you say and how you say it—will ultimately make or break your presentation. In this chapter, we'll investigate the "how" aspect of words: how to type, edit, and format text on slides.

First, a little background. The most efficient strategy for creating slide text is to let Persuasion's outliner and your slide placeholders (based on slide masters) do the work for you. You can either build your presentation using the outliner, or you can type directly into placeholders on individual slides. The interactive link between placeholders and outline ensures that whenever you make any changes to text content—either on the slide itself or in the outline—both outline and slide reflect the change. Text that flows between placeholders and the outline is referred to as "dynamic" text.

Besides using the outline and placeholders to work with dynamic text, you can also create text blocks directly on your slides. Such text blocks, referred to as "static text,"are not linked to the outline. This technique works best for an occasional caption, quote, or label.

Regardless of which of the two kinds of text (static or dynamic) you choose to create on your slides, the same techniques are used for editing and formatting it.

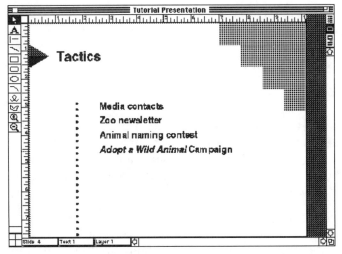

Figure 7.1.   Text flows between the outliner and a slide's text placeholders.

Adding Text to a Slide

Persuasion offers two approaches to working with dynamic text. Most often, you'll create text for your presentation in the outline, and then format it in slide view using slide masters and placeholders. In other words, you'll work with *content* in outline view, and then switch to slide view to work with *form*. Although efficient, this approach separates working with form from working with content.

If you prefer to work simultaneously with form and content (if you like to see exactly how text will look on a slide as you type it), you can type directly into a placeholder on a slide, either to replace the dummy placeholder text ("Title" or "Body text") or to edit text flowing from the outline. Of course, whatever you type in a slide placeholder automatically updates the outline.

Adding Text to a Placeholder

Since every placeholder contains dummy text, (for example, "This is a Title Placeholder"), you must select the dummy text before you can add your own.

Choose the text tool, select the dummy placeholder text, and then type the replacement text. As in all Macintosh applications, whatever you type replaces the highlighted text—no need to delete it before typing.

Tip: To help your screen display its best approximation of finished text, work at Actual size (choose *Actual size* from the Draw menu). Text is especially sensitive to the subtle distortions that can occur in other display sizes.

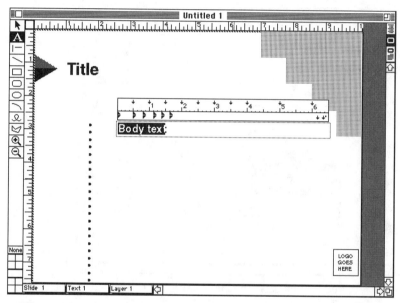

Figure 7.2.   To replace placeholder text, select it, and then type the new text.

Adding a Static Text Block to a Slide

Select the text tool, and then position it where you want the text to begin, or drag a rectangle the size of the desired block. If you've selected *Grid snap on*, the text tool will snap to the nearest grid division (so that the baseline of the first line of text will align with the grid). Click once to create the text block. A dotted line will indicate the initial boundary of the text block. If *Show text ruler* is turned on in the Text menu, you'll see the text ruler above the text block.

If you just click (instead of dragging a rectangle), the width and position of the text block depends on what's currently selected in the Alignment submenu. *Align left* and *Justify* will give you a text block that extends from where you click to the right edge of the slide, *Align right* will produce one that extends from click point to the slide's left edge, and *Align center* will center the text block on the click point.

To control the width of the text block yourself, start by clicking and dragging to the desired width. To alter the width of an existing text block, select the block with the text tool, hold down the Command key, and drag an edge. You can also resize a text block as you would any other object.

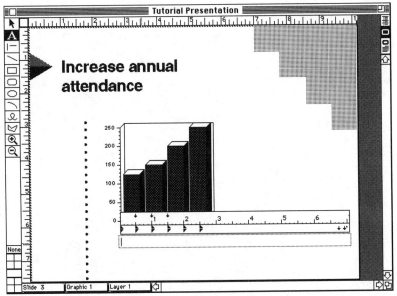

Figure 7.3.　A dotted line indicates the initial boundary of a new text block.

To type within a graphic such as a rectangle, double-click the graphic. Persuasion will center the text block vertically and horizontally within the graphic. This technique works best with a regular shape, but you can use it for any graphic (for example, labeling individual states on a map of the United States).

Once you've created the text block, go ahead and type. Your words will wrap to fit the width of the text block, and new lines will be created as required. Persuasion automatically makes the text block as deep as necessary to accommodate the text within it.

To change the width of an existing text block, click on it with the text tool, press the Command key, and then drag either side to the desired width. You can also resize it with the pointer tool as you would any graphic. Either way, text will automatically reflow to fit the text block's new dimensions.

Figure 7.4.   Double-click on a graphic to create a text block its width.

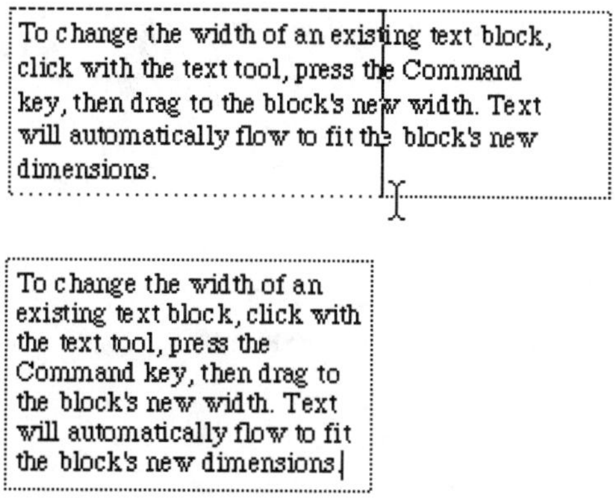

To change the width of an existing text block, click with the text tool, press the Command key, then drag to the block's new width. Text will automatically flow to fit the block's new dimensions.

To change the width of an existing text block, click with the text tool, press the Command key, then drag to the block's new width. Text will automatically flow to fit the block's new dimensions

Figure 7.5.   To change the width of a text block, hold down the Command key and drag with the text tool.

Editing text
Selecting Text

Selecting text in Persuasion follows standard Macintosh procedures. We've summarized them briefly here as a review for those of you who are newcomers to the Macintosh.

To select a range of text, choose the text tool from the toolbox, and then click the text box to select it. It will respond by displaying its dotted boundary, an insertion point (a blinking vertical line), and, if *Show text ruler* is selected from the Text menu, a text ruler. Then, you can select elements of the text, using one of the following techniques.

Table 7.1

To select	Do this
An insertion point	Click
A character or short phrase	Drag to highlight it
A word	Double-click the word or drag to highlight it
A range of text	Click one end, then press Shift key and click the other end
All text in a text box	Click insertion point, then choose *Select all* from Edit menu (*Command+A*)

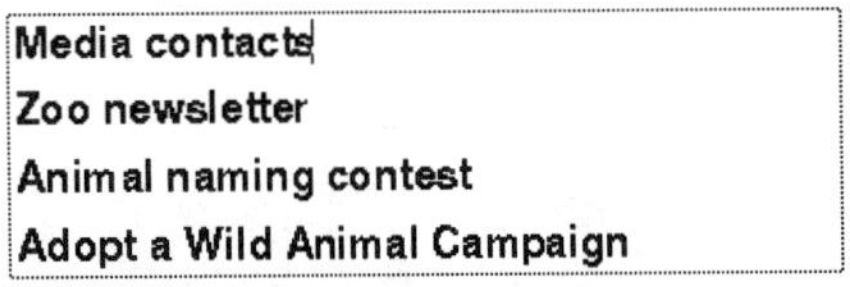

Media contacts|
Zoo newsletter
Animal naming contest
Adopt a Wild Animal Campaign

Figure 7.6.   When selected, a text box responds by displaying a dotted boundary and an insertion point.

Inserting Text

To insert text into an existing text block, click an insertion point, and then type. As with all Macintosh applications, what you type enters to the left of the insertion point. If the text block is a placeholder linked to the outline, whatever you type on the slide will flow back to the outline. The current width of the text block will control how text wraps; its depth will change to accommodate the new text.

Copying, Moving, or Deleting Text

To copy or move text from one location to another within a text block or between text blocks, first select the text, and then choose *Copy* (*Command +C*) or *Cut* (*Command+X*) from the Edit menu. A copy of the text will be placed in the Clipboard. If you chose *Copy*, the original remains untouched. If you chose *Cut*, the original vanishes from the slide. Click an insertion point at the text's new location, and then choose *Paste* (*Command+P*) from the Edit menu. The pasted text will appear to the left of the insertion point.

To delete all the text in a placeholder, you must go to Outline view or delete the placeholder on the slide master. If you try to delete all a placeholder's text in Slide view, the text will vanish obediently. But if you switch to Outline view, you'll see the text is still in the outline. And then, when you switch back to Slide view, the text will mysteriously reappear. This feature prevents you from inadvertently deleting an entire slide when you're editing text. Also, if you have been experimenting with formatting for a particular text block, you can revert to your original formatting by pressing the Delete key. If you go to Outline view, you'll see the text is still here, and, when you return to Slide view, the deleted text appears with its original formatting (the formatting called for by the placeholder on the slide's master.)

Formatting Text

Persuasion offers several techniques for formatting text. We'll summarize them here, then investigate each in detail.

1. Format a text placeholder on a slide master. In this case, title, subtitle, and body text flows from the outline into placeholders and takes on their formatting. This works dynamically so that all slides created previously and based on that master are also formatted.

2. Format text on a slide.
   a. Set formats before you type.
      - Set temporary text tool defaults; and
      - Set presentation defaults.

   b. Format existing text.
      - Apply options one at a time from the Text menu;
      - Apply multiple options from the Text format dialog box; and
      - Define and apply named text formats.

Since we'll cover how to create and format slide masters in Chapter 13, *Building an AutoTemplate*, let's begin here with the two basic ways to format the text on a slide: (a.) set up formats before you type, or (b.) format existing text.

Setting Formats before You Type
Setting Temporary Text Tool Defaults

"Default" is merely a fancy way of saying current setting. Tool defaults are applied to a particular tool for a one-time use. To set temporary text tool defaults, select the text tool from the toolbox and then choose formatting options from the Text menu. Any text you type immediately after specifying the format will reflect your choices. These tool defaults are temporary, however. Once you deselect the text tool, it will reassume the presentation defaults, as described just below. Tool defaults are indicated by checkmarks in the Text menu.

Tip: If the defaults you're after are the same as those of an existing placeholder or text block, you've got it easy. Select the text tool and then click in the appropriate placeholder or text block. The text tool will take on its attributes.

Setting Presentation Defaults

Presentation defaults are settings that are saved with the presentation. To set presentation defaults for text, make sure that the pointer tool is active and no object is selected. Open the Text menu and choose the format options you want. From now on, each time you select the text tool, it will reflect your choices. (Of course you can always temporarily override these presentation defaults by setting up temporary tool defaults, as just described.) Presentation defaults are indicated by diamonds in the Text menu.

Rule of thumb: set presentation defaults to the text formats you'll use most frequently in the current presentation. If most of your slide text will be black, left-aligned, 24-point Times bold italic, set your presentation defaults accordingly. Make sure the pointer tool is active and nothing is selected, and then choose the appropriate attributes from the Text menu. Each time you use the text tool, that's what you'll get. But for the occasional 18-point Helvetica caption, override the presentation defaults with temporary tool defaults: select the text tool, choose 18 from the Size submenu, Helvetica from the Font submenu, and type the caption. The caption will look just the way you want, and the next time you choose the text tool, you'll be back to typing with the Times bold italic presentation defaults.

Formatting Existing Text

So much for ways to format text before you create it. How do you handle type that's already on the slide? To make one or two changes—for example, to choose a different font or a larger size—apply options one at a time from the submenus and dialog boxes in the Text menu. To make sweeping changes, use the Text format option, which combines several options in one dialog box. For formats you intend to use repeatedly (for example, for captions), you may wish to define a text format so that it can be applied as needed.

Tip: If you intend to apply the same format to all text in a text block, you may find it easier to use the "text as object" approach. Choose the pointer tool from the toolbox, click to select the text block as a whole, and make your selections from the Text menu. Any formatting options you choose will apply to all text in the selected text block. (Of course, if you want to format only some text in a text block, you'll have to use the "text as text" approach. Use the text tool and drag to select the text you want to format.)

Applying Options from the Text Menu

To apply options one at a time, select the text you want to format, and then choose the appropriate command from the Text menu.

Checkmarks next to options in the submenus reflect the current attributes of the selected text. If the text you've selected includes two or more attributes (for example, if you select two words of different sizes), the submenu will reflect the attributes of the first character in the selected text.

Font

The names you see in the Font submenu reflect the fonts installed in your System file as well as those in any font suitcases you may have opened with a font management utility. Many variables will affect your choice of font, some of them aesthetic and some of them technical. The aesthetic aspects of presentation typography are covered in great detail in Chapter 15, *Designing Effective Presentations*. Technical considerations are addressed in Chapters 17–19, which cover producing presentations for different output devices.

As a quick rule of thumb, choose a simple font supported by your output device. Times and Helvetica, which come with Persuasion, are both excellent choices.

Size

Choose one of the point sizes displayed in the submenu, or choose *Other* to open the Other text size dialog box. Type the size you want and click *OK.* (Although the largest size you can enter is 256 points, you'll rarely want more than 72 points.) Point sizes that are outlined are those which have screen fonts installed; unless you're using Adobe Type Manager or Apple's System 7 to get smooth outline fonts at all sizes, be sure to choose an outlined size for an on-screen presentation. Otherwise, your carefully crafted words will appear with unsightly "jaggies." (To install additional screen fonts, follow the procedure for installing fonts described in Chapter 1, *Installing Persuasion.*)

Tip: Persuasion displays the last size you entered in the Other text size dialog box at the bottom of the Size submenu. If there's a nonmenu size you use often, enter it once in the Other text size dialog box. From then on you can select it directly from the Size submenu.

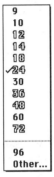

Figure 7.7. Outlined sizes are those for which screen fonts are installed.

Style

The Style submenu governs the style of selected text. It contains seven options, as shown in the figure below. Of these options, you'll probably use bold and italic most frequently. Since the commands are buried a couple levels deep in Persuasion's menus, we recommend committing their short-cuts to memory. (They're standard Macintosh shortcuts, so you may already know them by heart.)

Plain	⇧⌘
✓**Bold**	⇧⌘B
Italic	⇧⌘I
Underline	⇧⌘U
Outline	⇧⌘O
Shadow	⇧⌘S
Superscript	⇧⌘H
Subscript	⇧⌘L

Figure 7.8. Keyboard shortcuts speed up applying styles.

As its name suggests, *Plain* simply removes any styles already applied to the selected text. Its keyboard equivalent is *Shift+Command+Spacebar* (the spacebar icon doesn't appear in the submenu). To choose a bold weight of a font, choose *Bold* or *Command+Shift+B*. To italicize text, choose *Italic* or *Command+Shift+I* (but use italics sparingly because italicized text is relatively difficult to read).

Additional Style Options

The remaining five style options should be used in small doses for special effect.

Underline (Command+Shift+U) applies a solid, unbroken underline (including the spaces between words) to selected text. As a tool of emphasis, an underline is less effective than bold weight type. From a typographical standpoint, underlining is inelegant because you can't control the weight of the rule or its distance below the text. (The color of the underline will be the same as the color of its text.) Use the underline with discretion.

Outline (Command+Shift+O) outlines the letter forms and leaves their bodies hollow. Since outlined text is transparent, background color or pattern shows through it. Color applied to outline text affects only its outline, not its fill. Because outlined letters are more complex visually than solid letters, they're harder to read. For this reason, use outlining only for larger type sizes (for example, slide titles and subtitles 36 points and above). Make sure there's enough contrast between the outline text color and the slide background color so that the text is clearly visible.

Figure 7.9.   Outlined text is transparent.

Shadow (Command+Shift+S) applies a shadow to selected text. When used properly, a shadow can be a dramatic way of calling attention to a slide title or a short, bulleted point. Like any powerful tool, however, it should be used in small amounts and for calculated effect. You can control the distance and direction of a shadow from its text. Choose *Preferences* from the Edit menu, and then select a *Text shadow offset* of *Small*, *Medium*, or *Large*.

Small and medium offset are predefined at two and four pixels, respectively. You can specify how large (or small) the large offset is by typing the appropriate measurements in the *inches down* and *inches right* boxes for *Object shadow offset*. Entering negative numbers will cast a shadow above and to the left of the text. Shadow offset measurements apply to all objects and all text in the presentation; there's no way to select different offsets for different text blocks in the same presentation.

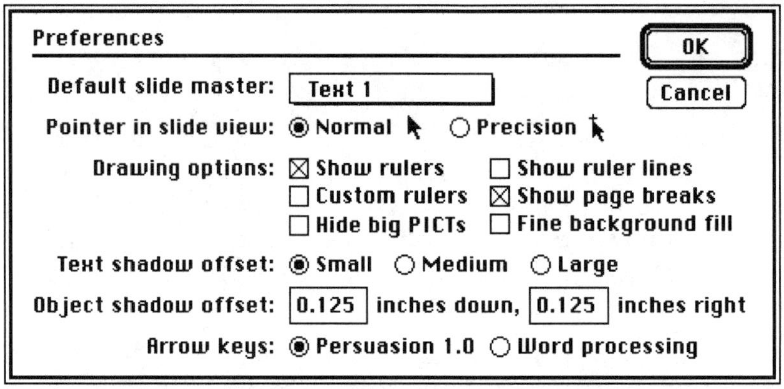

```
┌─────────────────────────────────────────────────────────┐
│ Preferences _____    ┌────────┐    │
│                                            │   OK   │    │
│ Default slide master: │ Text 1        │    └────────┘    │
│ Pointer in slide view: ◉ Normal ▶  ○ Precision ▶ │Cancel│ │
│ Drawing options: ⊠ Show rulers    □ Show ruler lines    │
│                  □ Custom rulers  ⊠ Show page breaks     │
│                  □ Hide big PICTs □ Fine background fill │
│ Text shadow offset: ◉ Small ○ Medium ○ Large            │
│ Object shadow offset: │0.125│ inches down, │0.125│ inches right │
│ Arrow keys: ◉ Persuasion 1.0 ○ Word processing          │
└─────────────────────────────────────────────────────────┘
```

Figure 7.10. Use *Text shadow offset* in the Preferences dialog box to control the appearance of text shadows.

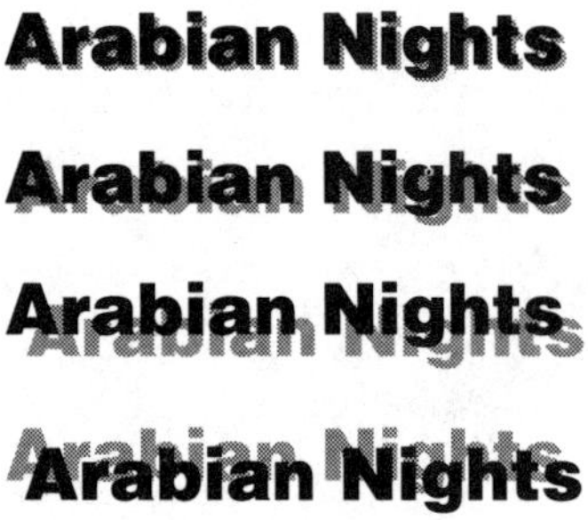

Arabian Nights

Arabian Nights

Arabian Nights

Arabian Nights

Figure 7.11. A small, medium, large, and negative text shadow offset.

Superscript (Command+Shift+H) and *Subscript (Command+Shift+L)* are special styles for occasional use: for register or trademark symbols, for chemical and mathematical formulas, and so forth. Superscripts and subscripts are about seven-twelfths of the type size of the related word. They're unique among text formatting commands in that they flow between slide text and outline. To help you remember the shortcuts, "H" is for "high" and "L" is for "low."

$$C_2H_{30}O_5$$

ZATCH[TM]

Figure 7.12. Subscript and superscript text is roughly half the size of regular text.

Color

Choose a color from the presentation's color palette (in the Color sub-menu of the Text menu), or choose *Other* to open Persuasion's color grid. Click the cell displaying the color you're after, and then click *OK*.

As we've already pointed out, color applied to outlined text affects the outline, not the fill. (The apparent fill color of outlined text will be the color of whatever's behind it, whether it's the slide background or a filled graphic.) Color applied to shadowed text affects the text, not the shadow. To change the color of a text shadow, choose the text block with the pointer tool, and then choose *Shadow color* from the Effect menu.

For more information on applying color to text, consult Chapter 9, *Working with Color*.

Alignment

Alignment controls how text aligns within its text block. Alignment options include *Align left*, *Align right*, *Align center*, and *Justify*. Although Persuasion offers you the typographic control you need for presentations, it's not a typesetting program. For best results, save justified text for the smaller type sizes called for by speaker notes or audience handouts.

If you apply an alignment option to a text block based on a placeholder (one that's linked to the outline), Persuasion will apply it to all paragraphs in the text block. Only with unlinked text blocks can you apply different alignment options to each paragraph. (This is hardly a limitation, though, since you'll rarely want to combine left and right aligned, or centered and justified text in the same text block.)

We the people of the United States, in order to form a more perfect union, establish justice, insure domestic tranquility, provide	We the people of the United States, in order to form a more perfect union, establish justice, insure domestic tranquility, provide
We the people of the United States, in order to form a more perfect union, establish justice, insure domestic tranquility, provide	We the people of the United States, in order to form a more perfect union, establish justice, insure domestic tranquility, provide

Figure 7.13. Alignment options include *Align left*, *Align right*, *Align center*, and *Justify*.

Line Spacing

To control the spacing between lines and paragraphs, choose *Line spacing*. In the Line spacing dialog box, enter the desired percentages for line and paragraph spacing. Although Persuasion will accept any value between 50 and 500%, a good range for line spacing is 90–150%, and for paragraph spacing 150–300%. Line spacing of 100% is equivalent to single spacing; paragraph spacing of 200% is equivalent to double-spacing between paragraphs.

Line and paragraph spacing are measured as percentages of type size. This means they vary with type size. If you apply 100% line spacing to 12-point type, the distance between lines of type (as measured from baseline to baseline) will be 12 points. If you apply 200% paragraph spacing to 24-point type, the distance between paragraphs will be 48 points.

For text flowing from the outline to text placeholders on a slide, line spacing controls the distance between lines of outline subheads that wrap to two or more lines. Paragraph spacing controls the distance between subheads within the same text placeholder. For text typed directly on the slide, line spacing applies to lines that automatically wrap to the width of the text block; paragraph spacing applies to paragraphs you create by pressing the Return key as you type.

Tip: To start a new line without starting a new paragraph, hold down the Shift key while pressing the Return key. Line and paragraph spacing are determined by the largest character in the line. With line spacing set to 100%, one 48-point letter in a line of 24-point type will produce line spacing of 48 points for that line.

Line spacing

| Line spacing: | 75 | % of normal |
| Paragraph spacing: | 100 | % of normal |

OK
Cancel

This is one paragraph. When line spacing is too small, the descenders of one line fuse with the ascenders of the line below it.
This is another paragraph. When line spacing is too large, lines of a paragraph may appear unrelated to each other.

Line spacing

| Line spacing: | 100 | % of normal |
| Paragraph spacing: | 200 | % of normal |

OK
Cancel

This is one paragraph. When line spacing is too small, the descenders of one line fuse with the ascenders of the line below it.

This is another paragraph. When line spacing is too large, lines of a paragraph may appear unrelated to each other.

Line spacing

| Line spacing: | 150 | % of normal |
| Paragraph spacing: | 300 | % of normal |

OK
Cancel

This is one paragraph. When line spacing is too small, the descenders of one line fuse with the ascenders of the line below it.

This is another paragraph. When line spacing is too large, lines of a paragraph may appear unrelated to each other.

Figure 7.14.   In the three samples above, line spacing varies from 75 to 150%, and paragraph spacing from 100 to 300%. In the first example, both line and paragraph spacing are too tight.

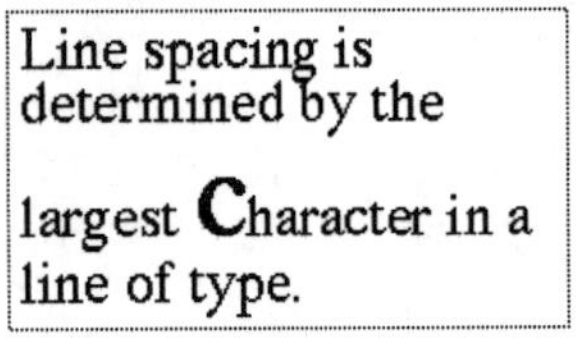

Line spacing is
determined by the

largest Character in a
line of type.

Figure 7.15   Line and paragraph spacing are determined
by the largest character in a line.

Bullet Marks

Bullet marks—whether, round, square, or a fancier shape—are an excellent way of guiding your audience's attention through the contents of a slide. When reading, the eye must sweep from the end of the line just read to the beginning of the next one; a bullet mark helps the eye reach its destination.

As you'll learn in Chapter 13, *Building an AutoTemplate*, you define and format bullets on slide masters. Once you've set bullets the way you want them on the slide master, you can turn them on and off for any particular slide. Select a text block, then select *Bullet marks* to hide or apply bullets for that block. To change the formatting of bullets, go to the current slide master (hold down the Option key while clicking the Slide view icon, remember?), and then choose *Define bullet marks* from the Master menu. For ideas and options on formatting bullets, consult Chapter 13, *Building an Auto-Template*.

Using the Text Format Feature

So much for the individual submenus and dialog boxes in the Text menu. When you want to change only one or two attributes, use a keyboard shortcut, if there is one, or choose a command from the Text menu. When you need to change several elements at once, choose *Text format*. The Text format dialog box not only lets you change font, size, style, and color all at once, it displays an actual-sized color sample of the choices you make. Along with its keyboard shortcut (*Command+T*), the Text format dialog box should be a well-used tool in your arsenal of formatting techniques.

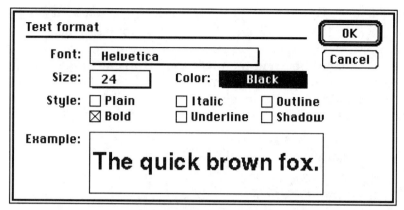

Figure 7.16. The Text format dialog box lets you change several text attributes at once, and displays sample text.

Defining and Applying Formats

If you've worked with page layout programs such as Aldus PageMaker or word processing programs such as Microsoft Word, you may be familiar with the concept of style sheets. Persuasion provides a sheet-like style feature called a format. A format is a named collection of typographic formats that you can apply repeatedly to different text selections. For example, you could define a format named "Caption" as 18-point white Times italic. Now, each time you want a white caption, instead of choosing all its attributes from their respective submenus, you'd just apply the format Caption—one step instead of many.

Formats are most appropriate for formatting static text blocks such as captions, legends, chart titles, and so forth. (Since you'll use text placeholders to format text linked to the outline, you won't need formats for this kind of text as often.)

Working with formats is a two-step process. First, you define a format, and then you apply it.

To define a format, choose *Define formats* from the Text menu. In the Define text formats dialog box, click *New*. This will take you to the familiar Text formats dialog box, in which you can specify the font, size, color, and style you want. Click *OK* when you've defined the format. Persuasion will display a default name (Format 1, Format 2, Format 3, etc.) in the *Rename* box. You can either accept this name or change it to a more descriptive name if you prefer.

To edit an existing format, click the name of the format you want to edit, and then click *Edit*. This takes you back to the Text formats dialog box—and you know what to do there! To rename an existing format, click its current name in the list box, and then type the new name in the Rename box. To remove a format, click its name, and then click *Remove*. When you're finished creating, editing, or removing formats, click *OK* to close the dialog box.

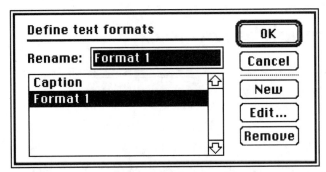

Figure 7.17. Create new formats or edit existing ones in the Define text formats dialog box.

Now what? To apply a format, select the text to be formatted, and then choose *Apply format* from the Text menu. A pop-down menu will display the formats you've defined. Unlike page layout style sheets, formats can be combined in the same paragraph or line. And, also unlike style sheets, editing a format won't affect text to which it has already been applied.

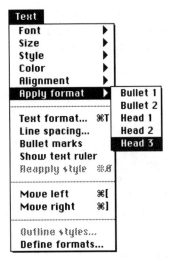

Figure 7.18. To apply a format, choose its name from the Apply format submenu.

Enhancing a Text Block

Usually a text block serves simply as a container for text. But sometimes you'll want to enhance a text block to call special attention to the text it contains. Besides holding text, a text block can also be treated as a graphic—you can frame it, fill it, color it, and shadow it. Furthermore, you can do this either to the placeholder in Slide master view (in which case every slide using that master will feature the enhanced text block), or to individual text blocks on a slide-by-slide basis in Slide view.

To frame a text block, select it with the pointer tool, then choose a line style and a line pattern other than *None*. You may then apply any other effects you desire. To control the left, right, top, and bottom margins within the text block, adjust the indent markers on the text ruler (we'll look at how to do that in just a minute). Unlike a box drawn with a drawing tool, a text block (and, of course, its frame) expands and contracts with its contents.

Feel free to apply other effects, including fill pattern and color, or a shadow. The Effects menu is covered in Chapter 9, *Working with Graphics*.

Working with the Text Ruler

Persuasion's text ruler provides a simple method for setting tabs and indents. To use the text ruler, choose *Show text ruler* from the Text menu. When you click on the slide with the text tool, the ruler appears above the text block (whether it's an existing text block or one you're about to create). On it, you'll see two types of markers. Along the bottom edge of the ruler, indent markers are composed of two stacked wedges; tab markers are the down arrows you see along the top edge of the ruler. In the bottom-right corner of the ruler, two tab markers sit side by side. These are used for adding more tab stops. The first is for adding left-aligned tabs, and the second is for right- and decimal-aligned tabs. The tabs that already exist on the ruler are all left-aligned and can be moved or removed. Although you can choose increments of inches, centimeters, or points for the rulers along the top and left side of the window, the text ruler is always calibrated in inches.

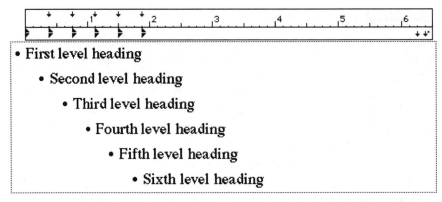

Figure 7.19. The text ruler appears above a selected text block. Down arrows indicate tab settings; pairs of wedges indicate indent settings.

Working with Tabs

To set a tab marker, click one of the markers in the lower-right corner and drag it into place on the ruler. The left tab marker will cause text to align to the left. The right tab marker will cause words to align to the right and numbers with a decimal point to align around the decimal point. If there's text already in the text box whose ruler you're tinkering with, changes will take effect immediately.

To move a tab marker, point to it, and drag it into its new position. To clear a tab marker, click it and drag it down off the ruler. There's no way to clear all tab markers simultaneously. You'll need to clear them one by one. To move an existing tab marker, click and drag it along the ruler to its new location. Once you've set up tabs to your liking, use the Tab key to move from tab to tab within the text block.

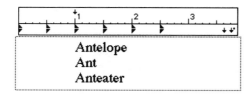

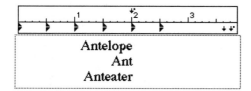

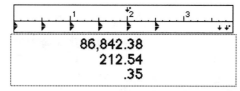

Figure 7.20. Text aligned with a left tab and a right tab, and numbers decimal aligned with a right tab.

Working with Indents

An indent marker is composed of two wedges, one balanced on top of the other. The six pairs of indent markers on the text ruler correspond to the six levels of indentation you can have in a text block. Changing any one of these pairs affects all of the paragraphs corresponding to that level. The top wedge, or first-line indent marker, controls where the first line of a paragraph begins. The bottom wedge determines where all subsequent lines of a paragraph begin. You can adjust them separately: if you drag the top wedge, the bottom wedge moves with it; if you drag the bottom wedge, the top wedge stays put. Click the indent marker you want to adjust and drag it into position.

To set up an indented paragraph or a hanging indent, drag the indent marker (top and bottom wedges together) to where you want the first line of the paragraph to begin, and then drag the bottom wedge left or right to where you want the remainder of the paragraph to begin. The line joining the top and bottom wedges tells you which pairs of markers go together.

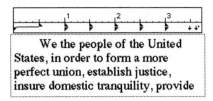

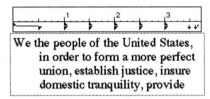

Figure 7.21. Use the first line and left indent markers to set up an
indented paragraph or a hanging indent.

Once you've set up indents, use the *Move left* (*Command+[*) and *Move right*
(*Command+]*) commands to move a paragraph one level to the left or to the
right. To change the indent level of existing heading, you need only click an
insertion point rather than select all of it. If you're working in a text block
that's linked to the outline, *Move left* and *Move right* will flow back and
change the text's heading level in the outline.

A few more facts and tips about working with the text ruler. You can set
tabs and indents on a slide master using a placeholder's text ruler (on a slide
master). In this case, outline text will automatically conform to the text
ruler settings as it flows onto a slide. If you set a tab marker at 1 inch, for
example, then any time you pressed the Tab key while typing in the outline,
that text will start one inch from the left of the text block; if you move the
second indent marker to 1/2 inch, all *B*-level headings will start half an inch
from the left of the text block. Of course, you can also adjust the text ruler of
a text block on an individual slide.

A paragraph's bullet hangs to the left of its indent marker; in other words,
the edge of the text block determines where the bullet will be, and the first
indent marker determines where *A*-level headings will begin.

If you discover a text block whose text ruler has no indent markers, don't
be alarmed: slide titles and subtitles typically have only one paragraph and
therefore do not display indent markers. Only body text placeholders show
indent markers in their text ruler.

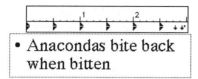

Figure 7.22. A paragraph's bullet hangs to the left of its indent marker.

Using Find/Change

Imagine the following chilling scenario: you've just put the finishing touches on a brilliant presentation to support your company's public relations campaign when you hear that the CEO has decided to change the company name from QuickCash to KwikKash. 150 of the most beautiful slides ever to grace a screen, pages of beautifully organized audience handouts...every one with the company name spelled incorrectly!

Fortunately, Persuasion provides a Find/Change feature that allows you to search for and replace words anywhere in a presentation, in slides, notes, or outline, and in charts and tables. And, of course, any changes made in your outline flow back to placeholder text, and vice versa.

To find and replace a word, choose *Find/Change* from the Edit menu (*Command+5*). Type the word you're after in the *Find* box (you can also paste copied text using *Command+V*), and then type (or paste) its replacement in the *Change to* box. (Of course, you can leave the *Change to* box empty if you just want to find a word but not change it.)

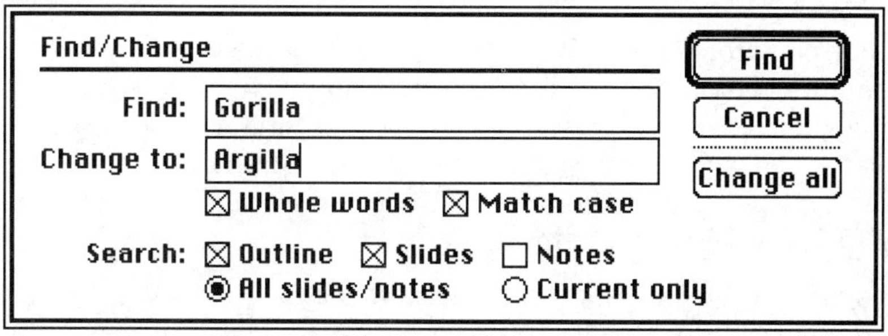

Find/Change		Find
Find: Gorilla		Cancel
Change to: Argilla		Change all
☒ Whole words ☒ Match case		
Search: ☒ Outline ☒ Slides ☐ Notes		
◉ All slides/notes ○ Current only		

Figure 7.23. Use the Find/Change dialog box to search for and replace words.

Next, give Persuasion the particulars. With *Whole word* deselected, Persuasion will find a string of characters or a word embedded in another word. For instance, by finding and replacing the character string *seperat* with *separat* (with *Whole word* deselected), you could correct the misspellings *seperate, seperated,* and *seperatist* with one Find/Change operation.

Click *Match case* to find words whose capitalization exactly matches what you type in the *Find* box. This is useful for instances in which you may have capitalized inconsistently.

Now you must select the parts of the presentation you want searched. You can search the outline, slides, notes, or any combination. You can also choose whether to search all or only the current set of slides and notes.

Once the dialog box is set up to your liking, there are a couple of ways you can proceed.

If you select *Find*, Persuasion will find and highlight the first instance of the word, so that you can review or edit it. Then you have several options:

- To find the next instance of the word, choose *Find again* from the Edit menu (*Command+6*).

- To change the current instance of the word, choose *Change* (*Command+7*).

- To change the current instance and find the next, choose *Change then find* (*Command+8*).

If you select *Change all*, Persuasion will ask for reassurance: "This action cannot be undone. Continue anyway?" Click *OK* to continue and replace all instances of the word in one pass. The Find/Change dialog box remembers what was last typed in it for the duration of a work session.

Using the Spell Checker

There's nothing more embarrassing than projecting the very first slide of your presentation on an 8-by-10-foot screen, only to discover your company's name spelled "Aceme" instead of "Acme." Fortunately, judicious use of Persuasion's spell checker can significantly decrease the risk of this sort of presentation nightmare. Persuasion's spell checker works like most word processing spell checkers. Here's how.

Choose *Spelling* (*Command+9*) from the Edit menu. If Persuasion can't find its dictionaries in the System or Persuasion 2.0 folders, it may ask your helping in locating them.

Choose the parts of the presentation you want checked. Your options include:

Outline

Slides (*All slides/notes* or *Current only*)

Notes (*All slides/notes* or *Current only*)

Click *Start* to get under way. Persuasion will search the parts you selected, cycling through Outline, Slide, and Notes view (in that order), beginning at your current location within the presentation. If you're on the 5th slide of a 10-slide presentation, Persuasion will check the remaining slides, and then ask whether you want to check the presentation from the beginning. When it finishes checking each section, it will ask whether to continue. When it has searched every nook and cranny, it will inform you, "Search complete."

Persuasion compares every word to its main and user dictionaries, and then highlights each unknown word and displays it at the top of the Spelling dialog box. There are several ways you can treat unrecognized words.

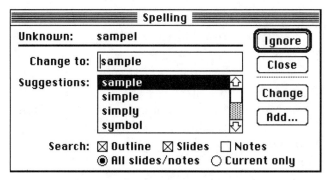

Figure 7.24. Persuasion displays an unknown word at the top of
the Spelling dialog box.

To ignore the word (along with subsequent instances of it) and continue the search, click *Ignore*. To change the word, type the new word in the box after *Change to*, or click the word you want in the Suggestions box, and then click *Change*. (Double-clicking the desired word is even faster.) If Persuasion encounters the same misspelling again, it remembers your previous correction and suggests it in the *Change to* box.

To add the word to the dictionary so Persuasion will recognize it in the future, click *Add*. In the Add word to dictionary dialog box, you're asked whether to add the word in lowercase letters, with a capital first letter, or exactly as it appears in the text box. Select the option you want, and then click *OK*. The word is added to the user dictionary, and spell checking continues.

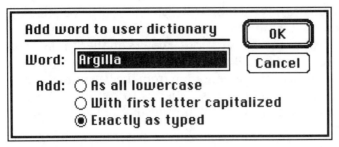

Figure 7.25. The Add word to user dictionary dialog box lets you control the capitalization of the words you add.

To end the search at any time, click *Close*. When Persuasion has finished checking the presentation, it will inform you, "Search complete." Click *OK* to close the Spelling dialog box.

Persuasion's user dictionary cannot be edited. If you accidentally add a misspelled word, your only choice is to replace the entire user dictionary with a correct backup copy. Because of this, we recommend you back up the user dictionary frequently. If you're using the United States version of Persuasion, your user dictionary is called *user1*; if you're using the International English or Canadian English version, it's called *userUK1*.

To back up the user dictionary, copy it to a folder outside the Persuasion dictionaries folder (somewhere else on your hard disk, or on a floppy disk). To replace a "corrupted" version of the user dictionary, delete it, and then copy the backup user dictionary to the Persuasion Dictionaries folder. Be sure to update the backup copy frequently.

One last word about Persuasion's spell checker: although it does what it's designed to do very well, don't rely on it exclusively. Like any spell checker, all it can do is tell whether a word is spelled correctly. It cannot tell if the word it's checking is the right word or not. You, not your spell checker, should be the final proofreader of your presentation.

Using Keyboard Shortcuts for Text Editing

Persuasion 2.0 provides two sets of keyboard shortcuts for text editing, an older set from Persuasion 1.0 and a new collection of word-processing-like shortcuts for Persuasion 2.0. Instead of forcing all Persuasion 1.0 veterans into the new mold, Persuasion lets you choose which set to use.

To change the current selection, choose *Preferences* from the File menu, and then, after *Arrow keys*, click *Persuasion 1.0* to use the Persuasion 1.0 shortcuts, or *Word processing* to use the Persuasion 2.0 set. The default setting is *Word processing*. (While most changes made in the Preferences dialog box apply only to the current presentation, a choice of keyboard shortcuts applies to all subsequent presentations.)

Here are the two sets of shortcuts:

Table 7-2

Action	Persuasion 1.0	Word processing
Move insertion point one character right	Right arrow	Right arrow
Move insertion point one character left	Left arrow	Left arrow
Move insertion point one word forward	Not available	Option + right arrow
Move insertion point one word backward	Not available	Option + left arrow
Move insertion point to end of paragraph	Option+right arrow	Command+right arrow
Move insertion point to beginning of paragraph	Option+left arrow	Command left arrow
Cycle between Outline, Slide, and Notes Views	Command+left arrow or right arrow	Command+>

Well, we've labored long and hard with words. Let's reward ourselves by learning how to work with graphics!

Chapter 8

Working with Graphics

"One picture is worth a thousand words." Have you ever wondered who did the calculations, and where the number "one thousand" came from? Of course, the actual word-to-picture ratio depends on the quality of the particular picture and words, but it's certainly true that a well-chosen image can enhance or even substitute for text.

When it comes to working with images, Persuasion is well-equipped. Not only can you import graphics from other applications, Persuasion provides tools for drawing graphics ranging from a basic rectangle to a three-story house. In this chapter, we'll explore how to use the drawing tools to create graphics, how to enhance graphics once you've created them, and how to import graphics from other programs.

Using Persuasion's Drawing Tools

Persuasion's toolbox contains eight tools for drawing graphics from straight lines to polygons. Using them is pretty straightforward; here's how they work.

Drawing a Line

Choose either the perpendicular line tool or the diagonal line tool. Position the crossbar where you want the line to begin, and then drag to the end of the line. The perpendicular line tool draws perfect vertical and horizontal lines. The diagonal line tools draws diagonal lines at any angle. Holding down the Shift key while drawing with the diagonal line tool constrains it to 45-degree increments. Holding down the Option key allows you to draw lines from the center. Remember, though, whenever you use the Shift key to modify a graphic as you're creating it, you must let go of the mouse button before you let go of the Shift key.

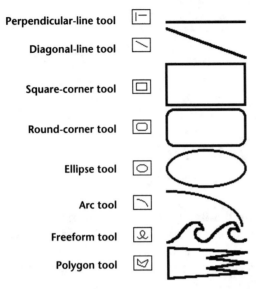

Figure 8.1. Persuasion's toolbox contains tools for drawing a wide selection of graphics.

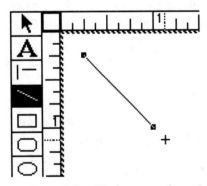

Figure 8.2. To draw a perfect 45-degree diagonal line, choose the diagonal line tool and hold down the Shift key while dragging.

Once you've drawn a line, you can use commands from the Effect menu to modify it as described further on.

Drawing a Rectangle or a Square

Choose the square corner tool, or, if you want rounded corners, the round corner tool. Position the crossbar at any one of the four corners of the rectangle and drag in the appropriate direction.

Here are a few techniques for modifying objects as you draw or resize them. (You may remember them from Chapter 6, *Working with Objects*.)

To draw a square, hold down the Shift key as you drag.

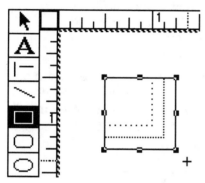

Figure 8.3.   To draw a perfect square, hold down the Shift key
while dragging.

To draw a rectangle from the center out, hold down the Option key as you drag. The crossbar's starting position establishes the center of the rectangle.

To draw a square from the center out, hold down both the Option and Shift keys as you draw.

Again, let go of the mouse button before you let go of the modifier keys! (Though this may seem a trivial detail, it will drive you crazy until you've made it a habit. There's nothing more frustrating than laboring over the exact position and size of a square drawn from the center, only to see it turn into a lopsided, misplaced rectangle when you relax the wrong hand first!)

To round off the edges of a rectangle's corners, select the rectangle you want to modify, and then choose *Round corners* from the Draw menu. In the Round corners dialog box, you can turn square-cornered into round-cornered rectangles or vice versa. Or, you can simply adjust the shape of a corner's curve.

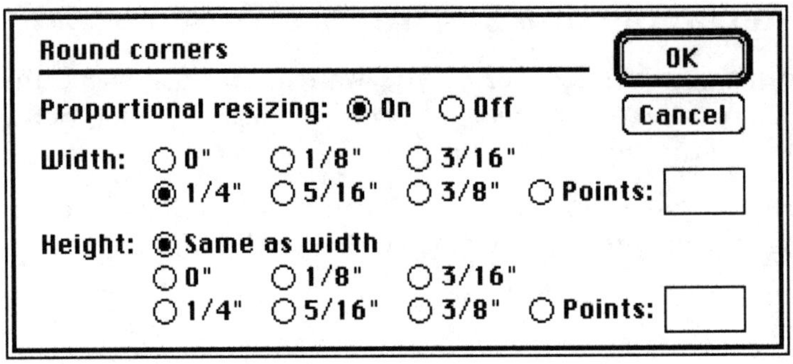

Round corners _____ (**OK**)

Proportional resizing: ⦿ On ○ Off   (Cancel)

Width: ○ 0"   ○ 1/8"   ○ 3/16"
        ⦿ 1/4"   ○ 5/16"   ○ 3/8"   ○ Points: [   ]

Height: ⦿ Same as width
        ○ 0"   ○ 1/8"   ○ 3/16"
        ○ 1/4"   ○ 5/16"   ○ 3/8"   ○ Points: [   ]

Figure 8.4.   The Round corners dialog box gives you precise control
over the appearance of a rectangle's corners.

To preserve even, round corners, select the same values for width and height. For unevenly rounded corners, select different values for width and height. If you don't see the size you need, type in a number in points (72 points to the inch, 18 points to the quarter inch). The corner size is equivalent to a radius of a circle inscribed in the corner.

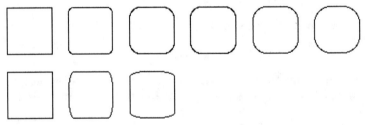

Figure 8.5.   You can create rectangles with even corners ranging from
0 to 3/8th inches (*above*) or uneven corners (*below*).

To change a round-cornered rectangle back into a square-cornered one, select *0 inches* for *width*, and *0 inches* for *height*.

When you're working with round-cornered rectangles or squares, you have several options when it comes to resizing them. These too are available from the Round corners dialog box.

To let corner size change in proportion to the rectangle as you resize it, select *On* for *Proportional resizing*. Persuasion will adjust both the width and height of the corners. Unless you're resizing the rectangle itself proportionately (by holding down the Shift key), corner width and height may differ, turning even corners into uneven corners. To keep corners even during proportional resizing, choose *same as width* for *height*.

To preserve the original corner size, select *Off* for *Proportional resizing*.

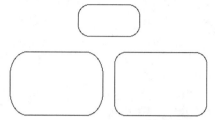

Figure 8.6.　A rectangle resized with proportional resizing (*below left*)
and without proportional resizing (*below right*).

Unless you're preparing lots of organizational charts, you may never need to exercise such fine control over a rectangle's corners, but it's good to know the resource is there when you need it.

Drawing an Ellipse or a Circle

Select the ellipse tool. Position the crossbar where you want to begin drawing, and then drag in any direction. And—no surprises here—to draw a perfect circle, hold down the Shift key; to draw an ellipse from the center out, hold down the Option key; and to draw a perfect circle from the center out, hold down Shift and Option keys simultaneously.

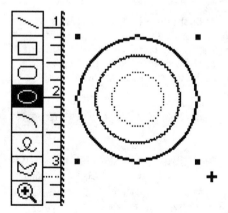

Figure 8.7.　To draw a perfect circle from the center, hold down the
Shift and Option keys while dragging.

Drawing an Arc

Choose the arc tool, position the crossbar where you want the arc to begin, and then drag in any direction. To force the arc tool to draw in quarter-circle increments, hold down the Shift key as you drag.

Once you've drawn an arc, you can modify it in two ways: you can resize it as you would any graphic, or you can reshape it. Resizing an arc shortens or lengthens it and changes its curve. Reshaping an arc, on the other hand, extends it along its original curve. For example, resizing an arc that begins as a quarter circle makes it elliptical; reshaping it preserves the circular shape and draws more or less of the circle.

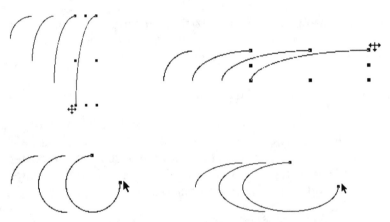

Figure 8.8.   Resizing an arc (*above*) lengthens or shortens it and changes its curve. During resizing, the cursor will appear as a two- or four-way arrow, depending on whether a side or a corner selection handle is chosen. Reshaping an arc (*below*) extends the arc along its original curve. When reshaping, the cursor will take the shape of a simple arrow.

To resize an arc, simply choose the pointer tool, click one of the arc's eight selection handles, and drag.

To reshape an arc, choose the pointer tool, select the arc, and then choose *Reshape arc* from the Draw menu. Instead of the usual eight selection handles around its perimeter, the arc will sprout two, one at each end. Click a handle and drag to extend or shorten the arc along its original curve.

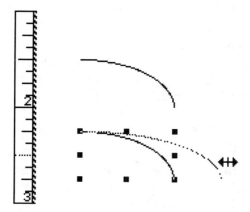

Figure 8.9.   Drag a selection handle to resize an arc.

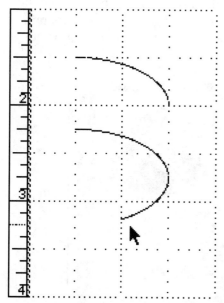

Figure 8.10. Use the *Reshape arc* command to extend or shorten
an arc along its curve.

Drawing a Freeform Line

The freeform tool is useful for drawing rough curves or loose, expressive sketches. If you've never drawn with a mouse or a stylus before, you may find it awkward at first. It requires a keen eye and a steady hand, and unless you're a graphic artist you may not use it as much as the other drawing tools. But if you're adventuresome, you may enjoy the variety of shapes you can create with the freehand tool and think of novel ways to incorporate them into your presentations.

Choose the freeform tool, position the crossbar at the starting point, and draw to your heart's content. For maximum freedom while drawing, check the Draw menu to make sure that *Grid snap on* is off!

Caution: Graphics drawn with the freeform tool are bitmapped. For that reason, they'll print at the resolution of your screen (generally, 72 dots per inch) rather than at the resolution of your output device. If you want more polished curves, consider using a dedicated program like Aldus Freehand to create the graphic, and then import it into your Persuasion presentation.

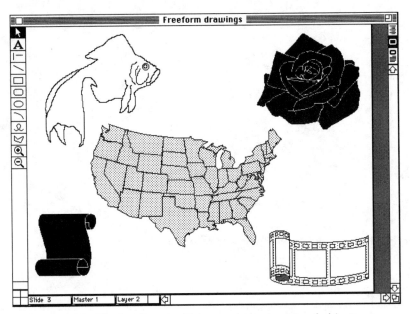

Figure 8.11. The freeform tool lets you draw a variety of objects.

Drawing a Polygon

Choose the polygon tool. Position the crossbar where you want to begin drawing, and then drag in any direction to draw the first side. Click to create a vertex, and then drag to draw a new side. Continue dragging and clicking to create as many sides as you wish. Double-click to complete the polygon.

Once you've drawn a polygon, you can reshape it. Select the polygon in question, and then choose Reshape poly from the Draw menu. (It's in the same place as the *Reshape arc* command will be if an arc rather than a polygon is selected.) Instead of eight selection handles around its perimeter, the polygon will sprout a selection handle at each vertex. To move a side of the polygon, drag the side you want to move. To move a vertex, drag any selection handle. To add a vertex, click any side. To remove a vertex, drag it on top of another one. When the polygon's shape meets your approval, click somewhere else to deselect it.

To draw equilateral polygons (for example, a perfect pentagon or hexagon), you'll need to rely on your eye; Persuasion can't guarantee that all sides will be the same length.

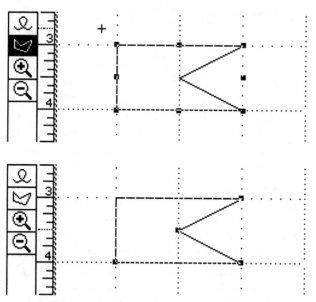

Figure 8.12. Reshape poly causes a polygon to sprout one selection handle at each vertex instead of eight handles around its perimeter.

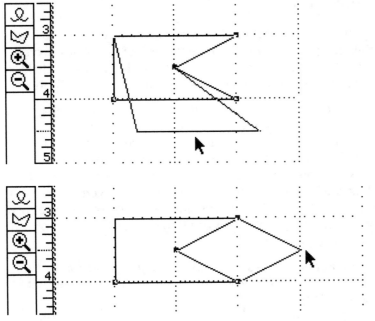

Figure 8.13. To move a polygon's side, click and drag the side. To move a
vertex, click and drag a selection handle.

That's it for Persuasion's drawing tools. If you've ever worked with a
drawing application, you'll find yourself instantly at home. Even if this is
your first time as an electronic draftsperson, you'll quickly learn the ropes.
Once you've drawn the basic shapes and modified them as just described,
you can apply fills and colors, and adjust the style and weight of the lines
that compose them.

Working with the Effect Menu

The Effect menu is where you go to fine tune the appearance of the
graphics you've created with the drawing tools. It's divided into three parts.
The top part, which includes four commands that control the weight of
lines and the pattern of lines, fills, and shadows, is what we'll explore right
now. The second and third parts, which consist of commands for applying
color to objects, are treated in depth in Chapter 9, *Working with Color*. (Some
people find the organization of the Effect menu a bit confusing at first. It
helps to remember that the second collection of commands all have to do
with color.) As always, select one or more of the graphics you want to
modify, and then choose one or more commands from the Effect menu.

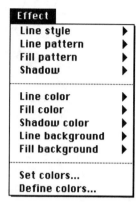

Figure 8.14. The Effect menu contains all the tools you'd ever want to control the look of graphics.

Line Style

To modify the width of any line, including the outlines of objects such as squares and circles, choose *Line style*. The Line style submenu is divided into three columns. Widths in the first column affect vertical and horizontal lines simultaneously. When applied to an oval shape, this option creates a gradually changing thickness from the sides to the top. Interesting effects can also be created with polygons and diagonal lines. The second and third columns let you set different widths for vertical and horizontal lines. (You have to open the submenu twice, once for each dimension).

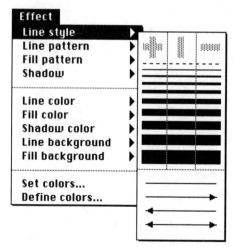

Figure 8.15. The Line style submenu lets you control vertical and horizontal widths independently of each other.

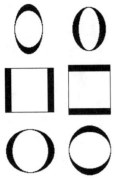

Figure 8.16. You can achieve interesting effects by applying different horizontal and vertical line widths.

When you select the dashed line from the Line style submenu, Persuasion applies a line thickness of zero to your object.

At the bottom of the Line style submenu, you can choose from four line styles, plain, right single-ended arrow, left single-ended arrow, and double-ended arrow. Combine different vertical and horizontal line widths with different arrows styles to increase the possibilities.

Figure 8.17. Different widths can be applied to vertical and horizontal lines.

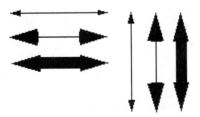

Figure 8.18. Combining line widths and arrow styles offers lots of possibilities.

Line Pattern

Not only can you choose from several line widths, you can apply different patterns to lines. Choose *Line pattern*, and then select one of the 39 patterns from the Line pattern submenu. To make the outline of a graphic such as a square or circle invisible, choose *None*. Obviously the thicker the line, the more recognizable the pattern will be. If you apply a checked pattern to a hairline rule, you'll simply get a dotted line.

To apply colors to lines, choose *Line color* or *Line background*, and then choose a color from the color palette. *Line color* affects the foreground, or the part of the pattern that appears in black. *Line background* affects the white part of the pattern. For more information about color, consult Chapter 9, *Working with Color*.

Fill Pattern

Persuasion lets you apply what it calls "fills" to the inside of any object, including squares, circles, closed polygons, open polygons, open arcs, freeform objects, and text blocks. You can control both the pattern and the color of fills.

To apply a fill pattern, choose *Fill pattern* from the Effect menu, and then choose one of the 42 patterns from the Fill pattern submenu. To make an object transparent, choose *None*.

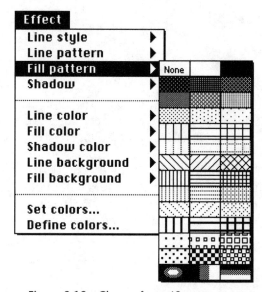

Figure 8.19. Choose from 42 patterns to apply as fills to objects.

To apply a graduated fill (a gradual transition from one color to another), choose one of the three patterns from the bottom row of the submenu. The larger the object, the more gradual will be the transition between the two colors.

To apply colors to fills, choose *Fill color* or *Fill background*, and then choose a color from the color palette. *Fill color* affects the foreground, or the part of the pattern that appears in black. *Fill background* affects the part of the pattern that appears in white.

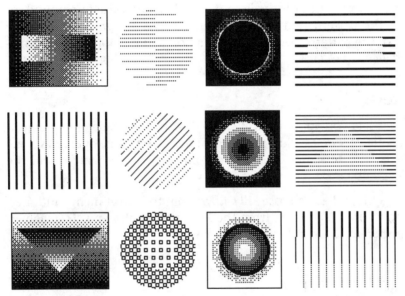

Figure 8.20. Combining shapes and fills gives you an unlimited range of drawing possibilities.

Note: Persuasion assumes that most often you won't want to apply a fill to a polygon or a freeform object, so it always sets the default fill for these objects to *None*, regardless of the presentation defaults. To work around this, you can either apply a fill to an existing polygon or freeform object, or you can set the tool defaults before drawing. Choose the polygon or freeform tool, select the pattern and color you want, and then draw. If you apply a fill to a freeform object, Persuasion will fill the shape created by joining the endpoints of the object.

Figure 8.21. If you apply a fill to a freeform object, Persuasion will fill the shapes above or below a line joining the freeform object's endpoints. If the endpoints overlap, the object will appear as a solid shape.

Shadow

Just as you can shadow text, you can add a plain or patterned shadow to any object. Choose *Shadow* from the Effect menu, and then choose one of the 39 patterns from the Shadow submenu. To remove a shadow, choose *None*.

To apply color to a shadow, choose *Shadow color*. Color is applied to the shadow foreground, or the black part of the pattern. In a patterned shadow, the background will always be white.

As we saw in Chapter 7, *Working with Text*, you can control where an object casts its shadow. Choose *Preferences* from the File menu, and then, after *Object shadow offset*, type in the distance you want for *inches down* and *inches right*. Experiment with negative numbers to move the shadow around the object. Settings for *Object shadow offset* apply to all objects in a presentation.

Figure 8.22   *(continued)*

Figure 8.22. Experiment with different shadow offsets. Shown above, -0.125 inches down and 0.125 inches right (*page 223, left*); 0.5 inches down and 0.5 inches right (*page 223, right*); -0.125 inches down and 0.125 inches right (*above*); and 0.5 inches down and -0.5 inches right.

Helpful Hints for Drawing Graphics

Persuasion provides several options that making drawing a breeze. In Chapter 6, *Working with Objects*, we explored how to use the grid and Persuasion's various alignment commands. Here are two subtle drawing features to help you work easily and efficiently.

Presentation and Current Tool Default Displays

The Presentation and Current tool default displays (in the bottom left corner of the presentation window) show you the relationship between presentation defaults and temporary tool defaults; this lets you anticipate the results when you work with Persuasion's drawing tools.

The Presentation tool default display tells you at a glance what line and fill attributes are in effect when you first use a drawing tool for your current presentation. The square at the bottom of the display shows a sample of the current settings in the Effect menu for lines: style, pattern, color, and background. The rectangle just above it shows a sample of the settings for fills: pattern, color, and background.

You may also remember that once you select a drawing tool from the tool box, the Current tool default display appears above the Presentation tool default display.

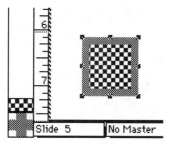

Figure 8.23. The tool default display in the bottom left corner of the presentation window tells you the current settings in the Effect menu for lines and fills.

At first, it looks exactly like the presentation tool display. But let's say you want to change the line and fill patterns temporarily to draw one particular object. With the drawing tool still selected, you open the Line and Fill pattern submenus and choose new patterns. When you close the dialog box, the Current tool default display will reflect the new, temporary settings for the drawing tool. When you draw the object, it too will reflect these settings. As soon as you deselect the drawing tool, however, the temporary tool settings are forgotten, and the Current tool default display disappears. You can also click on the current tool to restore the presentation defaults to the tool.

Note that you can always create new Presentation tool defaults for fills and patterns (just as you would for text attributes). Use the pointer tool, and without any object selected, make selections from the Effects menu. (You can also save these defaults in an AutoTemplate for future use.)

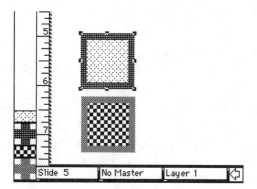

Figure 8.24. The presentation tool defaults (*below*) and the current tool defaults (*above*). The square at the bottom was drawn with the presentation defaults; the square above it was drawn with temporary tool defaults.

Icon Shape

Another visual cue: the crossbar changes shape and color depending on the current tool defaults. When you drag the drawing tool into the presentation window, it will display the current line, fill, and color settings. In fact, the size of the crossbar even changes depending on the view you're in. Since a line of a given weight will appear twice as heavy in 200% view as it does in 100% view; the crossbar will appear twice as heavy as well, to help you anticipate this.

Figure 8.25. The appearance of the crossbar helps you anticipate what you'll get when you draw.

Importing Graphics

Persuasion's drawing tools are powerful and versatile, but sometimes you'll need to use graphics that were created elsewhere. Perhaps you need to build a complex graphic in a specialized drawing application, or use the authorized version of your company's logo. Persuasion welcomes graphics from other programs in EPS (Encapsulated PostScript), PICT, and PICT II formats. If you want to import scanned images, make sure you save them in PICT format, since Persuasion cannot import TIFF images.

To import a graphic, go to the appropriate slide, choose *Import* from the File menu, and then use the list box to hunt down and double-click the name of the file you want. The graphic will appear in the center of the slide.

If it's in EPS format, you're limited to moving and resizing. If it's in PICT or PICT II (color) format, however, you can ungroup it and modify its elements as described in Chapter 6, *Working with Objects*.

When you ungroup a PICT graphic, Persuasion converts the graphic's elements into Persuasion elements. In others words, a PICT circle becomes a Persuasion circle, a PICT square becomes a Persuasion square, and so forth. Once converted, these elements can be modified just like any Persuasion graphic. You can apply a fill pattern or color, change the line weight, or even change the size and font of text. However, if the imported graphic contains certain elements that Persuasion can't create (such as rotated text), you won't be able to ungroup or modify it.

With Persuasion's eight drawing tools, nine line weights, and over three dozen line, fill, and shadow patterns, black-and-white drawing could keep you happily occupied for many an hour. Add the dimension of color, and the possibilities for persuasive presentations explode!

Chapter 9

Working with Color

Remember Dorothy's joy and awe when she left black-and-white Kansas for the full color world of the Emerald City? Dorothy's reaction wasn't unusual. Study after study demonstrates that color is persuasive, stimulating, and captivating, desirable qualities not only in an emerald city but also in a presentation. Fortunately, Persuasion 2.0 offers a rich array of tools for bringing the power of color to a presentation.

Many variables will affect your choice of colors, some of them aesthetic and some of them technical. In this chapter, we'll pause for a quick word or two about technical issues before focussing on how to use Persuasion's color tools. For more information about the aesthetics of color, consult Chapter 15, *Designing Effective Presentations*.

A quick word about the technicalities of producing color. When choosing colors for a presentation, you must consider two variables: what colors your monitor is capable of displaying, and what colors your output device can produce. For example, a Macintosh II can display 16.8 million colors, but some QuickDraw color printers are not capable of printing such an array of colors. Although you can choose from 200 colors on a Macintosh Plus or SE, many compatible output devices can only print eight of them. So, before you commit yourself to a color, make sure your computer and output device can deliver it to you.

Another tip. Even though a color monitor can pretty closely approximate output colors, the translation of color from one medium (video) to another (film or paper) is never perfect. Create a sample slide with your intended color palette, produce it on your intended output device, and compare colors. You may decide to compensate for color shift by changing some of the colors in your palette. At the very least, you'll spare yourself the nasty surprise of having 50 slides come back with your company's royal blue logo looking like a peacock! Much research is currently being done to improve fidelity between displayed and produced color, and solutions are appearing on the market. The TekColor Picker from Tektronix is one such solution. It matches monitor colors to its ink-jet printer colors. For more information about the vicissitudes of producing color, consult Part IV, *The Big Production.*

By the way, even if you're working with a black-and-white monitor, you can still mix and assign colors. Although they appear on screen as black, white, and patterned shades of gray, they reveal their true selves when output to a film recorder or color printer.

Using Persuasion's "Automatic" Color

With color, as with most parts of a presentation, you can let Persuasion's AutoTemplates do the work for you. Each of the 12 color AutoTemplates (S through X and GG through LL) includes a built-in color palette and slide masters featuring colored text, graphics, and slide background. Even tables and charts come with default line, fill, and text colors. Refer to the Persuasion *Desktop Reference* manual for illustrations of these templates; you should, however, expect some discrepancies between the printed samples and what you see on the screen or find coming out of your color printer or film recorder. Remember, the *Show thumbnail* option in the Open presentation dialog box lets you peek at different AutoTemplates.

You can either use an AutoTemplate right "out of the box" or as a jumping off point from which to modify and adjust color selections by following the procedures described below.

The Color Palette and the Color Grid

Persuasion's color system consists of two parts, the color palette and the color grid. The color palette contains your color scheme, up to sixteen of the colors you intend to use most frequently in a particular presentation.

Your presentation isn't limited to sixteen colors, however. In fact, the color palette is composed of colors chosen from the color grid, which is a matrix of 200 colors, 160 of which are predefined, and 40 of which can be edited. And, if you're working on a Macintosh II, you can replace the 40 editable colors from among the 16.8 million colors the Mac II can display, more than enough for most people's needs.

The color palette crops up as an option in several Persuasion menus. In the Text menu, the *Color* submenu and *Text format* dialog box both allow you to apply color to text. In the Effect menu, the five color submenus, *Line color, Fill color, Shadow color, Line background,* and *Fill background* control the color of different graphic elements. And, in the Master menu, the *Slide background fill* and *Define bullet marks* commands govern the background color and the color of bullets on the slide master.

Applying Colors to Existing Objects

As with formatting text, there are two ways to apply color: (*a*) apply color to existing objects or text from the color palette or color grid; (*b*) or set up default colors before you type or draw an object.

Applying Colors to Text

Use the text tool to select a little or a lot of text, or the pointer tool to select an entire text block or more. When color is the only attribute you intend to modify, choose *Color* from the Text menu, and then choose the color you want. The Color submenu menu displays palette colors by name, and, on a color monitor, in color.

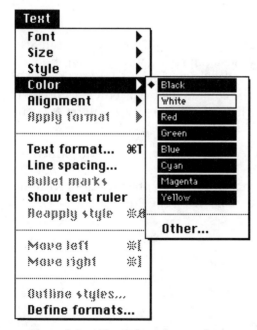

Figure 9.1.   The Color submenu lets you apply color to text.

The *Text format* option in the Text menu also allows you to specify text colors. Use this option if color is just one of several text attributes that you wish to change. Choose a color from the Color pop-down menu, make your other changes, and then click *OK* to close the dialog box. Of course, color is one of the attributes that you can build into the definition of a text format.

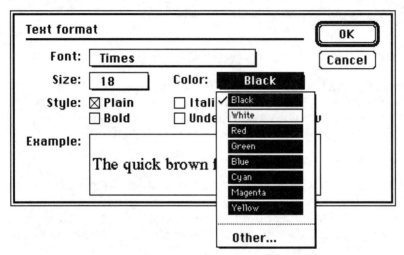

Figure 9.2.   The Text format dialog box displays an example of the current settings, including color.

As you may remember from Chapter 7, *Working with Text*, you can also set text tool defaults before you type. Select the text tool, and then choose a text color from the Color submenu or the Text format dialog box. Or, click an insertion point where you want the colored text to be entered, and then choose a text color. In either case, whatever you then type will reflect your choice of color.

Color applied to outlined text affects the outline, not the fill, which remains transparent. Color applied to shadowed text affects the text, not the shadow. To change the color of a text shadow, select the text block with the pointer tool, and then choose *Shadow color* from the Effect menu.

Applying Palette Colors to Objects

Persuasion lets you apply color to each of the following five elements independently.

- Line color;

- Fill color;

- Shadow color;

- Line background (if you've chosen a line pattern); and

- Fill background (if you've chosen a fill pattern).

This gives you the latitude to create a mauve and burgundy–striped rectangle bounded by a chartreuse and puce–checked line with a magenta shadow. So be careful!

To change the color of one or more elements, select the object(s) you intend to modify, open one of the five color submenus of the Effect menu, and then choose the color you want from the color palette.

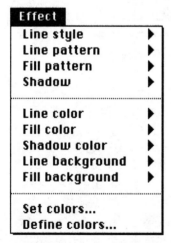

Figure 9.3.   To change the color of an object's elements, open one of the five color submenus of the Effect menu.

Applying Other Colors from the Color Grid

Ideally, the sixteen colors in your color palette will cover all your requirements for a given presentation. But from time to time you may want to apply a color that isn't in the palette. That's what the *Other* command at the bottom of each color submenu is for.

Select the objects you want to modify. Choose *Other* from the color sub-menu you're working with. You'll see the *Select text color* or *Select line color* (or whatever element you're modifying) dialog box, consisting of a grid of 200 colors. Click on any color in the grid, and then click *OK* to close the dialog box (or double-click the color to do it all in one step). The color is applied to the selected object. (The color won't be added to the color palette, though. That's customizing the color palette, which is covered below.)

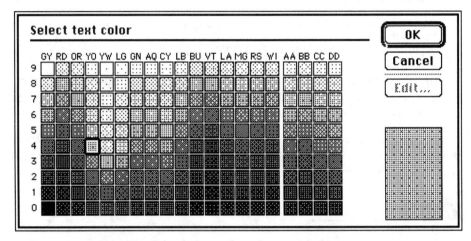

Figure 9.4.　Choosing *Other* from a color submenu gives you access to the color grid.

Using the Set Colors Option

To apply color to several elements at once, the fastest route is the *Set colors* option. Like the Text format dialog box, *Set colors* allows you to make many changes—in this case, to apply color to text and to the five elements of an object—without opening and closing lots of submenus. Save your mouse hand for more important tasks!

Select the text or object (or text *and* objects) you want to color, and then choose *Set colors* from the Effect menu. The Set colors dialog box displays six color boxes for text, fill, line, shadow, fill background, and line background. Each box reflects the current setting for the corresponding selected element. Click any box to display the color palette and choose a new color. The color you choose appears in the color pop-up menu you clicked on. The check boxes tell you what elements will be changed when you close the dialog box.

In the lower right corner of the dialog box, a sample rectangle reflects the current settings, including line, fill, shadow, and background colors, as well as the current line, fill, and shadow patterns.

When you've made the changes you want, click *OK* to close the dialog box. The colors of the text or object you selected before opening the dialog box will change to reflect your choices.

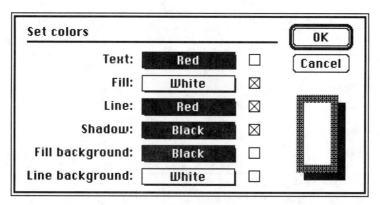

Figure 9.5.   The Set colors option allows you to change several color elements for an object at once.

Setting a Presentation's Color Defaults

The *Set colors* option can be used not only to modify particular text or objects, but also to set a presentation's default colors. Like text defaults that govern what you'll get when typing with the text tool, color defaults determine what colors Persuasion's drawing tools will produce. Notice that you can control the default color of text in two places: in the Text menu or in the Set colors dialog box.

Make sure that the pointer tool is active and no object or text is selected (or else you'll just be modifying a particular tool or object instead of setting defaults). Choose *Set colors* from the Effect menu, and then proceed as above.

When you set presentation color defaults in the Set colors dialog box, they'll be reflected in the Presentation tool display. In fact, the sample rectangle in the dialog box will match the tool display, as will any graphic drawn with a drawing tool.

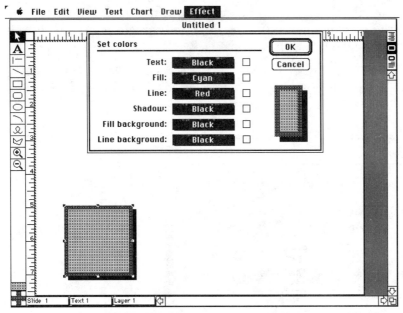

Figure 9.6. The selected square reflects the current default settings in the Set colors dialog box. These settings are also reflected in the Presentation tool default display in the bottom left corner of the presentation window.

Creating Your Own Colors

So far, we've looked at how to apply colors from the color palette to text and objects. Now let's move a little deeper and examine how colors get into the color palette in the first place. We'll explore how to add, remove, and rename colors in the color palette, and how to edit colors in the color grid. Armed with this knowledge, you can either customize one of Persuasion's AutoTemplates by editing its color palette, or build your own AutoTemplate and its color palette from scratch.

Customizing the Color Palette

To recompose the color palette, choose *Define colors* from the Effect menu. The Define colors dialog box appears, containing the color grid.

The 200-color grid is divided into two sub-grids, one consisting of 160 predefined colors and the other of 40 editable colors. In the left grid, columns are labeled with a two letter abbreviation (GY for gray, AQ for aqua, VT for violet, RS for rose, and so forth). In the right grid, columns are labeled AA through DD. Rows are numbered from 0 to 9, with darker colors appearing in lower rows with lower numbers, and lighter colors appearing in upper rows with higher numbers. Each color is identified by a three digit letter and number combination that indicates its position in the color grid, and, in case you're working in black-and-white, gives some hint as to its hue and brightness. (For example, LA9 is a very pale lavender, while OR1 is a very dark orange.)

The currently selected color (initially black) is represented in the *Color* pop-up menu above the grid and in the sample box on the right. It is also outlined within the grid, showing you its position in the grid and its relationship to other grid colors. The selected color's name is checked in the color palette that pops down in the Color box. Any changes you make, whether adding, renaming, or removing a color, will apply to the currently selected color.

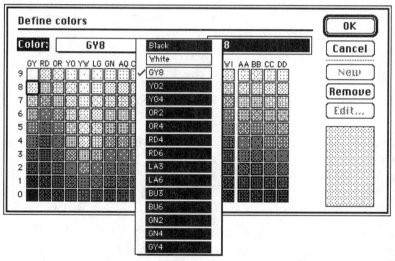

Figure 9.7.   The currently selected color appears in the Color box in the pop-down color palette in the sample box to the right and is outlined on the color grid.

To replace one palette color with another, choose the palette color you want to replace from the Color pop-up menu, and then click the new color on the color grid. For example, let's say you want to replace the color GY6, which is currently in your color palette, with RD6, which is not. Click the color box, and then select GY6 from the pop-down color palette. When the color palette closes, you'll see that GY6 now appears in the color box and is outlined on the grid. Next, click RD6 on the grid. RD6 replaces GY6 in the color box, and, when you open the color palette, you'll see that RD6 has taken the place of GY6. Remember, any change you make in the grid affects the color currently selected in the color palette. Any time you click a grid color, it will always replace the palette color that's currently selected. Sometimes this responsiveness can take you by surprise, so click the grid only with forethought.

To add a new color to the color palette, choose *New*, and then click the color you want to add. The new color and its three character name appear in the Color pop-up menu, and a sample appears in the sample box to the right of the grid. To add more colors to the palette, repeat the two step process of choosing *New* and then clicking the desired color. Persuasion will continue adding colors until the 16 positions on the palette are filled, at which point the *New* option will be dimmed and no longer selectable.

When you choose *New*, the color to the right of the currently selected color (the one you just clicked) is added to the palette and is now outlined. Be sure to choose *New* before clicking a color you want to add; otherwise the color you click on the grid will replace the palette color that's currently selected. As we've pointed out, this can be confusing at first.

Note: If *New* is dimmed, it means your color palette already contains the maximum 16 colors, so you'll need to remove some of the old to make room for the new.

When you've finished adding the colors you want, click *OK* to close the dialog box and save the changes to the color palette. To remove a color from the color palette, click the Color pop-up menu, choose the color you want to remove, and then click *Remove*. If you remove a palette color that's already been applied to objects on a slide, they won't be affected by the change.

To rename a color, choose the color that you want to rename from the Color pop-up menu. Its name will appear in the Rename box. Type the color's new name.

Customizing the Color Grid

If you're working on a Macintosh II, you've not yet exhausted the resources of Persuasion's color grid. The 40 colors on the right side of the grid can be edited using the Apple color picker. Here's how.

Choose *Define colors* from the Effect menu, and then click a color in one of the columns labeled AA through DD. (Remember to choose *New* first, or else you'll delete the color that's currently selected.) Click *Edit* to display the Apple color picker (also known as the color wheel).

Note: If you're working with an 8-bit color monitor, you may see the colors in your presentation shift dramatically as the color picker opens. This is entirely normal! An 8-bit color monitor can only display 256 colors at once. To represent the color wheel accurately, it has to adjust temporarily some of the presentation colors to keep within the 256-color display limit.

The sample box in the upper left corner of the color picker displays a swatch of the color before and after editing. To change the color's hue, hold down the mouse button and drag the pointer around the color wheel. To change the color's saturation, drag the pointer toward or away from the center of the wheel. To change the color's brightness, drag the scroll box up and down the scroll bar to the right of the wheel (or, either use the arrows, or click in the gray area above or below the scroll box).

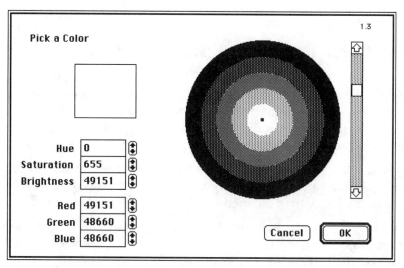

Figure 9.8.   Using the Apple color picker on a Macintosh II, you can add up to 40 of 16.8 million possible colors to Persuasion's color grid.

Note: For those of you who are new to the world of color, hue refers to a color's position on a color spectrum (whether it's red or blue or purple or yellow); saturation refers to how much "pigment" the color has (how red a red it is, or how blue a blue); and brightness refers to how dark or light the color is.

When you're satisfied with the color you're mixing, click *OK.* The Apple color picker vanishes, and your custom color replaces the old color in the palette and the grid.

To apply a custom color to a selected object or to select a custom color as a default, you can get to the color picker directly from all the color submenus (*Color* in the Text menu, *Line color*, and the others in the Effects menu). Choose *Other* from the submenu. In the *Select color (line/text/fill, etc.)* dialog box, click one of the 40 editable colors, click *Edit*, and then mix a color as described above. When you close the color picker, the color will be applied to the selected object, or saved as a tool or presentation default.

Note that if you edit a color that you've already applied to an object, the object will automatically reflect the edited color. For example, let's say you've applied a custom color called *Logo red* to all title text in your presentation. You decide to darken the red a bit, using the color editing feature just described. All the title text to which the color *Logo red* had been applied will automatically reflect the new, edited color. To preserve the color of existing objects, save the edited color under a new name, and then apply it to subsequent objects.

Creating Color Radial and Graduated Fills

As you saw in Chapter 8, *Working with Graphics*, Persuasion provides a wide selection of patterns—checks, stripes, and various textures—for filling lines and objects. But, once in a while, even checks and stripes won't do the trick. When that happens, a radial or graduated fill, suggesting a subtle blend from one color to another, is the only answer.

To apply a radial or graduated fill, select an appropriate object, choose *Fill pattern* from the Effect menu, and pick one of the three patterns from the bottom row of the Fill pattern submenu, radial, vertical, or horizontal.

When you close the submenu, the fill pattern is applied to the selected object. Pick colors from the Fill color and Fill background menus, depending on how you want the colors to blend. Table 9.1, below, explains where the Fill and Fill background colors will appear on the graphic.

Table 9.1

Pattern	Fill color will appear	Fill background color will appear
Radial fill	At the outer ring	At the center
Horizontally graduated fill	On the left	On the right
Vertically graduated fill	At the top	At the bottom

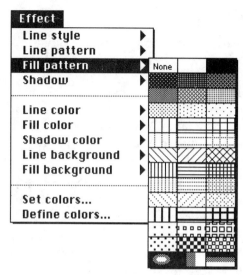

Figure 9.9. For a two-colored special effect, choose one of the three patterns from the bottom row of the pattern submenu.

For tips on how to create special effects by combining graduated backgrounds and objects with graduated fills, consult Chapter 13, *Building an AutoTemplate.*

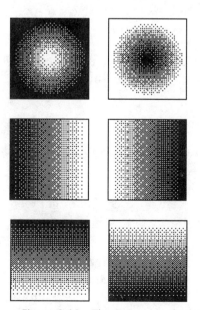

Figure 9.10. The squares in the left column have black as the Fill color and white as the Fill background color. The colors are reversed in the right column.

Importing Color Graphics

Persuasion doesn't force you to rely exclusively on its own drawing tools for color graphics. You can import or cut and paste color graphics from other applications. In fact, Persuasion can handle color graphics in PICT II and EPS (Encapsulated PostScript) formats, the two most popular formats for graphics applications. Once you get an EPS graphic into Persuasion, you can move and resize it as you would any any other. But you can't change its colors or edit its parts. Use a program like Aldus FreeHand to edit PostScript objects before importing them into Persuasion.

If you are using a 24-bit color monitor, Persuasion can display any imported graphic with true color fidelity. When you don't have 24-bit color, the Macintosh handles the display of an imported graphic's colors as follows. It compares each imported color to its own current color grid, and before display, it converts the imported color to the nearest available grid color. Depending on the graphic's colors and the grid, this may or may not produce acceptable results. If perfect on-screen fidelity to a graphic's original colors is crucial, consider editing the color grid (adding the graphic's colors).

Note: Unless you ungroup an imported graphic, only the color it appears on-screen—not its actual color—is changed. If an ungrouped graphic is subsequently output to a film recorder, its colors will match the originals more closely than will initially appear on a Mac screen. The bottom line? If printing the colors of an imported graphic exactly as they appeared in the originating graphics program is important, don't ungroup the graphic in Persuasion, and don't be concerned if the colors that you see displayed in Persuasion shift slightly from the original; they will print properly.

Matching an Imported Graphic's Colors

Converting a graphic's colors into Persuasion colors can be tricky. Most graphics programs use percentages of red, green, and blue, or degrees of hue and percentages of saturation and brightness, whereas Persuasion uses the Macintosh color numbers from 1 to 65535. Here are a couple of cumbersome but effective ways to convert a percentage color into a Persuasion color.

Open the graphic in the application that created it and find the percentages of red, green, and blue for each color you want to match in Persuasion. Then you can calculate the equivalent Macintosh color numbers by multiplying the percentage times the largest possible Macintosh color number (65535).

For example, let's say you have to match your company's logo color, PMS 200 (a bright red). You determine that it's 85% red and 20% blue, so you multiply (65535 × 0.85) for a red of 55704, and (65535 × 0.2) for a blue of 13107. Now you open Persuasion's Define colors dialog box, choose an editable color (AA9-DD0), click *Edit*, and type the numbers into the red, green, and blue boxes in the Apple color picker. When you import the graphic, Persuasion will discover the right red already on the color grid and match it perfectly.

See Table 9.2 below for the Macintosh color number equivalents of 48 popular PMS colors. (PMS stands for Pantone Matching System, a standard for matching colors in the printing industry.)

If you have Aldus PageMaker, you can use its *Define colors* option to match colors. Take the percentages of red, green, and blue from the original graphic and type them into PageMaker's Define colors dialog box (choose *Define colors* from the Options menu). Click the color you just defined, and then hold down the Shift key while clicking *Edit*. This displays the Apple color picker with Macintosh color numbers for red, green, and blue. Write them down, and then return to Persuasion and type them in as described above.

Table 9.2

Pantone color	Macintosh color numbers		
	Red	Green	Blue
Red			
Warm red	65535	13762	5898
185	65535	5898	15728
192	65535	3932	22937
199	65535	0	22937
206	65535	0	37355
213	65535	0	45875
Rubine red	65535	0	55705
Orange			
137	65535	43253	5898
151	65535	37355	8520

(continued)

Table 9.2 *(continued)*

Pantone color	Macintosh color numbers		
	Red	Green	Blue
158	65535	26214	3932
172	65535	22937	11141
Yellow			
Pantone yellow	65535	65535	0
109	65535	60292	3932
116	65535	55705	3932
123	65535	45875	3932
130	65535	47841	0
Green			
Pantone green	0	65535	22937
327	0	55705	24903
340	0	55705	10486
347	0	60292	8520
555	0	28835	0
562	0	45875	15073
569	0	53739	17039
Blue			
Reflex blue	0	14418	61603
286	0	22282	61603
293	0	28835	65535
300	0	37355	65535

(continued)

Table 9.2   *(continued)*

Pantone color	Macintosh color numbers		
	Red	Green	Blue
Purple			
Pantone purple	37355	5898	65535
259	13107	0	55705
266	3932	3932	65535
273	0	0	61603
527	13762	3932	65535
Gray			
Warm gray 3	53739	49807	49807
Warm gray 6	45875	40632	38666
Warm gray 9	34734	24903	22937
Cool gray 3	53739	53739	53739
Cool gray 6	40632	40632	40632
Cool gray 9	22937	22937	22937

Working with Color on Slide Masters

Slide background color and bullet color are set on slide and background masters. For the complete story on how to set up slide masters, see Chapter 13, *Building an AutoTemplate*.

Now that you've been immersed in words and dazzled by color, let's look at the world of charts and graphs, where words (or numbers) and colors come together.

Chapter 10

Working with Charts and Tables

An audience has only a short time to absorb information on a slide. For this reason, charts can be one of the most effective visual devices in a presentation. Charts represent information so that it is communicative and can be easily grasped. Charts turn data into information.

Persuasion has a most impressive chart making capability that makes creating charts as easy as organizing textual information in an outline. Before we explore Persuasion's charting features, however, let's discuss the various elements of a chart and how they can be used to communicate information and ideas.

Effective Charts

A successful chart is one that portrays information accurately and that holds a viewer's attention. Your chance of accomplishing these two goals is greatly increased if you take the time to plan and prepare each chart ahead of time. This means identifying the information you want to convey and then selecting the best chart format to get your message across. You can then spend some time adding more visual interest as well as highlighting the more important parts of the chart.

Chart Formats

Charts display quantitative data to prove or illustrate a point. The best chart format to use in a particular instance depends on what type of information you are working with. Persuasion includes eight of the most popular business charts (and their variations) in its drawing repertoire: pie, bar, column, line, area, scatter, high-low, and table. You can also customize any of these formats and save the custom format to use on other similar data at a later time. Figure 10.1 illustrates a typical column chart and its elements.

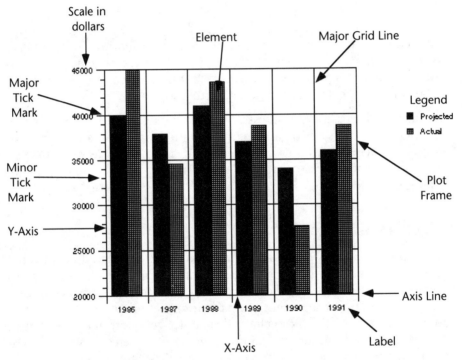

Figure 10.1. A column chart.

Axes

Nearly every chart type is plotted with two variables, each one measured in relationship to the other. One variable is the independent variable, referred to as the *category*, and the other, the dependent variable, is known as the *value*. In Figure 10.1, for example, the x-axis showing the years along the bottom of the chart is the category axis, and the y-axis along the left side is the value axis.

Most charts—in particular, the column, line, and area graphs—display the category variables along the horizontal axis, or x-axis, while the value is displayed along the vertical axis. One exception to this rule is the horizontal bar chart which reverses this relationship. It displays the categories along the vertical axis and the values along the horizontal axis. Other exceptions are the pie and scatter charts, which we will discuss in a few minutes.

Persuasion automatically takes the your categories and values and places them in the appropriate axis depending on which chart format you select.

Legends

Using a roadmap without a legend limits the usefulness of the roadmap. It is very hard to tell what every line on the map stands for. Likewise, a chart without a legend makes it difficult to understand the chart. The chart legend identifies the data plotted in the chart. In Figure 10.1, the legend shows what each column pattern represents.

Labels

Labels are used to title a chart or to identify parts of a chart, such as units of measure, that are not necessarily obvious. Include labels in your charts to make them clear, but be careful not to overdo it. When you use labels, strive to be consistent in font and size. Keep a label's size, weight, and shading proportional to its importance in the chart. Follow a hierarchy as you label a chart: start with relatively prominently sized text for the title and slightly smaller text for subtitles. Next in importance are labels to define lines and bars, and then labels for the horizontal and vertical grids and the scale captions.

For the best appearance, place labels for the horizontal axis under the axis, and centered between major tick marks. Place labels for the vertical axis exactly at the major tick marks down the axis.

Grid Lines and Tick Marks

Grid lines and tick marks are visual aids that help a viewer make comparisons among different sets of data, especially if the chart has lots of data. Persuasion can add two types of grid lines: major grid lines mark major divisions in an axis while minor grid lines mark in-between divisions in the axis. Usually major grid lines lines will suffice unless your viewers need to concentrate on a greater degree of detail. Use grid lines as required to help the viewer interpret the data. If the scale step is small, then the grid lines will clutter the chart rather than make it easier to interpret.

Tick marks are similar to grid lines, but tick marks only appear along the axis itself instead of extending across the entire chart.

Scaling

Scaling a chart is tricky because the scale profoundly affects how your viewers perceive the chart's information. For example, Figure 10.2 shows the identical set of data plotted against two different scales. The visual information conveyed by each chart is different.

Persuasion has a built-in scaling feature that automatically scales each chart. Persuasion scales a chart by looking at the data you want to chart and creating a scale that will place your data approximately in the midsection of the chart.

You can also customize the scale for any chart if you are not satisfied with Persuasion's automatic scaling. By increasing the maximum plot range, the chart will appear to diminish the comparative differences in values between your various data elements. Likewise, decreasing the maximum plot value will accentuate the differences among data.

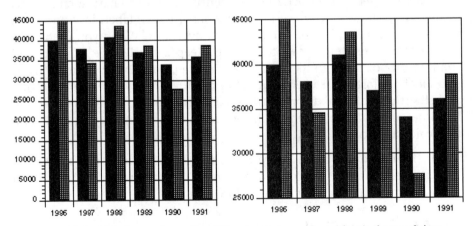

Figure 10.2. This figure shows the difference between two identical sets of data plotted using the same chart format but scaled differently. The chart on the left starts with a value of 0 on the y-axis, while the chart on the left starts with the value of 25,000 on the y-axis.

Design Considerations

As you create every chart your overriding concern should be how well it makes its point. A chart that is cluttered with unnecessary information is counterproductive. Keep in mind, too, that a presentation chart is projected on a screen of some sort. While certain details may have worked well for you in the past with charts in hard copy, they may now not work at all well on screen. Also bear in mind that a chart is projected for a limited period of time. The audience is not free to study and refer back to the chart at will. Therefore, you have to take great pains to be as explicit as you can. Use labels sparingly, but, if a label will clear up some uncertainty, use it.

Keep it simple. With all of the tools and options in Persuasion, it is tempting to overdo a chart with fancy embellishments and lose its clarity.

Your chart should have an overall sense of unity. Make a good contrast between each element of the chart. A single border surrounding the chart can keep the viewer's attention where it belongs. Also, be consistent in the patterns or colors you use through the course of your presentation. Use the same colors for similar information. For example, if you use red in one slide to show a negative number, don't choose red in the next slide to show a positive number.

Finally, when in doubt, it is best to err on the side of being too conservative rather than create charts that don't work as you intend.

Persuasion's Chart Formats

You can easily convert your own data into any of Persuasion's 10 different chart formats. And, if that's not enough, you can create your own custom formats by editing Persuasion's charts and adding the new format to the Chart menu using a unique name that you define.

Pie

A pie chart is a circle divided into pieces. A pie chart works best to show how various data parts relate both to one another and to a whole. Pie charts show proportionate relationships. They are not as numerically precise as bar charts because they don't show strict measurements on axes.

1990 Attendance Analysis

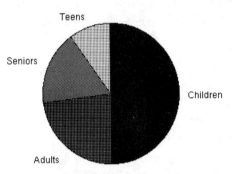

Figure 10.3. A pie chart is one of the more effective ways to visualize how individual parts make up the whole.

You can add emphasis to an element of the pie by selecting a piece and pulling it slightly away from the rest of the pie. This is usually called an "exploded pie chart." If you choose to use two pie charts on a single slide to show two different comparisons of identical data (such as the division of a budget for this year versus last year) there are a few rules to follow. First, be sure to maintain consistency in colors (if you used green to display salary information for last year's budget chart, then use green to show salary in this year's budget chart as well). Also, keep the order of chart elements the same among similar charts. If one chart orders salaries, rent, and then travel, the next chart should use the same order. This will help your viewers see the relationship between the two charts. In short, do everything you can to communicate to your viewers graphically since, by definition, you cannot communicate a chart with words.

Bar and Column Charts

Bar and column chart formats are probably the most commonly used. One reason for this is that they are inherently easy to comprehend. A simple bar chart is a good choice for showing the rank of similar items at a particular point in time. A clustered bar chart is effective for showing the rank of two or three similar items measured at various fixed points in time. For example, one glance at the clustered bar chart in Figure 10.4 tells you that projections for 1986 were the highest while actual attendance for the year was lagging.

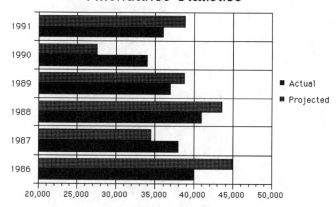

Figure 10.4. This bar chart shows the relationship between projected and actual attendance for a six year period. Notice the positions of data in the data sheet and how the data was transferred into a bar chart format.

The stacked bar chart is another variation of the bar chart. A single bar chart compares the difference between each individual data entry, while a stacked bar chart shows the accumulated contribution of each data element relative to the whole as you can see in Figure 10.5.

Attendance by Age Group • 1989-1990

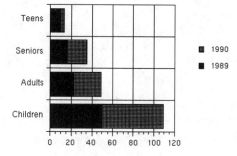

Figure 10.5. This stacked bar chart shows the cumulative attendance of four age groups over a two-year period.

The difference between a bar chart and a column chart is the orientation of their respective base lines. A standard bar chart uses the vertical axis along the left side, and a column chart uses the horizontal axis along the bottom of the chart. The chart type you choose will depend on the data you need to display. A bar chart usually compares different items at a specific point in time, and a column chart shows variations in one item over a period of time. A column chart is particularly effective for displaying negative numbers, as you can see in Figure 10.6. A viewer can easily see any deviation from the "zero" point, which is in this case the difference between profit and loss.

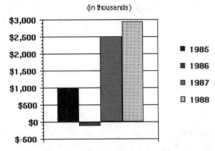

Figure 10.6. This column chart highlights the problem the zoo had in 1970 because of fuel shortages forcing people to cut their travel.

Tip: If you want to compare parts to the whole choose either a pie chart, stacked bar, or stacked column. Pie charts work best if you have between two and six "pieces" in the pie. If you have more than six data elements to chart, use a stacked bar chart format.

Line

Line charts are suitable for showing the continuous effects of trends or changes over time. This format suggests movement and encourages the viewer to speculate on a direction for the future.

You can plot either a single set of data or several sets of data on a line chart. Using a line chart to plot multiple data makes it easy for the viewer to see if there are similar trends among the different sets of data.

Line charts are also appropriate for showing projections or plans. Use a solid line for showing "actual" and a dashed line for plotting "projections" (see Figure 10.7).

Yearly Attendance

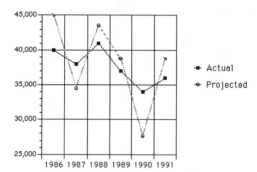

Figure 10.7. Using a contrasting weight lines for the projected and actual attendance helps the viewer differentiate between the two comparisons.

Note: One thing to be sure of when you work with line charts is not to use too many lines on one chart. Even with using color and assigning symbols to identify each line, any more than five lines makes the chart difficult to follow. Don't use spaghetti charts!

Area

The area chart (also called a surface chart) is closely related to the line chart, only instead of connecting dots, the area chart fills in the area below the lines. While this difference may seem subtle, this type of chart focuses the viewer's attention on the composition of the quantitative data in the chart, rather than on the trend the data suggests.

When you create an area chart, place the most important data element against the horizontal baseline since this is the only element that is viewed against a straight line.

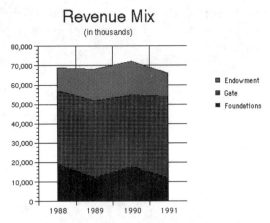

Revenue Mix
(in thousands)

Figure 10.8. An area chart can show the effects of separate related data elements against the whole and then plot different sets of data to span a period of time.

Scatter

Scatter charts are related to line charts; instead of using lines to display data, however, they use individual points plotted against the horizontal and vertical axes. Use a scatter chart to illustrate the correlation between data points. The viewer will mentally connect the dots, but the main point of a scatter chart is to see how closely the dots are positioned to each other. The purpose of the scatter chart is to help a viewer determine whether a relationship exists between the two plotted variables, and, if so, what the relationship is and how dependable it is. The straighter the line of dots the more dependable the relationship.

Figure 10.9 shows the relationship between gross attendance and gate proceeds. Someone in the audience could see that there is a strong correlation to attendance and proceeds, but the correlation is not perfect. The number of senior discounts and children admissions skews the correlation slightly, but the numbers average out overall.

If you want to show the difference between two sets of data, choose the scatter chart. Because by nature a scatter chart is meant to be interpreted by a viewer, use this format to illustrate correlation only.

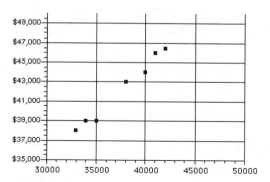

Figure 10.9   A scatter chart is best for showing correlation of a group of data. The scatter chart format lends itself to a more analytical view compared to other types of charts.

High-Low

High-low charts are also related to line charts. The most common use for high-low charts is in stock market reports that show a stock's high and low range for a period of time.

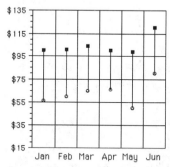

Figure 10.10.   The high-low chart format is appropriate to show a range of values for a single data element.

Table

Sometimes it is appropriate to supplement a chart with a table and to place them side-by-side on a slide. A chart gives the viewer a visual representation of the relationship between data while a table supplies the details.

Tables are useful to draw a viewer's attention to relationships among related facts. For example, a table can be as simple as a bulleted list or as complex as a train timetable or list of competing products in a buyer's guide magazine.

The point to remember when using tables is to be consistent throughout the table. Make sure to keep the syntax in each column consistent as demonstrated in Figure 10.11.

Friends of Argilla Zoo

Attendance Statistics

	Actual	Projected
1986	40,101	40,000
1987	34,567	38,000
1988	43,567	41,000
1989	38,765	37,000
1990	27,654	34,000

Figure 10.11. A table is a useful vehicle for helping a viewer categorize related facts.

Planning Pointers

As you can see by now, choosing the best chart format for your presentation is not an exact science. There are not hard and fast rules for which chart format to choose. Experience and a critical eye will be your best judge.

Whichever format you choose, there are a few guidelines that will make any chart most effective. The first is to keep it simple. One of the biggest problems with charts is trying to cram too much information within the confines of a single chart.

Make sure each chart has a single message. The visual impact of a chart will be blurred if you try to say too much in a chart. Use separate charts for each message. If need be, you can place another chart on the same slide.

Be consistent. An effective chart looks pleasing to the eye with proper proportions given to the data and different sizes and styles of type according to the text's importance in explaining the chart. Use the same patterns and colors for identical information that you use in different charts.

If your presentation will be in color, make best use of that color. Since dark colors dominate a chart, use a dark color for the most important chart elements. When you are comparing elements, use contrasting colors to drive the comparison home. For example, blue and orange are contrasting colors as are red and green. Colors also have certain psychological effects. Red is hot and active, whereas green is cool and relaxing.

The most important caveat for using color as well as other chart enhancements is moderation. Too many colors will have a negative effect on your audience.

Data into Charts

Now that we have covered some of the basics of chart terminology and formats let's roll up our sleeves and see how Persuasion measures up to the task of creating charts.

There are five or six basic steps to creating a chart in Persuasion. Note that the selection of a chart format (e.g., pie, bar, stacked bar, column, or stacked column) can be made at various points throughout the chart creation process.

1. Go to the target slide (the one on which you want the chart to appear). Or, if you are in the outline view, you can click on any heading for that slide. At this point, too, you might change the master slide assignment to one that contains a chart placeholder and choose a default chart format for that master.

2. Open a data sheet and type your chart data in the data sheet "work area." If the data already exists in another file (in .WKS or ASCII format, such as a database, spreadsheet, or word processor), you can import data into the data sheet to save retyping. Note too, that you can simply open an external data sheet and select data directly from the external source. In this case you will see a "temporary" data sheet in Persuasion with the data from the external file (although you cannot edit it.).

3. Specify a different chart format from the Chart menu. You can choose one of ten chart types in the Chart menu: pie, bar, stacked bar, column, stacked column, line, area, scatter, high-low, and table.

4. Select the data you want included in the graph and plot the chart by clicking the *Plot* button on the data sheet. The data will be graphed on the target slide. Once you plot selected data from an open external file, Persuasion copies it into the Persuasion data sheet where you can modify it if necessary.

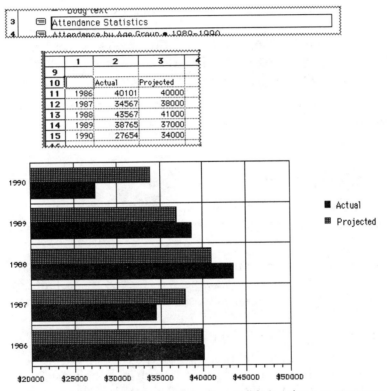

Figure 10.12. Creating a basic chart on a slide is a three step process: selecting the target slide in the outline (*shown*) or slide view, selecting the data for the chart, and viewing the data on the target slide.

5. Once Persuasion has translated your data into a basic chart, the possibilities for enhancing the chart begin. You can add graphic and text elements to the chart. You can add arrows, text, and other visual aids to emphasize the message that you want the chart to communicate. Persuasion gives you extreme control, allowing you to modify individual elements in a chart that are not typically modifiable in other programs.

6. If you think that another format would suit your purpose better, you can change the chart format by simply selecting the chart and choosing another format from the Chart menu.

Persuasion always maintains a warm link between the data in the data sheet and a chart. This means that if you change the data all you have to do is check the *Replot* button and Persuasion will update the chart with the new data sheet information.

The Data Sheet

The *Data sheet* command is found under Persuasion's File menu. This command is the foundation of every chart. If you have ever used a spreadsheet application such as Microsoft Excel, you are already familiar with the row-and-column structure of a worksheet. The Persuasion data sheet is structured very much like a worksheet. You enter data in a row and column format, then you select the data you want for the chart, and Persuasion will plot the chart. Once information is entered in a data sheet, you can use the same data (or just parts of it) over and over to create charts and tables within the presentation. Persuasion has just one data sheet per presentation; it contains all the data for all the charts and tables in the current presentation.

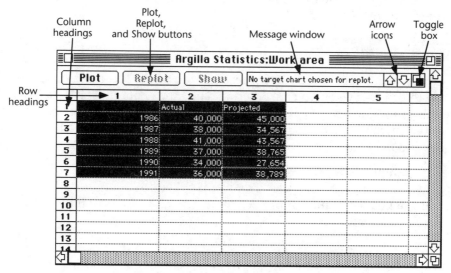

Figure 10.13. Data from the data sheet translates into a chart.

Methods for Entering Data into a Data Sheet

The first decision you need to make about your chart is how to get the chart data into Persuasion. If your data is not in any form of computer file, you must reconcile yourself to manually typing your data into a data sheet. If you are more fortunate, the data is already in another application and you can have Persuasion use it. Let's look at both possibilities.

The Manual Method

Let's say that you don't have the chart data available in any other electronic form. In this case you will need to open the Persuasion data sheet and manually enter the data. First choose *Data sheet* from the File menu, and then *Work area* from the submenu.

Along the top of the data sheet are basic chart commands that become active after you have entered some information. The plot button is what you use to first create a chart. The *Replot* button replots your chart if you have made changes to the data and want the chart updated. The *Show* button displays the slide on which a chart was already placed. We will discuss the rest of the data sheet window a little later.

> **Note:** If you are curious as to how much data you can fit in a data sheet, the answer is as many as 2,560 data points within a range of 256 rows and 32 columns.

What Goes Where

So, with the data sheet open where do you start? The most important thing to consider when you are entering data into a data sheet is which axis Persuasion will assign to column and row information (for most charts except pie charts). Persuasion needs to know what you want plotted as a category and as value data.

For example, let's say a zoo director wants to compare her annual gate attendance for the past six years. She wants to see both her projections and actual attendance numbers for each year. She chooses a column chart to make the comparison.

For her chart to plot properly, she needs to enter her information into the data sheet correctly. There is no iron-clad rule for which cells should contain value data and which cells category data. In Figure 10.15, you see a bar chart and a column chart both plotted from the identical set of data sheet cells. However, the categories and values are reversed for both chart types.

	1	2	3
1		Actual	Projected
2	1986	40000	45000
3	1987	38000	34567
4	1988	41000	43567
5	1989	37000	38765
6	1990	34000	27654
7	1991	36000	32000

Figure 10.14. The Persuasion Data sheet.

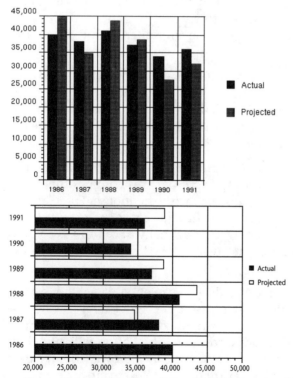

Figure 10.15. Both the column and bar charts in this figure were plotted from the same range of cells. Persuasion interprets the contents and location of information on the data sheet differently for different chart formats.

Note: If the data on the data sheet appears on the incorrect axis for the chart format you select, use the *Switch axes* command in the Axes submenu to swap axes. This does not affect the information on the data sheet, only on which axis the information is plotted on the chart.

If you leave the the top left cell in a cell range blank, Persuasion assumes the first row and column of the range contain labels and not data. If this is the case, the information appearing in the first column and first row appear on the chart as labels.

Selecting a Range of Cells

There are several different ways to enter data into a data sheet. The method you choose depends on personal preference and what works best for the project at hand.

One way to enter information in a data sheet is to click on an individual cell, type the data, and then click on another cell, and type the data. However, there are shortcuts that allow you to enter information into the data sheet more efficiently especially when you are entering lots of data at one time.

For example, once you type in data, you can always press the Return key to select the next cell down or press the Tab key to select one cell to the right. The problem with this technique is that your hands have to leave the keyboard each time you reach the last cell in the column or row to use the mouse to select the next column or row.

The fastest way to enter data for the first time is to select the entire range of cells in the data sheet before you start to type. This confines the cursor to the selected range of cells until you click with the mouse. For example, to select the range of cells in Figure 10.14, the zoo director clicked in cell location row 1–column 1 and dragged diagonally to cell row 7–column 3. When she released the mouse, the cursor moved to the first cell in the selection.

Once you have selected a range of cells, you can enter data either by row or by column, whichever suits your pleasure. To enter data row-by-row use the Tab key (or right arrow) to move right to the next cell in the row. When you reach the end of the selected range, Persuasion will automatically move the cursor to the beginning of the next row. To enter data column-by-column, use the Return key (or down arrow) to move down each column cell-by-cell. When you reach the end of the selected range of cells in the column, Persuasion automatically moves the cursor to the top of the next column.

Note: If you want to move backwards in a selected range of cells without deselecting the range, use the Shift-Tab or Shift-Return key combination to move the cursor in reverse.

By the way, don't worry about formatting numerical data in the data sheet. That formatting is done when you plot the chart itself. Persuasion can automatically format numbers to set the number of decimal places, insert commas, and convert numbers to scientific notation. We will discuss these options later when we cover formatting a chart later in this chapter.

Editing the Data Sheet

Once you have entered information in the data sheet work area you can add, delete, move, or make other changes to it. Note that you can also edit any data that has been brought into the Persuasion data sheet with the *Import* command from the File menu. This data does not, however, maintain its link to the external file. When you open an external file and plot data directly from its data, you cannot edit that *original* file. But once the data from the external source has been plotted, Persuasion moves *a copy* of the data in the data sheet work area and you can edit that copy.

Inserting or Deleting a Row or Column into the Data Sheet

1. Click the number at the beginning of the row or column to select the entire row or column as shown in Figure 10.17.

Figure 10.16.   Select an entire row by clicking at the left side of the row or the top of a column. This figure shows a row selected.

2. Choose *Insert* or *Delete* from the Edit menu. If you insert a new row, it will appear directly above the row you have selected; a new column will appear to the left of the selected column.

Adding, Changing, or Deleting Data in a Cell

1. Click the cell where you want to insert text, or double-click the cell you need to change.

2. Type the new information or type over the existing information.

Moving or Copying Data to a New Location

1. Select the cells that you want to move or copy.

2. To move cell data to a new location choose *Cut* from the Edit menu. Or, to duplicate cell data choose *Copy* from the Edit menu.

3. Click the upper rightmost cell where you want to move or copy the data.

4. Choose *Paste* from the Edit menu.

Using External Chart Data

Typing data directly into a Persuasion data sheet is only one way to get chart data into Persuasion. Opening and reading from an external file, or actually importing entire files from other applications into the Persuasion datasheet are two other very useful ways. If the information has already been typed in another application, it is a waste of time to rekey that information in Persuasion. In this section, we will discuss several ways to use existing data from other applications within Persuasion, so that you can avoid duplicating your work.

Persuasion can read files saved in two common file formats, .WKS and text (also known as ASCII). Before we begin a discussion of procedures for getting access to external data, let us briefly review what these two file formats mean.

.WKS File Format

The .WKS file format is the native format for Lotus 1-2-3 files. Because of the popularity of Lotus 1-2-3, this format has become a standard for most spreadsheet applications on both the MS-DOS and Macintosh hardware platforms. If you want to chart information in Persuasion using information from a Microsoft Excel worksheet, it is easiest to save the Excel worksheet using Excel's .WKS format. If you save the worksheet in Excel using the .WKS format, you can still work on the worksheet in Excel if you need to update the information.

ASCII File Format

The other native format that Persuasion reads is ASCII (or text, as it is more commonly known). ASCII is a universal file format on both Macintosh and MS-DOS computers. Word processors, spreadsheets, and other text-based applications invariably offer text as a save option. When you save a file in text format it is a good idea to type "text" as part of the file name so you will know what type of file it is.

When you save a file as text all formatting codes are stripped from the file, leaving only alphanumeric characters, spaces, and carriage returns. Persuasion divides an imported text file into rows and columns according to its arrangement of tabs and carriage returns. Each time Persuasion encounters a tab, it moves to a new column; for each carriage return in the text, it starts a new row.

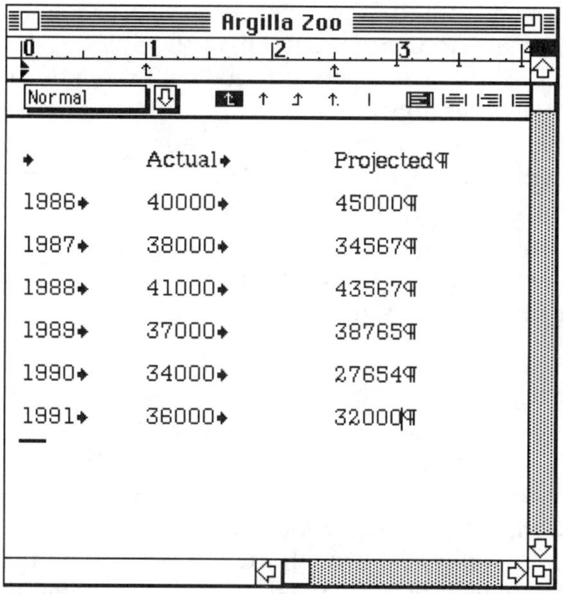

	1	2	3
1		Actual	Projected
2	1986	40000	45000
3	1987	38000	34567
4	1988	41000	43567
5	1989	37000	38765
6	1990	34000	27654
7	1991	36000	32000
8			

Figure 10.17. When importing a text file, Persuasion moves a column for each tab character in the text and starts a new row for each return.

Opening External Files for Charting Information

Persuasion will read directly from any external .WKS or ASCII file you specify. Simply choose *Data sheet* from the File menu, then *Open external* from the submenu, and select the appropriate file from the list box.

When you choose the file you want, it appears in a Persuasion data sheet format. You cannot edit any of the information there. You may drag over the data you need from it, however, and then plot the chart by pressing the *Plot* button. When you plot a chart from an external data sheet, a copy of the selected data is appended to Persuasion's own internal data sheet. Also, the name of the external data sheet is appended to the data sheet *open external* submenu. Thereafter, anytime you choose *Data sheet* in the File menu, its submenu will give you a list of all external data sheets that have been used to plot charts in the current presentation. Choosing any one of those data sheets will open that data sheet. Note, too, that selecting any chart from your presentation in the Slide view and choosing *Set external data* from the Chart menu will accomplish the same thing.

Whenever you open an external data sheet and plot a chart, Persuasion remembers the location of the data and the target slides that have been plotted from that data sheet. Thus, it is easy to update your charts to reflect any new data from the source files. First, open the file by name in the *Data sheet* submenu and refresh the data links. The chart will be updated, retaining all visual enhancements, fills, and positions. Click on the small arrows to the right of the message window to cycle through the plotted data on the data sheet. The message window will give the name of the target slide as well as the chart's location on that slide (just in case you have more than one chart on a slide). Thus, while there is no automatic replotting, you can update your charts by refreshing the links.

Importing a File

To import a file, open the data sheet work area and select a cell to serve as the top left cell for the imported data. Choose *Import* from the File menu. All of the data from the imported file will be brought into the work area. No link will exist to that external file.

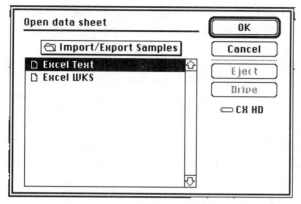

Figure 10.18. The Open data sheet dialog box lists the files that Persuasion recognizes as being either WKS or ASCII format for importing into a data sheet.

Cutting and Pasting

While not an optimal method, you can use the standard Macintosh *Copy* and *Paste* commands to import an entire chart image directly into a Persuasion slide from another application. For example, let's say that you use Microsoft Excel and that you have a fancy macro that automatically grabs data from several worksheets and draws a chart of that data in Excel. Rather than import the data into Persuasion and redraw the chart from scratch, you can select and copy the chart in Excel and then paste it directly onto a Persuasion slide.

The caveat is that your chart is no longer linked to any data. If your data changes, you will have to return to Excel, edit the worksheet, recreate the chart in Excel, and then copy and paste the chart into Persuasion again.

If you have a series of charts that you want to bring into Persuasion, copy the charts to the Clipboard and then paste them into the Scrapbook. Then, when you open Persuasion, you can copy the charts out of the Scrapbook and directly into each slide.

Once you have pasted a chart in Persuasion, you can use the *Ungroup* command to separate its elements, and then you can use Persuasion's editing tools to change the imported chart's fill pattern, add color, and change the fonts.

If you want to copy data into the data sheet instead of copying a chart onto a slide, open the application with the data you want to import (in this example, we use Microsoft Excel). Then select the range of cells that you want copied and choose the *Copy* command from the Edit menu.

If you are using Multifinder, make sure that your Persuasion presentation is open and make Persuasion the active application by clicking somewhere on its window or by clicking on the icon in the far right of the menu bar until the Persuasion icon appears. Then, from the data sheet submenu in the File menu choose the *Work area* command. Click on the upper left cell in the Persuasion data sheet where you want the data to appear and choose *Paste* in the Edit menu. If all goes well, your Persuasion data sheet will contain a copy of the values from the Excel data sheet. Keep in mind that there is no hot link between the Excel spreadsheet and the Persuasion data sheet. If you change the data in the Excel worksheet, you will have to repeat this process to update your Persuasion chart.

Even if you are not using Multifinder, you can still use the Macintosh Clipboard to move data, since the Clipboard holds data until you switch the Macintosh off or you perform a subsequent cut or copy operation. The steps are the same as for using the Multifinder except after you copy the Excel data quit Excel, and open the data sheet in your presentation file. Then click in the upper left cell of where you want the Clipboard data to start and choose *Paste* from the Edit menu.

Plotting a Chart

After you've finished entering (or importing) and editing your data or once you've selected your external data, it is time to plot your chart. The first thing you have to do is tell Persuasion which slide you want the chart placed on. You can do this in two ways. In the outline view, click the outline heading (slide title or body text) of the slide where you want the chart to appear. Or, bring the chart destination slide into view. The slide where the chart is to appear is also referred to as the target slide.

Once you have selected a target slide, bring the Data sheet window back into view, if it is hidden, by choosing it from the Data sheet submenu. Next, drag over the range of cells that contains the data you want to chart, and click the *Plot* button. That's all there is to it. When you move the data sheet window out of the way, you will see the chart on the slide.

Persuasion creates the chart and positions it on the target slide. The chart is formatted according to whatever chart settings are selected in the Chart menu or, if the slide has an assigned master slide that contains a chart placeholder, then the newly created chart is formatted according to the specifications of the chart placeholder.

To see the results, click on the slide area at the bottom of the screen; this will bring the slide in front of the data sheet.

Data Sheet Commands

A chart always remains linked to a data sheet. Now that you have seen how to create a basic chart let's return to the data sheet to discuss some of its more advanced capabilities. Whenever you have to edit data and then replot your chart, you will have to return to the data sheet.

The *Plot, Replot,* and *Show* buttons at the top of the data sheet provide a close link between your data sheet and presentation slides. They help immensely in the task of managing your charts. Likewise, the arrow icons and the toggle box help you navigate through the sets of data on the data sheet that you have used to plot charts. Clicking on either the up or down arrow icons in the upper right corner of the data sheet window scrolls among the various sets of selected data throughout the data sheet. Each click brings you to a another set of data. The slide location of that selected data appears in the message window. The toggle box toggles between the currently selected data and the target chart's data set. Use the arrow icons and toggle box to quickly locate match data sets with their respective slides, or to plot a different set of data with an existing chart format.

All these tools make it easy to copy chart formats, review which charts belong to which data sheet information (especially helpful when you use the data sheet to plot several charts), and more. Before we discuss how to do all this, let's look at the data sheet itself and the commands and tools that you see there.

Plot Button

We have seen that after you select the data you want to chart, you click the *Plot* button to tell Persuasion to create a chart. By choosing a different chart format from the Chart menu, and then using the *Plot* button a second time, you can place more than one chart representation on a slide. Figure 10.19, for example, shows how helpful it can be to have a stacked column chart next to a standard column chart. Although the information presented is the same, the viewer gets two different perspectives of that information.

You can also use the *Plot* button to place an chart using the same data set on another slide in the presentation. To do this, just select the destination slide and click the *Plot* button. Persuasion will create a chart using the same data on another slide. If you choose a master slide with a chart placeholder, the new chart will conform to the format specified by the slide's chart placeholder. If you aren't using a chart placeholder you can format your chart before you click the *Plot* button by first selecting the data you want to chart, and then making the various format choices in the Chart menu before you click the *Plot* button. Of course, you can always change your mind later and replot the chart.

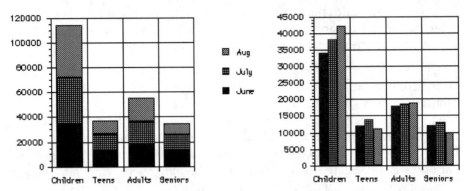

Figure 10.19.   You can use the *Plot* button to place separate charts on a slide using the same data but different chart formats.

Replot Button

Next to the *Plot* button is the *Replot* button. The *Replot* button serves two purposes. First, it updates and redraws a chart based on any changes you make to the data sheet, since Persuasion does not replot charts with new data until requested to do so. Second, you can use the *Replot* command to change a chart format. Select the data set for the chart you want to change and then make all format changes in the Chart menu. When you then click the *Replot* button, Persuasion will replace the older chart with the new format. If you click *Plot* instead of *Replot* Persuasion will add another chart to the slide in addition to the one that's already there. Let's go back to our example.

The zoo director realized that her attendance income for February was understated by $5,000. To update her chart, she must first select the chart in with the incorrect figure and then choose *Get data* from the Chart menu. Persuasion will open the data sheet window and automatically select the data set that was used for this chart. She then clicks on the cell with the erroneous number and types the correct number, and the *Replot* button becomes dimmed. As she starts to type the new figure, however, the old number disappears.

Before she can replot the chart with the new data she has to select the range of cells for the entire chart again. Rather than figure out the range mentally, she only has to click on the toggle box icon in the upper right of the data sheet window to have Persuasion automatically reselect the entire data set for the chart. Now, with the *Replot* button active again, she only has to click on *Replot* and Persuasion replots the chart taking into account the revised data. You can use the toggle box icon any time you edit a chart to switch between the currently selected data (in this case the single cell she edited) and the entire data selection range for the chart.

The zoo director knew which chart she wanted to replot before she made the edits. But what if she didn't know where the chart was located? In this case, she could have clicked on one of the arrow icons next to the toggle box. Each time you click the arrow icons Persuasion moves you from data set to data set. Each time you click on an arrow, Persuasion highlights another data range. And for each selection, chart format and chart location appears in the message box next to the arrows. The arrows and toggle box let you review and keep track of what data goes with what charts.

The *Replot* command has other uses, too. You can replot after you diminish or add to the selection range of a chart, or after you select an entirely new set of data to replace the present data. Let's say that the director wants to replace the current chart with figures for 1990 and 1991 only. First, she selects the six cell block of data in the data sheet. Then, she clicks the *Replot* button. The new data immediately replaces the old with the chart format intact.

The difference between *Plot* and *Replot* is that the *Plot* button always creates a new chart, whereas the *Replot* button is for changing a chart or its data.

The *Replot* command is only available when a target chart is specified in the message box next to the arrow icon. If the target chart description in the message box is italicized, Persuasion is warning you that the current selection range is different from current chart you are about to replot.

Show Button

The *Show* button is a navigational command that brings you from a data sheet selection to the slide on which the corresponding chart is displayed. Using the arrows in the data sheet window, you can move from data set to data set. To view the chart for a particular data set, highlight the appropriate data set and then click the *Show* button. Persuasion immediately moves to the target slide for that data set. To view the chart click anywhere in the slide window (or choose the slide view from the Windows command under the Apple menu) to bring the chart's slide in front and move the data sheet to the background.

Reusing a Chart's Format on Another Slide

Once you have spent the time creating and customizing a successful chart, you may look for an opportunity to reuse the chart format elsewhere in your presentation. There are two ways to do this. You can use the *Define format* command in the Chart menu. This lets you save the format of a selected chart simply by giving it a name. The names of any defined chart formats you have saved will appear as choices in the *Chart format* submenu.

Second, you can copy a chart format from one slide to another. First, and most simply, select the slide where the new chart is to appear. (If you are in the outline view, select the slide title; or, if you are in the slide view, display the target slide for the new chart.) Then, in the data sheet window click on the up or down arrow icons to cycle through the plotted sets of data. As you cycle through the data sets, the text window text box describes the type of chart assigned to each data set. Stop when you see the chart format you want to copy. Now, drag through the new data you want to plot and click the *Plot* button. Persuasion will plot an entirely new chart using the chart format displayed in the data sheet text box.

Note: Persuasion places no limit on the number of times you can use the same data for different charts on different slides. You can also create a chart or several charts based on portions of a single data set.

Customizing Charts

Often you may have special needs that require more than the the basic repertoire of chart formats. For example, if you are drawing a pie chart you may want to separate one piece of the pie for special attention. Or, you may want to change the pattern or color of a bar or column, or even change a single line width. Persuasion provides special procedures and tools for making both small and large scale changes to a chart. The number of changes you can make to your charts are limited only by your imagination rather than by any constraints within Persuasion.

Selecting and Subselecting

When you click once on a chart it becomes selected. You can tell because the chart is surrounded by eight small black boxes, or handles. But what do you do when you want to make a change to just one part of the chart, say to change the type face of the chart's labels? In Chapter 6, *Working with Objects*, you learned how to select and then manipulate objects in Persuasion. Working with a chart is similar to working with other types of objects. But before you can edit a chart, you need to learn Persuasion's special techniques for selecting particular chart elements.

The technique you will normally use to edit a chart is known as subselection. By subselecting a chart, you have access to three normally invisible levels of chart detail. You can progressively select *a)* an entire chart; *b)* all elements of the same type; or *c)* an individual element. Imagine you wanted to change the color assigned to one series of values in a stacked bar chart. You would use the *Subselect* command to select all the bar segments of that color and change the color just once. The new color would affect all of the selected bar segments at once.

Parts that you can subselect include fill patterns, fill colors, line patterns and line colors, text, font, and style for any of the following:

- Any graphical element of a data series (also including face, depth for a whole series, or one element of a series);

- Labels, headings, legends, or legend items;

- Grid lines and axes.

The *Subselect* command works by a series of clicks and double-clicks that effectively let you access different levels of chart detail. Before you use the *Subselect* command, select your chart as a single unit by clicking once anywhere on it. It should be selected as in Figure 10.20.

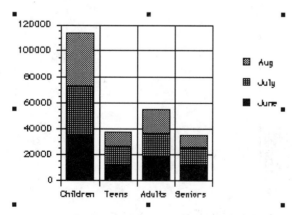

Figure 10.20. Clicking once on a chart will select the chart as a single unit.

Then select the first level of detail by double-clicking on the object you want to get at. In this example we double-clicked on a bar. When you double-click, more of the chart's elements become "selectable" as in Figure 10.21.

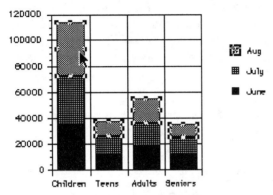

Figure 10.21. Double-clicking a chart that is already selected subselects another level of the chart.

Finally, to break the chart down into yet one more level of detail, point to the single element you want to change and double-click on it (see Figure 10.22). Note that you can also go right to this third level by triple-clicking on it.

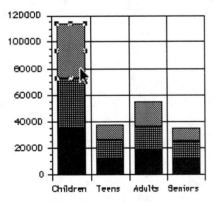

Figure 10.22. The third level of subselecting allows you to access smaller elements of the chart.

After you have made your changes to a particular element in the chart, you only need to click once anywhere in the slide window and Persuasion will regroup all of the chart elements together into a single unit again. To edit another element on the chart, follow the subselect steps again to get to that particular element.

The trickiest thing about the *Subselect* command is getting your point and click technique perfected. Each time you point and double-click, you have to be sure to keep the mouse pointed at the element you want to edit. Otherwise, Persuasion will restore the chart to a single object instead of bringing you to a deeper level of detail.

Here are a few of the cases when the subselect command is useful:

- Change the color or pattern of all bars of a single category. Click to select chart and then double-click while pointing to any of the bars in the category you want to change. Use the Effect menu to choose a new color for the set of selected bars.

- Change the color or pattern of a single bar within a category. Double-click on the element or click to select the chart. Then double-click again while pointing to any of the bars in the category you want to change. So far, these steps are the same as in the example above. Now point to the single bar you want to edit and double-click again. Just that one bar should be selected at this point. Choose the new color or pattern from the Effects menu.

- Change the font of all labels in both the x- and y-axis. Click once to select entire chart, and then double-click on any label. All labels should now be selected. Select a new font from the Text menu and both axes' labels will take on the new font.

- Change the font of just the labels on the horizontal axis. Click to select entire chart, and then double-click on any label in the horizontal axis. Both sets of labels should now be selected. Now point to the horizontal labels and double-click again. Select a new font from the Text menu and it will be applied to just the category labels.

Grouping and Ungrouping

The *Subselect* command is a great convenience. There will be times, however, when you need to edit a particular chart detail that is too small to get at with the subselect command. For these occasions, you need to use the *Ungroup* command successively to break down the chart into its smallest selectable parts and then the *Group* command to restore the chart to one unit. The *Ungroup* and *Group* commands operate with charts as they do with other objects in Persuasion as we have already discussed in Chapter 6, *Working with Objects*.

Note that ungrouping allows you to make any sort of change and by regrouping, your change is reattached. However, if you replot the chart, you will lose the enhancements you made by ungrouping.

Regrouping

After you have ungrouped a chart and made your changes you should regroup the chart again immediately. Choose *Regroup* from the Draw menu (or press *Command-R*). The *Regroup* command takes the newly edited element and incorporates it back into its original group.

You must often use *Regroup* more than once. Successive regroups take you in effect back through the group levels you used to ungroup the chart.

Enhancing Your Chart

Once you know about how to break down a chart into its component parts with subselection and the *Ungroup* command, you are ready to apply some customization to your charts. With a little tweak here and there, you can tailor your charts to highlight the information that's most important for your audience.

For example, you can use the Effect menu to change the chart's line styles, patterns, and colors, or the Text menu to change fonts, sizes, styles, and text color.

The Chart Menu

The Chart menu, as seen in Figure 10.23, has several commands that are used specifically for enhancing charts. On occasion, some of these command are dimmed when you call up the Chart menu. Either you have forgotten to click on the chart you want to change, or the command you are trying to use does not work with your particular chart's format.

Throughout this chapter, we have discussed what some of the Chart menu commands do. For example, we have shown how to use the *Chart* format command to change how a chart looks and the *Get Data* command to call up the data sheet window and highlight the range of cells that comprise a particular chart. Now let's take a moment to see the other commands.

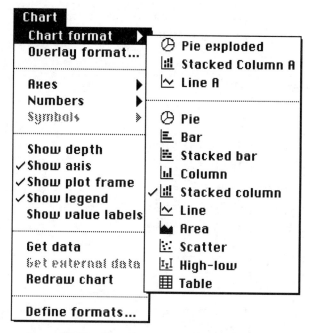

Figure 10.23. The Chart menu lists all of the chart formats available in Persuasion.

Overlay Format...

Sometimes it is effective to overlay two types of charts to make a point. One chart can have one set of data, and the other chart another set. Or, you can use the same data charted in two different formats, one overlaying the other. Table 10.1 shows the combinations of overlay charts that Persuasion allows.

To combine charts, start by plotting your primary chart. Open the data sheet, select the data you want to plot, and choose your chart format for the primary chart. By default, this primary chart appears behind the next chart you create.

The next step is to create the overlay format. From the Chart menu choose Overlay format..., and make your format choice for this second chart. Any formats that are incompatible with the primary chart format appear dimmed in the pop-up menu. (Refer to the charts in Table 10.1. Next, you will need to type the number of data series that you want to appear in the overlay (the default is 1) and click OK. Finally, click *Plot* in the data sheet window, and then close the data sheet work area to see your results.

You can always add an overlay to an existing chart. Click on the primary chart to select it, choose the *Overlay format* command from the Chart menu, and proceed as above.

Table 10.1.   Chart overlay type matrix.

	Pie	Bar	Stacked bar	Column	Stacked column	Line	Area	Scatter	High-low	Table
Pie										
Bar	X	X								
Stacked bar	X	X								
Column			X	X	X	X		X		
Stacked column			X	X	X	X		X		
Line			X	X	X	X		X		
Area			X	X	X	X		X		
Scatter										
High-low			X	X	X	X		X		
Table										

Axes Submenu

Switch Axes

This command rotates the chart 90 degree. Horizontal and vertical axes are exchanged so that column charts become bar charts and vice versa. Note that the *Switch axes* command affects the chart only leaving data sheet itself unchanged.

To use this command, simply click on a chart and then choose the *Switch axes* command. Persuasion immediately redraws the chart with the axes values switched.

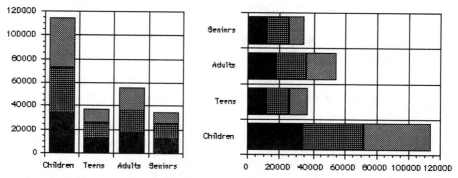

Figure 10.24. The *Switch axes* command, before and after.

Grid/Tick Options...

The options in this dialog box allow you to set where you want the chart's tick marks and grid to appear and whether you want major or minor marks in the chart.

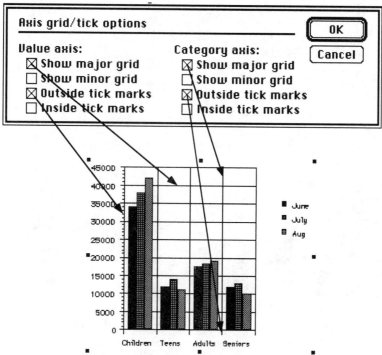

Figure 10.25. The Axis grid/tick options dialog box allows you to define the specifics for a chart's grid and tick marks.

Value/Category Axis Format...

The options in the value and category axis format dialog boxes allow you to change the plot range, tick mark spacing, and scale type for the chart.

Whenever Persuasion creates a chart it makes some assumptions about the plot range—the minimum and maximum values on an axis. It computes the minimum and maximum values for each axis based on the minimum and maximum values in the data set for the chart. You can override its calculations by typing your own minimum and maximum values. If you manually override Persuasion's settings the *Auto* box becomes unchecked. If you change your mind and want Persuasion to scale the axis then check the *Auto* box.

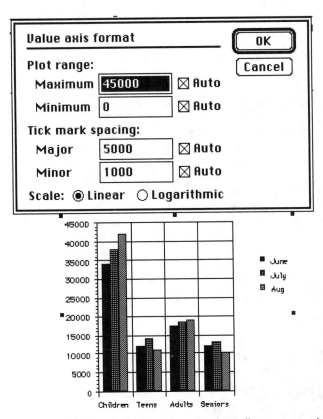

Figure 10.26. The Value axis dialog box allows you to change the default plot range, tick mark spacing, and scale for a chart.

Tick marks come in two sizes. Major tick marks are larger than minor ones. The values you enter in the tick mark text boxes let you define what are major and minor tick marks. If you check the *Auto* box Persuasion will make the calculation for you. You actually turn tick marks on and off in the Grid/Ticks dialog box.

Checking the *Linear* or *Logarithmic* buttons can radically change the scale of a chart. Choosing logarithmic values is convenient for displaying data points that span a great range of values.

Label Options

You can use the *Label options* command to define what ranges in the data sheet you would like to use as category and value labels. By default, in any selected range Persuasion expects to use the data in the top row as value labels and data in the first column as category labels.

Shortcut: You can open the Label options dialog box by holding the Option key while you click the Plot button in the data sheet window.

Note: For pie charts, Persuasion uses the information in the first column as labels since a pie chart has no axis per se.

Numbers Submenu

When you enter numerical information into a data sheet you don't have to worry about formatting numbers because Persuasion will do that for you automatically. You can always reformat numbers by selecting a chart and then picking a new format from this menu. Persuasion will update the chart with the new formatting. Format changes you make from this menu do not appear on the data sheet, only in the chart.

Table 10.2 shows the result of each formatting command after we simply enter "12345" into a data sheet cell.

You can select a combination of *Format*, *Negative values*, and *Commas*. For example, when you check *Currency*, you can also type the number of decimal places, and check *Commas*. Using multiple formatting commands allows you to further customize numerical information.

Table 10.2

Option	After formatting
General	12345
Fixed (if set for 3 decimal places)	123410.000
Currency	$123410.00
Scientific	1E+04
Percent	1234500%
Negative values*	-12345 or (12345)
Commas*	12,345
Decimal places*	Works in combination with the fixed or currency options

*   These formatting options can be used in combination with other formatting commands.

Symbols

The *Symbols* command on the Chart menu changes the style of an entire series of a selected symbol for line, scatter, or high-low charts. Figure 10.27 shows the symbol icon options that are available. To change a set of symbols, you must double-click on one of the symbols you want to change. This automatically selects all of the symbols of the chosen series.

Show Commands

The group of *Show* commands are pretty much self-explanatory. Choosing a combination of these commands hides and displays different parts and dimensions of a chart.

Show Depth

The depth command is effective if you don't have too many plotted points to start with. Otherwise, it can add to the confusion of trying to understand the chart. Depth works particularly well with pie, bar, and column charts.

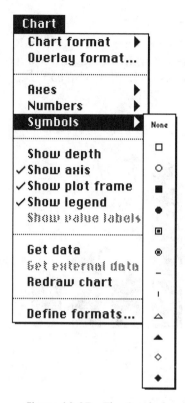

Figure 10.27. The Symbol menu is only available for those charts that use symbols. Select the value whose symbol you want to change, and then choose the new symbol from the Symbol menu.

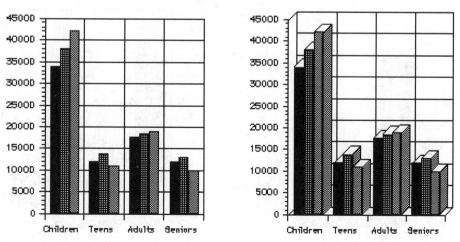

Figure 10.28. The *Depth* command, before and after.

Show Axis

This command shows and hides the axis and grid lines of a chart. Ordinarily you will want the axis to be visible. However, in instances where axis values are less important that the bars or columns in a chart, you can elect to make the axis invisible.

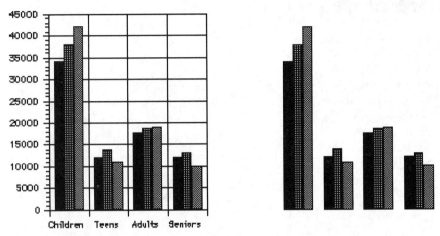

Figure 10.29. The *Axis* command, on and off.

Show Plot Frame

When this command is checked, Persuasion displays lines marking the top and right boundaries of a chart's plot range.

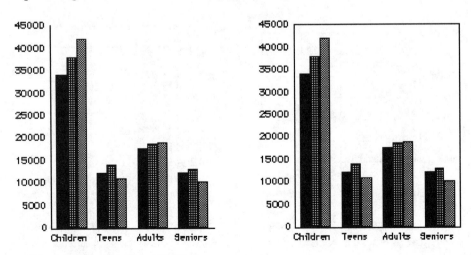

Figure 10.30. The *Show Plot frame* command.

Show Legend

A legend is a very important element of a chart. In a pie chart you don't need a legend because Persuasion labels each piece of pie automatically. You also don't need a legend with other simple charts. However, if there is information to be shared using a legend, be sure to turn on the *Show legend* command.

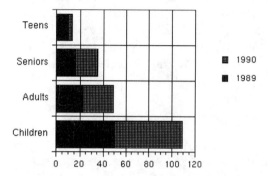

Figure 10.31. The *Show legend* command displays the legend alongside the chart to identify the bars.

Show Value Labels

The *Show value labels* command adds the numerical values to each bar or pie piece. Thus, a viewer is not only able to see the relative size of each chart element, he/she can also see the exact value of the element. If your viewers need to see exact information but your chart is already crowded, consider adding a table next to the chart. The task of the table is to convey the numerical information while the chart would show the numbers graphically.

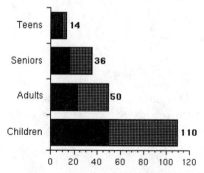

Figure 10.32. The *Show value labels* command places actual values on the chart giving the viewer both a numerical and graphical representation of the data.

Get Data and Get External Data

These two commands on the Chart menu are similar: *Get data* opens Persuasion's internal data sheet and *Get external data* opens a data file from an external application, allowing you to refresh the links to your chart. Both commands will bring you to the appropriate data series for the currently selected chart. (This is in contrast to the *Data sheet* command in the File menu, which simply brings up the work area sheet with no selection.) If your chart was plotted using data from an external source, both *Get data* and *Get external data* will be available. (*Get data* allows you to edit the current data for the chart internally; *Get external data* lets you update the links.) Unless you have a chart selected, the *Get data* and *Get external data* commands are dimmed.

Redraw Chart

When drawing programs such as Persuasion resize a chart, line ends may be scaled less than perfectly. This command lets you recalculate the chart optimally for its new size. Use this command after doing a significant amount of resizing if you feel your chart looks flawed. Small resizing doesn't need a redraw, and also the process causes you to lose enhancements you may have made when you ungrouped the chart.

Other Chart Enhancements

In addition to the commands in the Chart menu, there are commands scattered in other menus that are useful for adding additional interest to a chart.

The *Flip* commands found in the Draw menu can have a dramatic impact on a chart. Choose one of these commands when you need to reverse the order of an axis.

Flip Horizontal

This command inverts a selected chart horizontally. For example, if your chart is labeled left to right, from January to December, and you choose the *Flip horizontal*, Persuasion reverses the orientation of the chart so it reads from December to January along the horizontal axis. The vertical axis also moves from the left to the right side of the chart

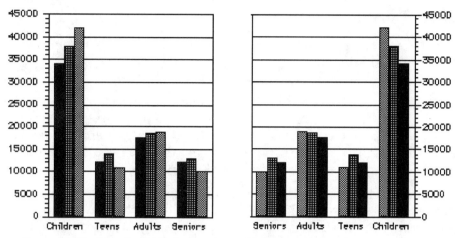

Figure 10.33. The *Flip horizontal* command before (*left*) and after (*right*).

Flip Vertical

This command inverts a selected chart vertically. For example, instead of pushing columns in a column chart upward, the columns all hang from the top like icicles. This command also moves the horizontal axis to the top of the chart. This command gives you a choice of how to present deficit information, either by using the standard format that shows the deficit's "growth" or flipped vertically to illustrate how far from zero deficit the budget has fallen.

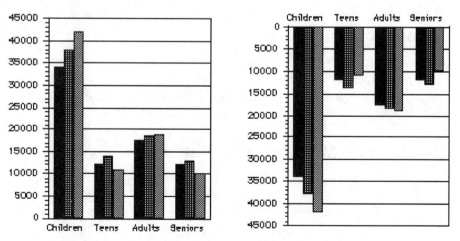

Figure 10.34.   The *Flip vertical* command before (*left*) and after (*right*).

Text Tables

So far we have discussed conventional charts that use bars, columns, and data points to bring information to life. There is one other chart type in Persuasion that merits special discussion. This is the table.

Why have a special table format when you can use text and lines to build a table from scratch? Because the table format simplifies the hassle of aligning text and lines that make up a table. By simply entering your table information into a data sheet (exactly as you do when you are plotting a chart), you can let Persuasion do the work.

Like a chart, a table helps the eye connect relationships, albeit not as dramatically as does a standard chart. But unlike a chart, a table is more precise since the viewer sees the actual data instead of a graphic interpretation of that data. In situations where you want both the visual power of a chart and the data to back the chart up, set up a chart and table side-by-side on the same slide.

Charts and tables have similarities, too. Both use a combination of text and graphics to help the viewer group the information at hand. For the most part, Persuasion treats charts and tables alike. Both use the data sheet as their foundation. And, like a chart, you can specify a table's position on an actual slide or via a table placeholder on a master slide. Tables are more precise because they use actual values in cells instead of converting the values to bars or the like. Charts are more effective, however, in illustrating trends over time.

Anatomy of a Table

At first glance, a Persuasion table looks like a simple array of rows and columns and in some senses it is. But, a Persuasion table also has some underlying intelligence that makes manipulating tabular information easier. This intelligence makes it easier for you to format a table.

Selecting and Subselecting a Table

Select and *Subselect* commands work the same way with tables as they do with charts. Using the *Subselect* commands gives you an appreciation for the underlying definitions that Persuasion attaches to different parts of the table. For example, if you double-click on any cell in the top row of a table, the entire row becomes selected because Persuasion assumes that you want to make a change to the labels in the top row. Likewise, double-clicking on any cell (except for the top left cell) in the first column selects all of the cells in the first column. Double-clicking on any cells elsewhere in the table selects the entire table (except for the first row and column). Double-clicking again on that cell selects the cell's entire column (or all cells in the same column).

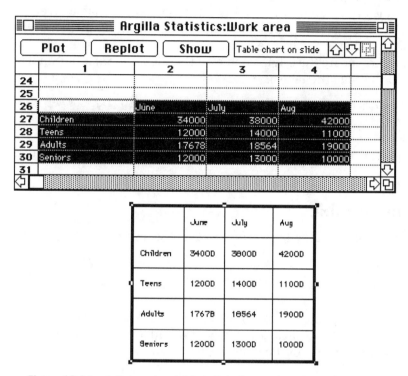

Figure 10.35.   A Persuasion table is based on a data sheet the same as a chart is.

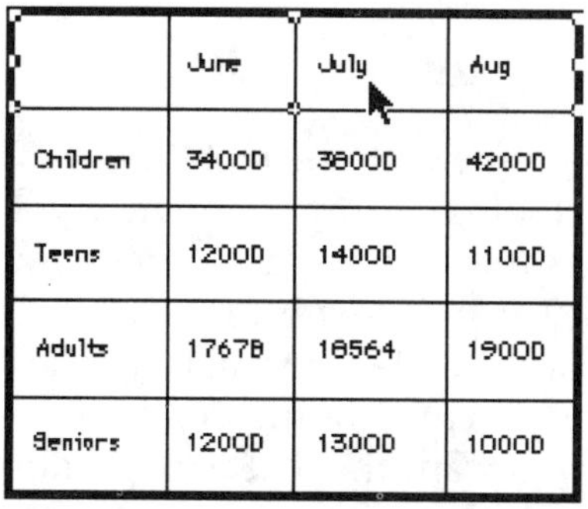

Figure 10.36.   You can subselect parts of a table as you can with a chart. For example, double click on any text in the top row and Persuasion selects the entire top row. You can then change the attributes of the top row all at once.

Plotting a Table

You create a table exactly as you plot a chart—by opening a data sheet, entering data, and selecting the data range by dragging over it. Then, once you choose the target slide, you click on the *Plot* button. After Persuasion draws the table on the slide, you can drag it to position the table precisely where you want it. The *Replot* and *Show* buttons also working the same way for tables as they do for charts. Use *Replot* if you change the data in the table and you want to update the original table on the slide; the *Show* button will move you to the slide the table is on.

The same rules of simplicity apply to tables as apply to charts. Keep your table as small as possible, about five columns by five rows. If you cannot live with those constraints, then see if you can break your table data into subsections that will allow you to create tables small enough for easy comprehension.

Enhancing a Table

After Persuasion creates a table, you can exercise a number of customizing options.

Editing Table Data

There are two ways to edit tabular data in a table. You can change table data on the data sheet and click *Replot* (as you would for a chart), or you can make the changes directly in the table itself.

Note: Persuasion maintains a dynamic link between a table and data sheet. When you make a direct change to a table, that change is automatically made to the data sheet as well.

To edit the text in the table, view the target slide with the table you want to change, and click on the text tool in the toolbox. Now click where you want to insert text, (or double-click if you want to replace text) just as you would in a word processing document. Type the new text into the table. If the new text becomes wider than the width of the table column, Persuasion automatically wraps the text to the next line, increasing the depth of the row to accommodate the additional text. If you want the text to appear on a single line you can increase the width of the column.

Changing Column Width

Changing the width of a column in a table is as easy as double-clicking on the border you want to change and then dragging the border left or right to its new position. After you have finished moving it, Persuasion automatically rewraps the text in each affected column to fit the new width as you can see in Figure 10.37.

	June	July	Aug
Children	3400D	3800D	4200D
Teens	1200D	1400D	1100D
Adults	1767B	18564	1900D
Seniors	1200D	1300D	1000D

Figure 10.37. Note the selected column border. You can change the width of a column by dragging its right column divider to the left or right.

Changing Text Appearance

You can change the font, style, size, color, and alignment of text in a table by first selecting the text and then making the change. The *Subselect* command comes in handy for these changes because instead of having to select individual cells to change, you can click on the section of the table to subselect the particular section and then choose the command you want from the Text menu. For example, if you select the entire chart and then change the font, the entire chart will have the new font. If, however, you subselect just part of the table, such as the value section, and then you change the font, Persuasion will change the entire selected section's text at once.

You can have a large degree of control over text attributes in table cells by using the text tool. You can change the font and style attributes of individual cells and text characters. Note, however, that these enhancements are not retained if the table is replotted.

Adding a Shadow to a Table

To get an added feeling of dimensionality, you can, depending on the effect you seek, use either the Chart menu's *Add depth* command or the *Shadow* command from the Effect menu.

The *Add depth* command does not offer any options. It is either on or off. You cannot combine *Add depth* with the *Shadow* command. In addition to the depth, top, and sides of a table, there are three regions in a table that can be filled and colored: the top row, the leftmost row (exclusive of the top left cell), and all remaining cells.

To add emphasis to a table, you can also add graduated fill patterns to either the first column, first row, all other cells, or any combination of these by selecting the area and then choosing one of the graduated fill patterns from the Effects menu.

	June	July	Aug
Children	3400D	3800D	4200D
Teens	1200D	1400D	1100D
Adults	1767B	18564	1900D
Seniors	1200D	1300D	1000D

	June	July	Aug
Children	3400D	3800D	4200D
Teens	1200D	1400D	1100D
Adults	1767B	18564	1900D
Seniors	1200D	1300D	1000D

Figure 10.38. The Shadow command provides 39 shadow pattern choices. You can also combine a pattern with a color from the Shadow color command.

On the other hand, the *Shadow* command offers a palette of patterns and colors, making it the better choice if you want more than just depth lines added to the table. To add shadow, select the chart and then choose the *Shadow* command. If you want to use colored patterns, refer to the *Shadow color* command also in the Effect menu. You can choose a combination of pattern and color for shadows. If you want a color other than the eight listed in the *Shadow color* command, select *Other* and choose from the full palette or the Macintosh color picker.

Saving Chart and Table Formats

So far in this chapter we have discussed how to format individual charts and tables. But what if you use the same format over and over? Or what if you customize a chart format of your own? Do you have to reformat manually every chart you use in your presentation? Hardly!

There are two ways to reuse chart formats in Persuasion. The first option is to set up a chart placeholder on a master slide. Whenever you choose to use this particular slide, Persuasion applies the format of the chart placeholder to the data you select in the data sheet. A full discussion of placeholders appears in Chapter 13, *Building an Autotemplate*. However, to summarize the steps for creating a chart placeholder, move to the master slide where you want the chart placeholder to appear and choose *Add chart* from the Master menu. Then enter the number of columns and rows that you want to plot and click *OK*. Don't worry about exact numbers here—you can change the data range on a slide-by-slide basis while retaining the same chart format. Persuasion needs to know the approximate dimensions of the chart so that it can estimate the size of the chart on the slide.

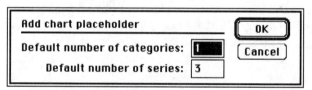

Figure 10.39. The chart placeholder dialog box permits you to enter the default number of categories and series that will appear in a new chart. You can always edit these choices on an individual slide.

Persuasion positions the chart placeholder on the master slide. Position the placeholder and make whatever custom changes you want in the Chart menu. If you want to add depth, then choose that command. You can also add special effects by using commands from the Effect menu or change the font and style of labels or text. Basically, whatever changes you make to the chart placeholder will take effect each time you use the placeholder in your presentation. Note too, however, that all formatting for a placeholder can be changed for individual slides. You are never bound to the placeholder format.

You can also create a table placeholder. But, instead of entering the number of categories and series to be plotted, you enter the number of rows and columns you want in the default table. Then you dress up the table with special shadow effects, a new font, and any other embellishments you care to make.

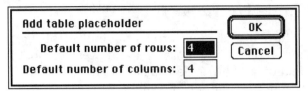

Figure 10.40. The Add table placeholder dialog box asks you to define the dimensions of the table. Later, you can insert and delete rows and columns as your needs require.

Custom Chart Formats

Creating a chart placeholder is one solution for customizing your tables and chart. However, charts take up a lot of memory. The more changes, and the more categories and series you allot to them, the more overhead you have to have to pay. You can use the *Define formats* command on the Chart menu instead to specify a format with all the attributes you want and then save it. From the menu you can apply it to a chart placeholder making less demands on your system's memory.

The *Define formats* command saves a custom chart format and places the name of this custom format in the Chart format menu together with Persuasion's own formats. You can then use this custom format on any chart in your presentation, or you can even apply the custom format to a chart placeholder.

Let's look at an example. Say that you need several pie charts in a presentation. Each chart has different data, but the data is related so you want each chart to share the identical format.

The first step is to customize the first chart exactly as you want it. Edit the patterns, move the piece out, and format the text.

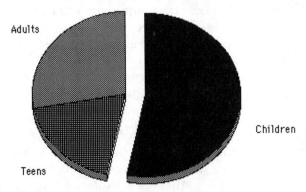

Figure 10.41. A custom pie chart.

When you are finished customizing the chart, choose *Define format* from the Chart menu. Notice that Persuasion has already attached the pie chart icon, so all you have to do is name the chart—try something like "Exploded pie"—and click OK.

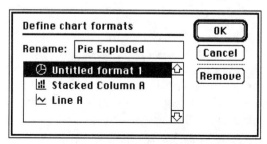

Figure 10.42. Persuasion allows you to save chart and table formats using the Define formats command.

Now take a look in the Chart format submenu, and you will see that Pie exploded has been added to the list of chart formats.

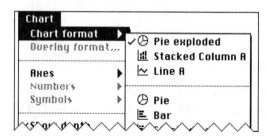

Figure 10.43. The name of the custom chart format has been added to the top of the Chart format submenu.

If you want to remove a custom chart format, choose *Define format* from the Chart menu, click on the format you want to erase, and click the Remove button.

Organizational Charts

In addition to being able to include a conventional chart or table on a slide, Persuasion also has the capability of creating what we commonly think of as an organizational chart. This particular chart format is often used to display a company's hierarchy of power. However, the organizational chart can also be useful when you want to illustrate a point using a conceptual model.

The method for creating organizational charts in Persuasion is different than for other types of charts. Typically, though, you can do as follows. Type your hierarchy on a slide, as you would for body text. Change the master for that slide to "Org. master" and you are done. (An organization chart master is any master with an organizational chart placeholder on it. Each of Persuasion's Autotemplates have one.

When you are creating organizational charts, you cannot place a free-hand organizational chart on a slide; you can only create an organizational chart via a master slide with an organizational chart placeholder. Also, you enter the information for an organizational chart using the structure of a standard presentation outline. If you make changes to the outline headings, those changes automatically update the related organizational chart.

Figure 10.44 shows the relationship between outline headings and levels in the organizational chart. The default number of levels for an organizational chart is 3. The default number of boxes (or entries) per level is 5. In all, you can have up to 10 levels in an organizational chart.

As you can see, the slide title becomes the title of the organizational chart. The next level heading becomes the summit. Each level after that (until you reach the maximum level of 10) becomes another row in the chart.

Creating an Organizational Chart

There is more than one way to create an organizational chart in Persuasion. Perhaps the easiest way is simply to use one of the organizational chart masters that come with each of Persuasion's AutoTemplates. If need be, you can edit the organizational chart placeholder. In situations where you need more than one organizational chart format, it is useful to base your new org. chart master on the existing one and then make the changes to the new organizational chart master placeholder.

To copy an organizational chart master, choose *New* from the *Go to master* command in the View menu. The dialog box that appears gives you the opportunity to base the new master on an existing one. Choose a master with an organizational chart placeholder already on it (see Figure 10.45).

Another possibility is to make a new master slide with an organizational chart placeholder on it from scratch. When you create a new master, the Master menu appears on the menu bar. Choose the command called *Add org. chart*. Before placing the placeholder, Persuasion wants some general size information about the organizational chart. Type your best estimates in the box, but don't worry since you can always adjust the organizational chart on a slide-by-slide basis.

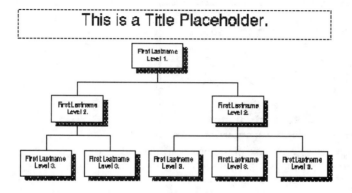

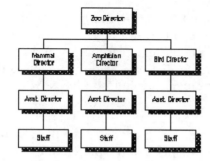

Figure 10.44. The underlying structure for an organizational chart is the outline. Each level in an outline becomes a different level in the organizational chart.

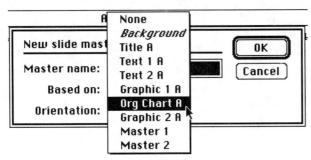

Figure 10.45. The New master dialog box gives you the chance to base
your new organizational chart master on an existing one.

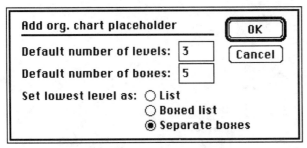

Figure 10.46. The choices you make in the org chart dialog box define
the size and box placement within the organizational
chart placeholder on the master slide.

Set the default number of levels, and the default number of boxes at each
level. Then choose to have Persuasion list the lowest level in the chart either
as a *List*, *Boxed list*, and *Separate boxes*. Click *OK*.

Note: Sometimes you may find the *Add org. chart* command dimmed in
the Master menu when you want to use it. This is because a master
slide cannot include both a body text placeholder and an organizational chart placeholder. If the *Add org. chart* command is dimmed,
select the body text placeholder and choose *Cut*. Now the *Add org.
chart* command is available.

Once Persuasion displays the organizational chart placeholder you can
change its defaults by subselecting parts of the placeholder and making edits. For example, to change the font for the second level select the org. chart
and then double-click on a box in the second level. Persuasion will select all
boxes in the level. Any changes you make at this point will affect all boxes
in the level in every slide that uses this master.

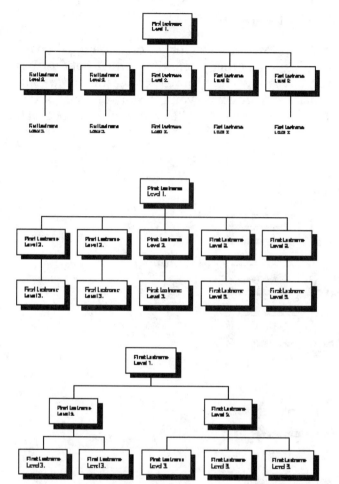

Figure 10.47. The list, boxed list, and separate box options in the Add
org. chart dialog box give you choices for displaying the
lowest level in the organizational chart.

You cannot edit an individual box at the master slide level, but you can
edit a one on an individual slide. To make such an edit move to normal slide
view and use the standard select and subselect techniques that you would
use for charts and tables to isolate elements of the org. chart. The subselect
commands let you tinker with almost every level of an org. chart. Try to
avoid using the *Ungroup* command at any cost since once you ungroup an
org. chart it loses its link with the outline. If you ungroup an org. chart and
then make changes in the outline, the changes will not be carried over to
the chart. You will have to delete the old chart and create a new org. chart to
have the new edits automatically appear in the org. chart.

Organizational Chart Formats

The "top-down" format is most common for an organizational chart. However, Persuasion provides some other interesting format options that can extend the usefulness of the org. chart format. Using the *Rotate* commands, Persuasion will rotate a chart giving you far more options for displaying organizational chart data. Figure 10.48 illustrates the results of each of the rotate commands on a single organizational chart.

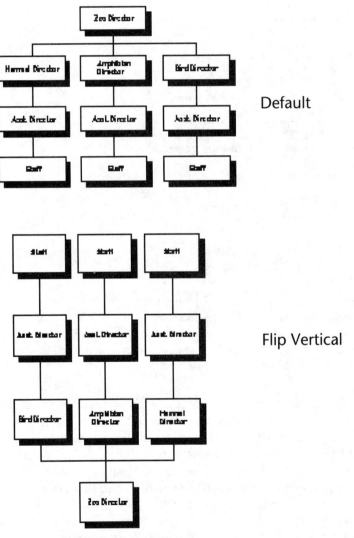

Default

Flip Vertical

Figures 10.48 and 10.49.   *(continued)*

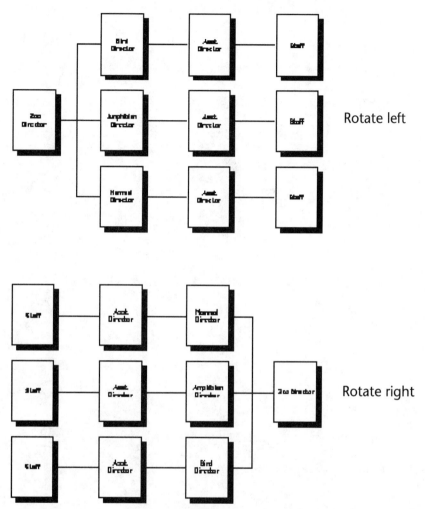

Rotate left

Rotate right

Figures 10.48 and 10.49. You are not limited to one organizational chart format. Using the *Flip vertical, Rotate right,* and *Rotate left* commands you can reorient your chart.

As you can see, Persuasion provides tools that go far beyond merely placing text on slides. Its charting capabilities rival those of stand-alone products. However, as you can see, there are many reasons to create your charts within Persuasion. You will benefit the most from its charting abilities if you take some time to experiment with its various charting tools. The payoff will be charts, tables, and organizational charts that improve both the effectiveness and the appearance of your presentation.

Chapter 11

Rearranging Your Presentation

Weary from lack of sleep, you've worked late into the night to meet your deadline. But, before you send your presentation for final output, you must take a final look at the show to check that the slides are in the best possible order. Slides can be out of order all too easily. Fortunately, it takes only a few clicks of the mouse to reorder your presentation, until it meets your satisfaction. Then you are ready to send it for final output.

Persuasion provides you with two methods for rearranging finished slides in a presentation. To view a presentation for content, the outliner is the best tool. To see how the slides segue graphically from one to the next, use the slide sorter which shows you several miniature slides on screen at once. Each of the methods has its strengths, and you should use both methods for reviewing every presentation.

Order by Outline

Regardless of whether or not you care to start building your presentation with the outliner, the outline view plays an important role toward the end of the presentation process. Using the outliner, you can review the presentation for clarity, consistency, and word choice, and make sure the slide sequence follows a careful step-by-step logical progression.

Let's say you are about done with your presentation and you want to double check to make sure the content of the presentation makes logical sense. To do this, return to the outline view from the View menu or by clicking on the outline icon in the slide window.

Sequencing slides using the outliner is identical to using the outliner to first organize a presentation. In fact, you may not have realized that each time you moved an outline heading as you created your presentation, Persuasion was quietly rearranging the order of the presentation itself. Detailed information on moving outline headings can be found in Chapter 5, *Working with the Outliner*. However, when you are using the outline to review the structure of a finished presentation there are two particular commands that will help you focus on the big picture rather than on individual outline headings. These are the *Hide body text* and *Hide notes text* commands.

Hiding Body and Notes Text

Sorting slides with the full outline in view can be as difficult as trying to see the forest through the trees; it is hard to concentrate on your slide titles when subtitles, multiple levels of body text, and several notes are also displayed on the display. To help you focus on the big picture, Persuasion allows you to hide the detail levels of your outline. Use the *Hide body text* or *Hide notes text* commands from the Outline menu to simplify your outline view. You can also click either or both of the body text and notes text icons in the lower left of the outline window. The result is a streamlined outline view with only slide titles showing. In a way, these commands are most useful for examining the logic of your presentation at several levels. As you sight inconsistencies in flow, you only have to drag the slide titles to new locations, and all of the slide's text and graphic elements will follow automatically.

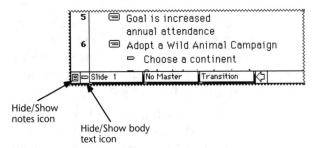

Figure 11.1   In the lower left of the outline view are the notes and body text icons. Clicking on either of these icons toggles all of the outline's notes or body text respectively.

Using the Slide Sorter

The outline view is perfect for getting a feel how your presentation flows from a content standpoint. But graphics also play an important role in how your audience perceives your presentation. For editing your presentation visually you can turn to the slide sorter view which displays as many ordered slides as will fit on your particular monitor. In the slide sorter view, you can both rearrange slides and you can reassign master slides. Since the outline and slides are dynamically linked, if you move slides in the sorter, Persuasion will automatically update the outline accordingly.

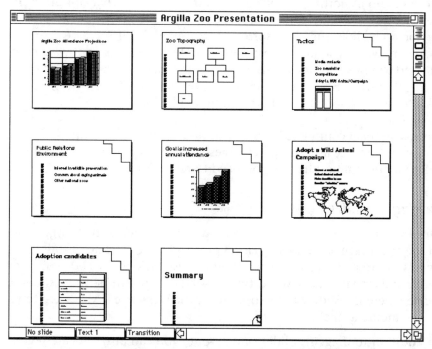

Figure 11.2   The slide sorter displays as many slides as will fit on your display. This view is on a standard Apple 13-inch monitor with the slide sorter window open as far as possible in Normal magnification in the Sorter menu.

Choose *Slide sorter* from the View menu to preview your presentation. In a few moments, the slide sorter window will open with several rows of miniature slides of your presentation reading left to right in their present order. The number of slides that fit in your display at one time depends on the size of your display and slide sorter window. To maximize the number of slides on the display, be sure the sorter window is open as large as possible. If you narrow the slide sorter window, Persuasion will display fewer slides across. If you want to view more slides at once, choose one of the sizes in the Sorter menu, 66%, 50%, or 20%. You compromise detail for smaller size, of course.

Those with color or gray scale monitors will find that viewing slides is a memory intensive operation that can radically slow your Macintosh's performance. In extreme cases where available memory is critically low and you have a lot of color in your presentation, your Macintosh may even grind to a complete halt. There is a "work-around," however.

When you use the slide sorter with a presentation that is color rich, do as much preliminary sorting as you can with the *Black and white* option in the Sorter menu selected. By eliminating the need for the Macintosh to process color for each slide, the slide sorter's performance will increase dramatically. Then, when you are almost done, deselect the *Black and white* command and review your slides. This way you can make sure you haven't made any ghastly mistakes with color choices. The rule of thumb is to keep the *Black and white* option checked for as long as possible.

> **Note:** The *Undo* command does not undo a sorting procedure! Before you start to make any drastic changes in your presentation, save the original presentation in case you need to return to it later.

Rearranging Slides

Once the slide sorter window is in view, you are free to rearrange slides with the advantage of seeing the visual progression from slide to slide. Let's say you want to make a change in the order. Just click on the slide you need to move and drag it to its new location. A solid bar appears between slides to indicate where the slide will be inserted in the sequence if you were to release the mouse at that moment.

In addition to dragging slides one-by-one, you can also relocate several slides at once. For example, let's insert slide 7,11, and 15 after slide 2. First, select the three slides you want to move using the shift-click technique. Then click and drag any of the select slides until the vertical bar appears between slide 2 and 3, and release the mouse. Voila! Persuasion moves all three slides to the new location and renumbers the rest of the slides in the show. The only thing you have to be aware of when you select several slides at once is that Persuasion will keep the sequential order of the slides you select when you move the set to its new location.

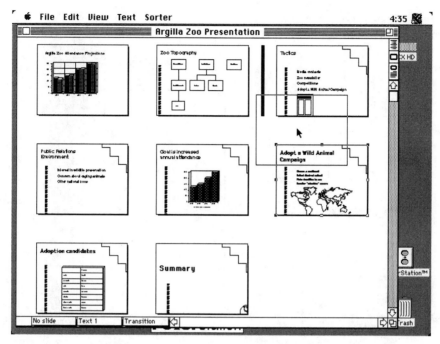

Figure 11.3   A solid bar between slides indicates where the dragged slide will be positioned if you release the mouse at that moment.

Reassigning Master Slides

In addition to rearranging slides, you can use the slide sorter to reassign slide masters. Viewing your slides side-by-side and being able to shuffle master slides gives you an opportunity to make some aesthetic transitions using different master slides.

To see what slide master is attached to a particular slide, click on a slide to select it. In the bottom left of the window, the middle pop-up box displays the master currently assigned to the selected slide. To change the master slide, click on the pop-up and choose a new master. You can also assign a single master to several slides at once by selecting more than one slide using the shift-click technique, and then choosing a new master from the assign master pop-up menu in the slide sorter window.

Not only can you assign master slides in the slide sorter view, but you can also assign transition effects to slides. Chapter 17, *Producing Overhead Transparencies*, describes transition effects in full detail.

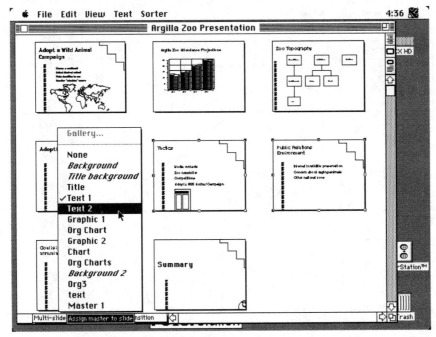

Figure 11.4　You can change the master slide on multiple slides by
selecting the slides using shift-click and then choosing a
new master from the master pop-up menu.

If you want a closer look at a slide in the sorter you can always double-click on the slide and Persuasion will immediately move you from the slide sorter view directly to the standard slide view where you can examine and edit the slide by itself.

The slide sorter is a valuable view that gives you final control over how you want the presentation sequenced, and it gives you a preview of how each slide leads visually from one to the next.

Chapter 12

Working with Speaker Notes and Handouts

In addition to producing the presentation slides themselves, Persuasion automatically produces two other ancillary presentation tools—speaker notes and handouts—based on your finished slides.

Speaker Notes

Notes are invaluable as prompts for a speaker, reducing the need for him or her to squint at the screen as they give their presentation. This way, too, the speaker can make sure he or she doesn't forget to mention any major points about the current slide on view.

A typical speaker note has a miniature of the presentation slide as well as speaker notes that the presenter can use to amplify his discussion of the slide's significance. For example, if an on-screen slide displays a chart, the speaker note for that slide might include the chart in miniature, alone or with information and further details about the purpose and importance of that chart.

Creating Speaker Notes

You create speaker notes by defining a master slide, similar to the way you create a master slide for your presentation itself. But there are a few differences that we need to explain.

The first thing is to place the notes master slide in view by choosing *Notes master* from the View menu. If you are using one of Persuasion's Auto-Templates, a few placeholders will already be on the page as shown in Figure

12.2. As you can see on the master, if you change nothing, the default notes master will print a miniature of the slide followed by the slide title. However, if you are creating a template from scratch, the notes master will be blank. In either case, you can edit or position placeholders (just as you would a slide master) to design a useful notes page.

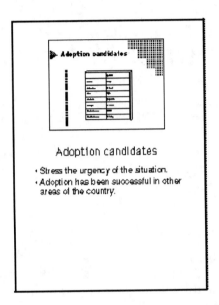

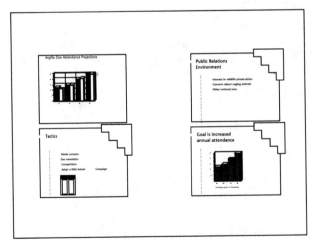

Figure 12.1   Notes from the outliner appear only on the speaker's printed copy of the presentation (*above*). They add comments or information to the slide for the speaker's benefit. Handouts are perfect for providing the audience with a copy of your presentation for their own note-taking or as a "take with" summary of your presentation (*below*).

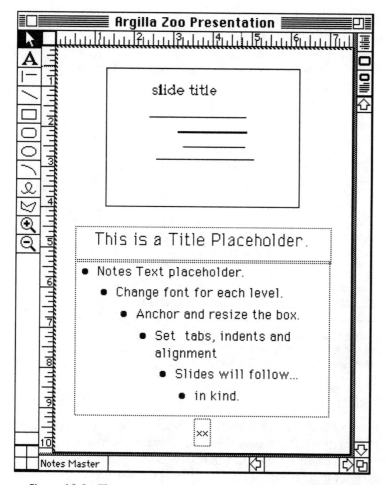

Figure 12.2   The notes master from any Persuasion AutoTemplate
includes the slide copy placeholder and a title placeholder.

Before you start to design a notes master, you need to decide whether you want your notes to have a tall or wide orientation. This selection on the Master menu pertains to notes master pages only. Therefore, you can use a tall orientation for notes while keeping a wide orientation for the slides themselves.

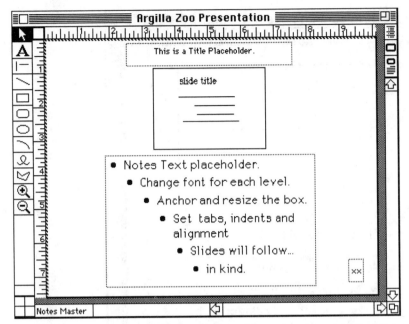

Figure 12.3   You can produce a set of speaker notes that are tall while your slides themselves are wide by checking the *Tall* orientation box in the Master menu.

Notes Placeholders

Once you have settled on the notes page orientation, you can place, reposition, or format the note master's placeholders. Persuasion gives you four placeholder choices: title, page number, slide copy, and notes text. Like many other placeholders, the title and notes text copy are drawn from outline headings of the same name. If you use the page number placeholder, Persuasion will generate a page number and then dynamically update the page number to keep your notes in sync with the order of your presentation slides.

When we design a presentation, we usually make use of each of the four placeholders. We place the title placeholder at the top of the notes master and format it in 24- or 36-point bold type. Considering the pressure on the presenter, having the title prominently displayed makes it easier for him or her to locate a particular note page easily.

The slide copy placeholder places a miniature version of each slide on each note page. If you wish, you can resize the slide copy placeholder by selecting it and dragging one of its handles. If you shift-drag a corner handle, you resize the slide while keeping its proportions intact.

Notes placeholders are most like body text placeholders on standard master slides. You can format the text however you like from the Text menu, changing font, size, style, color, or alignment. The difference between formatting a notes master and slide masters is in how both pages will be ultimately used. It is important to choose and use type that is suitable for projection when you create slides, but notes masters are always printed on standard pages and read by the speaker.

We suggest formatting the notes text with a readable font such as Orator, a particularly readable font designed for presenters. Keep in mind that the sole purpose of speaker notes is to make it as easy as possible for the speaker to do their best job.

Adding Emphasis

In addition to placeholders, you can add graphic elements to a notes master. As with other masters, any graphic that you add will appear on all notes pages. A good rule of thumb is to keep the master slide simple. If the sole purpose of the notes master is to serve the speaker, don't clutter the page with a logo or other distracting objects.

Don't forget that you can edit note pages just as you can edit slides. Feel free to make connections between a speaker's note text and points on the miniature slide by using the line tool to draw a visual link between the note and a specific point on the slide itself.

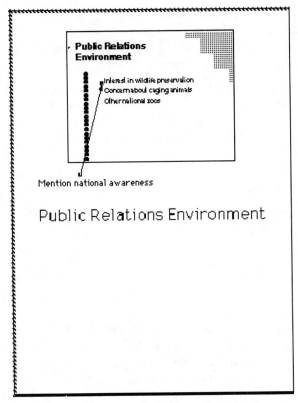

Figure 12.4. Use an arrow line to draw a connection between a point
on an individual speaker's note and the corresponding
point on the slide miniature.

Audience Handouts

Persuasion's handout feature makes it convenient to give your audience a
set of slides to take with them. Handouts relieve the need for your audience
to take copious notes, because each person has their own set of the presentation. They can then mark up their set of handouts with their own notes as
they wish.

Creating Handouts

Like slides and speaker notes, Persuasion formats handouts according to
the specifications you make on a master. However, unlike slide and notes
masters, there are a few eccentricities about creating a handout master that
can be a little confusing at first. Let's review the process of creating audience
handouts.

The first step in creating a handout master is to choose *Page setup* from the File menu. This command gives you access to both page orientation and the number of handouts you want to appear on each handout page.

To change the page orientation of handouts check the *Tall* or *Wide* option in the *Page setup* dialog box. (This is in contrast to the orientation command for both slides and speaker notes that is in their respective Master menus.) Once you click *OK* in the page setup dialog box, Persuasion displays the Presentation setup dialog box. The only command in this box that you need to be concerned with at this point is for choosing the number of slides you want to appear on each handout—1, 2, 3, 4, or 6. Once you have made this selection, click *OK*.

Now choose *Handout master* from the View menu. A master handout slide appears in the orientation you chose in the *Page setup* dialog box, and with the number of slides per page you chose in in the *Presentation setup* dialog box. If you change your mind about either orientation or number of slides on a page, you can still make those changes. However, if you have edited or added to the handouts master, you may have to make adjustments to be sure everything is still on the page in a proper position.

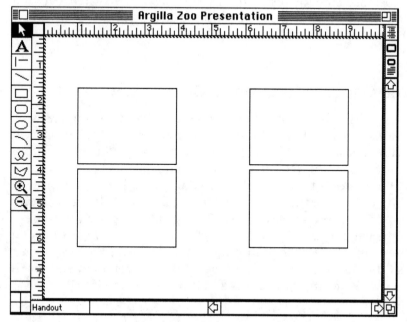

Figure 12.5   The default master page for handouts places miniature slides on a blank page according to your choices from the Presentation setup dialog box in the *Page setup* menu.

You may have noticed already that the handouts master does not have its own Master menu as do the slide and notes masters. Therefore, you will have to limit any changes to using the Text or Draw menus or the toolbox. Since the Master menu contains mostly placeholders that you can't use in a handouts master anyway, the only feature you may miss is the automatic page numbering. What you can do is resize and move the miniature slides around the master page. You can also use the Scrapbook or *Import* command to place graphics on the master. And, you can draw borders or other graphic enhancements using the drawing tools in the toolbox.

Printing Notes and Handouts

Printing notes and handouts is managed through the Print dialog box in the File menu regardless of the medium of your final presentation output. The same print command controls notes, handouts, and even slides. The difference is in which options you check off from the Print dialog box—whether Persuasion prints slides, notes, handouts, or a combination.

If your presentation is split between two different output devices, say a film recorder for slides and a LaserWriter for notes and handouts, you may have to make some adjustments as you make the switch between devices. You will have to change the output device with the Chooser, review the Page setup commands, and then make some changes in the Print dialog box.

Using the Chooser to Change Output Devices

If you are going to print out slides, notes, and handouts on the same output device, then you do not have to go through this step. However, if you have just sent a presentation file to a film recorder or other output device and now you want to print a set a notes and handouts, you must tell Persuasion that it needs to send the file to your printer in place of the film recorder. To do this, use the Chooser in the Apple menu. In the Chooser dialog box, click on the appropriate icon for the output device you want to use. Close the window to affirm your selection. Now go to *Page Setup* and click *OK* to confirm the change in output device within your *Page setup* dialog box. The Adjust graphics dialog box will now come up and you'll want to choose *Yes* to adjust handouts and leave slides unselected.

Once you have chosen a printer (in this example we have chosen the LaserWriter), choose the *Print* command from the File menu. The top line of the Print dialog box will confirm the name of the output device currently selected. If the wrong device name is listed, return to the Chooser and re-select the correct one.

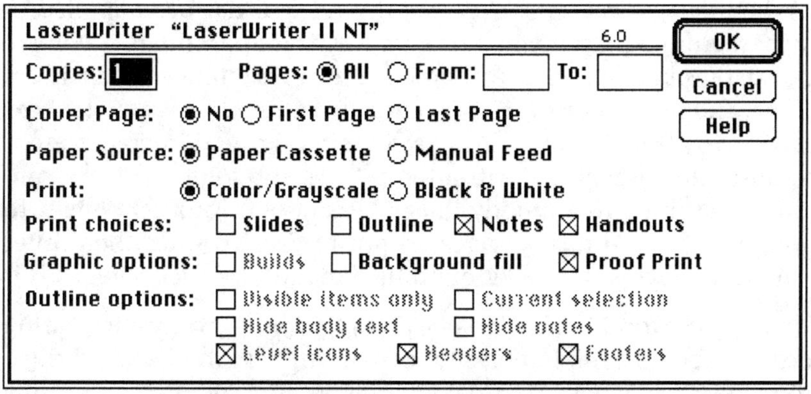

```
┌──────────────────────────────────────────────────────────────┐
│ LaserWriter  "LaserWriter II NT"           6.0    ┌────────┐  │
│                                                   │   OK   │  │
│ Copies:[1█]        Pages: ◉ All  ○ From:[  ] To:[  ] └────────┘ │
│                                                   ┌────────┐  │
│ Cover Page:   ◉ No ○ First Page  ○ Last Page      │ Cancel │  │
│                                                   └────────┘  │
│ Paper Source: ◉ Paper Cassette  ○ Manual Feed     ┌────────┐  │
│                                                   │  Help  │  │
│ Print:        ◉ Color/Grayscale ○ Black & White   └────────┘  │
│                                                               │
│ Print choices:    □ Slides  □ Outline  ⊠ Notes  ⊠ Handouts   │
│                                                               │
│ Graphic options: □ Builds   □ Background fill  ⊠ Proof Print │
│                                                               │
│ Outline options: □ Visible items only  □ Current selection   │
│                  □ Hide body text    □ Hide notes            │
│                  ⊠ Level icons   ⊠ Headers   ⊠ Footers       │
└──────────────────────────────────────────────────────────────┘
```

Figure 12.6   The Print dialog box contains options that govern how your notes and handouts will print, particularly if you have a color presentation that you want to print on a single color printer such as a LaserWriter.

The top part of the Print dialog box has the standard Macintosh print choices. You can choose the number of copies and a page range. Likewise, you have options for changing the cover page, paper source, and print. Select the *Color/Grayscale* option to get color output on a color PostScript printer and grayscale output on a monochrome PostScript printer. Selecting the *Black & White* option will produce black & white output on all PostScript printers. If you are using a standard LaserWriter it doesn't matter which selection you check, since the printer is only capable of printing in black and white. The more significant choices for printing notes and handouts are under the *Print choices* and *Graphic options* categories.

Print Choices

Persuasion will print any combination of slides, outlines, notes, or handouts. If you make more than one choice, Persuasion will print all of one type of output followed by the next. For example, if you check both notes and handouts for a specified range of pages, Persuasion will first print out the notes for the range and then the handouts.

Background Fill and Proof Print

Your choices in the Print dialog box for background fill and proof print have a direct impact on the legibility and printing speed of notes and handouts that are sent to a LaserWriter for output.

The *Background fill* option tells Persuasion whether or not to print background. When *Background fill* is checked, the fill that has been applied to the entire background master will be printed. This is appropriate if you are printing to an output device that will produce the presentation media itself. For handouts and notes, however, it is generally better to uncheck the box. This is particularly true if you are using a color background in your presentation because the LaserWriter will attempt to print colors in black and white, usually resulting in a muddy, illegible handout. Another benefit to not printing background fills is increased printing speed since the printer does not have to process the background information for each slide.

Proof print goes beyond the *Background fill* option by not only eliminating each slide's background fill, but also by converting text to black and filled objects to white. It gives a good readable representation of a color slide in a black and white medium. All fills print white and all lines print black. Checking *Proof print* is the fastest way to print a set of notes or handouts because it eliminates both color and fills information from being set to the printer. Figure 12.7 shows the difference between printing a note with *Proof Print* unchecked and checked.

Proof print and *Background fill* are mutually exclusive. Therefore, you cannot check both choices at the same time.

Once you have made your printing choices, click *OK* or press the Return key. Persuasion will then print your notes and handouts.

Warning: If you are sending your presentation to a slide service bureau, be sure to uncheck the notes and handouts options. Otherwise, you will receive separate 35-mm slide sets of notes and handouts (and you will be charged for them besides!).

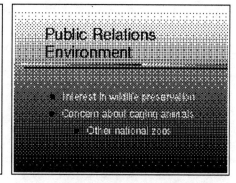

Figure 12.7 Unchecking *Proof print* will probably make color presentations look better on a black and white printer, as well as improve printing times.

That's all there is to preparing notes and handouts. As you can see, once you have set up a master for notes and handouts, Persuasion does all the work for you. Think of using notes and handouts in your production cycle. They are an efficient means of getting hard copy of a presentation. For a presentation itself, notes will make the speaker's job easier, and handouts will leave a lasting impression of the presentation with your audience.

Chapter 13

Building an AutoTemplate

If you've worked your way through this book, you now know all the basics of building a presentation with Persuasion—how to organize an outline, how to arrange and format text and graphics on slides, how to build charts and tables, how to apply color—an impressive list of skills!

In this chapter, we're going to learn how to integrate all these elements into an AutoTemplate. We'll start by looking at the 36 AutoTemplates that come with Persuasion 2.0, and then we'll turn our attention to how to build your own AutoTemplate from scratch.

Choosing an AutoTemplate

As you know, Persuasion 2.0 comes with 36 professionally designed AutoTemplates. With such a rich selection, how do you choose the right one for the job? The discussion below outlines some things to consider when making your selection. The table that follows it provides a brief description of each AutoTemplate. Use the table along with the Persuasion *Desktop Reference* to help you decide.

Presentation Medium

Some of the templates (A-R and AA-FF) are designed for black-and-white overheads, while others (S-X and GG-LL) are intended for color slides. Choose an AutoTemplate to match the medium you plan to use for your presentation. For an on-screen presentation on a black-and-white monitor, choose a black-and-white overhead AutoTemplate; for a color monitor, choose a color slide AutoTemplate.

Although every color slide AutoTemplate has a black-and-white overhead equivalent, not every black-and-white overhead AutoTemplate has a color slide equivalent. If you want to produce a color slide presentation based on an black-and-white overhead AutoTemplate for which there's no color slide equivalent, you can always modify the black-and-white overhead AutoTemplate by changing its slide shape and adding color. Equivalent black-and-white or color AutoTemplates are listed in parentheses in the table below.

Caution: Remember to select an output device from the Chooser and specify the correct presentation setup before beginning to work with the AutoTemplate of your choice. Consult Chapter 4, *Setting Up a Presentation*, if you need a refresher on how to do this.

Text and Graphic Elements

The text and graphic contents of your presentation will also determine what AutoTemplate you select. If the contents are simple, feel free to choose an AutoTemplate with a complex design, such as AutoTemplate B or X. By contrast, if your presentation includes many charts and graphics, avoid clutter by choosing a simple AutoTemplate such as A or G. If many of your slides contain lots of text, choose a spacious AutoTemplate such as A or H; if, on the other hand, your titles and subtitles will be short, you can use an AutoTemplate such as E or F that provides limited space for text elements.

Ease of Use

How much time do you have to put together your presentation? Some of the AutoTemplates are truly ready to go: you type text into the outline, assign slide masters, and print. These are labeled *Quick* in the table below. Others require a bit more work. Several contain logo placeholders or a line of static text that must be replaced with your own logo or text or removed altogether from the slide masters before you begin. Some, because of their complex design, require some tinkering to get the balance and alignment of elements just right. These are labeled *Moderate*.

Design Tone

Some of the AutoTemplate designs are formal, some are informal, some are warm, some are cool, some are traditional, some are contemporary, and so forth. Choose the AutoTemplate whose character best matches the tone you desire for your presentation. For more information on audience, design, and tone, consult Chapter 15, *Designing Effective Presentations*.

AutoTemplate Selection Guide

Table 13.1 lists each of Persuasion's 36 AutoTemplates, the presentation medium for which it was designed, and a brief description of its typographic and graphic elements. In addition, the table ranks each template's ease of use and design tone, and includes cautions and tips where appropriate.

Building Your Own AutoTemplate

With such a rich array of "built-in" AutoTemplates, you may never need to build your own AutoTemplate at all. You may find that one or more of Persuasion's AutoTemplates—as is—meet all your presentation needs. Or you may get by quite nicely just adding an occasional slide master, editing a color or two, or rearranging elements slightly in an existing AutoTemplate.

But the day will probably come when none of Persuasion's own Auto-Templates quite fits the bill, or when you're just feeling creative and adventurous. Then, you can open a new presentation, set up slide and background masters, add text placeholders, and build your very own, original AutoTemplate.

When would you want to build your own AutoTemplate from scratch? You may wish to set up one or more custom AutoTemplates for use by everyone in your department or your company. By incorporating your corporate logo, typefaces, and colors, presentations can reinforce your corporate identity. If you work for a design studio or ad agency, you may wish to include custom AutoTemplates as part of a corporate identity package you market to your clients. Or, as we've said, you may just be ready for the challenge of building from the ground up.

To give you a preview, here's a quick summary of the steps involved required to construct an AutoTemplate:

- Open a new presentation and save it as an AutoTemplate;
- Set up background and slide masters;
- Add placeholders and anchor them;
- Create or import text and graphics;
- Define automatic slide builds

Of course, some of these techniques, such as setting up slide masters, can be used to modify existing presentations as well to build new ones.

Table 13.1

AutoTemplate	Presentation medium	Typographic elements	Graphic elements	Ease of use	Design tone
A (S)	B&W OH	Times Title and text centered	Centered horizontal rule Static text	Easy Spacious, flexible	Very simple, formal
B (T)	B&W OH	Helvetica Title and text aligned left	Thick, horizontal, patterned and shadowed bands, top left and bottom right. Horizontal graduated rule Logo placeholder Static text	Moderate *Tip:* Keep text and graphics to a minimum to avoid clutter *Tip:* Be sure to balance elements	Strong, energetic, informal
C (U)	B&W OH	Helvetica Centered title Text aligned left within centered placeholder	Patterned background Shadowed boxes for title and body text No static text	Easy, quick *Tip:* Keep title text short to fit within box	Bold, heavy, informal

Table 13.1 *(continued)*

AutoTemplate	Presentation medium	Typographic elements	Graphic elements	Ease of use	Design tone
D	B&W OH	Times Centered title Text aligned left within centered placeholder	Thick and thin border rules Logo placeholder No static text	Easy	Ornamental, formal
E	B&W OH	Times, Title and text aligned left	Patterned, shadowed bands top left and bottom left Logo placeholder Static text	Moderate *Tip:* Keep titles short to fit within band	Strong, energetic, contemporary, informal
F (V)	B&W OH	Times Title and text centered	Decorative borders top and bottom Centered, shadowed squares	Easy, quick *Tip:* Watch placement of text in relation to graphic elements	Contemporary, sophisticated, informal

Table 13.1 *(continued)*

AutoTemplate	Presentation medium	Typographic elements	Graphic elements	Ease of use	Design tone
G	B&W OH	Helvetica Title and text aligned left	Thick horizontal rule Logo placeholder	Easy spacious, flexible	Very simple, informal
H	B&W OH	Helvetica Centered title Text aligned left within centered placeholder	Black and gray horizontal bands and rules	Easy *Tip:* Keep titles short to fit within band	Striking, authoritative
I	B&W	Helvetica Centered title Text aligned left within centered placeholder	Patterned background Rotated, shadowed box	Easy, quick	Dynamic, informal
J	B&W	Times Centered title and text	Gray triangular graphic above horizontal decorative band	Easy, quick	Contemporary, delicate, informal

Table 13.1 *(continued)*

AutoTemplate	Presentation medium	Typographic elements	Graphic elements	Ease of use	Design tone
K	B&W OH	Helvetica Title and text aligned left	Horizontal rule above title Light gray box with horizontal rule along top Logo placeholder	Easy *Tip:* Watch placement of title text in relation to horizontal rule *Tip:* Watch readability of text and graphics against gray background	Bold, clean, informal
L	B&W OH	Helvetica Centered title, Text aligned left within centered placeholder	Thick horizontal rule Static text Logo placeholder	Easy	Very simple, clean, informal

Table 13.1 *(continued)*

AutoTemplate	Presentation medium	Typographic elements	Graphic elements	Ease of use	Design tone
M	B&W OH	Times Title and text aligned left	Diagonal line divides slide into gray and white areas Thick black band along left edge	Easy, quick *Tip:* Be sure to balance elements in relation to gray background *Tip:* Watch readability of text and graphics against gray background	Unusual, dynamic, informal
N (W)	B&W OH	Helvetica Title and text aligned left	Band composed of horizontal rules along right edge Logo placeholder	Easy	Simple, vibrant, informal

Table 13.1 *(continued)*

AutoTemplate	Presentation medium	Typographic elements	Graphic elements	Ease of use	Design tone
O	B&W OH	Times Centered title Text aligned left	Round-cornered box rule border Logo placeholder	Easy *Tip:* Leave adequate white space between border and elements	Traditional, formal
P	B&W OH	Helvetica Centered title Text aligned left within centered placeholder	Thin box rule border with thick rule across top Logo placeholder Static text	Easy	Clean, strong, informal

Table 13.1 *(continued)*

AutoTemplate	Presentation medium	Typographic elements	Graphic elements	Ease of use	Design tone
Q	B&W OH	Helvetica Title and text aligned left	Stairstep gray graphic in upper right edge Triangular accent graphic on left edge, Dotted vertical rule Logo placeholder	Moderate *Tip:* Watch placement of title in relation to triangular accent *Tip:* Watch placement of text in relation to dotted vertical rule	Striking, dynamic, contemporary
R	B&W OH	Times Title and text aligned left	Nested gray borders Irregular "torn-edge" graphic in upper left corner Logo placeholder	Easy *Tip:* Keep text and graphics to a minimum to avoid clutter	Very unusual, busy, informal

Table 13.1 *(continued)*

AutoTemplate	Presentation medium	Typographic elements	Graphic elements	Ease of use	Design tone
S (A)	Color slide	Times, yellow and white Title and text centered	Blue background, Centered horizontal rule Static text	Easy spacious, flexible	Very simple, clean, formal
T (B)	Color slide	Helvetica, white Title and text aligned left	Blue background Thick, horizontal, shadowed bands top left and bottom right Horizontal graduated rule Logo placeholder Static text	Moderate *Tip:* Keep text and graphics to a minimum to avoid clutter *Tip:* Be sure to balance elements	Strong, energetic, informal
U (C)	Color slide	Helvetica, white Centered title Text aligned left within centered placeholder	Green background Blue shadowed boxes for title and body text No static text	Easy, quick *Tip:* Keep titles short to fit within box	Bold, heavy, informal

Table 13.1 *(continued)*

AutoTemplate	Presentation medium	Typographic elements	Graphic elements	Ease of use	Design tone
V (F)	Color slide	Times, white Title and text centered	Graduated purple-to-black background Decorative borders top and bottom Centered, shadowed orange squares	Easy, quick *Tip:* Watch placement of text in relation to graphic elements	Contemporary, sophisticated, elegant
W (N)	Color slide	Helvetica, white Title and text aligned left	Graduated red-to-black background, Band composed of red horizontal rules along right edge Logo placeholder	Easy	Vibrant, warm, informal

Table 13.1   *(continued)*

AutoTemplate	Presentation medium	Typographic elements	Graphic elements	Ease of use	Design tone
X (Q)	Color slide	Helvetica, white Title and text aligned left	Blue background Stairstep light blue graphic in upper right edge Triangular yellow accent graphic on left edge Dotted vertical rule Logo placeholder	Moderate *Tip:* Watch placement of title in relation to triangular accent *Tip:* Watch placement of text in relation to dotted vertical rule	Cool, striking, contemporary
AA (GG)	B&W OH	Times Title and text aligned left	Graduated horizontal rules top and bottom	Easy, quick spacious, flexible	Simple
BB (HH)	B&W OH	Times Title and text aligned left	Black asymmetrical shape along top edge	Easy, quick *Tip:* Keep titles short to fit within graphic	Bold, contemporary

Table 13.1 *(continued)*

AutoTemplate	Presentation medium	Typographic elements	Graphic elements	Ease of use	Design tone
CC (II)	B&W OH	Times Centered title Text aligned left within centered placeholder	Medium gray background Large dark gray box for title Smaller light gray box for subtitle White box for text	Easy, quick *Tip:* Keep titles and subtitles short to fit within boxes *Tip:* Watch readability of titles and subtitles against gray background	Strong, heavy
DD (JJ)	B&W OH	Times Title aligned left Text aligned left within centered placeholder	Background composed of vertical rules against patterned field White, shadowed box for text Graduated circle graphic	Easy, quick *Tip:* Keep graphics simple to avoid clutter	Striking, dynamic, informal

Table 13.1 *(continued)*

AutoTemplate	Presentation medium	Typographic elements	Graphic elements	Ease of use	Design tone
EE (KK)	B&W OH	Times Title and text aligned left	Background composed of diagonal rules against gray field White box with vertical black rules for text	Easy, quick *Tip:* Keep graphics simple to avoid clutter	Striking, dynamic, informal
FF (LL)	B&W OH	Helvetica titles Times text Title and text aligned left	Thick black border Horizontal rule	Easy, quick *Tip:* Watch alignment of titles and subtitles with left end of horizontal rule	Simple, strong, authoritative
GG (AA)	Color slide	Times, yellow and white Title and text aligned left	Graduated aqua background Graduated horizontal rules top and bottom	Easy, quick Spacious, flexible	Simple, warm, light

Table 13.1 *(continued)*

AutoTemplate	Presentation medium	Typographic elements	Graphic elements	Ease of use	Design tone
HH (BB)	Color slide	Times, white Title and text aligned left	Graduated gray-to-black background Dark red, shadowed, asymmetrical shape along top edge	Easy, quick *Tip:* Keep titles short to fit within graphic	Bold, contemporary
II (CC)	Color slide	Times, white Centered title Text aligned left within centered placeholder	Graduated purple background Large dark gray box for title Smaller purple box for subtitle Purple box for text	Easy, quick *Tip:* Keep titles and subtitles short to fit within boxes	Strong, heavy, rich
JJ (DD)	Color slide	Times, white Title aligned left Text aligned left within centered placeholder	Pinstriped gray background graduated gray box for text Graduated red circle graphic	Easy, quick *Tip:* Keep graphics simple to avoid clutter	Striking, dynamic, informal

Table 13.1 *(continued)*

AutoTemplate	Presentation medium	Typographic elements	Graphic elements	Ease of use	Design tone
KK (EE)	Color slide	Times, white Title and text aligned left	Diagonal gray pinstripes on a dark blue field Light blue box for text bordered by gray vertical rules	Easy, quick *Tip:* Keep graphics simple to avoid clutter	Cool, contemporary
LL (FF)	Color slide	Helvetica titles, white Times text, white Title and text aligned left	Light gray background with thick dark gray border, Horizontal aqua rule	Easy, quick *Tip:* Watch alignment of titles and subtitles with left end of horizontal rule	Simple, warm, casual

A Little Background

Constructing your own AutoTemplate requires really getting into the nuts and bolts of how a presentation is built. Let's review a few basics before we dive into production. After all, it's important to build on a solid foundation.

What exactly is an AutoTemplate? An AutoTemplate is simply a presentation that's been saved in a special way—as an AutoTemplate! When you open a presentation that's been saved as an AutoTemplate, you get an untitled copy of the presentation, not the original. This preserves the original AutoTemplate unchanged, so that you can return to it again and again to base new presentations upon it.

Building your own AutoTemplate is just a matter of designing the "shell" of a presentation, with appropriate masters and default settings but without any particular outline text, and then saving it in an AutoTemplate so that you can base new presentations on it.

And what exactly is a slide, from Persuasion's point of view? A slide is like a two- or three-layer sandwich. You have an optional bottom layer, a background master that can carry a fill pattern or color, your company's logo, or a repetitive design element such as a rule. Elements that are common to most or all of the slides in a presentation can be placed on the background master. The middle layer of the slide-sandwich is the slide master. It includes placeholders for various kinds of text, charts, or organizational charts, as well as graphic static elements appropriate for a particular slide layout. The top layer of the slide contains only ingredients unique to the individual slide, such as the text flowing from an outline heading, or a chart that plots data from the data sheet, and so forth. The background master, the slide master, and the slide can all contain static text and graphics.

It's up to you how broadly you want to apply such static elements to your presentation. If you want a small geranium on every slide, place it on all the background masters you intend to use. If you want the geranium only on a particular slide layout, place it on the slide master(s) for that layout. If the geranium need appear only on an occasional slide, place it directly on the slides themselves.

Most presentations will have only one or two background masters, if any. The background master provides a consistent background for all your slides so that you don't have to create it separately for every slide master.

On the other hand, most presentations will have half a dozen or more slide masters. You can apply different background masters to the various slide masters, and go on to apply different slide masters to slides. Mixing and matching background and slide masters gives you many possibilities without sacrificing consistency or making lots of work. So much flexibility is also a challenge. In fact, it may take you a while to develop a feel for what to put on a background master and what to put on a slide master.

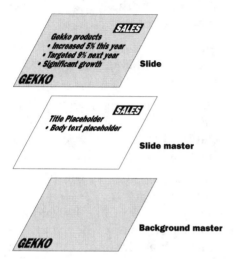

Figure 13.1.   A slide is composed of as many as three layers: a background master, a slide master, and a layer containing individual slide elements.

Although the process of creating and editing background and slide masters is nearly identical, we'll treat them separately just to avoid any possibility of confusion. But before we can work with masters, we have to have a presentation to work in!

Starting a New AutoTemplate

As you know, the very first thing you do when beginning a presentation is to select an output device. This is true whether you're opening an Auto-Template that came with Persuasion or constructing your own. Your choice of output device tells Persuasion what dimensions and proportions to use in formatting your presentation. Select *Chooser* from the Apple menu, and click on the icon of the output device you intend to use.

Once you've chosen an output device, there are two ways to start your AutoTemplate. (These are the same alternatives you have for beginning any presentation.)

  1. Choose *New* from the File menu. This opens an untitled presentation based on your default presentation, *Persuasion Prefs*. What will you get? Well, it depends on what's in *Persuasion Prefs*.

Here, there are two possibilities. Usually, *Persuasion Prefs* will be the Persuasion AutoTemplate you specified as the default when you installed Persuasion. As you may remember from Chapter 1, *Installing Persuasion*, AutoTemplate A is the "default default." Alternatively, if you've saved a presentation of your own under the name *Persuasion Prefs*, you'll get a copy of that presentation.

Use this starting point when the default presentation contains some of the same elements, such as color palette or background and slide masters, as the AutoTemplate you're building.

2. Open a brand new, "empty" presentation by holding down the Shift key while choosing *New* from the File menu. This opens a presentation with the basic application defaults that ship with Persuasion. These are listed in Appendix A of the Persuasion User Manual.

Holding down the Shift key to override the *Persuasion Prefs* file gives you the simplest presentation possible—no static text or logo placeholders, only black and white for colors, and just one background master and one slide master. Use this starting point when your *Persuasion Prefs* file contains elements such as graphics or colors that you don't want in the AutoTemplate you're building.

Once you've opened a presentation, choose *Page setup* from the File menu, and then make the appropriate selections in your output device's Page setup and Persuasion's own Presentation setup dialog boxes. If you're not sure how to do this, refer back to Chapter 4, *Setting Up a Presentation*.

Finally, you must save this presentation as an AutoTemplate. Choose *Save as* from the File menu. In the Save presentation as dialog box, type in a new name for your AutoTemplate. Below the list box, be sure select the *Save as AutoTemplate* option. This ensures that when you open your AutoTemplate in the future, you'll get an untitled copy rather than the original. Click *OK* to close the dialog box.

What does your AutoTemplate consist of at this point? No matter which of the two starting places described above you chose, your AutoTemplate already contains one or more background and slide masters. If your *Persuasion Prefs* file is based on a Persuasion AutoTemplate—for example, if you selected AutoTemplate A as the default presentation during installation—your new AutoTemplate will have two background masters (*Background* and *Title background*) and six slide masters (*Title, Text 1, Text 2, Graphic 1, Graphic 2,* and *Org Chart*). If you pressed the Shift key while choosing *New*, your presentation will have one background (*Background*) and one slide master (*Master 1*).

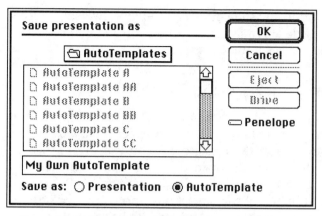

Figure 13.2. Enter the name of your new AutoTemplate and click *Save as AutoTemplate*.

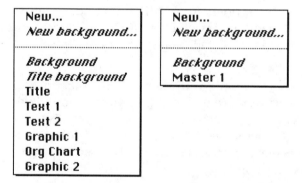

Figure 13.3. Each Persuasion AutoTemplate includes six default slide masters and two default background masters (*left*). Even an empty Shift-*New* presentation contains two default masters (*right*).

Your new AutoTemplate also contains default settings for text, color, fill patterns, and so forth. These defaults will be either those of your *Persuasion Prefs* presentation, or, if you held down the Shift key while selecting *New*, the initial application defaults.

Setting Up Background and Slide Masters

As we've already seen, the function of a background master is to carry elements common to all, or most, of the slides in your presentation. Generally, this means a background color and/or fill, graphics such as a rule or a logo, and text such as a company name or presentation title.

Working with background and slide masters is usually a two-step process. First you edit any existing default masters, and then you add new masters as necessary. Let's begin with background masters.

Editing an Existing Background Master

As you know, there are several paths you can take to get to an existing background master. The most common way is to select *Go to master* from the View menu, and then select the background you want from the submenu. Or, from Slide view, you can open the *Go to slide master* pop-up menu. Finally, when you are in a Master view, you can open the *Go to master* pop-up menu (at the bottom left of the screen) and choose the background you want. In all the menus listed above, the names of background masters are italicized to distinguish them from slide masters. Choose a default background master to edit, usually either *Background* or *Title background*.

From the Master menu, specify the orientation of the background master. For a vertical slide, one that's taller than it is wide, select *Tall orientation*. For a horizontal slide that's wider than it is tall, make sure *Tall orientation* is turned off.

Although Persuasion allows you to mix vertical and horizontal orientations within the same presentation, do so with caution. Most 35-mm slides are horizontal; switching back and forth between orientations can disorient your audience. Overheads can be either vertical or horizontal. With the exception of "portrait" monitors that are tall and narrow, all on-screen presentations require horizontal orientation.

If you change the orientation of a master that already contains text or graphic elements, you may need to adjust them to fit the master's new proportions.

Now let's look at how to create a new background master. Then we'll discuss techniques for editing background masters—whether existing or new—including how to add or remove text, graphics, and slide background fill.

Creating a New Background Master

From any view, choose *Go to master* from the View menu and *New background* from the submenu, or, while in Master view, choose *New background master* from the *Go to master* pop-up menu in the left-most menu at the bottom of the window.

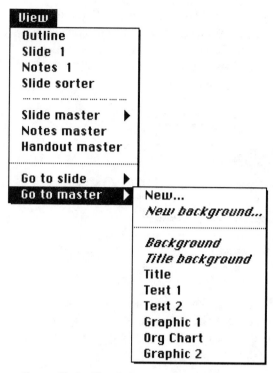

Figure 13.4. The Go to master submenu lets you create a new
background or slide master, or go to an existing master.

In the New background master dialog box, you'll see a suggested name for the background master. Persuasion automatically suggests numbered master names, beginning with the first unassigned number (e.g., *Background 2*). Generally, you're better off naming your masters something descriptive; it's a lot easier to remember what *Gray bkgd* is than *Background 5*. Type in a name for the new background if you wish.

For the *Based on* option, choose *None* to get a new blank background master. If the background master you're creating is similar to an existing background, however, you can save yourself some work. Select the name of the "model" background from the pop-down menu following *Based on*, and you'll get a copy that you can edit as you wish. (By the way, the *Based on* option just gives you a simple copy of the background in its current form: if you edit a master, any masters based on it will be unaffected by the changes.)

Select an orientation, *Tall* or *Wide*, and then click *OK*. (If you've based your master on an existing master, an orientation will already be selected.) Your master will appear before you, ready for adding text, graphics, and slide background fill as described below. And its name will appear in the Background pop-up menu in the lower menu bar.

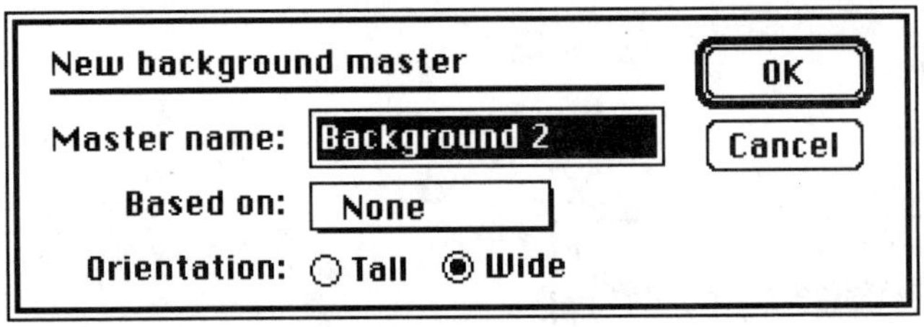

```
┌─────────────────────────────────────────────────┐
│ ┌─────────────────────────────────────────────┐ │
│ │                                             │ │
│ │  New background master           ┌────────┐ │ │
│ │  ─────────────────────           │   OK   │ │ │
│ │                                  └────────┘ │ │
│ │  Master name: │Background 2│     ┌────────┐ │ │
│ │                                  │ Cancel │ │ │
│ │  Based on:  │  None  │           └────────┘ │ │
│ │                                             │ │
│ │  Orientation: ○ Tall  ◉ Wide                │ │
│ └─────────────────────────────────────────────┘ │
└─────────────────────────────────────────────────┘
```

Figure 13.5. The New background master dialog box lets you name a new background master, base it on existing master, and select its orientation.

So much for the basics of setting up background masters. The procedures for slide masters are nearly identical, but there are a few additional options. Let's walk through them, just to avoid confusion.

Editing a Slide Master

As with background masters, every new presentation will have at least one slide master. First you'll edit the existing slide master(s), and then you'll create new ones as necessary.

To go to the slide master of an existing slide, select *Slide master* and then *Current* from the View menu, or press Option while clicking the Slide icon.

To edit an existing slide master other than the current one, choose *Go to master* from the View menu, or, in Master view, open the Go to slide master pop-up menu at the far left of the bottom menu bar. If you began your presentation with the Shift-plus-*New* option, choose the default slide master *Master I*. A blank slide master appears.

If you began with a copy of *Persuasion Prefs*, choose any one of the six default slide masters to edit. You may need to delete existing graphics and placeholders.

To edit the slide master, change its orientation as described above, and add or remove text, graphics, and slide background fill as described below.

Creating a New Slide Master

From any view, select *Go to master* from the View menu, or, from Master view, open the Go to slide master pop-up menu. Choose *New*. (If you're in Master view, you can also choose *Define masters* from the Master menu, and then choose *New*.)

The New slide master dialog box is identical to the New background master dialog box. Type a name for the new slide master. If you want to base the new master on an existing one, choose its name from the Based on pop-down menu. Select an orientation, and then click *OK*. If you base a new slide master on a slide master with a background master applied to it, the orientation options are dimmed because they can only be changed by changing the background master.

Your new slide master is now ready for editing.

Adding a Slide Background Fill

To add a fill pattern or color to a background master or a slide master, choose *Slide background fill* from the Master menu. Choose a pattern from the now familiar selection in the fill pattern pop-up menu. Then select a color from the color palette for *Color 1* and *Color 2*. (Or, as you learned in Chapter 9, *Working with Color*, you can click *Other* to select a color directly from the color grid.) *Color 1*, the foreground color, affects the parts of the patterns that appear black in the menu. *Color 2* affects the parts that appear white. The sample box displays the pattern and colors you specify.

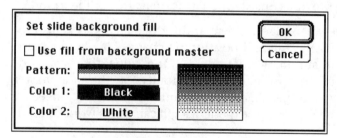

Figure 13.6. In the Set slide background fill dialog box, choose a pattern and colors for the slide background fill.

If you're working with a slide master, check *Use fill pattern from background master* to let the fill of any background master you might apply take precedence over the slide master's fill. To preserve the slide master's fill no matter what background master you apply to it, leave the option unchecked. (If you're working on a background master, it will be dimmed.) Click *OK* when you're satisfied with the fill.

Note: Persuasion gives you a choice as to how slide background fills are displayed on the screen in Slide view: dithered (that is, coarsely) or smoothly. If you're working with a 24-bit color monitor (in 24-bit color mode), you'll automatically get smooth background fills. If you're working with an 8-bit color display, however, you'll automatically get dithered background fills. To change this, choose *Preferences* from the Edit menu, and then click *Fine background fill*. Although smooth background fills are pretty to look at, they may slow performance. Backgrounds are always displayed smoothly during an on-screen slide show.

Adding or Modifying Placeholders

Next on the agenda: adding placeholders to slide masters. As you know, placeholders specify how text that flows from the outline will be formatted. They can also specify how charts should be plotted from a data sheet. The placeholder on a master slide "turns into" a text block or a chart on an individual slide.

Placeholders are dynamically linked to both the outline and the data sheet, so that changes in content you make in one place show up in other appropriate places. You can't get outline text onto a slide without the right placeholder on a slide master; there's no conduit for it. Although worksheet data can be displayed on a slide without requiring a chart placeholder, chart placeholders do help provide consistent chart formats from slide to slide.

Finally, the link between placeholders and individual slides is also dynamic in this sense: formatting and positioning changes made to a placeholder at any time will automatically update all individual slides based on that slide master. Thus, by reformatting placeholders on the slide master, you can retroactively reformat elements on multiple slides at once. For those of you with some PageMaker experience, placeholders work similarly to Master Pages.

There are as many types of placeholders as there are kinds of text and charts. Here's a list of all nine:

- Title
- Subtitle
- Body text

- Chart (formats and displays data from the data sheet)
- Table
- Organization chart
- Page number (automatically numbers slides and speaker notes pages)
- Slide copy (places a miniature slide on the speaker notes master)
- Notes text (moves speaker notes from the outline to speaker notes pages).

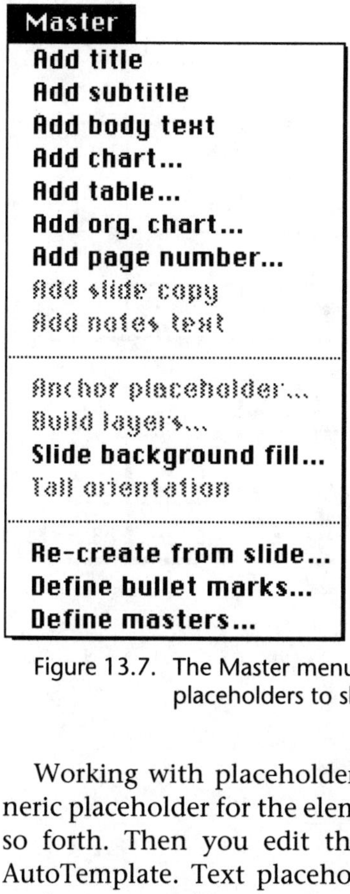

Master

Add title
Add subtitle
Add body text
Add chart...
Add table...
Add org. chart...
Add page number...
Add slide copy
Add notes text

Anchor placeholder...
Build layers...
Slide background fill...
Tall orientation

Re-create from slide...
Define bullet marks...
Define masters...

Figure 13.7. The Master menu allows you to nine types of placeholders to slide masters.

Working with placeholders is a two-step process. First, you place a generic placeholder for the element you want—title, subtitle, chart, table, and so forth. Then you edit the placeholder to suit the demands of your AutoTemplate. Text placeholders require the additional step of "anchoring", i.e., controlling how outline text will actually flow into placeholders.

In this section, we'll cover how to add all the various types of placeholders, and what to consider when modifying them. Then we'll take up how to control the flow of outline text into placeholders. Refer to Chapter 15, *Designing Effective Presentations*, for tips on font, size, and color selections for text and charts.

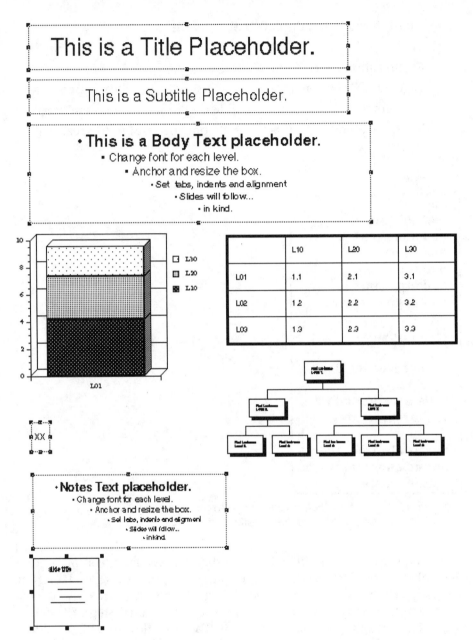

Figure 13.8. Nine types of placeholders address the needs of different
presentation elements.

To add a placeholder, go to Slide master or Notes master view, and then
stand by to open the Master menu in the upper menu bar.

Adding or Modifying a Title Placeholder

To add a title placeholder, choose *Add title* from the Master menu. A title placeholder will appear in the center of the master slide. If necessary, drag to move it, or grab a side selection handle and drag to change its width. (Its actual size on a slide will be determined by the amount and attributes of the outline text it contains.) Position the placeholder so as to leave enough room for the title text. Usually this means centered or flush left in the upper quarter or third of the slide.

To change the font, size, style, or color of placeholder text, use the individual submenus in the Text menu, or open the Text format dialog box. Although you can use either the pointer tool or the text tool to select a placeholder for text formatting, we recommend the pointer tool because it's faster. If you do choose the text tool, however, you'll notice that you can't select just a word or two in a placeholder. Clicking once selects all the text. (Changing just a word or two must be done on individual slides.)

To add a fill pattern, a text block color, a line pattern or color, or a shadow, select the placeholder with the pointer tool and choose the options you want from the Effect menu.

Adding or Modifying a Subtitle Placeholder

To add a subtitle placeholder, choose *Add subtitle* from the Master menu. Modify the placeholder if necessary, using your wealth of moving, resizing, and formatting techniques. As for the subtitle's position, don't let it crowd the title, but make sure the two elements aren't so far apart they appear unrelated to each other.

Adding or Modifying a Body Text Placeholder

To add a body text placeholder, choose *Add body text* from the Master menu. Modify and format to your heart's content.

In a body text placeholder, you can select and format each heading level independently. For example, you can make all first level headings bold, all second level headings regular, all third level headings italic, and so forth. (But don't overdo it!) To do this, choose the text tool, and then click on the level you want to format (you needn't drag or click more than once). Selecting the whole placeholder with the pointer tool is the easiest way to format all levels at once.

If there is too much text in your body text placeholder, you can select any number of levels with the text tool and delete them with *Cut, Clear,* or *Delete*.

Bullets

Bullets, those small but important visual signals, get special attention in Persuasion. In fact, each outline level's bullet can be defined independently. Although bullets are defined for each slide master with body text placeholders, their display in individual text blocks in any graphics view can be controlled by selecting that text block and choosing *Bullet marks* from the Text menu to turn bullets on or off.

To define the character, font, and color for bullets for a master, choose *Define bullet marks* from the Master menu (in Master view). In the Define bullet marks dialog box, *Level 1* is already selected. Type the character you want as the Level 1 bullet, and then choose a font and color from the Font and Color pop-up menus.

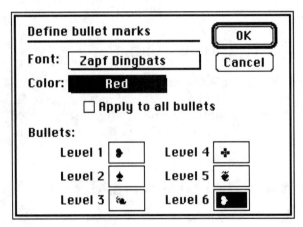

Figure 13.9. The Define bullet marks dialog box allows you precise control over the appearance of bullets in body text.

Click *Apply to all bullets* to apply the changes to all six bullet levels. If you click *Apply to all bullets* when more than one font or color has already been assigned, the word *Mixed* appears in the font or color box. This is Persuasion's way of prompting you to decide on one font or color for all the bullets. Simply open the appropriate pop-down menu and make your selection.

To define each bullet level independently, uncheck *Apply to all bullets*, click to select another level, and then define its character, format, and color. Continue until you've defined all six levels. To delete bullets for an individual level, select the level whose bullets you want to delete, and then press the Delete/Backspace key.

You can use different characters and fonts for each level. For example, six Zapf Dingbat characters are shown in the example below. (Whether you'd actually want to do this from an aesthetic point of view is debatable, but technically it's feasible.)

Table 13.2

Level	Character	Keyboard combination	Level	Character	Keyboard combination
Level 1	★	Shift + h	Level 4	☛	Shift + 8
Level 2	♠	Option + e	Level 5	❏	o
Level 3	♣	Option + r	Level 6	❖	v

Tip: The font Zapf Dingbats should be in every desktop presenter's arsenal. Using the standard alphabet plus Option- and Shift-key combinations, you can generate more than 100 interesting characters ranging from a tiny airplane to a pair of scissors. Also, besides symbols, the Symbol font offers some interesting dingbats, such as © (Option + g), ⌘ (Shift + Option + k), and ™ (Option + 2). Use the desk accessory Key Caps in the Apple menu to figure out what keys or key combinations produce what dingbats on your computer.

Adding or Modifying a Chart Placeholder

To display charts on your slides, you do not in fact need to have a chart placeholder. Once your data is in the data sheet, you can simply choose a chart format directly from the Chart menu. Chart placeholders, do however, help maintain consistent chart format among slides.

To add a chart placeholder, choose *Add chart* from the Master menu. Type in the default number of categories and series you want. (The defaults that appear in the dialog box when it opens are the same numbers you last specified as defaults.)

A chart placeholder appears on the slide master. To select a different chart type for the placeholder, choose *Chart format* from the Chart menu, and then select the chart or table format you want. If necessary, drag to reposition the chart or resize it as desired. Use commands from the Text and Effect menu to modify text and graphic components of the chart. You can also alter any part of a chart by double- or triple-clicking to subselect the part you want to modify.

The format of the chart placeholder that first appears on the slide master is the chart format last selected from the Chart menu. In other words, Persuasion remembers what chart format you last chose and assumes you want it again. For example, let's say you're creating two slide masters, one for a pie chart and one for a column chart. You add a chart placeholder to the first slide master, choosing *Pie* as the chart format from the Chart menu. Then you create a second slide master and add a chart placeholder to it. This time, Persuasion will use a pie chart as the default chart format. In fact, instead of asking you for the default number of categories and series, it will ask for the default number of pie slices.

For charts, the defaults you enter for categories and series (or pie slices) are not critical. Regardless of the defaults you enter for the placeholder, you can use any number of categories and series in the data sheet for a given slide. In fact, the placeholder will be the same size, no matter what numbers you enter.

More important than the defaults for categories and series is the match between the format of the chart placeholder and the data you want displayed on individual slides. For best results, create one slide master for each chart format you anticipate using. For example, if your presentation includes both column and bar charts, set up one master slide for each.

Tip: To streamline the process of creating several slide masters for different types of charts, use the *Based on* option in the New slide master dialog box. For example, let's say you want to set up two slide masters with identical formatting, one for column charts and one for bar charts. Set up a Column slide master, specifying Column as the chart format for the placeholder, and choosing colors, styles, and patterns for line, fills, and shadows. Then create a new slide master. In the New slide master dialog box, for the *Based on* option, choose *Column* from the pop-up menu of existing slide masters. The new slide master will be identical to the one you just created; it will include a chart placeholder with exactly the same formatting. Now all you have to do is to change the chart format from column to bar! Two harmonious, consistent slide masters for little more than the price of one!

Adding or Modifying a Table Placeholder

To add a table placeholder, choose *Add table* from the Master menu. Type in the number of default rows and columns you want, then click *OK*. The numbers you enter do not limit you. Rather, they give you a good basis for determining the format and look of the table. If you'll be using the same slide master to format several slides with tables on them, enter the number of rows and columns required by the largest table.

Unlike chart placeholders, table placeholders are finicky about the defaults you enter. In general, the closer the default number of rows and columns to the actual number of rows and columns required by data on individual slides, the better the result. If an individual table has more columns than specified in the placeholder, the additional columns will appear slightly compressed. If the table has fewer columns than the placeholder, they'll be narrower than is optimal for the available space on the slide. Of course, you can always adjust column width manually, but it's just not as efficient as letting Persuasion do it for you.

Once you've added the table placeholder, you can reposition or modify it using the same techniques described for the chart placeholder.

Adding or Modifying an Organization Chart Placeholder

To add an organization chart placeholder, choose *Add org. chart* from the Master menu. Enter the number of levels and boxes you want, and indicate whether you want the lowest level set as a list, boxed list, or as separate boxes. Click *OK* when you're through.

Be sure that the default number of levels and boxes you specify matches the actual number of levels in the outline as closely as possible. Persuasion uses these numbers to determine both the overall size of the organization chart as well as the size of the individual boxes that compose it. If there's too great a discrepancy between the placeholder setup and individual organization charts, the results will not be optimal.

Again, you can use commands from the Text and Effects menus to tailor the organizational chart to your taste.

Adding or Modifying a Slide Number Placeholder

Next to losing your voice or falling backward off the podium, what could be worse that dropping a pile of unnumbered overheads in the middle of a presentation? Fortunately, Persuasion's automatic slide numbering feature transforms certain disaster into mild hardship. You can add a slide number placeholder to slide and notes masters, but not to background masters.

To add a slide number placeholder to a slide or notes master, choose *Add page number* from the Master menu. The slide number placeholder appears on the master. Position it and format its text as you wish. When you switch to slide or notes view, the slide's number miraculously appears in place of the placeholder's "xx."

Tip: Page numbers will only appear on slides whose masters have a slide number placeholder. For best results, then, you must remember to include one on every slide master, and to position and format it consistently. To speed up text formatting on several masters, use the *Formats* command in the Text menu to define a format for the slide number.

Adding a Slide Copy Placeholder (Notes Master)

To add a slide copy placeholder to a Notes master, go to Notes master view, and choose *Add slide copy* from the Master menu. A miniature of a slide appears on the Notes master. Drag to move or resize it. If you want the slide to be legible on the notes pages, make the slide copy placeholder large. If you anticipate having lots of notes, make the slide copy placeholder small to leave adequate room for them. For more information about notes, consult Chapter 12, *Working with Speaker Notes and Handouts*.

Adding a Notes Text Placeholder (Notes Master)

To add a notes placeholder to the Notes master, with the Notes master on the screen, choose *Add notes text* from the Master menu. Position and format its text as you would any placeholder. A word of caution: make sure you can read the text! In most cases, you'll be shifting back and forth from your notes to your audience. In many cases, you'll be working with low or even little light. Your notes text should be large and legible enough for you to keep your place without losing your balance. Times Roman, a very legible typeface, set in 12 points or larger, is a good place to start.

Anchoring Text within Placeholders

What happens when the actual text flowing from the outline into the placeholder on a particular slide is much longer than the the dummy placeholder text? When your slide's title is *A Proposal for Public Relations for the Argilla Zoo* and not *This is a title placeholder*? When your subtitle is two lines rather than one line long? How does Persuasion accommodate the extra text? As usual with such critical decisions, Persuasion turns to you for help.

The *Anchor placeholder* command allows you to control the direction that text will flow within the placeholder. For example, will it enter the top left of the placeholder and flow down to the right? Or will it enter the bottom right and flow up to the left? Just as an anchor holds the bow of a boat in position while allowing the the boat to adjust to the flow of the tide, the placeholder anchor is the fixed point from which the placeholder will adjust to accommodate the flow of text.

To anchor the text within a placeholder, select a placeholder with the pointer tool, and choose *Anchor placeholder* from the Master menu. The Anchor content to placeholder dialog box lets you select a vertical anchor site (*Top*, *Center*, or *Bottom*) and a horizontal anchor site (*Left*, *Center*, and *Right*). When you select a new anchor site, the placeholder and the outlined arrows around it move to indicate the direction of text flow. The nine possible pairs of vertical and horizontal anchor sites give you nine anchoring possibilities.

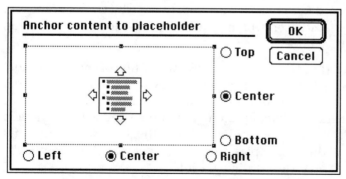

Figure 13.10. The Anchor content to placeholder dialog box illustrates how text will fit and flow within a placeholder.

Understanding anchoring takes concentration. It helps to consider the relationship between placeholders and text blocks. On each slide, text based on the placeholder is converted to a text block that's as large or small as needed to accommodate that slide's text. Sometimes the text block will be smaller than the placeholder and sometimes it will be larger.

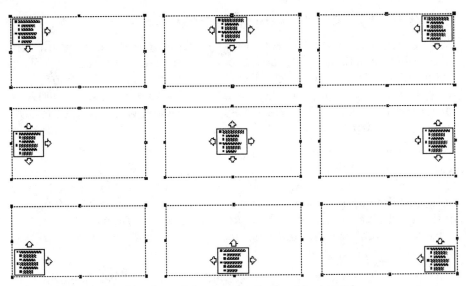

Figure 13.11. Combinations of the three vertical and horizontal anchoring sites yield nine anchoring possibilities.

Anchoring determines where a text block is placed in relation to the placeholder that it's modeled on. For example, if the placeholder is centered-anchored both vertically and horizontally, all text blocks based on it, whether large or small, will be centered on the same point as the placeholder. If the placeholder is top left–anchored, the top left corner of the text block (no matter what its size) will appear in the same location as the top left corner of the placeholder.

When anchoring, the frame of reference is the outline of the placeholder itself. In the following figure, we've applied a gray fill to a title placeholder on a slide master to show its outline. Below it, three examples show the relationship between the original placeholder outline and actual slide text when the placeholder is anchored horizontally at the top, at the center, and at the bottom. (In all three examples, the placeholder is anchored vertically at its center, and the text itself is aligned center.)

Figuring out the best anchor site for a placeholder takes practice, but here are some guidelines to help you start. For a slide title above a rule, anchoring at the bottom will cause slide title text to flow upward, rather than down over the rule. For a subtitle underneath a rule, anchoring at the top will cause text to flow down, leaving the rule unscathed. Anchoring body text at the top will usually give the best results.

This is a Title Placeholder.

**A PR Campaign
for the
Argilla Zoo**

**A PR Campaign
for the
Argilla Zoo**

**A PR Campaign
for the
Argilla Zoo**

Figure 13.12. The placeholder appears outlined at top and, in the three examples below it, in gray. The three examples show how text will flow when the placeholder is anchored bottom center, center center, and top center.

Although people sometimes confuse anchoring placeholders with aligning text inside a text block, they're really quite different operations. Anchoring determines the position of individual text blocks in relation to the placeholder when the text blocks are smaller or larger than the original placeholder. With anchoring, the frame of reference is the placeholder. By contrast, the alignment commands in the Text menu control how text aligns within a text block.

Figure 13.13 shows three text blocks based on the placeholder at the top of the figure. The placeholder has been filled with a pattern to show its dimensions. It is anchored top center. The three text blocks below it are all based on the top center–anchored placeholder, but each has a different text alignment command applied to it. Text is aligned left in the first, centered in the second, and aligned right in the third. Although the shape of the text blocks varies slightly to accommodate the differing alignments of their text, all three text blocks are anchored top center in relation to the original placeholder.

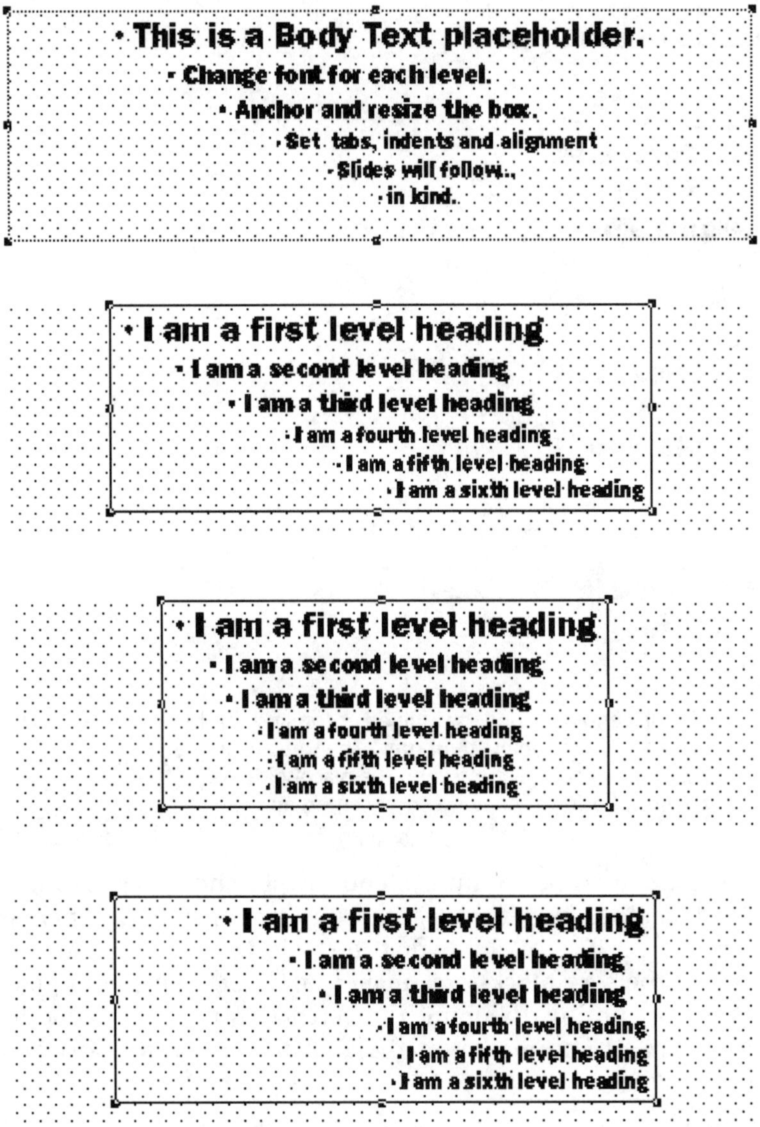

Figure 13.13. The placeholder appears outlined at top and, in the three examples below it, in gray. The three examples show the size and position of text blocks and text when the placeholder is anchored top center and the text is aligned left, center, and right.

Adding Other Text and Graphics

You can add freestanding text and graphics to a background or slide master just as you would to any slide. The advantage of adding elements to a master is that they'll appear on every slide to which the master is applied.

Use Persuasion's text and drawing tools to create and format text and graphics, or use the *Import* or *Copy*-and-*Paste* features to import text and graphics from other sources.

Defining Slide Builds on a Master

A slide build, as its name suggests, is a technique that gradually reveals information, or, you might say, information is "built," bit by bit, bulleted point by bulleted point, chart column by chart column, and so forth. It's a way of controlling your audience's attention, even of "building" suspense.

Let's say you're presenting your organization's marketing plan to the board of directors, and you intend to discuss four target market segments. The conventional way to present this information would be to list all four market segments on one slide. The slide goes up on the screen, and you begin to explore the first segment. Where is your audience's attention? Not with you! In fact, they're way ahead of you, reading what the second, third, and fourth market segments are. But by using a slide build, you can reveal the four market segments one by one. This way, you—not your slides—are running the show. You can also use builds to control the presentation of information in charts; you can build a pie chart slice by slice, a bar chart bar by bar, or a column chart column by column.

As its name suggests, a build is cumulative. That is, each slide adds to or builds on the information on the previous slide. In our example above, market segment one is joined by market segment two, which is then joined by market segment three, and so forth. Builds can be used effectively in all three presentation media, on-screen slide shows, 35-mm slides, and overhead transparencies. Working with overhead builds requires the use of a frame to ensure the precise registration of the building image. For more information on producing builds in different presentation media, consult Chapters 17–19.

There are two ways to define a build in Persuasion. One technique is to work on each slide individually, using the Layer pop-up menu to assign elements to different layers. The more efficient technique is to set up a slide build on a slide master; builds will be created automatically for any slide assigned that slide master. ("Automatically" here refers to the creation process, not to the presentation itself. You can still add each build layer manually when you give your slide show.)

Apply the master to any slide on which you want a build. Persuasion lets you define builds for body text, chart, and organization chart placeholders. Then, during a slide show, each slide is gradually revealed for body text builds, bulleted item by bulleted item; for a chart build, series by series or category by category; and for an organization chart, layer by layer.

To define a slide build, go to Master view, and use the pointer tool to select the body text, chart, or organization chart placeholder you want to work with. Choose *Build layers* from the Master menu. The dialog box you'll see depends on what kind of placeholder you selected.

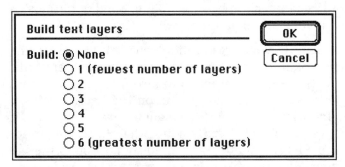

Figure 13.14.   In the Build text layers dialog box, you can specify that
text slides build layer-by-layer for up to six layers.

For a body text placeholder, select from one to six layers after *Build*. What does the number of build layers do? Each build layer corresponds to an outline level; if you specify five build layers, every heading in your outline down to the fifth level, will be revealed one at a time. In other words, the greater the number of build levels you specify, the finer the increments in which information builds on the slide.

Let's say you're running an on-screen slide show and you're showing slide 1, whose master calls for *one* build layer. The first time you click the mouse to display slide 1, the slide title and the first heading—along with all its subordinate headings—appears. The second time you click the mouse, the second heading and its subordinate headings appear, and so forth. In Figure 13.15 below, the slide at the top calls for one build layer.

How would calling for *two* build layers change how the text is revealed? The first time you click to display the slide, its title and the first heading— *without* any subordinate headings—appears. The second time you click, the first subordinate heading appears. The third time you click, the second subordinate heading appears, and so on. In Figure 13.15, the slide at the bottom calls for two build layers.

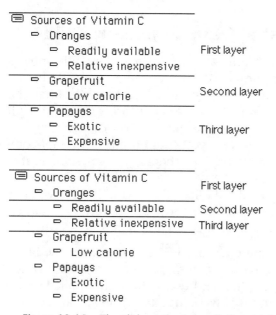

Figure 13.15. The slide at the top calls for one build layer. The slide at the bottom calls for two.

For a chart placeholder, indicate whether you want the chart built series by series or category by category. To turn off an existing build, choose *None*.

For an organization chart placeholder, select *Build layers for org. charts* to build the chart organization layer by organization layer. Deselect it to turn off an existing build.

How do you actually "produce" a slide build once you've defined it on a slide master? For an on-screen slide show, choose *Slide show* from the File menu. In the Slide show dialog box, enter the delay in seconds you want between build layers. To turn slide builds off altogether for the entire presentation, enter a 0-second delay.

When working with slides or overheads, to print a separate slide or overhead for each build layer, choose *Print* from the File menu. In the Print dialog box, choose *Builds* for *Graphic options*. (Leaving *Builds* unchecked produces a composite slide with no builds.)

Note: These two options control builds for the entire presentation. There's no way to turn builds off temporarily for an individual slide whose slide master calls for a build. If you want some slides with builds and some without, set up a separate slide master for each.

Creating a Slide Master from an Existing Slide

Not only can you save yourself some work by basing a new slide or background master on an existing master, you can create a new slide master based on an existing slide. Imagine you've been laboring long and hard on a particularly ingenious slide, and only when you're nearing the end does it occur to you that it would make a great slide master. How do you convert a plain old slide into a slide master? Well, you could use the *Select all* command to select all the slide elements and copy them to a blank slide master. But you'd still have to replace text blocks with true placeholders, and you'd probably have to add a slide background fill; in short, you'd still have to do quite a lot of tedious and time-consuming tinkering. Fortunately Persuasion provides an elegant, if complex, solution to this problem.

Working within an existing presentation, you can create a new, blank slide master, and then use the *Recreate from slide* feature to specify which elements of an existing slide—graphics and text—you want applied to the new slide master. Or you can use this technique to "recreate" an existing master; that is, to add elements to an already-created master.

To create or recreate a master based on an existing slide, go to Master view. Set up a new, blank slide master or choose the master to be recreated. Choose *Recreate from slide* from the Master menu. In the Choose master elements dialog box, use the Slide pop-up menu in the lower left corner to choose the slide whose ingredients you want to use. The dialog box's window will display a slide miniature that is large enough for you to see what you're doing.

Check *Create master from this slide*. Now you will have to select elements from the slide on display and assign them a placeholder role for your master. Click a slide element that you want on the new master, and then indicate what part you want it to play there. Usually, the best place to start is by identifying the text on which you want to base a title placeholder and then clicking *Title*. There are six "roles" that a slide element can play on a recreated master:

- Title placeholder
- Subtitle placeholder
- Body text placeholder

- Slide number placeholder
- Static element (any graphic or text not linked to the outline or data sheet)
- An element to be ignored

You can only identify one slide element per placeholder; in other words, no master can have more than one title, subtitle, body text, or slide number placeholder. Each slide element you identify as a placeholder will appear on the master in the same place and with the same text specifications as on the original slide.

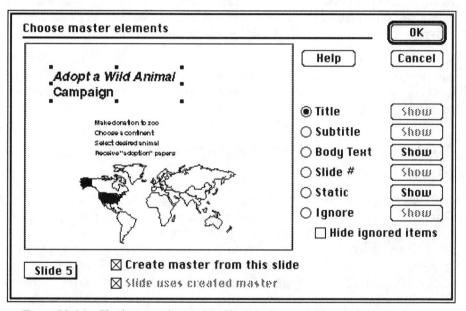

Figure 13.16. The large and complex Choose master elements dialog box lets you build a new master based on an existing slide, and apply the master to slides.

The available roles depend on the type of element you select. You can assign any text element the role of title, subtitle, body text, or slide number placeholder. Charts, tables, and graphics, however, can only be assigned the role of a static element, or ignored.

If there are slide elements that you don't want on your new master, select them, and then click *Ignore*. To avoid the distraction of looking at elements you're trying to ignore, check *Hide ignored items*.

To find out what role slide elements have been assigned on the new master, click the appropriate *Show* button in the list to the right of the thumbnail window. For example, to see which element you've identified as a subtitle, click the *Show* button after *Subtitle*. If no element has been assigned a particular role, its *Show* button will be dimmed.

Once you've finished setting up the new slide master, you can apply it to existing slides in the presentation before you close the Choose master elements dialog box. Choose the slide you want formatted with this new master from the slide pop-up menu, then check *Slide uses created master*. (The names of unmodified slides are italicized in the pop-up menu; slides to which you've assigned the master appear in regular roman style.) When you close the dialog box, Persuasion constructs the new slide master and applies it to any slides for which you've clicked *Slide uses created master*.

By the way, in tacit recognition that re-creating a slide master can be complex, the Choose master elements dialog box includes a direct line to the Persuasion's Help menus. Just click on the *Help* button and read on—never be too shy to ask for help!

Applying or Removing a Background Master to a Slide Master

Here's where you get to mix and match background and slide masters. You can, if you wish, apply a background master to a slide master. Let's say you've set up one background master with a graduated dark-to-light-blue fill pattern (called *Blue Bkgd*) and another with a radial mauve-to-violet fill (called *Mauve Bkgd*). Now you're setting up a slide master for a title slide (called *Title*). You have a choice. You can apply background color directly to the slide master, or you can apply color by assigning one of the two background masters. The second option gives you more flexibility. You can assign the background-plus-slide-master combination *Blue Bkgd-plus-Title* to some slides and *Mauve Bkgd-plus-Title* to others.

To apply a background master to a slide master, go to the slide master you want to work with, then choose a background from the Background pop-up menu. If the slide master already has a background master assigned to it and you wish to remove it, choose *None*.

Assigning background masters to slide masters can occasionally create conflicts. For example, what happens when you apply the mauve-and-violet background master to a pink-and-chartreuse slide master? In general, Persuasion assumes you want the background fill to take precedence (otherwise, why would you apply a background master in the first place?). But you can set up a slide master whose fill takes precedence over its background master's fill. To do this, when you apply a slide background fill to the slide master, uncheck *Use fill from background master*. We'll come back to slide background fills in just a minute.

Figure 13.17. Use the Background pop-up menu to apply background masters to slide masters.

What do you get if you cross a tall background master with a wide slide master? Two medium-sized masters? Nope, the slide master's orientation changes to match its background master. And, if you open the Master menu, *Tall orientation* will be dimmed because the only way you can change the slide master's orientation is by changing its background master's orientation (or by removing the background master altogether).

Renaming and Removing Masters

A few last words about masters. To remove or rename a master, choose *Define masters* from the Master menu. The Define masters dialog box includes a list of all the presentation's slide and background masters.

To rename a master, click its name in the list box and type the new name in the *Rename* box. To remove a master, select it, and click *Remove*. Persuasion removes the master from all menus and from any slides to which it has been applied.

To create a new slide master, click *New*, then proceed as described above. This is equivalent to choosing *New* from either of the Go to master menus.

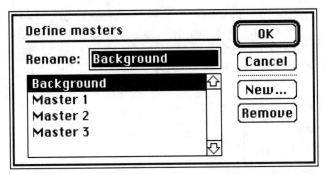

Figure 13.18. Use the Define master dialog box to rename and remove slide and background masters.

Congratulations! You're now an expert on creating simple and not-so-simple presentations with Persuasion. Practice and experience will hone your skills and take you to ever greater heights of presentation prowess!

Chapter 14

Importing and Exporting

Despite the extensive graphics, chart, and text capabilities that are built into Persuasion, you will often want to import text and graphic elements from other applications. This will relieve you of the rather burdensome task of rekeying data, or recreating graphics in Persuasion. Persuasion is conversant with text and graphics formats used in many word processing, spreadsheet, and graphics programs; it also allows you to import templates from other Persuasion presentations including those from its MS-DOS counterpart, PC Persuasion. Persuasion can even import entire presentations created in Microsoft PowerPoint.

Exporting is just about as versatile as importing. You can save all or part of a Persuasion presentation in commonly used text and graphics formats that can be read by a majority of text and graphic applications. Persuasion does not exist on an island! Its purpose is to allow you to put together your presentation as easily as possible, using data from any number of sources. Let's discuss how to make Persuasion talk to other applications first. Then we will explain how to borrow parts of one Persuasion presentation and use them in another.

Importing Text Files

Persuasion can also read text-only files that can be created by virtually any word processor, spreadsheet application, and other text-oriented application using that application's text (also called ASCII) Save option.

Importing an Outline

Persuasion can import outline files in their native formats from Acta 2.1, and 3, MacWrite 4.0, and More 1.0, 1.1, or 1.1c; it will retain the heading levels. If you are using a version of More (in particular, More 2.x or later), you will have to save your outline within More 2.x using the *More 1.x Save* option that comes with the More 2.x package. That way Persuasion will import the file without any problem.

Importing Outlines Saved As Text

Persuasion will also import a word processing outline saved as a text file. Persuasion will place imported text on different levels depending on the number of tab keystrokes contained in the imported file. Persuasion will format the imported text according to the number of tabs that precede each line of text. Each tab in the imported outline indents a level in Persuasion. For example, if an imported outline begins with three tabs, Persuasion will place the line on level three, and two tabs place the line in level two.

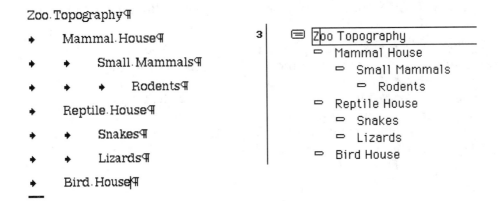

Figure 14.1   You can import a text file from Microsoft Word directly into Persuasion. The number of consecutive tabs in the Word file determine the heading level within Persuasion.

Importing from the Clipboard

A quick way to import an outline is to use the Clipboard. You can also copy all or part of another outline or tabbed text to the Clipboard and then paste that outline directly into your Persuasion outline. Persuasion will maintain all the heading and subheading information from the original outline.

Importing other Presentations

Persuasion 2.0's importing feature is particularly capable when it comes to importing a presentation created in another application, in particular Microsoft PowerPoint. The import process is a two-step one. First, you use the original presentation software application to save the file in Scrapbook format. When you use the option in Microsoft PowerPoint to save a presentation in Scrapbook file format, the program places each slide on a separate scrapbook page. Persuasion will then import the scrapbook by converting each Scrapbook page into separate slide. So far so good. Here is a step-by-step explanation of how this procedure works.

First, open Microsoft PowerPoint and the PowerPoint presentation that you want to import into Persuasion.

Then choose *Save As* from PowerPoint's Edit menu. Click on the *Save slides as pictures in a scrapbook* option, and name the file. That completes your work with PowerPoint. Quit PowerPoint.

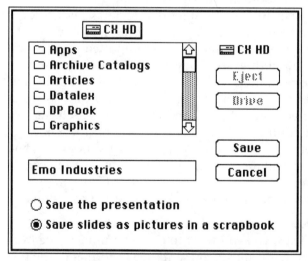

Figure 14.2   Save the Microsoft PowerPoint presentation using the Scrapbook option to import the file into Persuasion.

Now your presentation file is ready for Persuasion. Open Persuasion and either start a new presentation or open an existing one. If you are starting a new presentation, you can simply choose *Import* from the File menu. For an existing presentation, click on the heading in the outline view above the spot where you want to insert the imported presentation.

When the Import dialog box opens, Persuasion lists all files in the open folder that it has identified as importable. Open the folder that contains the Scrapbook you created in PowerPoint and then open this Scrapbook. In a few minutes, the *Choose master elements* dialog box will appear. The choices you make next within this dialog box are important. The Choose master elements dialog box gives you the option to import the entire presentation by pasting the contents of each Scrapbook page onto a slide, as a static object. Or, you can actually convert it to a more fully functioning Persuasion presentation.

If you make no choice at all and simply click *OK*, Persuasion will import the file, pasting the contents of each scrapbook page on separate Persuasion slides. Persuasion will treat the text and graphics elements on each slide as static objects, that is with no dynamic links to an outline or to a master slide. Each text and graphic element exists as though you created them freehand on each slide. If you need to change titles or body text you will have to so directly on the slide rather than within an outline.

Instead, you can use the Choose master elements dialog box to actually define text and graphic elements on the imported slide as placeholders, similar to defining placeholders on a standard Persuasion master slide. The advantage to making placeholder assignments for an imported presentation is that by defining the title, subtitle, and body text they automatically become part of the Persuasion outline with all of the advantages of being able to use the outliner in the creation and editing process. This process works fairly well, but it isn't perfect, since Persuasion has to define each element on each imported slide according to its relative position on that slide. Assuming that there is a general pattern for the position of various text and graphics elements in the presentation you are importing, Persuasion can do an adequate job of defining the parts of each slide. After the importing process is complete, however, be sure to recheck Persuasion's assignments.

Persuasion only creates one master slide initially when importing a Scrapbook presentation. Thus, you will want to choose a model slide from the imported presentation that is most representative in format of the presentation as a whole. (We will discuss the procedure for creating more masters from the imported presentation later.)

To choose an imported slide as a model master slide for your Persuasion presentation use the pop-up menu in the lower left of the dialog box. This should be a slide typical in terms of positioning of title, subtitle, and body text. Don't pick a slide with a graphic or chart unless it is typical of the rest of the presentation. By default, Persuasion chooses slide two from the imported presentation. (Persuasion assumes that slide one is a title slide and, therefore, not typical of the other slides in the presentation.) Once you decide on a slide to use as the master, check *Create master from this slide*. The name of this slide becomes underlined in the pop-up menu to remind you of your choice, and the *Slide uses created master* option dims.

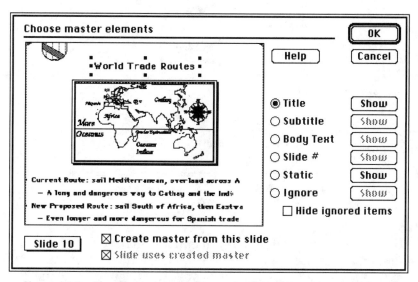

Figure 14.3   The Choose master elements dialog box presents options for defining Persuasion placeholders for a typical imported slide.

Now it's time to start the definition process itself. Click on the element in the miniature slide that you want to define as a master slide placeholder, and then click the corresponding placeholder radio button along the right side. For example, click on the element in the miniature slide that you want to define as Title and then click on the *Title* button. Continue defining elements on the model slide by selecting an element in the slide and then defining it by clicking on a definition button to the right. Figure 14.4 shows how you might define placeholders for an imported slide.

When you first designate an imported slide as a model for a master, Persuasion treats all text and graphic elements on that slide as static unless you define them otherwise. Any items you do not define are static items, and become the master slide's background. If you want Persuasion to ignore extraneous slide elements, and not make them part of the master, select them, and then click the Ignore button. Those elements will not be part of the master at all. You can confirm this visually by clicking on the *Hide ignored items* box. When checked, you will view all elements that have been defined.

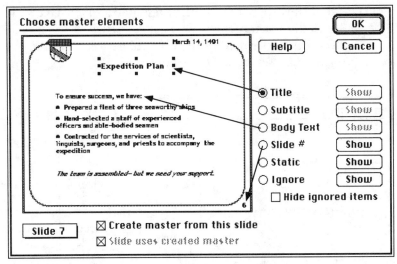

Figure 14.4   This slide is typical of most slides in this particular presentation so we've chosen it as the master mode.

Note: Sometimes a presentation that you import will have a solid white background that lies hidden in the background of the master slide. If you don't notice the solid background and leave it defined as Static it may cover some of your slides when you finish the import procedure. You can identify this type of background by clicking the *Show Static* button and then observing whether there are selection handles in each of the four corners of the definition slide. If you see these four extra handles in the corners, click anywhere in the slide to deselect everything in the slide and then click in a corner of the slide to select only the solid background. Then click the *Ignore* button.

You may assign only one element from the model slide as a title, subtitle, body text, and slide number placeholder, just as you would for a normal Persuasion master slide. However, you can assign multiple elements as static elements or as elements to be ignored. To review your assignments for each type of element, select an element, click the *Show* button, and Persuasion will select any item(s) in the slide display that conforms to that type.

If you've defined an element and you then change your mind and want to redefine it, all you have to do is select the element and make your new choice from the list of definitions along the right. Persuasion will automatically redefine the element.

Once you define a model master slide, you can then go through each slide in the imported presentation and decide whether or not to apply that master. Use the pop-up slide menu in the lower left to view each slide and check or uncheck the *Slide uses created master* option for each individual slide. However, there are a few things to bear in mind as you make your decision about using the master.

If you do *not* check the *Slide uses created master* for a particular slide, then all text and graphics elements on that slide will be static as though you added them directly on the slide. They will not appear in the outline. You can tell at a glance which slides are assigned to the master by the slide number that appears in the pop-up list: slides that do use the created master appear in the pop-up menu in italic type.

The best advice is to use the created master whenever possible. Although a slide may not exactly match the model, you can always switch master slides once the import procedure is complete.

When you have assigned the master to all the appropriate imported slides, you can click *OK* in the Choose master elements dialog box. Depending on the size of your presentation, Persuasion will continue the process of importing the presentation and, in a few minutes, will open into a normal looking Persuasion presentation.

When you import a presentation into a new Persuasion file, Persuasion will use the AutoTemplate you selected for the presentation (or it will use the default one if you haven't chosen one). For either a new or existing presentation, Persuasion will add a new name to the list of master slides. This new name is the name of the import file itself. If, by chance, there is already a master slide with the same name, Persuasion will append a number to the master slide name such as .0, .1. so as not to overwrite one master slide name with another.

Touch-ups

Unless every slide in your imported presentation happens to be identical in format (which isn't very likely), Persuasion will probably have difficulty making a perfect correlation between the newly created master slide and each individual slide in the presentation. It is imperative that you review your Persuasion presentation—slide-by-slide—to make adjustments. Once the presentation is imported into Persuasion, you can create additional master slides or reassign the imported slides to existing master slides.

For a discussion about importing data sheet information for charts and tables from other applications, refer to Chapter 10, *Working with Charts and Tables*.

Adding and Modifying Imported Masters
Importing Graphics

In addition to converting scrapbook files to presentations, Persuasion can also import PICT, PICTII, and EPS (Encapsulated PostScript) graphics as individual images on specific slides. You can also import scanned images if you save them in one of these graphic file formats.

To import a graphic, it is imperative that you be in the Slide view with the destination slide before you and choose *Import* from the File menu. Bear in mind that you cannot place a graphic in the Outline view. Using the *Import* command in this view will only display text files in the Import dialog box even if there are graphics files in the same folder.

In the slide view, Persuasion lists all the PICT, PICTII, and EPS graphics files in that folder. Select the graphic you want, open it, and Persuasion places it on the slide. You can drag the graphic's handles to resize or scale the graphic. If you keep your finger on the Shift key while resizing the graphic, Persuasion will resize it while maintaining the graphic's proportion.

> *Note:* When you import a PICT graphic, you can use Persuasion's graphics tools to ungroup and edit the graphic. However, you cannot ungroup an EPS image—you can only resize it. Note that when a PICT graphic is ungrouped, its elements are converted into Persuasion elements.

Importing from other Persuasion Presentations

In addition to importing slides and graphics from other applications, Persuasion 2.0 also lets you import slide masters, background masters, the notes master, defined text formats, colors, and chart formats from another Persuasion presentation or an AutoTemplate.

Importing Master Slides from Another Persuasion Presentation

In the course of preparing a presentation, it is not unusual to want to borrow some or all of the master slides from another presentation or from an AutoTemplate file. After all, why should you have to spend time reinventing a presentation format.

To import a set of master slides from another Persuasion presentation or an AutoTemplate, choose *AutoTemplates* from in the File menu. The Select AutoTemplate dialog box that appears lists all of the Persuasion files in that folder, both presentations and AutoTemplates.

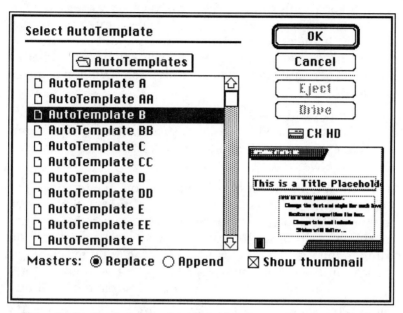

Figure 14.5 The AutoTemplate dialog box has options for appending or replacing a presentation's master slides with another presentation's.

If you check the *Show thumbnail* box, you can see a miniature of a master slide that is associated with the highlighted Autotemplate. (The master slide shown is the one—usually a title master—for that particular presentation or template.) When you find the file you wish to import, you have two choices: you can replace the masters in your existing presentation with the masters from the selected file, or you can append the master slides from the other presentation to your existing presentation. In either case, you will be importing all the masters, and the text and chart formats from the other template or presentation. Here is how *Replace* and *Append* work and their ramifications.

Note: The action of replacing master slides is not undoable. Save a copy of your original presentation just in case the replacement does not work as well as you had expected.

Replace

If you choose to replace your master slides with those from another presentation, all new masters are imported as follows. If the imported master has the same name as one in the current presentation, the imported master replaces the current one. Only the slides whose masters were overwritten by the imported masters will be changed. Persuasion will recreate the presentation accordingly. If the new, imported masters are of a different size than the ones in your current presentation, however, you will be asked whether you want Persuasion to adjust graphics of the current presentation to match that of the imported file.

Retained text formats will also be imported along with the master slides. If a text format in the imported presentation has the same name as one in the current presentation, the imported text format will replace that text format.

With the *Replace* option, the set of color names from the imported presentation will replace the color names in the current presentation. The effect of this can be difficult to predict. Each of the 40 colors in the imported presentation will replace those in the current presentation according to its relative position in the Persuasion color grid. Thus, the imported color grid is simply overlaid on the current one. Any objects that you have colored will take on the new imported color that now occupies that grid location.

When you select *Replace*, Persuasion replaces any chart formats in the menu that have the same name as any of those of the imported presentation. Any charts that you have already drawn, however, will not change. If you have any masters with chart placeholders that have been replaced, all charts based on those masters will be redrawn according to the new format.

Append

Using the *Append* command is by definition more controllable than the *Replace* command. Instead of arbitrarily replacing masters with the same name, the *Append* command adds formatting information to the existing presentation.

If you append master slides from another presentation to the current presentation, all of the masters from the external presentation file are added to the active presentation. In cases where master slide names are the same in both presentations, Persuasion modifies the duplicated names to keep them separate.

Table 14.1 summarizes the effects either *Replace* or *Append* has on your presentation.

With the *Append* option, the rule for master slide names also holds true for text formats. Imported text formats are added to those in the current presentation. In cases of conflict where two text formats share the same name, Persuasion renames the imported text format so that you can tell the difference between the imported text format and the original format.

Colors and color names are not imported, and chart formats are listed as additional choices in the Chart menu of the current presentation.

If Persuasion sees that the appended masters are in a different format (for a different output device) from those in the active presentation, the Adjust graphics dialog box will appear. If you want to adjust the size of the appended masters, click *OK.* In any case, the best advice is to flip through your slides one-by-one when you have made any change to your templates. It is easier to catch any change that may have slipped by before you produce the actual show.

Table 14.1

Element	Replace	Append
Slide masters Background masters Notes masters	All masters will be imported into the current presentation. If two masters have the same name, the imported master will automatically replace the current one. All slides based on replaced masters will be recreated according to the imported file's specifications.	All masters will be added to those in the current presentation. If an imported master has the same name as the one in the current presentation, Persuasion will change the name of the imported master so that you can distinguish it from the master in the current presentation. Persuasion will append a decimal number to the duplicate master names (.0, .1, .2,)

(continued)

Table 14.1 *(continued)*

Element	Replace	Append
Defined text formats	All text formats will be imported. If two text formats have the same name, the imported text format will replace the one in the current presentation.	The imported text formats will be added to those in the current presentation. If two text formats have the same name, Persuasion will change the name of the imported text format so that it you can distinguish it from the text format in the current presentation.
Colors	The set of color names will completely replace the color names in the current presentation. The 40 editable colors in the selected AutoTemplate will replace those in the current presentation. The new color replaces the color that was located in the same location in the color grid. Objects using an old color will be changed to the new color that now occupies that location in the grid.	Colors and color names are not imported.
Chart formats	The chart formats in the selected presentation will replace those in the current presentation. However, any existing charts whose format is replaced will remain unchanged unless you replot them. Any charts based on changed placeholders will automatically replot. Other charts will remain unchanged unless you explicitly replot them.	All chart formats will be added to those in the current presentation.

Click *OK* to complete the operation (or *Cancel* if you change your mind and want no changes to the current presentation).

Exporting from Persuasion

The *Export* command offers you four export options. You can export a slide, a group of slides, an outline, or a group of selected outline headings. The more presentations you create, the more you will come to appreciate the *Export* command. Instead of having to recreate slides or reenter outline text from scratch, the *Export* command is perfect for porting graphics and text to other Persuasion presentations. You can use the same commands to export Persuasion elements for use in other applications, too, since Persuasion can save both outlines and slides in popular text and graphics formats.

Exporting Slides

It is common to want to reuse slides from one presentation in another presentation. You can export a single slide or an entire slide show for use in another presentation. When you click either the *All slides* or *Current slide* button, the choices in the Format pop-up menu at the right of the dialog box will display the available graphic file formats, namely PICT and Scrapbook. The *Background fill*, *Builds*, and *Fewer colors* options also become active.

Select *Background fill* to export the slide's background fill, as well as the slide's contents. If left unchecked, the slide's fill will not transfer. Do not check the background fill option if you plan on using another background fill in the new presentation. Select *Builds* to create a separate slide for each build layer; that is, one slide from layer one and a second slide for layers one and two. If *Builds* is left unchecked, Persuasion will export a single slide with composite builds. Check *Fewer colors* to reduce the number of colors exported for slides with graduated fills. This will reduce the quality of the slide, but will increase the printing speed.

Once you have made your option choices, choose a file format from the Format pop-up menu. The choice is either PICT or Scrapbook as shown in Figure 14.6. If you choose PICT, Persuasion will create a separate PICT file for each slide you export. The slides will be labeled with the file name you type together with sequential numbers that Persuasion adds. For example, a 23-slide presentation called Budget saved in PICT format will be saved as separate files labeled Budget.000, Budget.001, Budget.002, etc., all the way to Budget.022. If on the other hand, you check the *Builds* option and have builds within the presentation, then the number of PICT files will exceed the number of slides you selected for export.

If you choose the Scrapbook format, then Persuasion will save the presentation as a single Scrapbook placing one slide on a page.

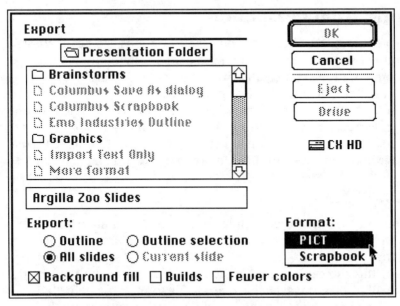

Figure 14.6   When you select to export slides, the choices in the Format pop-up menu change from those of the outline formats.

Exporting a Persuasion Outline

Exporting an outline from Persuasion is as easy as importing one. The list of applications Persuasion supports for exporting is identical to importing: text (ASCII), Acta 2.01, or More 1.0, 1.1, or 1.1c formats.

To export an outline choose *Export* from the File menu. The dialog box in Figure 14.7 appears.

The first thing to do is to type the name of the export file and choose what folder you want it placed in. Then you need to choose what part of the Persuasion file you want to export, the entire outline or just a selection. If you want to export a selection, then you need to make the selection before you open the Export dialog box. Use Persuasion's multiple selection techniques (refer to Chapter 5, *Beginning with Ideas*) if you want to export non-contiguous parts of the outline. Once you select the outline headings, click the *Outline selection* button. Persuasion then saves the selected headings and their respective subordinates.

If, on the other hand, you want to export an entire outline, just check the *Outline* button in the dialog box and Persuasion will do the rest.

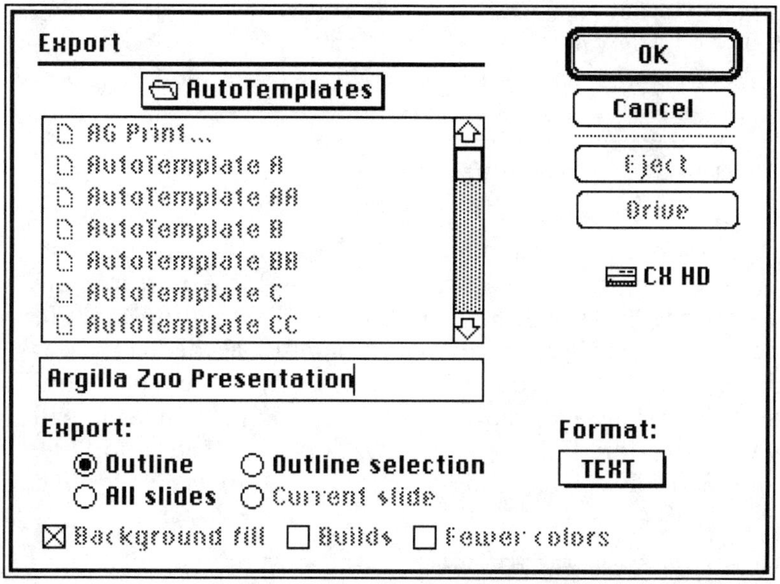

Figure 14.7   The Export dialog box presents the options for exporting your outline to another application or as a text file.

The last choice in the Export dialog box is to choose the format you want to save the outline in. As you can see in Figure 14.6, you can choose either Text, Acta, or More. Choose an export format that the receiving application will understand. Unless the destination application specifically supports Acta or More, choose Text. Persuasion places a tab in the export file for each level in the outline.

If you want to use an exported Persuasion outline file in Microsoft Word, for example, just save the file as text and you will be able to directly open it in Word. Once in Word, you may want to turn on the invisible characters (*Command-Y*) to see the tabs so that you can adjust the tabs in the ruler for best display.

Argilla Zoo Presentation

Export:

⦿ **Outline**   ○ **Outline selection**

○ **All slides**   ○ Current slide

☒ Background fill ☐ Builds ☐ Fewer c…

Format:

| **TEXT** |
| Acta |
| **MORE** |

Figure 14.8   Outline export choices are text, Acta, or More.

Note: Just as you need a workaround when importing a More 2.x out-line into Persuasion, there is a similar workaround to export to More 2.x. First, save the Persuasion in More format. Then, within More II, choose *Open* from the File menu and select More 1.x as the file type, as shown in Figure 14.7. If you don't select the More 1.x file type within More, the outline you saved with the More option in Persuasion will not appear in the More II dialog box. Then, open the Persuasion file. More II automatically converts earlier More outlines to its own format.

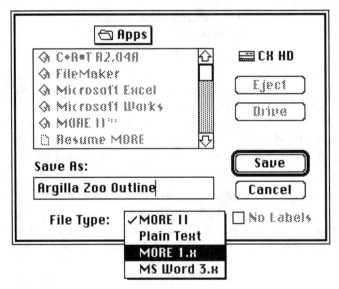

📁 **Apps**

◇ C◆R◆T A2.048
◇ FileMaker
◇ Microsoft Excel
◇ Microsoft Works
◇ MORE II™
🗋 Resume MORE

⊟ CX HD

[Eject]

[Drive]

Save As:

Argilla Zoo Outline

[**Save**]

[**Cancel**]

File Type: ✓MORE II
                Plain Text
                MORE 1.x
                MS Word 3.x

☐ No Labels

Figure 14.9   More 2.x can import other More file formats. Be sure to choose the More 1.x format within More 2.x. For this option to appear, you will need to have the More 1.x filter in your System file (this filter comes with More).

Exporting a Data Sheet

Persuasion also allows you to export a data sheet into a text file; it can then be used within a spreadsheet, word processor, or any other application that can read a text file. Each column of the exported data sheet is separated by an embedded tab character, and each row is separated by a carriage return.

To export a data sheet, open the data sheet you want to export and then choose *Export* from the File menu. The data sheet export dialog box will appear as illustrated in Figure 14.8.

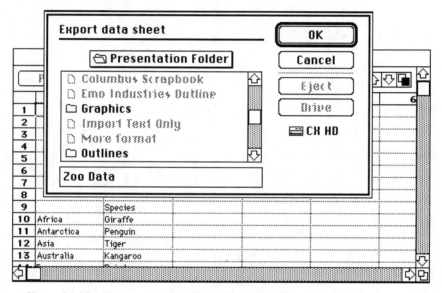

Figure 14.10   To export a data sheet, open the data sheet and then choose *Export* from the File menu.

Name the file and choose the folder you want the new file placed in. Then click *OK*. Persuasion saves the entire data sheet as a text file. It is not possible to save just a selection from the data sheet.

As you can see, Persuasion is pretty good at moving information in and out of a presentation. In a corporate environment, this makes it easier for several people to work on a presentation using the tools they know best. The presenter might use More, Acta, or a word processor to capture the text for the presentation. A designer can use any popular drawing package such

such as MacDraw or SuperPaint, or a professional level product such as Aldus FreeHand or Adobe Illustrator to generate professional looking artwork. The presentation production person can then integrate all of the text and graphics files into a presentation with the added flexibility of being able to work with the text in Persuasion outline form.

Part III ◆ Behind the Scenes

Chapter 15

Designing Effective Presentations

Reflect for a moment on your experience as a presentation audience member. Remember when you strained from the back row to see type that's too small to be read by the naked eye farther than 10 inches away? Struggled to speed read a slide that looks like the first page of a novel, only to have it vanish before you get to the end of the first sentence? How about the slide whose type fades into the background so it's like trying to read an unlit billboard at midnight? Or the slide that looks like a supermarket advertising flyer, so cluttered with "specials" that you have no idea what to look at first? Or the graph that plots airplane departures against chickadee births on a polka dot background? Or the presentation in which each slide looks like the work of a different first grader, each contributing their own unique vision of the subject? Or slides that are so boring, you wish they'd turn off all the lights and let you sleep in peace?

We laugh, of course, but partly it's a laugh of recognition: we know it's really not that hard to be the poor, misguided presenter in these extreme examples. Mastering the science of Persuasion is one thing, but mastering the art of Persuasion as quite another. Just because you have the tools doesn't mean you're born knowing how to use them effectively.

As you've seen, Persuasion's AutoTemplates provide you lots of guidance. But inevitably the day will come, when, either because you've grown tired of the AutoTemplates or because you're just feeling adventurous, you'll want to design your own presentation from scratch. And unless you're trained in graphic design and typography, you may suddenly find yourself confronted with questions you've never considered before. How do I make sure type is readable? What colors are good? What colors are bad? Is there an alternative to centering everything?

This section is a quick-and-dirty guide to designing effective presentations. It's organized as a series of practical tips—do's and don'ts—so you don't have to wade through a treatise on the aesthetics of design and typography before finding the answer to your question. At the same time, we give reasons for our recommendations on the assumption that, though you're busy, you're also curious about why certain things work better than others.

Before we get into the tips, though, just a few words to put presentation design in its proper place. Consider why you're using visuals in the first place: to clarify your message; to support your argument; to highlight critical information; to focus your audience's attention. And some "non-reasons": to decorate, astound, awe, overwhelm, or just generally impress your audience with the technological prowess of your desktop presentation equipment.

Visuals are meant to help you communicate more effectively. To do this, they should reinforce, rather than overwhelm, your spoken presentation. If people get more interested in looking at the intricate flowers on the bar chart than they do in understanding that they're headed toward bankruptcy unless they follow your recommendations, you may win the battle but lose the war. You may get named *Presenter of the Year* for a company that's just gone belly up. Design is the business of communicating visually, not decorating or making things pretty.

Okay, so much for the pep talk. Here are the tips. They're divided into four sections: layout, type, color, and graphics.

Layout

Layout is the process of arranging elements on the page. Ideally, layout is a conscious, intentional process rather than accidental and chaotic. A slide's layout should be appropriate for the number and kind of elements it contains, and layout should be more or less consistent from slide to slide. Here are some specific guidelines for effective slide layouts.

Keep Slides as Simple as Possible

Your audience should be able to make sense of a slide in 10 seconds or less. If it takes any longer, they'll still be reading while you're talking. Since very few people can read and listen effectively at the same time, your audience will probably not be paying much attention to you for the first few seconds they see each new slide. Try to minimize that lost attention by keeping the slide as simple as possible.

Here's how.

Every slide should focus on a single idea, and should include no more than one illustration, graphic, or chart. For text slides, use a maximum of six to seven words per line. Since the average person can take in about 40 characters, or six to seven words, at a glance, they can digest your slide one complete line at a time, fast and efficiently.

Use a maximum of six to seven lines per slide, including the slide title. This means no more than five to six bulleted items. Four is ideal.

If you have lots to say on one topic, divide it among two or more slides rather than cramming it onto one. Repeat the title on each continuation slide, and use the same layout and type specs. Place the word "continued" in small type after the slide title or in a corner.

Avoid the "Rambo" approach to presentation design. Don't haul out every visual tank and cannon you own. Just because you have a portfolio of 100 typefaces and an extensive clip art library doesn't mean you have show them off in every presentation. Keep what's most important, and let go of the rest. The old adage "Less is more" applies especially well to designing presentations with persuasion.

Keep slides simple

Focus on a single idea
One graphic, chart, or table
Maximum 6-7 words per line
Maximum 6-7 lines per slide

Avoid the Rambo approach to presentation design

Don't feature every typeface you've ever bought
Don't show off your clip art collection
Don't try to fit an entire report on a single slide or else your audience will still be reading long after you're ready to switch to a new slide, and they won't have heard a word you've said

Figure 15.1. Keep slides as simple as possible. Avoid the Rambo approach to presentation design.

Use Visual Emphasis to Support Your Argument

Use the power of "optical weight" to control what your audience looks at, and in what order. Optical weight is the power of an element to attract the eye's attention. The tools you have at your disposal are size, weight, color, shape, and "white" or background space.

A large square has more optical weight, or visual attraction, than a small square. Bold weight type has more optical weight than light type. Against a dark background, a light, bright color has more optical weight than a darker color. An unusual shape, like a starburst, has more optical weight than a square or a circle. And a graphic floating in space has more optical weight than one that's drowning in a sea of clutter.

Make the most important element largest, heaviest, most brightly colored, and don't make it compete with anything else for your audience's attention. Emphasize key points, and deemphasize subordinate points. Avoid crying wolf; i.e., visually insisting that everything's equally important. (Of course, if you haven't established your priorities, you won't be able to communicate them clearly to your audience.)

Create Unity by Being Consistent

"Consistency is the hobgoblin of small minds," goes the saying. Hobgoblin or not, consistency is the spirit of communication. In a way, design is a teacher. It teaches your audience what to expect. Good design quickly establishes rules, raises expectations, and meets them consistently. In an effective presentation, by the third or fourth slide, people will already understand the visual "language" of the presentation: for example, the most important ideas appear in bold white type, subordinate ideas appear in regular yellow type, and reference material like labels and legends appear in blue italic type. Consistency makes communication very effective because the audience doesn't need to reorient themselves for each new slide.

Establish a set of rules and stick to them. Use all design elements consistently, including

- Line style, pattern, color, and background;
- Fill pattern, color, and background;
- Shadow pattern and color

Assign rules and borders the same weight and position on every slide. Use one format for all titles, another for all subtitles, another for all level one headings, and so on. Place elements consistently, for example, all titles centered 2 picas above a 2-point rule; all body text aligned 6 picas from the left edge; and the logo 3 picas in from the bottom right corner.

Try to fill an equal area on each slide. If necessary, adjust type size slightly, but make sure it doesn't fluctuate wildly slide to slide. Use color consistently as well.

Consider the transition between slides: if the placement of repetitive elements such as the title or a logo changes from slide to slide, you'll have the presentation equivalent of a flip book—one of those little books whose contents appear to move when you flip the pages fast. This can be very disconcerting to an audience. Use Persuasion's slide sorter and view all slides at once to test for consistency.

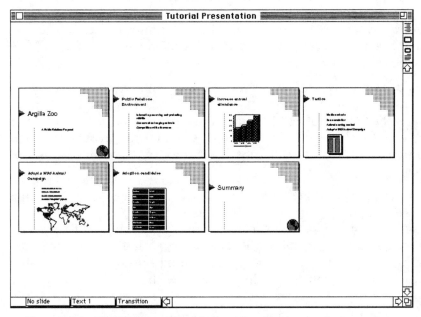

Figure 15.2. The Slide sorter can help you assess the consistency of your presentation.

The more consistent you are, the more opportunity you have to be inconsistent for a purpose. If the background of the first ten slides has been deep blue, consider the impact of an eleventh slide with a fiery red background. When you want to startle your audience, stir them up, set them off balance, or just plain wake them up, break the rules you've established. Reverse the foreground and background colors to change moods or signal a transition. Change the title font for an especially critical point. But, be sure to break your rules only intentionally for a clearly defined purpose that you're sure you're achieving, rather than out of boredom or carelessness.

Persuasion's slide master system makes consistency easy to achieve. Determine in advance what types of layouts your presentation will require, set up slide masters for each layout, and then apply the slide masters without too much variation to each individual slide of your presentation. Use the

Based on feature to base new slide masters on existing ones, to ensure consistent placement of repetitive elements. And use the *Formats* and *Set colors* features to ensure a consistent typographical and color palette.

Balance Your Slides

Consider the kind of tone you want your presentation to convey. Do you want a presentation that's dignified, formal, staid, and authoritative? Use a symmetrical layout, one in which every element is mirrored across a central axis. Or do you want a more casual, dynamic feel for your presentation? Use an asymmetrical layout.

No matter which type of layout you choose, symmetrical or asymmetrical, it must be balanced. Balancing symmetrical layouts is simple: whatever you put on the left side of a slide, put on the right side too, and then center all the type. Voila, a perfectly balanced, symmetrical layout! Although symmetrical layouts convey dignity and authority, they run the risk of being boring.

Asymmetrical layouts are harder to do well. They depend on balancing the optical weight of elements. If a large object has more optical weight than a small object, and a bright color has more optical weight than a dark color, then a small bright object will balance a large dark object. Obviously you can't go out and buy a scale for measuring optical weight. But the concept of optical weight can help you analyze the effectiveness of your layouts.

Some people, drawing on their innate ability to perceive balance, can move elements around the screen until they just "feel" right. Most of us, however, have to develop a sense of balance consciously. Ask yourself whether one side of the slide looks "heavier" or more crowded than the other, or whether it's top or bottom heavy. Learn to distinguish between chaos masquerading as an asymmetrical layout and a layout that's truly balanced.

Why bother with asymmetrical layouts if they're difficult to get right? In contrast to symmetrical layouts, asymmetrical layouts can be more casual, energetic, dynamic, and visually interesting. And, once you get the hang of it, they're fun to work with.

One last tip regarding balance: keep all slides in a horizontal layout. If you have a strong vertical graphic—a diagram of the Empire State Building, for example—don't center it on the slide and leave dead space to the left and right. Instead, put the graphic to one side or the other, and fill the remaining space with appropriate text or a solid color.

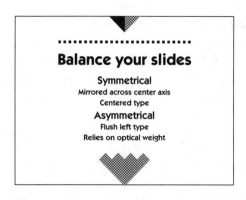

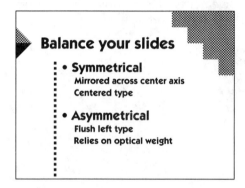

Figure 15.3. A symmetrical layout and an asymmetrical layout.

Avoid Layout Claustrophobia

This is a corollary of the first rule, "Keep it simple." Layout claustrophobia is a serious but preventable condition that arises when every square inch of a slide is full, with lots of big type, borders, graphics, clip art, and so forth. In print design, we talk about leaving white space—unfilled, open, airy territory on the page. Since more often than not a slide's background won't be white, we'll call it background space. But whatever we call it, the principle of white space still applies to presentation layout, and the principle is, leave lots of it.

Some people approach laying out a slide as if they were packing for a very long trip. The slide is a suitcase, and unoccupied space is a missed opportunity. This approach is dead wrong. First of all, anything surrounded by background space will be much more prominent than if it's crowded by other elements all clamoring for your attention. If there's just one word on a slide—even if it's a very short word in very small type—it will stand out dramatically. By contrast, even a very long word in very large type can be drowned out by too many patterned graphics, dingbats, and whatnot. The more important something is, the more wide open space it deserves.

Finally, space is not just what's left over when all the important things have been placed on the slide. Space itself is an important participant in visual communication. Space implies relationship. If you place three elements on a slide, two related and the third not, indicate the relationships by leaving less space between the two related items and more space above the third, unrelated item. For example, lines of body text should be closer together than the title and the first line of body text. When you're finished laying out a slide, sit back and ask yourself, what's my use of space implying about the relationship among these elements? Then, move things around until the spatial relationships reflect your intentions.

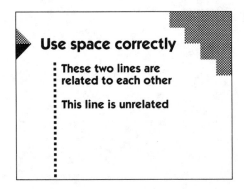

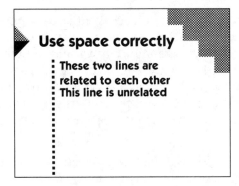

Figure 15.4. Use space to indicate relationships.

Type

Nothing can doom your presentation to failure faster than poor typography. The surest sign of excellent typography is when you can understand text quickly and easily without noticing the type at all. Here are some guidelines for using type for rather than against you.

Choose One or Two Simple, Legible Fonts

If you're printing slides to a non-PostScript film recorder, your typographic selection is limited. But if you're printing overheads on a PostScript laser printer, you can select from a dizzying array of downloadable fonts from vendors like Adobe, Bitstream, and Letraset, with alluring names such as Balloon, Bison, Blippo, Cabaret, Hobo, Revue, and Vegas, just to mention a few. Generally, the more exotic the name of a font, the more inappropriate it is for presentations.

Presentations demand legible type. By legibility, we mean how easily the eye recognizes letters and words in a given typeface. Legibility is a function of typeface design, with the most legible typefaces reflecting the most restrained design. There are hundreds of faces—script, cursive, novelty, outline, shadow, and others of their kind—that are lots of fun to look at, but will absolutely guarantee that nobody will be able to read your slides. Avoid them.

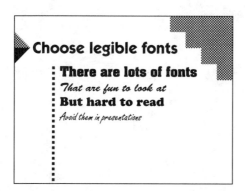

Figure 15.5. Use simple typefaces and avoid decorative faces for presentations.

Typefaces—legible or otherwise—come in two varieties: serif and sans serif. Serifs are the horizontal flourishes that end vertical and diagonal strokes in letters such as *H* and *M* and *b* and *l*. In smaller type sizes, they aid reading by guiding the eye horizontally along lines of text; in larger sizes they may actually become distracting.

Sans is merely the French word for "without"; a sans serif face has no serifs. Sans serif type is read faster, if less accurately, than serif type. In printed documents, you'll often see headlines, which are intended to be read quickly, set in a sans serif font, and body text, which is intended to be read relatively slowly but accurately, set in a serif face. You can apply these principles to slides by choosing a typographic palette of two fonts, one serif and one sans serif. Use the sans serif font for slide titles and subtitles, and the serif face for body text. Consider a condensed sans serif face for slide titles. Especially in larger type sizes, you can get more characters per line with a condensed face.

Serif	Sans serif
Bookman	Avant Garde
Palatino	Franklin Gothic
Times Roman	Helvetica

Figure 15.6. Sans serif and serif type.

Here's a list of over two dozen legible typefaces suitable for use in presentations (providing your output device supports them). They're divided into three categories: serif, sans serif, and condensed.

Serif

- Bitstream Amerigo
- Baskerville
- Bookman
- Century Oldstyle
- Century Schoolbook
- Bitstream Charter
- Cheltenham
- Garamond
- Goudy Oldstyle
- Lucida
- Palatino
- ITC Stone
- Times Roman (sometimes known as Dutch)

Sans serif

- Antique Olive (sometimes known as Provence)
- Avant Garde
- Eras
- Franklin Gothic
- Frutiger
- Futura
- Helvetica (sometimes known as Swiss)
- Kabel
- News Gothic
- Optima
- Univers

Condensed

- Futura Condensed
- Helvetica Condensed
- Univers Condensed

Most serif faces mix reasonably well with most sans serif faces. Mixing two serif or two sans serif faces is dangerous, though. It's often the typographic equivalent of combining plaids and stripes.

Make Sure the Type Is Large Enough to Read

How large is large enough to read? Well, it depends on whether you're creating slides or overheads, and how large they'll be projected. But here are some general rules of thumb.

Table 15.1

Text element	Recommended type size
Slide title	36–56 points, 72 for a very short headline
Subtitle	24–56 points, at least one screen font size smaller than slide title
Body text	24–40 points
Footnotes, axes labels, column heads	12–18 points

Tip: For those of you new to the world of graphic arts, type is measured from top to bottom in points, with 72 points to an inch. That means that 36 point type measures about half an inch from the top of a capital letter or an "ascender" (the long vertical strokes on the lowercase *b, d, f, h, k,* and *l*) to the bottom of a "descender" (the stroke that descends below the baseline on a lowercase *g, j, p,* and *q*).

The range of legible sizes will depend on what font you're using, and, if you're using color, on the contrast between text and background colors. If you produce a lot of presentations under a variety of conditions, consider creating some sample visuals showing a range of fonts in different sizes, weights, and colors. Project the slide or overhead under conditions similar to the anticipated presentation, look at it from different locations in the room, and see for yourself which sizes are most legible.

If you're creating a presentation to be displayed on your monitor or by a projection panel or video projector, remember to select only sizes for which you have screen fonts installed (unless you're using Adobe's Type Manager). Persuasion's presentation fonts, Times, Helvetica, and Symbol, include screen fonts in the following point sizes: 12, 14, 18, 24, 36, 40, 48, 56, and 72.

Use no more than four sizes of type per slide, one for the title, one for the subtitle, one for body text, and one for labels, legends, footnotes, and captions. Using many sizes reduces their impact: instead of signaling levels of importance, the type blends gradually from large to small. Avoid combining sizes less than 4 points apart in size; most people won't notice the difference between, say, 18- and 20-point type.

Most people
Won't notice the difference
When type size varies by only
One or two points

Instead,
Make relative importance clear
By obvious distinctions
In type size

Figure 15.7. Avoid combining fonts that are too close together in size.

Use Different Styles for Emphasis

Not only can you vary size to indicate relative importance, you can apply the following styles from the Text menu:

- Plain
- **Bold**
- *Italic*
- <u>Underline</u>
- Outline
- Shadow

If you're using one typeface for all slide text, use a bold version for titles and subtitles, and plain for body text.

Italics are difficult to read, so avoid them except for an occasional touch of emphasis, and for technical terms, foreign words, publication names, and so on. Use them sparingly in on-screen presentations, since the diagonal lines in italics accentuate the "jaggies."

Wherever possible, avoid underlining. To emphasize a word, set it in bold instead. Underlining is a relatively ineffective tool of emphasis, a holdover from the days of the typewriter (when there was no alternative), and it's unappealing visually as well.

Outline type is tough to read, so use it only occasionally, and in larger type sizes. When you choose *Outline* from the Style submenu, Persuasion applies the text color to the outline, making the text itself transparent and revealing the background color. You can't control the weight of the outline. Depending on text and background colors, outline type may nearly vanish. Even when there's adequate contrast, it's relatively busy and hard on the eyes.

Of Persuasion's text styles, *Shadow* is the most dramatic and the most potentially compromising to legibility. A shadow works best when applied to larger sizes of bold, sans serif type (for example, in titles). Large amounts of shadowed text interfere with reading, so avoid it in body text.

For bold, sans serif type, set the *Text shadow offset* to *Medium* or *Large*. (Remember, when you choose *Large*, you can control the direction and degree of offset by typing in the appropriate positive or negative numbers for *Object shadow offset: inches down* and *inches right*. Of course, shadowed objects will also reflect these values.) For serif type, keep the shadow offset set to *Small*, or else you'll see distracting background-colored gaps between the text and its shadow. Check the upper inside arc of a rounded letter like *o* to make sure there's no background peeking out between the letter and its shadow.

For an occasional startling special effect, choose both *Outline* and *Shadow* from the Style submenu. Persuasion will outline both the text and its shadow, producing a double exposure composed of three colors: the text color, the shadow color, and the background color. For best results, use a large font size (48 point or greater), and set *Text shadow offset* to *Small* in the Preferences dialog box.

Figure 15.8. Apply both *Outline* and *Shadow* to large, bold, sans serif type.

Set Headlines and Body Text in Upper- and Lowercase

For maximum readability, avoid setting text in capital letters. First of all, text set in all caps requires as much as 30% more space than its upper and lower case equivalent, and space on slides is usually at a premium. More importantly, though, all cap text is more difficult to read. Studies of the mechanics of reading have shown that one of the subtle cues the eye depends on for quick comprehension is the silhouette of a word. Compare the same headline set in all caps and in upper and lower case. In the all cap version, the silhouettes of all words are identical, making them indistinguishable from each other. By contrast, in the upper and lower case version, each word has a unique silhouette, which speeds comprehension.

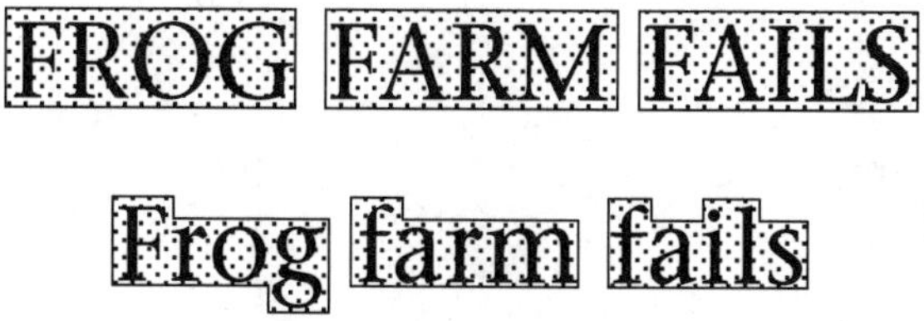

FROG FARM FAILS

Frog farm fails

Figure 15.9. Because the silhouettes of words set in all caps are
identical, word recognition is slower.

For titles and subtitles, you can choose one of two capitalization styles: capitalize the first letter of each word, except articles and prepositions such as *"a"*, *"the"*, and *"to"* (unless it's the first word of a line); or, capitalize just the first word of each line. For body text, choose the second capitalization style. Capitalizing every word of body text creates visual "hiccups"—Every Word Clamors For Your Attention As If It Were Just As Important As Every Other Word. Don't do this to your audience.

Choose Appropriate Alignment and Spacing

Although the Text menu offers four choices for alignment, most of the time you'll use only two of them: *Align left* and *Align center*. For titles and subtitles, either is fine. (Remember, though, that centered layouts tend be to formal and static compared to asymmetrical layouts with text aligned left.)

For body text, *Align left* (also called flush left) is preferable to *Align center*. Centering body text creates a ragged left margin; when the eye sweeps from the end of one line to the beginning of the next, it has to hunt for a different starting point for each new line. This makes reading that much harder. (Right aligned text is difficult to read for the same reason.)

To center an entire block of flush left body text on its longest line, center the body text placeholder on the slide, center anchor it, and choose *Align left* from the Alignment submenu. Persuasion will size the placeholder to accommodate the text, center it on the slide, and set the text within it flush left.

Justified type, in which space is added or subtracted between words and letters to create an even right margin, has no place on slides. Even in printed documents, the irregularities in word and letter spacing in justified type can be distracting and unappealing. The larger the type, the more pronounced these irregularities become, and when projected onto a screen, they're magnified even more. Apply the *Justify* command only to text on audience handouts, and, even then, consider sticking with *Align left*.

With centered text,
each new line
has a different starting point.
This can confuse the eye.

Never justify text on a slide. The
variations   in   word-   and
letterspacing required to justify the
type create distracting rivers and
lakes of white space. Besides, you
should never use this much text.

Figure 15.10.   Centered body text requires the eye to find a different
starting point for each new line. Justifying text creates
uneven word and letter spacing.

Persuasion's default line spacing of 100% and paragraph spacing of 200% are generally perfect for body text. With 100% line spacing, the distance between lines will be 100% of type size: 24 points for 24-point type; 48 points for 48-point type; and so forth. 100% line spacing is equivalent to single spacing in the world of typewriters and word processors.

For multiple line titles, consider reducing line spacing to 90% or so. This helps the lines hang together as a unit and conserves space. But watch for fusion, which happens when the descender of one line overlaps an ascender of the line below it; fusion creates a vertical line that interrupts the horizontal motion of reading.

Keep Text Background Simple

Even under the best of circumstances, reading requires effort. Make it as easy as possible for your audience. Don't run type across two colors, because it forces the eye to readjust in midstream. And don't place type over a complex graphic; the type and the graphic will compete for the eye's attention, and your audience won't know what to look at first. Keep the background behind type to a solid color or a simple pattern, or apply a solid fill color to the text block itself.

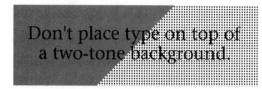

Figure 15.11. Don't make text compete with the background.

Color

Color can make or break a presentation. Used effectively, color can guide your audience's attention, signify importance, and set emotional tone. Used ineffectively, color can aggravate, intimidate, frustrate, or even hypnotize an audience. Set up a color palette of no more than 5 major colors (10, if you're working with charts or graphics), and apply them consistently. If you use more than that, you'll end up with a carnival, not a presentation.

Choose a Slide Background Color to Set the Tone

The color you choose for the background of your presentation provides the visual foundation on which text, charts, and graphics will be built. It must be dark or light enough to contrast with these elements so that they stand out clearly and can be easily read. For slides, choose a dark color from the bottom row or two of Persuasion's color grid; for overhead transparencies, choose a very pale color from the top two or three rows; for on-screen presentations, choose a mid-range color. Cool colors such as blue tend to recede in space (like sky or water in a landscape), making them especially appropriate background colors. Warm colors, such as red, orange, and yellow, come forward and compete with foreground elements such as text and graphics.

Background color not only provides contrast with foreground elements, it sets the overall mood of your presentation. In a sense, the background color is like paint color in a room. Think how differently you feel in a bright yellow room than in one that's gray or dark green. Background color has a similar environmental impact on your presentation.

To make the background color work to your advantage, ask yourself what tone you want to set. Do you want to create a sense of luxury? Try a deep purple background. Do you want to convey drama and urgency? Choose a dark red. Is your presentation a pitch for environmental conservation? Choose a lush, deep green background. To help your selection, consider some of the common color associations listed below.

Table 15.1.

Color	Associations
Red	Danger, excitement, warmth, energy, passion, blood, indebtedness
Orange	Warmth, earthiness
Yellow	Warmth, comfort, cheerfulness, sunshine, youth, richness
Green	Growth, fertility, nature, life, money, security, calmness, quietness
Blue	Serenity, restfulness, intellectualism, rationality, detachment, coolness
Purple	Royalty, luxury, power
Brown	Earth, organic
Black	Nobility, luxury, power, death
White	Purity, truth
Gray	Formality, neutrality, coldness, drabness

Here's another way of classifying colors that may help you choose the one that's most appropriate for your purposes.

Table 15.2.

Green/blue/purple	Red/orange/yellow
Cold	Warm
Shadow	Sun
Transparent	Opaque
Soothing	Stimulating
Airy	Earthy
Watery	Fiery
Far	Near
Light	Heavy
Wet	Dry

Whatever background color you choose, be sure to choose just one. Using one, consistent background color establishes unity and helps your presentation flow smoothly from slide to slide. Changing the background color randomly and frequently can be irritating and distracting because the eye has to adjust to the color intensities and contrasts of each new color palette.

There are only two good reasons to use more than one background color. Use a second background color on slides that signal transitions or begin new sections or topics. For an occasional, especially dramatic effect, reverse the foreground and background colors you're using. For example, if your basic color palette consists of yellow type on a blue background, make transition slides yellow with blue type.

The second reason to vary the background color is to distinguish among different kinds or sources of information. For example, if your presentation combines contributions from several departments in your company, you might assign one background color to marketing, a second to sales, a third to r&d, and so on. Remember, though, that a presentation occurs in time. When people see a new slide, their eyes are still remembering the last one. Make sure the transition between slides is harmonious. Don't move from fire engine red to magenta, or from orange to green.

When it comes to color selection, graduated fills require special care. Choose two related colors, such as light blue and dark blue, or light red and dark red. Persuasion's color palette makes this easy because all colors in the same column are related. Choose one color from the bottom row or two (Rows 0 and 1) of the palette, and a second color from Row 2 or 3 in the same column: GY 0 and GY 3, for example, or RS 1 and RS 4. If the lighter background color is too light, you'll have trouble reading type that's placed on top of it. Colors in adjacent rows, such as GY 0 and GY1 or RS 3 and RS 4, are too similar to show a perceptible gradation. Blending colors from different columns can produce some hideous combinations, and make finding harmonious type colors nearly impossible.

Consider the effects of different foreground and background color combinations in graduated fills. In a horizontal fill, for example, a dark-to-light fade might suggest a sunset or a hidden glow beneath the slide, while a light-to-dark fade might look like an underwater scene.

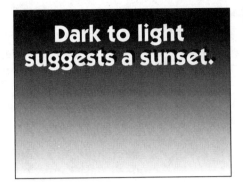

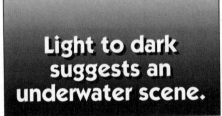

Figure 15.12.   A graduated fill from dark to light creates a different effect than one from light to dark.

Select Text Colors for Greatest Readability

Once you've picked a background color, you must choose one or more colors for slide text. If the most common symptom of a mediocre presentation is slides that are hard to read, the most common diagnosis is poor contrast between text and background colors.

For slides, choose a light color (from the top two or three rows of the color grid). For overheads, choose a very dark color. If you like, you can choose two text colors, one for slide titles and subheadings, and one for body text. Remember, though, that different colors have different "optical weights." Against a dark background, the lighter and brighter the color, the greater its optical weight. Correctly chosen colors should draw the viewer's eye to the most important element first (usually the slide title), then to a subtitle, then to body copy. The brightest, lightest color should be used for the most important text elements, and so on. Yellow and white are the safest choices for text on slides, dark blue and red for color overhead transparencies.

Avoid choosing a text color that's a complement of the background color. Complementary colors are located across from each other on a color wheel. When juxtaposed, they vibrate and interfere with reading. The effect is especially pronounced with two complementary colors of the same intensity (for example, dark blue and dark orange, or medium green and medium red). Red type on a dark blue background is especially overpowering, and should be avoided.

Avoid color combinations with irrelevant connotations. Don't use red, white, and blue unless you want to be patriotic; steer clear of red and green unless you're a Christmas tree company. Of course, sometimes these associations may be exactly what you're after.

Choose Accent Colors to Guide the Eye

Finally, you'll want to choose a color or two to use as accents in shadows, bullets, rules, boxes, and other graphic devices you use for emphasis and interest. Since accent colors are meant to draw attention to themselves, choose warm colors such as red, orange, and yellow to take advantage of their urgency. Choosing an accent color that's a complement of the background color can be very dramatic and effective, provided you use it in small doses.

Shadow colors call for special attention. A dark shadow color applied to a light object will make it appear illuminated from above, while a light shadow applied to a dark object will make it appear illuminated from below. Make sure there's enough contrast between text and its shadow, otherwise they'll merge and make reading impossible. Of course, a shadow color must show up against the slide background. Black is a foolproof if conservative color for shadows (except on a black background, in which case dark gray or red will do). Another way to select a shadow color is to choose in the color grid from the same column as the shadow's object.

Charts

Charts present complex data in a form that's easy to understand. They translate data into spatial relationships—the length of a bar, the height of a column, the size of a pie slice—that are more easily comprehended than the numbers they represent. Every element of a chart, from gridlines and tick-marks to color and text, should contribute to making it easy to understand. Here are five tips for making your charts as clear as day.

Choose the Right Type of Chart

As you know, Persuasion offers you nine different types of charts, including tables and organizational charts. With so many formats to choose from, how do you know what type of chart to use for your data?

The first question to ask yourself is what you want to illustrate. The same information will often lend itself to several different types of charts. Your choice of a chart format should reflect what you want to communicate to your audience. Take the three charts below. Although all three present exactly the same data, each suggests quite different conclusions. Which one is the best format? It depends on the point you want to make.

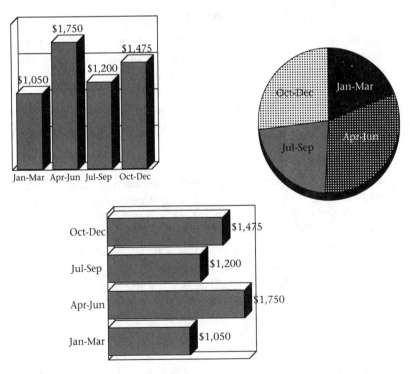

Figure 15.13. Different chart formats convey different impressions of the same data.

The following table provides guidelines for selecting a chart format.

Table 15.3.

To show	Use
Relationship of parts to the whole for a single item	Pie chart
Relationship of similar types of things to each other Trends over time	Column chart
Relationship of similar types of things to each other (especially when category labels are longer than 9 characters) Relationships of different items at the same time	Bar chart
Relationships of parts to the whole of several items Comparative relationships among similar whole items	Stacked bar chart or stacked column chart
Trends over time	Line chart
Trends over time, and totals as well as fluctuations	Area charts
Relationships between two ordered pairs of data	Scatter charts
Compare ranges of data to some other value	High-low chart
Hierarchical relationships and procedures	Organization chart
Specific numbers rather than the trend they represent	Table

No matter what chart format you choose, scale and proportion will influence its message. Although both the charts below plot the same data, they paint very different pictures of it. Which is telling the truth? Again, that depends on the point you're trying to make. Once you've determined what value scale will best illustrate (without distorting) your point, be sure to apply that scale for all charts in your presentation.

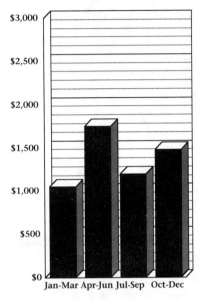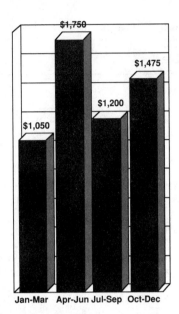

Figure 15.14. Avoid choosing a scale to mislead or exaggerate. The different scales in these charts lead to quite different conclusions about the data they present.

Keep Charts Simple

Cluttered charts are one of the most common and deadly presentation sins. In general, use as few elements—data points, colors, labels, gridmarks —as possible while still getting your point across. When in doubt, leave it out.

In bar, column, and pie charts, show no more than six bars, columns, or slices. If you need to show more than six data points, choose a line chart instead. Otherwise, your chart will look more like a city skyline or a work of modern art than numerical data.

In pie charts, combine slices comprising less than 10% of the pie into one "miscellaneous" or "other" category. In line charts, plot a maximum of four to five lines per chart and use only as many data points as are needed to show trends. Remember, if you're using a line chart, your purpose should be to illustrate trends, not specific data points. If the numbers themselves are what's important, rather than the trends they represent, choose a table instead.

Finally, use only as many grid lines, major and minor, and as many tickmarks as are absolutely essential to convey your message. You're better off showing value labels and keeping gridlines to a minimum. Start by choosing *Grid/Tick options* from the Axes submenu in the Chart menu, and deselect everything but *Show major grid* for the value and category axes. Then, if the specific numbers represented by the column or bar are important, select *Show value labels* from the Chart menu. Ask yourself if your point is clear. If it is, try simplifying the chart even more by choosing *Value axis format* from the Axes submenu, and then increasing the intervals for *Tick mark spacing*.

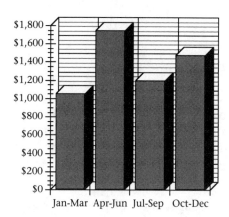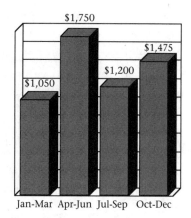

Figure 15.15. Use as few tick marks and labels as possible (*right*) while still communicating clearly.

Emphasize One Important Element

The standard practice in pie charts is to position the largest slice on top, or the line of the largest slice at 12 o'clock to make it most prominent. (Since Persuasion plots the first data point from 12 o'clock, enter the largest number first in the data sheet.) To emphasize any slice, drag it out of the pie. Choose *Show depth* to accentuate the isolated slice. (Remember, you don't need to ungroup the pie in order to move a slice.)

To emphasize a bar or column in a bar or column chart, apply a color or pattern to it and make all the others transparent. Or make all the columns and bars one color, and then apply a brighter shade of the same color (or a complementary color) to the one you want to emphasize.

When it comes to spacing, columns and bars should be wider than the "negative" space between then, or else your audience's attention will end up falling into the cracks between the bars and columns.

Choose Harmonious Fill Colors and Patterns

Even the most well-constructed chart can be demolished by clashing colors and jarring patterns. Chart colors should clarify and support the chart's message; they should not fight with chart elements or detract from the chart's focus.

In pie charts, choose one color for each slice, following one of the following two strategies. Strategy number one: choose colors of equal intensity (from the same row of the color grid, OR2, YO2, BU2, RS2, for example). Lighter colors tend to move forward and darker colors recede; choosing colors of equal intensity will make all the slices appear to be resting on the same plane.

Strategy number two: use different shades of the same color (from the same grid column, RS0, RS2, RS4, RS6, for example). Apply the lightest shade to the largest or most significant slice, and then work around the pie applying the next darker color from the column you've selected. (If you're working with overhead transparencies, move from dark to light.) This technique creates a gradual spiral from the lightest foreground color to the darkest background color, with each pair of adjacent slices appearing to be in the same plane. The overall effect is smooth and harmonious.

For regular and stacked bar and column charts, choose one color for each data series using one of the pie chart color strategies just described. For stacked bar and column charts, or bar and column charts showing two or more data series, make sure the color steps for each data series are the same. Avoid the color red for displaying financial data unless you intend to show a loss.

Apply a lighter shade of the background color to gridlines, tickmarks, and the chart frame. Make sure there's just enough contrast so that they're visible but not so much that they jump forward and overpower other chart elements.

When working with three-dimensional charts, experiment with applying different shades of the same color to the three surfaces (front, side, or top). The side with the lightest color will appear closest to the suggested light source. For example, if the lightest colored surface of a bar chart is the top, the chart will appear to be lit from above.

If possible, choose solid rather than patterned colors as chart fills because they're easier to read. If you do use patterns (if you're preparing black-and-white overhead transparencies), avoid ones that conflict with each other (checks and stripes, for example). Patterns from the first four rows of the Fill pattern submenu are the most appropriate. Applying a vertical pattern to one column and a horizontal pattern to the column next to it will exaggerate the differences between them.

Make Chart Type Legible

When it comes to type in charts, simplicity is the best principle. Use one font, style, size, and color for all chart text—axis labels, value labels, legend, and caption. Follow the guidelines for legible type we've already presented, making sure to use a size of at least 18 points. Whatever typographic palette you set up, apply it consistently to all the charts in your presentation.

Abbreviate labels and column titles whenever necessary to keep them short and quickly digestible (for example, Jan, Feb, and Mar instead of January, February, and March). Limit category labels to nine characters or fewer. In pie charts, place labels on top of or as close as possible to the slice they represent.

When it comes to tables, make sure entries are very short. Remember, you don't want your audience reading while you're talking. Text should be left aligned, and numbers right or decimal aligned. Keep column titles short and to the point, and align them left or centered. Round out big numbers—20,000 is much easier to grasp than 19,978—and don't include any more numbers than absolutely necessary to make your point.

If you're a newcomer to presentation design, don't expect yourself to produce an award winning presentation the first time out. Wean yourself gradually from Persuasion's AutoTemplates. In the long run, armed both with these tips and your Persuasion skills, and fortified by experience, your presentations will grow ever more persuasive. Good luck!

Chapter 16

Preparing and Delivering an Effective Presentation

What's the very worst thing you can imagine going wrong during your presentation? The first slide of the day appears on the screen upside down and backwards? Midway through your introductory remarks, you realize the ornithologists convention next door has broken down into bird mimicking sessions? Your microphone gives you so much feedback it's like being on the tarmac as a B52 comes in for a landing? You trip over an extension cord, yanking the overhead projector off the table, breaking the bulb for which you have no replacement, and scattering your unnumbered transparencies? Speaking in front of a group is harrowing enough without having to worry about nightmares like these!

This chapter offers you a range of tips on how to prepare and deliver the most effective, trouble-free presentation possible. We'll begin in the ethereal world of ideas, and finish up in the material world of extension cords and light switches.

Define the Purpose of Your Presentation

No matter how powerful your presentation software and hardware, great presentations start in the mind, not in a machine. Before you even turn on your computer, you must ask yourself a few very basic, very crucial, very easily overlooked questions.

First of all, why are you giving this presentation in the first place? What is the opportunity here? What outcome do you want to achieve? What will you see or hear that will let you know you have achieved it?

Write down the purpose of your presentation. Start out with a brief phrase, such as:

- To inform;

- To educate;

- To sell;

- To persuade;

- To motivate;

- To win a contract;

- To defend a position; and

- To introduce an idea.

But don't stop there. Be as specific and detailed as possible. Inform whom? Educate whom about what? Sell what to whom? Persuade whom of what? For example:

- To inform people about the severity of environmental problems...

- To educate our sales force about our product's new features...

- To persuade a potential client that our proposed public relations strategy will best meet their needs....

Finally, be sure to consider what action you want your audience to take in response to your presentation. Possible actions include:

- To donate money;

- To sign a contract;

- To spread the word;

- To approve the budget;

- To allocate resources;

- To perform more effectively;

- To follow a new procedure; and

- To change their opinion.

As you build your statement of purpose, push your thinking as far as possible. The more specific and detailed your understanding of the purpose of your presentation—including its desired outcome—the greater the odds that the presentation will actually do what you want it to do. For best results, the desired outcome should be one whose success or failure you can evaluate. Generally, this means building in a date, a dollar amount, or some kind of observable behavior, such as signing a petition or agreeing to a proposal. Here are some examples of detailed, outcome-oriented statements of purpose:

- To educate our sales force about our product's new features, so that they can sell it more effectively and *increase sales 5% in the next quarter.*

- To persuade a potential client that our proposed public relations strategy will best meet their needs, so that they'll *sign a three-year contract* with us.

- To inform people about the severity of environmental problems, so *30% of them will donate $5* to our environmental preservation fund *tonight,* and *30% of them will speak about the problem* to someone else *within the next month.*

Identify Your Audience

After asking what you want from this presentation, the next most important questions to ask yourself are, what does your *audience* want from this presentation? Why are they coming to hear you speak? What's in it for them?

The most common and most serious obstacle to effective communication—no matter what mode of communication you're using—is the assumption that the minds of those in your audience are like your own, and that their interests are identical to yours. Just because you believe that an expensive new corporate identity program is absolutely essential to the continued growth of the company doesn't mean your board of directors sees it that way too. Just because you think that the yellow-bellied sapsucker is the most remarkable bird in the world doesn't mean your audience shares your passion. Just because you know everything there is to know about diisopropylfluorophosphates or antialiasing algorithms doesn't mean your audience would know if they were bitten on the ankle by one.

Consider the presentation from your audience's point of view. Do they care about the subject? Do they know how they'll benefit from hearing you out? If you answer no to either question, you must convince your audience of the relevance of your presentation from the very beginning in order to hold their attention.

Consider opening with an audience-oriented statement of purpose, such as:

- Our goal here today is to teach you techniques that will help you close 20% more sales.

- This morning, we're going to explore the pros and cons of the new technology so that you can make a better-informed buying decision for your organization.

- My purpose this evening is to explain why this is such a serious problem for all of us, and what we can do to make a difference.

If members of your audience are coming to your presentation under duress—for example, if they could lose their jobs if they didn't attend—it's especially crucial that you explain how they'll benefit from the time they spend with you. If your goal is to sway your audience's opinion, what are their current views on the subject? You must know what they believe now and why, so that you can raise and meet their possible objections to your argument.

Speak your audience's language. What do they already know about the subject? Are they experts or novices? Be sure to use an appropriate vocabulary. Don't use words they may not understand, or technical terms they may not recognize. On the other hand, don't bore them or condescend to them. If your audience's background on the subject is mixed, use asides to fill in the gaps in their knowledge quickly. For example, "For those of you who aren't familiar with the term *leading*, it refers to the amount of white space between lines of type...."

How much information can your audience absorb, and how fast? If they're familiar with the subject, they'll be able to retain more in a short period of time than an audience completely new to the subject. Adjust the amount of information you deliver and its pace accordingly. There's nothing worse than sitting through a three-hour presentation that proceeds at a snail's pace, unless it's sitting through a presentation like a flip book—images and information that whiz by so fast you're left gasping for breath after the first five minutes.

Choose a Presentation Medium

The medium you choose for your presentation depends on a number of factors, including what the purpose of your presentation is, how large your audience is, what equipment you have, and so forth. Each medium offers a different combination of benefits and limitations. Your objective should be to choose the medium that best matches the circumstances and objectives of your presentation.

Let's take a look at the strengths and weaknesses of each medium. They're summarized in Table 16-1.

Overhead Transparencies

Overhead transparencies are most appropriate for small-to-medium–sized audiences (no more than 50 people). Informal in tone, they're perfect for a presentation to a staff meeting, to a task force, or to a small group of peers whose goal is to reach consensus, solve a problem, brainstorm, and so on.

Overheads make interacting with your audience easy. Because overheads can be seen clearly in a well-lit room, you can continue to make good eye contact with your audience during the presentation. You can write on overheads to emphasize a point. In fact, you can even use them to collect and display your audience's comments or ideas—all it takes is the proper pen or marker to turn an overhead from a presentation graphic into a working document.

Overheads allow you to follow a more leisurely pace than a slide presentation. You can linger longer on an overhead than on a slide; because you're still visible to your audience, they have two things to occupy their attention, you and the overhead. When they've finished looking at the overhead, their attention returns to you. In the darkened room required by slides, only the slide is visible. Once your audience has digested your slide, they may start thinking about digesting lunch. Slides require a faster pace to keep your audience's interest.

Overheads give you lots of room to maneuver: you can easily skip a transparency if you run out of time, or jump forward or backward to respond to a question or your own change of course. And you can make last minute changes easily. Just edit the slide in Persuasion, slip a new sheet of transparency film into your printer or plotter, and you have your new transparency in minutes.

Overheads do have a few drawbacks. Flipping overheads can be cumbersome, especially if you're nervous, or if the surface holding the projector won't hold two stacks of overheads—shown and to be shown. Enclosing transparencies in cardboard frames makes them easier to handle and gives you room to write notes to yourself, but the frames add bulk and weight to the already heavy overheads.

Make sure you number overheads—there's nothing worse than watching your stack of overheads reshuffle themselves on their way to the floor in the middle of a presentation.

Most overheads are black and white. Although you can use a color printer or plotter to produce color overheads, their color will never be as rich and saturated as those of 35-mm slides (although the darker the room, the more vivid the colors will be).

An overhead projector must be placed closer to the screen than a slide projector. Be sure to set up the room so that the projector doesn't block your audience's view of the screen.

Slides

When you're making a formal presentation to a medium-sized or large audience (25 people or more), choose slides to convey your message. With their vivid, saturated colors glowing in a darkened room, slides always make a strong impression. If you're presenting to a board of directors or to potential customers or clients and your goal is to impress as well as to convince, slides are the way to go.

Because they require more advanced preparation, slides are rarely appropriate for a last minute, impromptu working session. Save them for when the stakes are high and you really want to impress your audience.

Because they require a darkened room, slides allow less interaction between you and your audience than overheads. This puts more pressure on the slides to be attention grabbing, since the slides (and your voice, but not your face) are the only things your audience has to focus on. It also requires that you use your voice as effectively as possible. Nothing puts an audience to sleep faster than boring slides being discussed in a montone voice in a darkened room.

As a result, the pace of a slide presentation must be faster than one using transparencies. As a rule of thumb, an average of two slides per minute is an appropriate pace. It's a good idea to begin the presentation at a brisk pace, slow down a bit in the middle, and gather momentum again at the end. An average of two slides per minute means you might have three to four slides per minute in the beginning and at the end, and three slides every two minutes during the middle.

Slides are portable. Although cumbersome, a carousel tray with 80 slides isn't nearly as heavy as 80 overheads with cardboard frames. They're also easier to handle during the presentation than overheads—no flipping, just clicking. You can move freely about the room while advancing the slides instead of being anchored to an overhead projector.

But as always, freedom comes at the price of flexibility. You can't write on slides, nor can you unobtrusively skip ahead if you run out of time. When you advance the remote control device, each slide appears at least momentarily on the screen; your audience will know they're missing something.

Because they take longer to process, slides require more advance planning than overheads, and changes can't be made up until five minutes before curtain call. As far as changes go, it's also harder to match colors exactly if you add slides at some point during the future. (Consult Chapter 18, *Producing 35-mm Slides*, for tips on slide production.)

On-screen Slide Shows

Because of their relative novelty, on-screen presentations of any kind will pique your audience's curiousity.

With a standard large-screen monitor (19 or 21 inches), you can present to a small group of people (usually no more than four or five). The larger the monitor, of course, the more people you can address. Monitor screen presentations are excellent for product demonstrations in a sales setting or for self-paced instruction.

A projection panel or an RGB projector can accommodate an even larger audience. Like overheads, a black-and-white or gray-scale projection panel creates an informal tone, suitable for a presentation to a working group such as a staff meeting or task force. Furthermore, they can be used in a medium lit room, making some eye contact possible. A color video projector, on the other hand, creates a formal atmosphere like that of a slide presentation; i.e., color in a darkened room.

Table 16-1.

	Overheads	Slides	On-screen slide show	Projection panel	Color video projector
Audience size	Small to medium (5–25)	Medium to large (25+)	Small (5–6)	Medium to large (25+)	Medium to large (25+)
Tone	Informal, spontaneous, working	Formal	Semi-formal	Semi-formal	Formal
Room size	Small to medium	Medium to large	Small	Medium to large	Medium to large
Lighting	Visible in well-lit room; maximum interaction with audience	Requires dark room; minimal interaction with audience	Visible in well-lit room; maximum interaction with audience	Requires dimmed lighting; moderate interaction with audience	Requires dark room; minimal intraction with audience
Black and white or color	Black and white or color	Color	Black and white or color	Black and white	Color

Table 16-1. *(continued)*

	Overheads	Slides	On-screen slide show	Projection panel	Color video projector
Ease of making last-minute changes	Very easy	Requires processing time	Very easy	Very easy	Very easy
Ease of use during presentation	Cumbersome; requires flipping transparencies; requires presenter to stay close to projector	Easy, with especially remote controller	Easy, if equipment is reliable	Easy, if equipment is reliable	Easy for presenter, but usually requires a technician to operate

Whether you're using a monitor, a projection panel, or a video projector, you'll need to make sure the equipment is set up and thoroughly tested in advance. Although you may carry your own projection panel with you on the road, you probably won't want to transport a color video projector and a Macintosh II. Be sure to work out the logistics of acquiring and setting up the equipment very carefully. If you're renting equipment, make sure the rental company sets it up and tests it before vanishing. If you intend to use a video projector, hire a technician to install and run it for you, unless you're a techno-wizard.

Once the equipment itself is taken care of, the actual presentation is relatively portable. All you need is your floppy or portable hard disk with your presentation on it. Make sure you have a backup of your presentation, and that Persuasion 2.0 and all the fonts you'll need are installed on the computer's hard disk.

On-screen slide shows, of course, are very flexible. You can jump forward or backward just by typing the number of the slide you want to display. As for last minute changes, you can still be editing slides as the audience files into the room.

Once you've determined which medium will best meet your needs, you must choose an appropriate AutoTemplate. Consult Chapter 13, *Building an AutoTemplate*, for tips on AutoTemplate selection.

Generate Content

Although Persuasion automates and streamlines the process of assembling a presentation, it cannot think for you. So what do you do once you've established the purpose of your presentation, identified your audience, and chosen a presentation medium and an AutoTemplate?

Go to outline view of your AutoTemplate, and proceed to do a "brain dump." Just empty the contents of your mind onto the screen. Type in your ideas, in whatever form they occur to you. Don't worry about their soundness, or about logic, sequence, or flow. Just keep your mind moving. Include presentation text, as well as notes for graphics, stage directions, and anecdotes.

But what about my outline? you may be asking. Isn't working in an outline all about logical thinking? Shouldn't I be considering main and subordinate ideas? Shouldn't I progress in linear fashion from beginning to end?

Eventually yes, but not at the beginning. Most people find it very helpful to segregate idea generation from idea evaluation, to separate creative from analytical thinking. Rare is the person whose thoughts naturally arise in perfect I, A, 1, a... outline form. If we force ourselves to think this way from the start, we freeze. When an idea occurs to us, instead of welcoming it, we judge it—it doesn't belong here, it's not logical, it's a lousy idea, it's too obvious, it's not relevant, and so forth. Try to hold such critical thoughts at bay. Once you've emptied your mind, you'll still have lots of time to give your critic free reign.

The brain dump is especially useful when you're suffering from a mild or severe writer's block. For most of us, the most excruciating moment in the creative process is the initial confrontation with a blank piece of paper or its electronic equivalent, a computer screen. Usually, once we have something—almost anything—to work with, our performance anxiety diminishes, and we can think clearly and effectively.

Organize and Refine Content

Once you've got most of the raw material you need, it's time to call on your critical, analytical faculties to organize and refine your presentation.

Review the material you've generated, looking for possible organizing schemes. Here are some possibilities:

- Geographical (e.g., sales figures by territory);

- Organizational (e.g., revenue by operating unit);

- Chronological (e.g., past, present, future; before, during, after; short-term, medium-term, long-term);

- Evolutionary (e.g., background, evolution, present circumstances);

- Argument (e.g., issue, argument and supporting evidence, position; main idea, corollary, supporting details);

- Problem solving (e.g., recommendation, conditions corrected, feasibility; strategy, logistics, tactics; recap, update, forecast; observation, analysis, decision);

- Pros and cons (e.g., options, evaluation, selection);

- Product or service introduction (e.g., product or service, marketability, profit potential); and

- Features/benefits.

Using Persuasion's outliner, begin to drag headings and subheadings into logical relationships, following your organizing scheme. How is this idea related to that idea? What should come first? What second? What should be a slide title? A subtitle? What should be body text? Will this information fit comfortably on one slide, or should it be divided between two slides? Some people prefer to rough everything out, and then go back and refine until they have exactly what they want. Others prefer to work sequentially from beginning to end, moving on to the next slide only when this one's perfect.

Be sure to include an introduction and a conclusion or summary. Remember the old presentation rule, "Tell 'em what you're going to tell 'em" (*introduction*). "Then tell 'em" (*body*). "Then tell 'em what you told 'em" (*conclusion*). Roughly 10% of your presentation should be devoted to an introduction and 20% to a conclusion, leaving about 70% for the meat of your presentation. The introduction should address your audience's primary concerns: *What can we expect from this presentation that will benefit us? Who is the presenter, and what qualifies him or her to speak on the subject?* The conclusion should review the facts or arguments given in the body of your presentation and demonstrate how they lead to the goal or statement of purpose announced in your introduction.

Once you've worked out the overall structure of your presentation, it's time to edit. Look at your material from your audience's point of view. Will this sequence make sense to them? Is this slide absolutely necessary? Does it contribute to the purpose of your presentation? Cut every inessential word. Find simpler synonyms for technical terms. Consult Chapter 15, *Designing Effective Presentations*, for guidelines on how much text should appear on each slide.

Next, print out a copy of your outline. Determine what should appear on slides and what should be set as speaker notes. Make notes of any stage directions you may want, such as *Collect survey here*, or *Tell anecdote about elephant eating hay here*, or *Slow down and emphasize!* Do a graphic analysis. That is, review your material for points that can be enhanced with a well-chosen visual. If you're presenting financial or statistical information, translate it into a chart or a graph. If you're listing pros or cons, set up a table. To control your audience's attention, reinforce previous points, and generate suspense, use a slide build.

Proofread your outline for spelling errors before you begin to build slides—it's quicker. Like all spelling utilities, Persuasion's spell checker can only tell you if a given word is spelled correctly, not whether it's the right word. Acne Construction will look just as right to Persuasion as Acme Construction.

Finally, review your material to see what additional slide masters you'll need, if any. How many slides call for charts, and what kind? Perhaps you need one slide master for a column chart, one for a bar chart, and one for a table. How much text do your slides contain? Perhaps you need one slide master for shorter amounts of text set in a larger point size, and another for longer amounts of text set in a smaller point size. Do you need a slide master for an organizational chart? Perhaps you need one master with room for a graphic in the bottom left corner. Do you need two different color schemes? You may want to make rough sketches, creating quick "storyboards" to help you visualize what you want.

Although a "slide master analysis" isn't absolutely necessary, we recommend it. If you launch into slide production without any forethought and create a new slide master whenever an existing one won't do, you may end up confusing yourself with a bewildering hodgepodge of ad hoc masters.

Now, go ahead and build slides, notes, and handouts, using the arsenal of skills you've developed in the previous chapters. Finally, print out a proof copy of your slides and review them one last time. Check every word and every number. Exercise your ruthless editorial eye. Ask yourself, "Why do I need this? What does it contribute?" Every word and every image on every slide should directly support the purpose of your presentation. If you're not sure exactly what a particular element contributes, leave it out.

Print and carefully proofread your speaker notes. Rehearse, making sure there isn't anything that will trip you up, like a typo that will make you guffaw at the wrong time, or a stage direction that will knock you off course. Make sure your notes are legible under the actual lighting conditions of your presentation. While 12-point type might be readable in a brightly lit room, a dark room may require 18-point type. Make sure your notes include the right amount of detail. Usually, one or two key words for each idea you intend to present will be sufficient. Notes that are too detailed, like a verbatim script, tend to make you "note bound" by drawing you into reading rather than presenting, and decrease the odds that you'll make good eye contact with your audience.

A quick word about audience handouts. The best time to distribute handouts is at the end rather than at the beginning of your presentation. If you distribute them at the beginning, you're giving your presentation away. Your audience may feel they already have what they came for, and that there's no point in hearing you say it. Tell your audience that you'll be distributing handouts at the end of your presentation. This frees them from the compulsion to take notes on everything they see and hear; instead, they can focus on you, noting an occasional especially salient point, confident that they'll receive notes at the end of the presentation. On the other hand, if you distribute notes at the end with no warning, people may feel all the note-taking they did was unnecessary. They may even resent you rather than being grateful for the handouts.

Take Care of Logistics

Once you've taken care of your slides, script, and handouts, it's time to turn your attention to a more mundane, but no less important matter, logistics.

Make sure the room has been booked and refreshments have been ordered. If you plan to provide coffee and tea, make sure it will be refreshed periodically throughout the day. If you're working with a hotel, make detailed arrangements well in advance with the catering or banquet services department, and then confirm the arrangements the day before the presentation.

Assemble name badges, tent cards, handouts, pens, pencils, pointers, chalk, and markers. Carry a spare projector bulb, and be sure you know how to unjam a carousel tray. If you're preparing an on-screen presentation, make sure Aldus Persuasion and all necessary fonts are loaded onto the computer's hard disk; bring a backup copy on floppy disk just in case.

If you must travel to the presentation, don't ship your presentation materials. Carry your slides, overheads, or electronic presentation file (whether on floppy or hard disk) with you. If possible, carry audience handouts too. If you have too many handouts to carry and so must ship them, be sure to bring the original with you so that you can have it xeroxed if the handouts end up in another city. Get the name of the person and the department to whom the materials were shipped, and arrange to have the materials delivered to the presentation room the night before. There's nothing worse than tracking down your audience handouts in the shipping department while your audience is starting to arrive.

Set Up the Room

It's all too easy to focus on the presentation itself—what you're going to say and how—and forget to consider the physical environment in which you'll be speaking. Although an idyllic environment won't guarantee that you'll be a star, a poor environment can undermine even the most compelling presentation. Here are some things to consider about the room itself.

Size

The room should fit the audience, and vice versa. It may sound obvious, but it's very important. Large rooms feel impersonal and intimidating, and discourage participation. And from the presenter's point of view, speaking to a very small audience in a very large room is a bit like delivering an oration into the Grand Canyon. If you must use a large room, partition one end, or seat people with their backs to the chasm.

On the other hand, if the room is too small, people will feel claustrophobic. This in turn may make them irritable and constrain their thinking to small thoughts. The air in a small, crowded room grows old quickly, and people tend to fall asleep. If the room is too small, try to limit attendance, take frequent breaks, and, if possible, leave doors and windows open to let the air circulate.

Ventilation

The perfect room for a presentation is neither too hot nor too cold. Unfortunately, a perfect room is hard to find. Locate the thermostat if there is one, and be prepared to use it. If you're giving a presentation in a hotel, get the extension of the maintenance department, and be prepared to call them. Depending on the season, you may find the room too cold during the morning and too hot during the afternoon. Ask participants to let you know during a break if the room is uncomfortable. Remember, you're standing, walking, and talking and they're sitting down. If you notice your audience shivering or falling asleep, call a break so they can warm up or wake up.

Make the room nonsmoking, but schedule breaks that are long and frequent enough to accommodate the smokers in your audience.

Acoustics

Don't wait to test the acoustics during your opening remarks. If no one farther back than the third row can hear you or if your own voice comes echoing back, your options are limited. Visit the room ahead of time. Set up a microphone, if you intend to use one, and have someone listen to you from different locations in the room. Remember, though, that when the room fills with people the acoustics will change. In fact, you'll need to speak more loudly because people and clothing absorb sound. If possible, visit the room when it's being used to get a feel for the acoustics when the room is full.

As for microphones, don't use them unless absolutely necessary. A static, lectern mike forces you to stand in one place to be heard. A hand-held mike occupies one of your hands all the time. This is especially troublesome if you're trying to flip overhead transparencies. A standard lavalier (a small microphone that clips to your clothing) comes with a cord that follows you around and can trip you like a dog on a leash. Even a remote, wireless lavalier can be a problem. All mikes are subject to technical glitches than can unbalance even the most seasoned presenter.

If you must use a mike, make sure you know where the volume controls are and how to use them. Check for interference or feedback from acoustical systems in adjacent rooms (this can be a problem with remote lavaliers). Test the volume in advance. There's nothing more oppressive than being assaulted by an over-miked speaker. You want people to leave your presentation with their imaginations ringing, not their ears.

Lighting

What settings are optimal for the medium you're using? As we've said, a dark room is a must for slides and color video, medium lighting for an LCD projection panel, and normal room light for overheads and monitor displays. Locate all the light switches, and test the lighting in advance to determine what settings will most enhance your presentation.

Access

Ideally, people should enter the room at the rear, from behind the audience. If there's a door near you at the front of the room, close it before you begin. Otherwise, you'll have to compete with every latecomer for your audience's attention.

Distractions

Find out what's going on in the rooms around you. Will there be a gospel choir assembly or a National Association of Cheerleaders reunion? Will the participants in adjacent rooms be miked? How soundproof are the partitions or the walls?

Avoid windows, if possible, particularly those that face a swimming pool or a golf course. Unless your presentation is especially riveting, you may find your participants paying more attention to diving and putting than to what you're saying.

Test, Test, Test

Finally, when you think everything is in order, go over the details one more time. Here are some additional things to look out for:

- Is the overhead projector on a table large enough for you to put your overheads on it when you've finished showing them?
- Can the screen be seen from every seat in the room?
- Can your voice be heard from every seat in the room?
- Is the lectern large enough for you to turn your notes?
- Is the angle so steep that they'll fall off the edge?
- Is all your presentation equipment in proper working order?
- Do you have enough extension cords?
- Are there enough electrical outlets in the right places?
- Is there an extra bulb in the projector?
- Is the focus sharp?
- Is the glass clean?
- Is there a surge protector for the computer?
- Is the computer up and running?
- Are the connections between the computer and the projection panel tight?
- Are the RGB "guns" of the color video projector properly aligned (and is your technician standing by in case of emergency)?
- Is the software loaded?
- Is the image on the screen symmetrical and sharp?

Make yourself a checklist before the day of the presentation, so that you can conduct a thorough and efficient run-through, even when you're slightly disorganized by anticipatory stage fright.

Niceties

If the presentation is being held off-site, give your audience good directions. Send a map, and then make sure the room itself is clearly marked. There's nothing worse than presenting to people who have spent the last half hour driving around in rush hour traffic trying to figure out which exit to take.

Tell your audience where to park, how much it costs, and who will pay. Tell them where to find the coat check, rest rooms, and telephones. If they're on their own for meals, recommend and give directions to nearby restaurants.

Whatever you can do to make the overall experience a pleasant one for your audience will translate into goodwill toward you and your presentation.

Deliver Effective Presentations

Your slides are perfected, all the logistics are taken care of, the audience is filling the room—you're on! Now what can you do now to make your presentation as effective as possible? Here are a few tips for winning your audience.

Start on time. Wait for people to quiet down before beginning. Stand at the lectern, look at the audience, and make it clear you expect them to pay attention.

State the purpose of the presentation, and introduce yourself, including your qualifications for speaking on the subject. Outline your agenda, and be sure to tell people when you'll break and when you'll end. One of our colleagues who gives day-long management development seminars begins the day by saying, "The first three things people want to know when they attend a presentation is when they can eat, when they can rest, and when they can leave." People always laugh in grateful recognition.

Take frequent breaks, at least one every hour and a half. Human beings are simply not meant to sit still and absorb information for long periods of time. The more breaks you take, the fresher and more attentive your audience will be.

Consider the time of day that you're giving your presentation. In general, earlier is better. If you're presenting just before or after lunch, remember this: if it's just before lunch, people's blood sugar levels are dropping, and they'll be more likely to think about eating than about what you're saying. Consider acknowledging that, and make your delivery as strong and forceful as possible. If it's just after lunch, people's blood will be in their bellies rather than their brains, and they may tend to be sleepy. Again, acknowledge that and keep your energy level high. Consider an exercise involving their participation to get them moving.

If you're one of several presenters on the agenda, try to be first or last instead of in the middle; you'll have the natural energy of novelty (if you're first) or climax (if you're last).

Vary the rhythm and pitch of your voice. There's nothing more hypnotic and sleep-inducing than a monotone voice in a darkened room. Pay attention to your energy level: when you feel yourself flagging, pick up your pace and raise your pitch. Speak from your chest, not from your throat.

Make eye contact with your audience at all times. Distribute it uniformly. You can establish an ally or two—the people who nod or smile at you inspire confidence and keep you going. But don't exclude everyone else. Make sure you establish eye contact that's meaningful—look into the eyes of the person you're speaking to for 5–10 seconds, and speak to that person as if he/she were the only person in the room. Don't just sweep your eyes across foreheads or noses. True eye contact transmits energy and warmth.

Pay attention to your body and be sure to keep moving. Avoid staying rooted to one spot. Consider walking down the aisle if you're presenting to a large audience. Even though motion is important, be sure it's intentional. Avoid pacing aimlessly. Any predictable, rhythmic motion—whether of your entire body or of your hand (to rub your eye, push back your hair, or adjust your tie)—will grab your audience's attention. They may become more fascinated by watching your "tick" than by listening to you speak.

Finally, finish your presentation on time. If you say you'll end at 4:30 and then keep on going until 4:45, your audience will feel you're holding them hostage. If you must run over, renegotiate. Say something like, "I know I said we'd be done at 4:30, but I'd like to take 15 more minutes of your time. Please stay if you can, but I'll understand if you need to leave." Running late or out of time is a common problem for novice presenters. Rehearse and time your presentation in advance, remembering that it never goes as smoothly in real life as it does in rehearsal. Watch questions, since they and their answers can easily make you run overtime. Figure out in advance what to omit and how, so that you have a plan if you find yourself running behind.

Above all, relax and try to have a good time. If you build your presentation around your audience's needs, and plan and rehearse extensively, you're all but guaranteed to make a persuasive presentation!

Part IV ◆ The Big Production

Chapter 17

Producing Overhead Transparencies

So far, we have discussed procedures for creating presentations within Persuasion. Now we turn to the issues involved in producing a presentation. Unless you plan to use your Macintosh's video monitor for an on-screen presentation, you will have to tailor your presentation for a specific presentation medium—overhead transparencies, a table flip-chart, or 35-mm slides. Each of these options has its pros and cons, and we will consider them in this section. But, before we get into specifics about each medium we need to consider a few technical issues that come into play regardless of the output media you ultimately choose.

WYSIWYG (What-You-See-Is-What-You-Get)

What-you-see-is-what-you-get (WYSIWYG) is one of the computer industry buzzwords, used when referring to a computer's output. Ideally, the image displayed on your monitor should exactly match the image you produce on a slide, overhead, or piece of paper. However, reality dictates otherwise. There are inherent visual differences between a screen display and every type of output medium. Some of the disparity is due to the methods each device uses to produce an image. For example, a video monitor creates color by shining three lights against the back of a phosphor tube, whereas a thermal printer produces color by overlaying three colors on top of one another. No matter how carefully you regulate color on your monitor there are bound to be differences in the final product.

In addition to the inherent differences in how images are created for each medium, there are other considerations that influence the fidelity between screen display and final output image.

The Macintosh uses one or both of two imaging models or languages to create an image on the video monitor and an output device. One is called QuickDraw, an imaging language built into every Macintosh and is used to generate images on the Macintosh screen. The other is PostScript, a rich page description language used to print the Macintosh screen image to an output device. Both of these languages have complicated command sets that manipulate fonts and graphics and that describe in minute detail what goes where on a monitor or other output device. As Macintosh users, we don't really have to know anything about what happens within the computer to generate images. But it helps to know enough about QuickDraw and PostScript so that we can better judge how what we see on the monitor translates into a printed page.

QuickDraw

The best guarantee for replicating the image that you see on a Macintosh screen to an output device, such as a printer, is to use an output device that shares the Macintosh's native imaging language, QuickDraw.

Up until fairly recently, QuickDraw output devices were unable to meet the demands of serious presentation work: QuickDraw had both a limited typographical repertoire as well as limitations in rendering some types of images (such as rotated text) in comparison to PostScript.

Over the past year or so, there have been an increasing number of high-quality devices that support QuickDraw, including laser, thermal wax, and ink jet printers in addition to film recorders. These imaging devices are traditionally lower in cost than the devices that support the other imaging model, PostScript.

Thanks to Adobe Type Manager (ATM), many of QuickDraw's typographical limitations have been resolved. ATM makes it possible for a user to expand his or her repertoire of screen fonts to include the thousands of PostScript fonts available from such vendors as Adobe Systems, Bitstream, Monotype, Agfa-Compugraphic, and other electronic foundries that produce PostScript fonts.

Note that when you use a QuickDraw output device, you must be careful not to incorporate PostScript-based encapsulated PostScript (also called EPS) graphics files into your presentation. These include graphics created using Aldus Freehand or Adobe Illustrator. While an imported graphic may look acceptable on the video monitor within Persuasion, it will not reproduce with a high quality in the final printed output. PostScript graphics files will simply not print on QuickDraw devices!

PostScript

We have seen that the native language of the Macintosh is QuickDraw. When you connect your Macintosh to a PostScript output device, the computer translates QuickDraw instructions into PostScript, otherwise the PostScript device could be unable to place an image on paper. The situation is a little like an American and a Russian trying to communicate. They eventually communicate, but sometimes they lose something in the translation. The same thing happens between QuickDraw and PostScript.

Macintosh always displays text and graphics on a monitor using its native QuickDraw (except when ATM intervenes and enables PostScript fonts to be displayed on the screen). When you send these images to a PostScript output device, unexpected things may happen in the translation to PostScript. For example, if you have graphics with unevenly rounded corners on your monitor, PostScript will print them as rounded. PostScript uses different algorithms than QuickDraw to create some types of graphic objects, this results in a slightly different appearance in your final output.

When you need a graphic on a slide, the best assurance you can have of matching screen image with video image is to use an EPS format graphic, since it requires no translation into PostScript. The file is, by definition, a PostScript file.

QuickDraw or PostScript?

If you already have a QuickDraw or PostScript output device your choice is already made for you. Use the device you have unless you cannot live without a feature that the other device has.

- If you have a choice of output device, QuickDraw, in combination with ATM, will assure you of faithful renditions between screen and output device (with the caveats noted above). If the QuickDraw output device does not support ATM, then you will be limited to a small selection of fonts, Times, Helvetica, and a few others. Unless things have changed, you will have these limitations as well, including Autographix.

- PostScript provides the best fidelity for any EPS graphics that may be included as part of your presentation. PostScript devices also give you the option of using hundreds of typefaces in almost any size you need. Use ATM even if you use PostScript output. ATM will generate any size font on your screen and will allow you to manipulate the type with the assurance that the printed output will closely mirror what you see on your screen. If you don't use ATM, you may notice slight discrepancies in spacing and appearance.

We'll be making some specific product recommendations in the following chapters as we discuss each of the major output technologies in more detail.

Overhead Transparencies

Over the past 25 years or so, the overhead transparency has become the veteran war-horse of presentation media. Since World War II, when the overhead projector rose in popularity, billions and billions of overhead transparencies have been produced world-wide. Transparencies are relatively inexpensive and are quick to prepare.

The overhead has suffered a reputation as a low quality presentation medium. However, its reputation has improved over the past few years now that you can run specially formulated transparency material through output devices that are computer operated. This, combined with the Macintosh's graphic output capabilities, have given transparencies new respect.

Transparency Films

The best way to generate overhead transparencies from a Persuasion presentation is to run the transparency material directly through your computer's printing device. This avoids the inevitable loss of quality that occurs if you print the presentation on paper and then make your final set of transparencies using a photocopier.

When you make a transparency directly from a printer, be sure to use transparency film specifically made for the type of printer you are using: laser, ink jet, dot-matrix, thermal transfer printers, or pen plotters. Each of these printer devices uses a different technology to create an image and thus makes an image using a technology that makes unique demands on transparency film. For example, transparency film for a pen plotter is designed to dry quickly using specially formulated plotter pens so that colors don't smudge and color contrast is high. On the other hand, transparency film for laser printers has to withstand very high temperatures while going through the printer.

Note: Be particularly careful of the type of transparency material you use in a laser printer. If you use the incorrect type, the transparency film will melt, possibly damaging your printer.

Transparency film is made by several manufacturers, most notably Avery and 3M. Avery makes a product called Laser Printer Transparencies (No. 5182, 50-sheet box; No. 5282, 20-sheet box). This product not only prints directly from a laser printer, but it also feeds automatically from the printer's paper tray, making it possible to print a presentation unattended. A special paper backing on each piece of transparency film reduces static, permits easy proofing and filing, and minimizes fingerprints and scratching on the film itself.

3M also markets special films and markers for printers including plotters, ink jet printers, impact printers, and thermal transfer printers.

Table 17.1 Film types for various output devices. These films are specially formulated for each specific device. Films are also made by other manufacturers.

Printers	3M	Avery
Laser printer	Type 154, 8803	Nos. 5182, 5282
Ink jet printer	Type 120, 8804	
Impact printer	Type 186	
Thermal transfer printer	Type 185	
Plotter	Types 073, 074, 075, 076, 077, 115	

Transparency Output Devices

One of the advantages of using overhead transparencies is their flexibility. As you can see in Table 17.1, you can image a transparency on a wide variety of different printing devices, such as laser, ink jet, dot-matrix, and thermal transfer, as well as on pen plotters.

Laser Printer

The most popular and widespread device for creating overhead transparencies is probably the laser printer. Compared to other hard copy devices it is easily available and gives high quality output not only for overhead transparencies, but for speaker notes and audience handouts as well. A Macintosh, Persuasion, and a laser printer can function as a kind of self-contained presentation production center.

Laser printers became popular in 1983 with the introduction of the Hewlett-Packard LaserJet. This machine represented a breakthrough in both price and technology. Before the introduction of the LaserJet, a laser printer could cost upwards of $10,000. However, at a price point less than $5,000, the LaserJet quickly became the de facto printer for MS-DOS computers. Apple bested the LaserJet when it introduced its own laser printer in 1985. Using the same imaging engine as the LaserJet, the LaserWriter added an important new capability to computer printers, the PostScript page description language. Compared to the LaserJet, which had limitations in the amount of text and graphics that could appear on a page, the LaserWriter gave Macintosh users free reign over how a page should look. The LaserWriter was and is a revolutionary piece of computer hardware.

There are several laser printer brands and models on the market today. And recently, the prices for laser printer prices have declined while the printing capabilities have increased. The Apple LaserWriter IINT has held its place as the mainstream PostScript laser printer. Its cousin, the LaserWriter IINTX is basically a higher performance version of the NT.

The main advantage of the IINTX is speed. Like the NT, the NTX comes with 2MB of RAM for storing downloaded fonts as well as for queuing pages that are waiting to print. The memory in the NTX can be increased to 12MB, however. This provides a dramatic increase in memory either for additional downloadable fonts or for queuing pages from the Macintosh. Pages can load into the random access memory (RAM) far faster than they print, and thus control of the Macintosh can be returned to the user much sooner.

The IINTX also has a SCSI interface port that accommodates external storage devices such as hard disks. The hard disks can be loaded with additional downloadable PostScript fonts that complement the 35 fonts already built into the printer. Using a hard disk in this manner spares you from sacrificing disk space on an individual Macintosh workstation in order to store downloadable fonts. The advantages of using a hard disk on the II NTX are particularly apparent with networked Macintosh installations; a hard disk that is attached to the IINTX can serve all the Macintoshes connected to a shared printer.

A lower cost PostScript printer is the GCC Business Laser Printer, by General Computer Corporation in Waltham, MA. This machine doesn't have the same lifetime rating as the LaserWriter, but, for lighter volume output demands, it produces output at least comparable to the more expensive LaserWriter II series of printers.

It you have a Hewlett-Packard LaserJet printer you can add PostScript capability by adding a QMS JetScript board to the LaserJet. This permits the printer to still function both in its native LaserJet mode, or in PostScript mode through the JetScript board.

If you choose to go the QuickDraw route, there are several QuickDraw laser printers on the market that can produce as high a quality output as a PostScript device. QuickDraw printers are generally less expensive than PostScript machines. Apple's LaserWriter II SC is one such device. This printer is identical to the other members of the LaserWriter family, except that the SC is a QuickDraw only machine. Another choice is GCC's Personal Laser Printer. You can later upgrade either of these machines to full-fledged PostScript printers if you decide you need PostScript.

The Technology

A laser printer (whether PostScript or QuickDraw) uses the same imaging technology found in many office photocopying machines. A laser printer works by reflecting a tiny beam onto a rotating mirror that in turn passes the beam through a lens and onto a photosensitive drum (see Figure 17.1). The drum then rotates through a bin of toner particles, and these particles are attracted to the exposed areas of the drum. Then, when the drum passes over a sheet of paper, the toner is transferred from the drum to the paper. Just before the page exits the printer, the printer melts the toner on the paper.

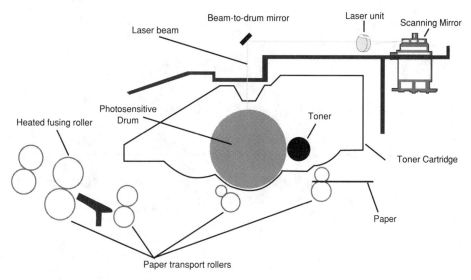

Figure 17.1. The laser printer imaging engine.

Cost

Laser printers can cost from about $1,500 to $9,000. The wide span of prices has nothing to do with the quality of the image on the page. The differences in price have to do with whether the printer supports PostScript and how much RAM it has. Most laser printers come with at least 2 MB of RAM, which is sufficient for even demanding presentation work. Adding more RAM will speed printing and return you the control of your Macintosh sooner.

All PostScript printers come with a minimum complement of 11 font families built into the printer. Including the standard variations for each family (Roman, bold, bold italic, and italic), a total of 35 typefaces are available, as illustrated in Table 17.2.

Table 17.2

Font	Roman	**Bold**	***Bold italic***	*Italic*
Avant Garde	X	X	X	X
Bookman	X	X	X	X
Courier	X	X	X	X
Helvetica	X	X	X	X
Helvetica Narrow	X	X	X	X
New Century Schoolbook	X	X	X	X
Palatino	X	X	X	X
Symbol	X			
Times	X	X	X	X
Zapf Chancery	X			
Zapf Dingbats	X			

QuickDraw laser printers start at about $2,000. You can find PostScript laser printers priced at about $4,200.

The per copy cost of running any laser printer ultimately depends on the average amount of text and graphics on a printed page: the more image area, the more toner the printer will use. As a rule of thumb, you can expect to spend about $0.04 per page, $0.03 for the toner and $0.01 for the paper itself.

Maintenance is usually a minor cost factor for the laser printer owner. On the one hand, you can usually purchase a service contract on your printer to cover the parts and labor for a set annual fee. However, from our experience, the failure rate of the laser printers is so low that the cost of the service contract may not be cost effective. In the several years we have owned LaserWriters, we have yet to take a printer in for repair. In fact, most malfunctions are likely to occur within the warranty period.

Multiple Color Output

Laser printers do have an Achilles heel. At present, there are no color laser printers priced for the consumer market. An inexpensive color laser printer is at least a few years away. Luckily, there are other alternatives for producing color transparencies. Pen plotters, ink-jet, and thermal wax transfer imaging devices are each capable of producing colored transparencies.

Color WYSIWYG

The addition of color to the what-you-see-is-what-you-get equation poses some additional problems regardless of the output medium you use. The main problem is this: there is no way to match accurately the color on a display with the color of hard copy. The reason is largely technical and has to do with the inherent differences in how each medium produces its color. A video monitor produces full color using three separate color guns, for example, but many printing technologies image color using a combination of four transparent process color inks (yellow, magenta, cyan, and black). The different methods cannot help but cause a mismatch between monitor and page.

One solution to the problem has been introduced by Tektronix. Its TekColor product for the Macintosh replaces the standard Macintosh color picker. This software product intercepts the color printer signal in the printer driver and analyzes all the colors that the printer can produce. The colors that can be produced by the printer are then compared with those available on the monitor. Those colors that match provide a common palette from which the user can choose.

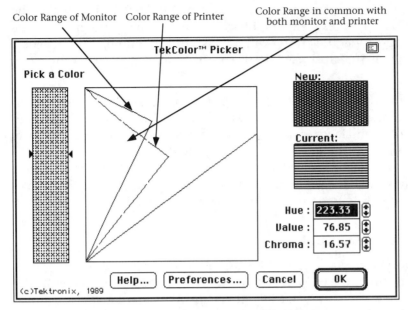

Figure 17.2. The TekColor Picker shows the difference between what colors are viewable on a display compared to a particular color output device.

TekColor Picker is a step in the right direction. However, at this time, the product only supports a limited number of Tektronix printers. Tektronix has made the TekColor system an open interface specification, however, so that other printer vendors can calibrate the Picker to work within the color constraints of their output hardware device.

Ink Jet Printers

One way to create impressive color presentations on a slim budget is to use a color ink-jet printer. The quality, performance and range of colors in color ink-jet printers is unmatched in the realm of color output devices that can reproduce the standard 256 Macintosh colors.

Tektronix makes a full feature printer, the ColorQuick, at a moderate price, about $2,500. The printer driver has two resolutions: 72 dpi for bit-mapped graphics (such as those imported from Pixel Paint or MacPaint), and 216 dpi for text or vector graphics (such as those created within Mac-Draw or Persuasion itself). The ColorQuick also works with the TekColor application.

Another strong color ink-jet candidate is the Hewlett-Packard PaintJet. The PaintJet is a serial device that can be attached to the printer port, or to the modem port. By using a network sharing device such as Shiva Corp.'s Net Serial (a unit that combines a serial port and an AppleTalk connector and allows any serial device to become a networked resource on an AppleTalk network), you can share the PaintJet among multiple users. Compared to the Tektronix ColorQuick, the PaintJet is slower, and, while its colors are not as saturated as the ColorQuick, nonetheless, they are quite good. The price of the PaintJet sets it apart from its competition. At a retail of about $1,500, the PaintJet is $1,000 less than the ColorQuick, which retails at $2,500.

The Technology

Ink jet printers propel fine droplets of ink through tiny holes in a print head toward the surface of the medium. The most popular ink jet technology is called drop-on-demand. Electronically pulsed transducers propel the ink whenever a drop is required. This method is more reliable than the continuous spray method, which shoots a continuous stream of ink while using a magnetic field to deflect the drops from areas where they are not needed.

Color ink jet printers blend the three primary colors (yellow, magenta, and cyan) plus black using a process called dithering, which creates a variety of colors and half tones. The quality of these colors and halftones is controlled by the dithering algorithms contained in the printer driver.

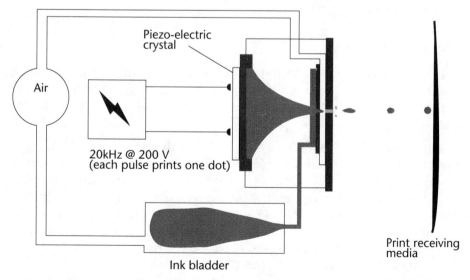

Figure 17.3 Ink jet technology depends on the accuracy of the printer to shoot droplets of ink toward the surface of a sheet of paper.

Early ink jet printers often used to have problems with messy ink and clogged jets. The current generation of ink jet printers has resolved these problems through improved technology. The major limitation for ink jet printers is their slow speed. The ink jet will print on any type of paper; however, specially coated ink jet paper and overhead transparency film yields the best color quality.

Cost

The cost per page for an ink jet printer ranges from $0.03 to $0.15, including ink and specially formulated paper. To make color overheads, the cost rises to about $1.00 per transparency because of the cost of the special film. The only maintanence you are likely to have on an ink jet printer is the periodic cleaning of the ink jets.

Pen Plotters

Pen plotters have been used widely in drafting and other fields in which the output is primarily composed of lines in a few colors, and often in a large format output. Plotter output can be up to several yards long if need be. Plotters are not intended for imaging presentation materials, and cannot be recommended for producing presentation materials except in instances where your design is extremely simple. Detailed graphics or fancy fonts do not play well on a plotter.

The Technology

Plotters use computer-controlled motors to guide up to eight separate colored pens. In a flat bed plotter, the pen moves back and forth over a sheet of paper or other material. Other types of plotters move the pen in one axis and the paper in the other.

Pen plotters are reliable devices notable for their crisp, sharp lines and their ability to image in color. However, they are slow, since they draw a line at a time and fill in solid areas by crosshatching. Also the range of colors is quite limited. They are primarily mechanical devices that require careful adjustment: the pens must be kept sharp and sufficiently loaded with ink. If you must print with more colors than the plotter can produce at one time, you will have to stand next to the machine to switch the pens manually with different-colored ones. The pen plotter has too many drawbacks to use to create high quality presentation output materials. Its use for presentation work should be limited to transferring standard plotter images such as engineering drawings, schematics, and architectural images.

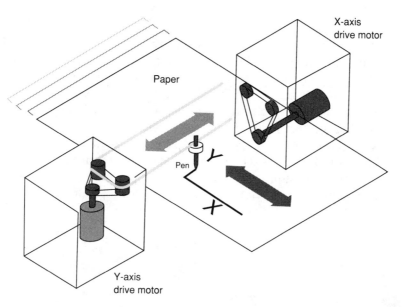

Figure 17.4   Pen plotters move pens and paper to create an image. They can produce crisp, sharp lines but have problems with complicated text.

Thermal Wax Printers

Thermal wax transfer printing is a reliable, proven technology capable of rendering excellent color quality at rapid print speeds. PostScript thermal wax printers offer a means for creating high quality color transparencies. Until now, they have been very costly (costing from $13,000 to more than $20,000). Their use was limited to high-end users, such as advertising agencies and large design studios needing to create color comps. With prices now around $10,000 for a PostScript thermal wax printer, and $6,000 for a non-PostScript one, these machines have increased appeal. For presentation work, thermal wax printers can image film in strong colors.

The QMS ColorScript 100 Model 10 printer is one of the market leaders in color thermal wax output. The Model 10 ships with 8 MB RAM, has high duty cycle, and print spooling capabilities for faster throughput. You can also connect an external hard disk drive for downloading additional typefaces, logos, or overlays. This printer has a duty cycle of up to 3,000 prints per month, comparable to the Apple LaserWriter II machines. In addition to PostScript, the printer is also licensed for Pantone matching color support.

For non-PostScript machines, Mitsubishi has a 300 dpi color printer for about $6,000. This machine is an alternative for users who cannot afford a PostScript machine.

The Technology

The basic thermal wax transfer process works by heating colored wax and fusing it to special, coated material. A thermal transfer roll is segmented into consecutive, page-sized bands of wax pigments. Hundreds or even thousands of individually controlled elements in the printer's thermal head melt spots of color onto the smooth surface paper. Variations in color are produced by taking primary colored wax and altering the size and spacing between the dots placed on the paper. Thus, purple is created by scattering red dots on a field of blue pixels. The page makes three or four passes under the print head, one for each primary color, plus an optional pass for a separate "true" black (similar to conventional process color reproduction).

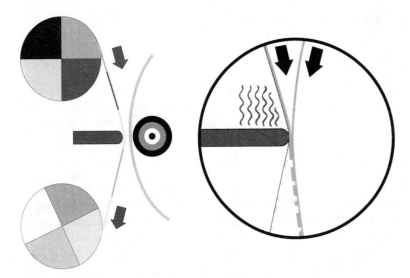

Figure 17.5   The thermal wax transfer process uses heat to transfer colors from ribbon to page.

Aside from cost of the printer itself, thermal wax transfer has many advantages that make it well suited for imaging color overhead transparencies. For one, it has a large color palette—you can use any of the Macintosh's 16.7 million colors and get a reasonably good rendition on a transparency. And, like a laser printer, thermal wax printers have a resolution of 300 dots per inch.

Cost

The cost for producing an image on paper is about $0.35. For an overhead transparency, it rises to about $1.25, which includes the transparency material and ribbon. Since thermal printers use special coated paper, you cannot use standard copier bond or transparency material. You must use special material specifically packaged for thermal wax transfer.

As far as repairs are concerned, thermal wax printers historically require little maintenance and have a long life. They make a good investment if you are looking to produce enough color high quality transparencies to warrant the machine's high initial cost.

Installing an Output Device for Producing Overheads

Now that we have discussed the pros and cons of hard copy output devices, let's look at how these devices connect to the Macintosh itself to produce overhead transparancies. All of these output devices physically connect to a Macintosh in a similar fashion—through the Macintosh's built-in AppleTalk network. The connection is not only easy and fast to make, but also allows several Macintoshes to share the same printer, making it easier to justify an expensive printer when you divide its cost among several users.

Every external output device comes with one or two special files, called printer drivers. These files reside in the Macintosh and allow the computer to talk to the printer. For example, a LaserWriter NT requires two driver files called LaserWriter and LaserWriter Prep. The QuickDraw-based LaserWriter SC comes with a driver of its own. Whatever the output device, the procedure for installing the software is identical: simply drag the driver file into the System Folder and restart your Macintosh.

Note: If you are sharing an output device with other users on an Apple-Talk network make sure each user is using the identical version of the driver files for the particular output device in their System Folder.

Selecting the Output Device for Your Presentation

To specify or change your output device, open the Chooser from the Apple menu. You can select the Chooser to change your output device at any time, even while you are using Persuasion or another application.

When the Chooser dialog box appears on your desktop, it will look similar to the one pictured in Figure 17.6. (Depending on what output devices you have available to your Macintosh, your Chooser dialog box may look slightly different than the one pictured.)

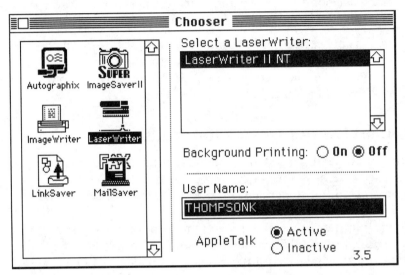

Figure 17.6   The Chooser dialog box displays an icons for each output device.

The icons at the left of the Choose dialog box represent each available output device. Select one by clicking on its icon. If you are connected to more than one device represented by that icon, the scroll box in the upper right will list the names of each device. Select the one you want to use. To confirm your choice, check the close box in the upper left corner of the Chooser window. Your choice will remain in effect until you return to the Chooser and make another choice.

The Page Setup and Print Commands

After you have specified a printer in the Chooser, select *Page Setup* from Persuasion's File menu. This is a two-step process. First, choose the physical page size from the standard device print dialog box. US Letter is the choice for a standard transparency. Other choices you may wish to make in this dialog box affect how your output device should handle special situations.

- **Font substitution:** This option converts the Macintosh fonts Geneva, New York, and Monaco into the LaserWriter II fonts Helvetica, Times, and Courier, respectively. The best advice is simply not to use the Macintosh fonts at all in a presentation.

- **Text smoothing:** This option minimizes jagged edges on Macintosh bit-mapped (screen) fonts that have no corresponding outline (printer) fonts installed. For professional looking presentations, however, be sure to have outline fonts installed on your Macintosh in addition to the bit-mapped (screen) fonts.

- **Graphics smoothing:** This option minimizes jagged edges on graphic images, in particular bitmapped images.

- **Faster bitmap printing:** This option speeds the printing of bit-map graphic images. This option entails a compromise: bitmap images will not print with the same quality as with the box unchecked. If you need to print bitmapped images, we recommend you do not check this box.

If you click the *Options button*, you will have more options:

- **Flip horizontal:** Reverses the page left to right.

- **Flip vertical:** Reverses the page top to bottom.

- **Invert image:** Prints white on black.

- **Precision bitmap alignment:** Reduces the size of the printed page by 4% for better representation of graphic images.

- **Larger print area:** This expands the print area by reducing the minimum margins required.

After you check *OK* in the Print dialog box, another dialog box, Presentation setup, appears. Click on the *Overheads* choice and then click *OK*.

Once you completed your presentation, you are ready to print, choose the *Print* command under the File menu. The Print dialog box itself will vary for each type of output device since each device has its own special options. For example, if you are using the LaserWriter SC, your dialog box will have one set of options, and, if you are using a LaserWriter the dialog box you will be presented with will have other options. The LaserWriter dialog box should look similar to the one in Figure 17.7.

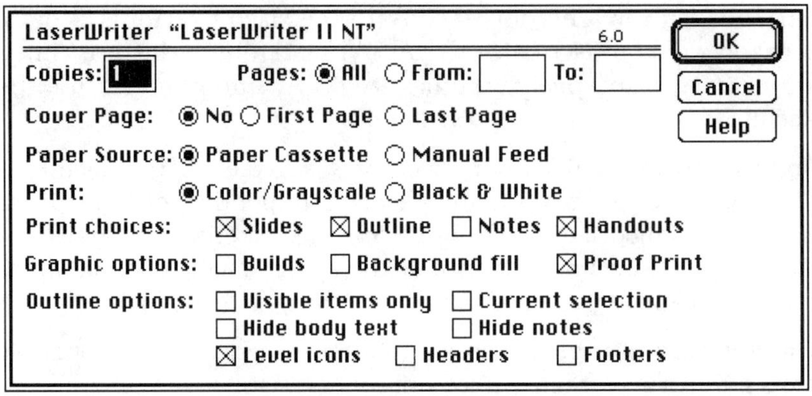

```
┌─────────────────────────────────────────────────────────────────┐
│ LaserWriter  "LaserWriter II NT"              6.0    ╭──────────╮ │
│                                                      │    OK    │ │
│ Copies:[1  ]        Pages: ⦿ All  ○ From:[   ] To:[   ]╰──────────╯│
│                                                      ╭──────────╮ │
│ Cover Page:    ⦿ No ○ First Page  ○ Last Page        │  Cancel  │ │
│                                                      ╰──────────╯ │
│ Paper Source: ⦿ Paper Cassette  ○ Manual Feed        ╭──────────╮ │
│                                                      │   Help   │ │
│ Print:         ⦿ Color/Grayscale ○ Black & White     ╰──────────╯ │
│                                                                   │
│ Print choices:    ☒ Slides  ☒ Outline  ☐ Notes ☒ Handouts        │
│ Graphic options:  ☐ Builds  ☐ Background fill   ☒ Proof Print     │
│ Outline options:  ☐ Visible items only  ☐ Current selection      │
│                   ☐ Hide body text      ☐ Hide notes             │
│                   ☒ Level icons  ☐ Headers    ☐ Footers          │
└─────────────────────────────────────────────────────────────────┘
```

Figure 17.7 The Print dialog box contains commands for sending your
presentation to the output device you have chosen with the
Chooser. In this example, you see the LaserWriter print dialog box.

The top half of the dialog box is identical to the standard dialog box for
the output device you have chosen. The *Print choices*, *Graphic options*, and
Outline options, however, are specific to Persuasion.

- *Print choices* are self-explanatory. Depending on which boxes you
  check, Persuasion will print slides, outline, notes, or handouts one set
  after the other.

- *Graphic options*

  Builds: This option lets you choose whether you want a separate overhead for each slide build or layer, or a single composite overhead. If
  you check Builds, Persuasion will print a separate overhead for each
  layer on those slides that use layers.

  Background fill: If your presentation is color and you are printing on
  a standard single-color output device, uncheck the background fill
  box. This will knock out the background for printing. Otherwise, a
  colored background could make your slides difficult to read.

  Proof print: This option will convert colors to black text and objects.
  Also use Proof print to more quickly produce a legible set of speaker
  notes and handouts.

- *Outline options* allow you to print selected parts of the outline.

  Visible items only: This options prints only those outline items that
  are expanded and thus visible on screen.

Current selection: Prints only the selection you have selected at the time you choose the Print command.

Hide Body Text/Hide notes: Prints the outline without including body text and/or notes. Check both if you want to print a list of your slide titles only.

Level icons: Prints the Persuasion icons alongside each heading. If you leave this unchecked the icons do not appear.

Headers/Footers: Will place headers or footers on each outline page. If you check Header, Persuasion places the file name on the top of every outline page; if you check Footer, Persuasion places a page number at the bottom of every outline page.

As you can see, there are many options for producing a set of professional looking overheads. Persuasion, coupled with a laser, thermal wax, ink jet printer, or plotter breathes new life into the medium of the overhead transparency.

Chapter 18

Producing 35-mm Slides

Of all the standard presentation media, 35-mm slides are probably the most impressive. At the same time, slides are the greatest challenge to produce. We have seen that on-screen presentations and presentations using transparencies presentation require only a standard Macintosh system. Imaging a presentation on a set of 35-mm slides, however, requires special file preparation procedures and then special hardware for producing the slides.

You have two choices for producing 35-mm slides. You can send your Persuasion file to an outside service bureau for imaging, or you can use an in-house film recorder to do the job yourself.

In-house or Service Bureau?

There is no right answer when it comes to deciding whether to buy a film recorder or to send your presentation file out to a service bureau.

Economically, a film recorder looks to be the best value for anyone who produces more than a few presentations a month. Compared to traditional costs that can be as much as $100 per slide, a film recorder costing about $5,000 can seem to pay back in as little as one or two presentations.

A film recorder gives you the control and convenience of having the output device nearby. You also get an added layer of security since more of your presentation production is handled internally.

However, film recorders do present some hidden costs in terms of time and hardware support. At this time there are few PostScript-equipped film recorders on the market, and those that are on the market are fairly expensive although prices are likely to decline over the next year or so as the competition for PostScript film recorders increases.

Non-PostScript devices usually use proprietary imaging schemes that limit the machine's graphic and text capabilities. You may be forced to draw on a small selection of fonts that come with the film recorder instead of the incredible variety of fonts available for PostScript devices. It also takes a great deal of time to produce a finished series of 35-mm slides. The average imaging time per slide on a film recorder is about 4 minutes; still, given a 20-slide presentation, it will consume more than an hour if all goes well. Then, you must add the time it takes to get film back from the processor. If you use more than one roll of film, you also run the risk of color shifts between film batches as well as variations in processing.

Note: When using a film recorder, buy film that has the same batch numbers. This assures that you will get more consistent results among rolls used for the same presentation.

Service bureaus are equipped to handle a large presentation expeditiously. They have the equipment and know-how to turn a presentation around in 24 hours or less, if necessary. The cost per slide is, of course, higher than it would be if you produced the slide in-house, but the advantage is that the service bureau takes responsibility for the entire production process: from imaging the slide to running the processing. Consider, too, that once you deliver a slide file to a service bureau your Macintosh can be used for other things. If you are producing slides with your own film recorder, your Macintosh is tied up for the time it takes to image the slides.

Before you choose either solution, you need to analyze your needs carefully. Think about your present and anticipated volume, quality requirements, and staffing resources. Some companies opt to use a film recorder for day-to-day presentation work and use a service bureau for rush or extraordinary presentations requiring extra production skills and time.

Film Recorders

The procedure for preparing a file for a film recorder is similar to a service bureau in that you must first convert the presentation to an intermediary file rather than send the file directly to the film recorder. For non-Postscript film recorders, the Macintosh scrapbook file format is the common format. For PostScript devices, there is a different format since the Scrapbook cannot accommodate PostScript effects.

To convert a Persuasion presentation into a Scrapbook format, follow the steps for exporting a presentation in Chapter 14, *Importing and Exporting.*

The Technology

Film recorder technology has taken a quantum leap in the last few years. The result is that an inexpensive film recorder can image surprisingly high quality 35-mm slides in a relatively short time. These recorders digitize the Macintosh display and transfer its image to high-resolution, color 35-mm transparency film. Earlier analog devices merely reproduced the low resolution image from a monitor directly onto film, in effect taking a snapshot of the screen at 72 dot per inch resolution. Digital film recorders, on the other hand, transform the image from a display into dots and lines at resolutions of up to 4,000 lines per inch, which is about the highest resolution a piece of film can record.

Digitizing film recorders contain a cathode ray tube (CRT) that displays a black-and-white version of the Macintosh's screen image. A 35-mm camera back mounted to the back of the film recorder takes three separate exposures of the CRT on the same frame of film: one exposure each with a red, green, and blue filter. The various shades of gray on the CRT translate to the millions of different colors the Macintosh II can generate.

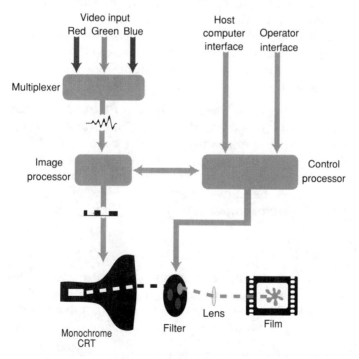

Figure 18.1   The film recorder takes three separate exposures of a slide displayed on a miniature CRT: one exposure each with a red, green, and blue filter.

Film recorders vary the most in two areas: CRT size and the type of rasterizing software used. The CRT sizes vary from 2 to 7 inches on the diagonal. Manufacturers who use larger tubes claim that they enable better resolution. Some recorders use rasterizing software that scans images as an array of lines and columns, rather than dot-by-dot. This scheme produces accurate detail, and the edges of text and graphics generally appear sharper on the slide. This system of scanning can also increase the image scanning speed. The software used by other film recorders is based on the QuickDraw raster image, which is a dot-by-dot representation of the Macintosh screen.

Tip: The SCSI interface cable that comes with a film recorder is usually too short, requiring the recorder to be located right next to the Macintosh. To locate the recorder more conveniently, you can buy a SCSI extension cable in several lengths.

Cost

Film recorder hardware itself is a relatively inexpensive item for anyone producing a few presentations a month. A film recorder includes a camera back and software for controlling the recorder from the Macintosh. Most units also offer optional camera backs, such as one for Polaroid, and different film size backs for special purposes. The units also come with a selection of outline fonts that you must use in your presentation, since you can not use your PostScript fonts on a non-PostScript film recorder.

Aside from the film and processing costs, a film recorder will probably run for some time without any problems. But since mechanical devices are prone to breakdowns and since film recorders are partly mechanical, you should beware of a few potential areas for problems over time. For example, over time, the filters will fade causing colors to shift. And, since the three filters are mounted on a turret that moves three times for each slide, eventually the turret can wear down or stop functioning properly.

Slide Bureau Output

The number of service bureaus that can accommodate Persuasion files is growing. At present, the major service bureaus, including Autographix, Genigraphics, and Crosfield-Dicomed, all can produce Persuasion presentations on 35-mm slides. (They can also provide overheads and color prints.)

In our service bureau example, we will use Autographix since each Persuasion 2.0 package comes with an Autographix Presentation kit that contains the software and documentation for preparing a Persuasion file for

35-mm slide imaging at an Autographix Service Center. Each of the other service bureaus use different but similar steps to image Persuasion files.

Hard Copy

Before you prepare a file for the service bureau, you may want to print a hard copy version of your presentation for proofing. Remember that you will need to print your copy as an Autographix-formatted presentation. You must not choose to have Persuasion reformat your entire file to accommodate the laser printer's page size.

From the Apple menu select *Chooser* and click on the LaserWriter icon. Select *Page Setup* from the File menu and change the entry in the *Reduce/Enlarge text box* from 100 to a percentage between 70 and 90 (you may need to experiment to find the best percentage within this range). By changing the percentage, your presentation reduces to fit on a page since the proportions for a slides and for a standard 8.5 × 11 page are different. In the subsequent Presentation setup dialog box, you'll see that *Custom* is selected. Select 35-mm slides that will change the format size to the Autographix dimensions.

That's all there is to it. Now you can print selecting either 35-mm slides, notes, or handouts. You may have to experiment with the reduction number in the Page setup dialog box.

Preliminaries

As we've mentioned before, if you are going to image a presentation onto 35-mm slides for Autographix, it is preferable to configure Persuasion for 35-mm slides output from the start (with the Autographix driver selected) so you are working in the appropriate dimensions as you design the presentation.

So, the first step is to make sure that Persuasion is aware that you are about to create a 35-mm slide presentation for Autographix imaging. (Note that other service bureaus may use slightly different dimensions, and so the "35-mm slide" is not a fixed item in terms of sizing.)

As an option, Autographix and most other service bureaus can also provide color overhead transparencies or 8 1/2 × 11 color prints. The steps for creating these alternative output media is identical as for 35-mm slides.

From the Apple menu, select the *Chooser*. If the Autographix driver is installed (Persuasion installs it automatically during the installation process), you will see the Autographix driver icon displayed on the left side of the

Chooser dialog box along with other output options (see Figure 18.2). Click on the Autographix icon to select it, and then click the *Continue* button in the warning dialog box that reminds you to update the settings in the Page setup dialog box. Close the Chooser when you've made your selections.

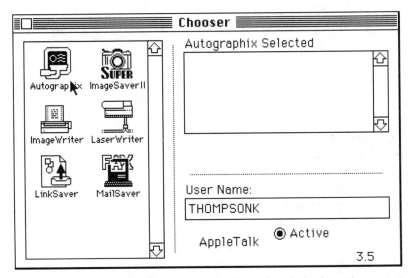

Figure 18.2   You choose the Autographix output driver from the
Chooser just as you would select a printer driver.

Normally, of course, you use the Chooser to select a printer. Similarly, by choosing the Autographix driver in the Chooser, you will "print" your presentation file to disk for later use by the service bureau. The service bureau will use the specially formatted print file and will print your presentation to its own slide imaging devices.

Now choose *Page Setup* from the File menu (as you were instructed to do when you selected the Autographix driver from the Chooser). The Autographix dialog box appears as shown in Figure 18.2.

Note: The orientation settings in the Autographix dialog box do not affect slide orientation. For example, to change orientation from portrait to landscape, choose *Tall orientation* from Persuasion's Master menu. You can mix horizontal and vertical slide formats in a single presentation by designating some masters as portrait.

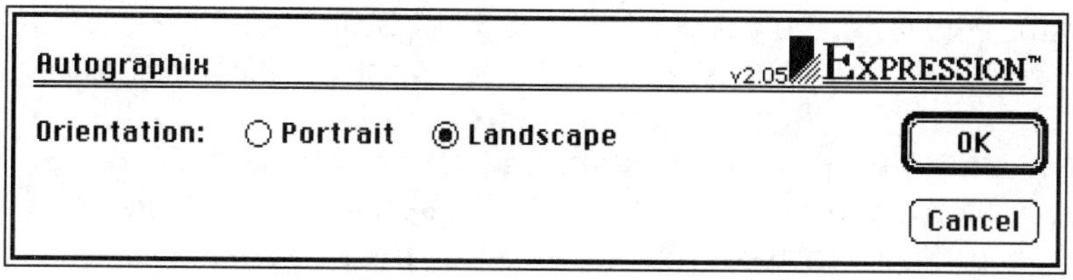

Figure 18.2. The Autographix dialog box appears when you choose *Page Setup* after you have selected the Autographix driver in the Chooser.

To remove the Autographix dialog box, either click *OK*, *Cancel*, or press Return. In the Presentation setup dialog box that then appears, click on the radio button for 35-mm slides. Notice that the dimensions in the *Custom text boxes* change to 13.81 × 9.21, the correct size for an Autographix 35-mm slide. If you set up your presentation for 35-mm slides before specifying the Autographix driver from the Chooser, you need to go to the Page setup/presentation setup dialog box to specify 35-mm slides again for Persuasion to update its dimensions to precisely match Autographix' dimensions.

Depending on what Persuasion's settings were before you choose the Autographix driver, Persuasion may display the Adjust graphics dialog box as shown in Figure 18.3.

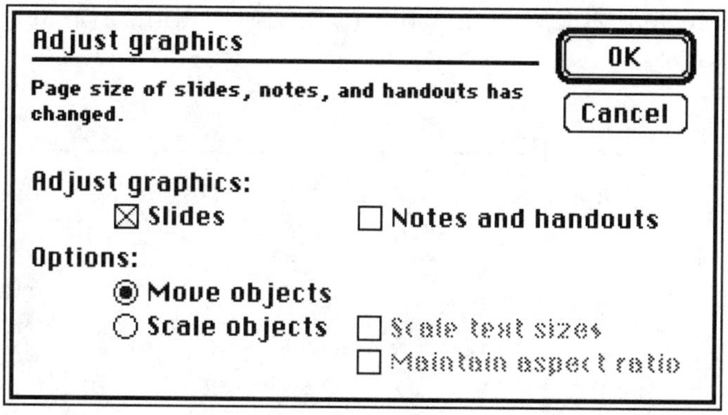

Figure 18.3 The Adjust graphics dialog box provides a way to have Persuasion automatically fit text and graphics elements on a slide.

Persuasion only displays the Adjust graphics dialog box when the size of slides or notes and handouts have been affected by any new settings you have selected. If you have only changed the size of slides, the *Notes and handouts* option will be dimmed. Likewise, if only the note and handout page size has changed, then the *Slides* choice will be dimmed.

If you want Persuasion to calibrate text and/or graphics for the new presentation size constraints, check off one of the *Adjust graphics* options. The *Options* choices below will then become active, allowing you to stipulate what kind of adjustments you wish to make to your slide images. For a more detailed discussion of these two options see Chapter 19, *Producing an On-screen Slide Show*. You can have objects moved with no resizing of text or objects, or you can have objects resized for the new slide area (including text or not).

If you choose to scale objects, you can also check *Scale text sizes*, and Persuasion will enlarge or reduce your text to fit. If you leave the box unchecked, Persuasion will not change the size of text, but it will scale other nontext items on the slide. So which options should you check? We recommend the *Move objects* option for most cases, and then suggest you review your presentation slide-by-slide since you will probably have to make some small position changes to some of the repositioned slide elements.

Fonts

At this time, slide service bureaus are just starting to support PostScript. In the meantime, you will have to limit yourself to the library of fonts that the particular bureau supports. Below is the list of the fonts that Autographix supports at this writing. It is typical of the selection you can expect from a slide bureaus. Note that the choices mirror the list of fonts available on a PostScript printer.

Table 18.1

Font	Roman	Bold	Bold italic	Italic	Outline	Shadow
Avant Garde	X	X	X	X	X	X
Bookman	X	X	X	X	X	X
Courier	X	X	X	X	X	X
Helvetica	X	X	X	X	X	X
Helvetica Narrow	X	X	X	X	X	X
New Century Schoolbook	X	X	X	X	X	X
Palatino	X	X	X	X	X	X
Symbol	X				X	X
Times	X	X	X	X	X	X
Zapf Chancery	X				X	X
Zapf Dingbats	X				X	X

While the choices are limited compared to the hundreds of fonts available with PostScript output devices, many of these fonts are effective for presentation work.

Note: If you use a font other than one of the supported fonts listed in Table 18.1, a bitmapped font will be substituted during the imaging process, and the text on your slide will probably come out with jagged edges, unsuitable for presentation.

While the variety of fonts is limited, there is no restriction on what size font you can use in a presentation. For best on-screen appearance, as you create your slide presentation be sure to install the appropriate size screen font. This way you won't be faced with output surprises. Persuasion 2.0 comes with a supplemental set of larger screen fonts to complement the smaller bitmapped screen fonts for Times, Helvetica, and Symbol (unless you are using ATM, in which case you don't need to install the additional font sizes). Persuasion's screen fonts for these fonts include 12, 14, 18, 24, 36, 40, 48, 56, and 72-point sizes.

To install the additional screen fonts, use the Font/DA Mover that comes with your Macintosh, or, better yet, use a desk accessory such as Suitcase II or Master Juggler, which eliminates having to install the fonts directly into the System file. Instead, you can temporarily open the larger size font suitcases that you need for the presentation and then close the suitcases after you are done. To conserve disk space, don't install sizes you aren't likely to use. For more information on installing fonts, refer to Chapter 1, *Installing Persuasion.*

Graphics

If you are going to use the Autographix or other service bureau, there are some limitations as far as what graphics you should use within your presentation. Some types of imported graphics look perfect within Persuasion but come out unacceptably jagged on the finished slide.

Just as service bureaus today do not support PostScript, they cannot accurately image a graphic that is in PostScript format. They are simply treated as bitmapped images by Autographix. The two graphic formats that you can use reliably are PICT and PICTII, standard file formats for any object-oriented draw program such as MacDraw, Cricket Draw, or SuperPaint. Most scanner software also will save graphics in PICT format; the appearance of the scanned image on a slide may not be of presentation quality.

If you import a bitmapped graphic, such as one created in MacPaint or imported from HyperCard, the resulting slide will have unacceptably jagged edges. You will also get unsatisfactory slides using a gray scale TIFF (tagged image file format) file in your presentation design.

Color

Using a color-equipped Macintosh II or a Macintosh SE/30, you can choose any color combination from the Macintosh's 16.7 million color palette. One thing to keep in mind, however, is the inherent difference in rendition between colors you see in on the computer display and what comes out on the slide. For numerous technical reasons, most colors do not match well between display and slide (or between the display and other hard copy media for that matter).

Autographix warns that nonrectangular objects that contain graduated color fills print with a jagged edge. To create objects that print with a smooth edge, Autographix recommends the following steps:

1. Draw the object.

2. Apply a graduated fill pattern to the object.

3. Apply a line style of *None* (the dotted line in the Line style menu) to the object.

4. Duplicate the object using the *Duplicate* command from the Edit menu.

5. Apply a line style at least 2-picas thick (the fourth solid line from the top of the Line style menu) to the duplicate object.

6. Apply a fill pattern of *None* to the duplicate object.

7. Drag the duplicate object on top of the original object so that the line around the duplicate object completely covers the edge of the fill on the original object.

Macintosh Plus and SE

If you preparing a presentation using a Macintosh Plus or Macintosh SE, there are severe constraints when it comes to color. First is the obvious problem of actually seeing the color choices on the display. Colors display as patterns of gray, which are difficult, at best, to visualize.

The larger problem is the choice of colors you can use in a presentation. If you are using one of these black and white Macintoshes, you can only choose from the basic QuickDraw palette of eight colors: black, white, red, blue, green, yellow, cyan, and magenta.

Note: With a monochrome Macintosh, you cannot apply horizontal or vertical graduated patterns or radial fills to a slide.

Tip: A workaround for producing color slides from a monochrome Macintosh is to complete the presentation with the monochrome machine, and then open the presentation on a color Macintosh and there apply color to your slides.

Slide Output

Once you've finished your presentation using a mix of supported fonts, graphic file formats, and colors, you need to save the file in special Autographix format whether you intend to transfer the file to Autographix by disk or by modem.

Preparing a presentation file for Autographix is a two-step process. First, you save the presentation as a print file using the Autographix driver you already chose in the Chooser. Then, whether you will be using a modem or sending a disk to Autographix, you use a separate utility program called "AGXit" to package the presentation along with billing and shipping information for Autographix. You cannot just send Persuasion files to Autographix. You must package your presentation using AGXit.

When your presentation is ready for imaging, choose *Print* from the File menu. A dialog box like the one in Figure 18.3 appears. This is similar to a standard print dialog box except that it is customized for Autographix.

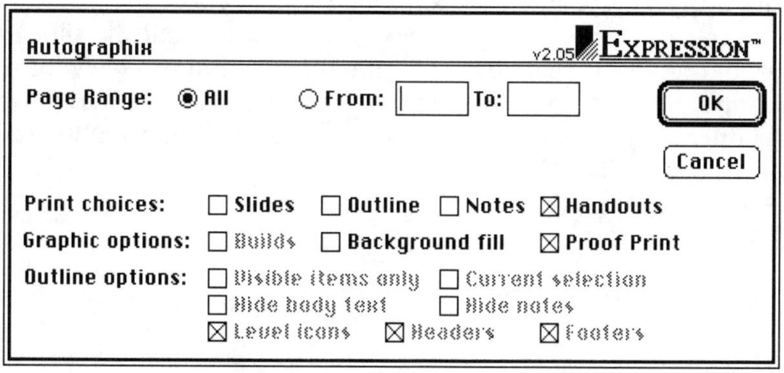

Figure 18.4   The Autographix print dialog box.

In the dialog box, you need to make some choices:

- If you want the entire presentation imaged, leave the *All* button checked. Or, if you only want to image part of a presentation, enter the range of slide numbers in the *From:/To:* text boxes.

- Be sure to uncheck *Outline*, *Notes*, and *Handouts*. The only checked item should be *Slides*. Since Autographix will image everything you have checked off, if you accidentally leave *Outline*, *Notes*, or *Handouts* checked, you will get 35-mm slides of these other items for which you will be billed accordingly by Autographix!

Enter a file name in the dialog box and click *OK*. Persuasion then prints your file in a special format for Autographix.

There's one last step after you have created your print file. You have to electronically package the presentation print file together with billing and shipping instructions for Autographix using a supplied utility called AGXit. (If the AGXit utility is not in the Persuasion 2.0 folder, you will need to refer back to the Persuasion installation process to install AGXit from the Persuasion disks.)

Turnaround

This chart gives you an idea of the type of turnaround service you can expect from a service bureau. The chart is a guide only. Contact the slide bureau directly to get an up-to-the-minute turnaround schedule.

Tip: If you live in the Eastern time zone and if you are using a modem to download files, you can save rush charges by sending your file to a slide bureau in the Western part of the US. For example, with a three hour time difference between Boston and San Francisco, you could send a file to San Francisco before 3 P.M. Eastern time, and the slide bureau would receive it before noon Pacific time, within its policy for standard rates. Since overnight couriers offer overnight service nationwide, the only additional cost would be for the long distance phone call to download the file.

Table 18.2

Type of Courier	Time at Slide bureau	Time of delivery or pick-up
Overnight courier		
Standard	In by noon	Delivered by noon, next day
Rush	In by 3 P.M.	Delivered by noon, next day
Local Pick-up		
Standard	In by 8:30 A.M.	Ready for pick-up by 5 P.M.
	In by 5 P.M.	Ready by 9 A.M. the next business day
Rush	In by 8 A.M.	Ready by 2 P.M. that day
	In by 10 A.M.	Ready by 4 P.M. that day
	In by 3 P.M.	Ready by 10 P.M. that day

Bear in mind the trade offs between an in-house film recorder and a service bureau. Don't make the mistake of creating a cost analysis based solely on the cost of the film recorder hardware. There's more to the picture than that.

Chapter 19

Producing an On-Screen Slide Show

With the slide show feature, you can use Persuasion to give a full-screen presentation, eliminating the distraction of menus and windows. With on-screen presentations, you can use Persuasion's special effects to add movement to otherwise inanimate slides. You can use special transition effects as you move from slide to slide, and you can use its screen-build feature to add text and graphic elements progressively to a single slide for added emphasis. Using the Macintosh for a slide show makes the Macintosh both a production and a presentation tool at once.

Besides using Persuasion's built in slide show for live presentations, you can preview or rehearse a slide show that will ultimately be presented on a big screen with overheads or 35-mm slides. You can get a sense of the flow of the show and, if necessary, can stop the presentation at any point to make changes.

This chapter is divided into two parts. First, we will discuss how to set up an on-screen presentation using Persuasion and consider the hardware issues that you will have to come to grips with. Then, we will explain the pros and cons of some of the hardware options available for an on-screen show.

Slide Show Set-up

If you are simply previewing your slide show and plan to print overheads or 35-mm slides don't make any changes in the Page setup dialog box. Simply choose *Slide show* from the File menu. If you make changes to the Page setup settings you risk making changes in your presentation that can affect

473

the positioning of text and graphics elements in the set of final overheads or 35-mm slides. Remember that Persuasion always reminds you of the final output device you've selected so that you don't accidentally create a presentation using the wrong slide sizes.

On the other hand, if you are using the on-screen slide show view as your final output, you want to be sure that your Macintosh is configured for the best possible display.

Fonts

We cannot stress enough the importance of having the correct set of screen fonts installed on the presentation Macintosh. This is almost as important as having the presentation file itself because without having a set of correctly installed fonts, your text will look jagged and will be in a position different from that when you created your presentation. Your audience will find the text hard to read, and amateurish, especially in the larger point sizes that are normally used for presentations.

Make sure that the presentation Macintosh has the necessary fonts and sizes for your slide show. It is best to go through a dry run on the presentation Macintosh to check that the correct fonts are installed. You may want to bring along and then install a set of the font suitcases from the machine that you used to create the presentation on. For more information about fonts, consult Chapter 1, *Installing Persuasion*.

Presentation Setup

Once you have the right set of fonts for your presentation, you should check that your presentation setup settings are correct. Hopefully, you specified these settings before you started to design your presentation.

To set the correct proportions for the monitor, open the Presentation setup dialog box using the *Page setup* command and choose *Screen*. You will have to enter custom dimensions, however, if you are preparing your presentation on one monitor and planning to show it on a different monitor with different dimensions. In this case, check the custom slide shape and enter the dimensions (in inches) of the presentation monitor for the slide show. These dimensions may be determined by either of these two methods:

1. Open Persuasion on a Macintosh with the same size screen as you will be using in the final presentation. Then, open the Presentation setup dialog box (via the *Page setup* command). Persuasion will automati-

cally enter the dimensions of the current monitor in the *Custom* edit boxes. Persuasion always reads the screen dimensions for the current monitor.

For example, if you will be presenting using a standard Macintosh II RGB monitor, you will have to edit the Custom size dimensions to read 8.88 by 6.66 inches. However, if you are actually creating that presentation on a Macintosh SE instead of the Macintosh II, you must edit the *Custom* dimensions of the SE (7.1×4.75 inches) inches shown on the SE to fit the larger RGB monitor (8.89×6.67 inches).

2. If you don't have access to the presentation monitor itself, you can refer to Table 19.1 for a list of Apple monitor dimensions, or refer to the monitor's owner's manual or manufacturer to find out the active image area of the monitor.

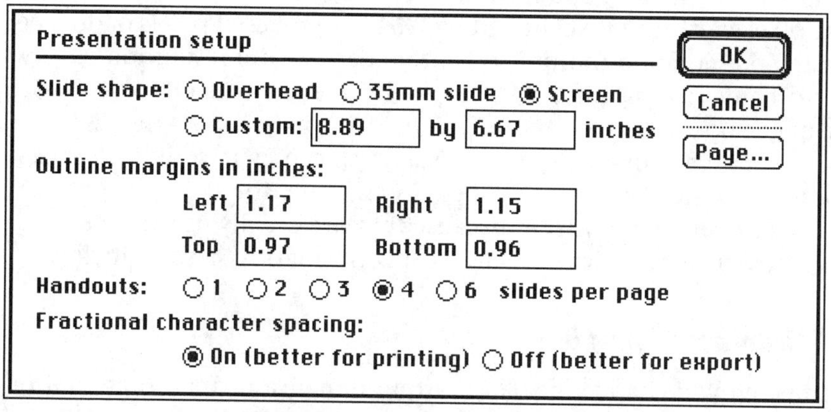

Presentation setup			OK
Slide shape: ○ Overhead ○ 35mm slide ⦿ Screen			Cancel
○ Custom: 8.89 by 6.67 inches			Page...
Outline margins in inches:			
Left 1.17	Right 1.15		
Top 0.97	Bottom 0.96		
Handouts: ○1 ○2 ○3 ⦿4 ○6 slides per page			
Fractional character spacing:			
⦿ On (better for printing) ○ Off (better for export)			

Figure 19.1   Choose *Screen* as the output device in the Presentation setup dialog box. If you are using a nonconventional size screen, enter the screen dimensions directly in the *Custom* text boxes. Otherwise, you can accept the values that Persuasion places in the *Custom* text boxes when you click the *Screen* output.

Table 19.1.

Apple screen dimensions	Pixels	Inches
Macintosh Plus or SE	512 × 342 (72 dpi)	7.1 × 4.75
AppleColor High-Resolution RGB	640 × 480 (72 dpi)	8.88 × 6.66
Macintosh Portable	640 × 400 (72 dpi)	8.88 × 5.55
Apple Macintosh Portrait Display	640 × 870 (80 dpi)	8 × 10.87
Apple Two-Page Monochrome	1,152 × 870 (77 dpi)	15 × 11.3

You can also calculate the dimensions with some simple math. As you know, the resolution (or the active image size) of a monitor is expressed in pixels rather than inches. You'll need to convert the pixels into inches. Divide the pixel width and pixel height by 72, the number of pixels or dots per inch, if the presentation monitor is the standard 72 dpi resolution. For example, to convert a monitor with a pixel dimension of 680 × 480 into inches, divide both dimensions by 72 to yield an answer of 9.4 inches by 6.6 inches. If you were going to present on such a screen, you would enter these two values into the *Custom* text boxes. As an aside, the fields for entering custom dimensions are in inches because they are usually used for tailoring the size of overheads. Overheads are most conveniently sized in inches.

Adjust Graphics Dialog Box

Often when you change media or output dimensions for a presentation that you have already prepared, you will have to make some compositional adjustments for the new size. If you change from overheads to a slide show with the Presentation setup box, an Adjust graphics dialog box will automatically appear as you exit the Presentation setup dialog box. This is Persuasion's warning that text and graphics objects on your slides may need to be adjusted or resized on one or more slides. Naturally, if your presentation was designed for overheads and you change to on-screen slides, the available image area will be different because overheads and monitors have different ratios of height to width. If you don't adjust objects at all, you may find that some objects appear to fall off the screen during the show.

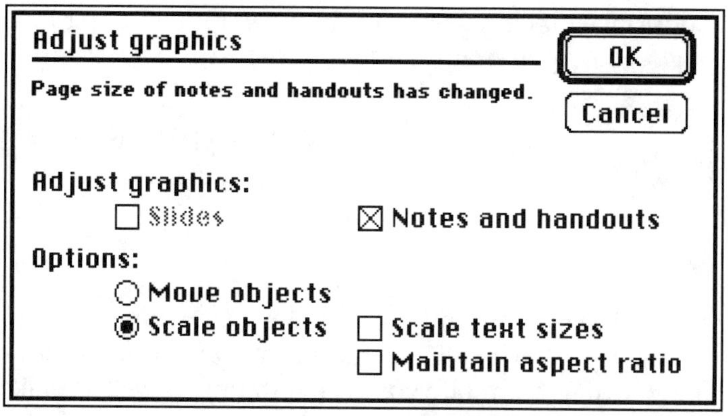

```
┌─────────────────────────────────────────────────────────┐
│  Adjust graphics ─────────────────    ╭──────────╮       │
│                                       │    OK    │       │
│  Page size of notes and handouts has changed.            │
│                                       ╭──────────╮       │
│                                       │  Cancel  │       │
│                                       ╰──────────╯       │
│  Adjust graphics:                                        │
│        ☐ Slides          ☒ Notes and handouts            │
│  Options:                                                │
│        ○ Move objects                                    │
│        ⊙ Scale objects   ☐ Scale text sizes              │
│                          ☐ Maintain aspect ratio         │
└─────────────────────────────────────────────────────────┘
```

Figure 19.2   The Adjust graphics dialog box will reformat a presentation and automatically adjust the graphics and text on each slide.

If you check either one of the Adjust graphics check boxes, (*Slides* or *Notes and handouts*), the options below become available for automatically reformatting the appropriate elements in your presentations.

If you choose the option *Move objects*, Persuasion does not resize any text or graphics elements, but it will treat all slide elements as a unit and center it for the new dimensions. If your new presentation format is smaller than the previous one (this is the case when you go from overhead to slide show), Persuasion will crop off any elements that extend beyond the dimensions of the new slide. Therefore, you should manually check each slide to be sure that all objects are still contained within the new boundaries. If, on the other hand, the new presentation format is larger than the old one, Persuasion will extend the background, if any, to fill the entire slide.

If you opt to *Scale objects*, Persuasion will resize text and graphics objects for the dimensions of the new slide, rather than simply move them.

The *Scale objects* option makes two other choices available. *Scale text sizes* will mathematically adjust your text size in the same percentage as the new slide format. It will then convert the scaled text to the nearest size displayed in the Font Size menu.

Select the *Maintain aspect ratio* option if your slides include graphics, such as circles, squares, or real life images; this way, when Persuasion scales elements for the dimensions of the new format, it doesn't tamper with the original height-to-width ratio of these elements. Circles can thus maintain a constant radius, and squares can remain squares.

Regardless of the options you choose in the Adjust graphics dialog box, be sure to flip through your presentation slide-by-slide to make a visual check of the changes.

Once your slides are all set and you have checked through them, you are ready for the slide show itself.

The Slide Show

Once you have specified the output monitor and its dimensions, you can proceed to set up the slide show itself. The Slide show dialog box is chock full of options that allow you to automate your presentation as well as make other adjustments to make your show run smoothly.

Choose the *Slide show* command from the Edit menu.

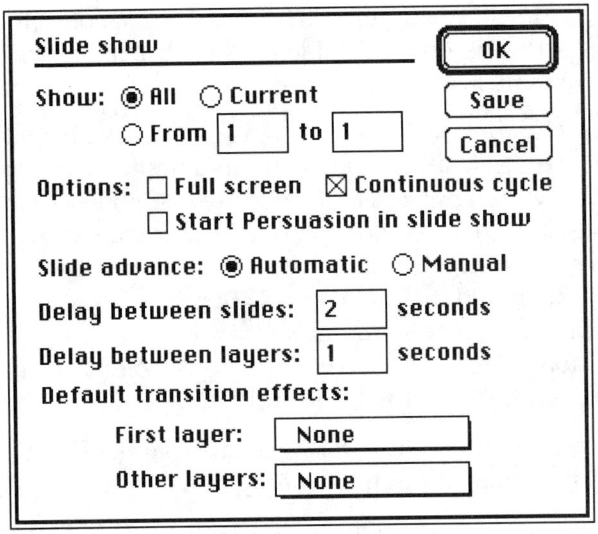

```
┌──────────────────────────────────────────────┐
│  Slide show                    ┌──── OK ────┐  │
│                                └────────────┘  │
│  Show: ◉ All  ○ Current        ┌─── Save ───┐  │
│         ○ From │1│  to │1│      └────────────┘  │
│                                 ┌── Cancel ──┐  │
│                                 └────────────┘  │
│  Options: ☐ Full screen  ☒ Continuous cycle    │
│           ☐ Start Persuasion in slide show     │
│                                                │
│  Slide advance: ◉ Automatic  ○ Manual          │
│  Delay between slides: │2│  seconds            │
│  Delay between layers: │1│  seconds            │
│  Default transition effects:                   │
│     First layer: │ None        │               │
│     Other layers: │ None       │               │
└──────────────────────────────────────────────┘
```

Figure 19.3   The Slide show dialog box contains all of the controls for
running an on-screen slide show on a Macintosh.

The Slide show dialog box is the command center with options for controlling the range, duration, and special transition effects for the show. The *Show* option allows you to select the slide or slides that you want in the show.

If you want to view the whole show, click on the *All* button; if you only want to see the currently displayed slide in full screen view, click the *Current* button. If you are reviewing a presentation and you want to focus in on one part of it, then fill in the *From* and *To* text boxes to specify what slides you want to review.

The *Full screen* check box determines whether you want the presentation to take over the entire screen, eliminating the menu bar for the duration of the show. For reviewing a show, keep this option unchecked, so that you have ready access to the menu bar to make any changes. Otherwise, when the curtain goes up on the final presentation, you should check the *Full screen* box to eliminate the menu bar which can be distracting.

If you check the *Continuous cycle* option, Persuasion will show your presentation continuously. When you reach the last slide, Persuasion will cycle around to the first slide again.

The *Start Persuasion in slide show* option makes a change to the presentation file so that the next time the file is opened, it opens in slide Show mode rather than in one of the other views. This option is useful if you have an assistant or colleague who is unfamiliar with Persuasion and who has to run the on-screen presentation. In any case, it can make your presentation a notch more professional by allowing you to avoid the slide dialog box at show time. Once you have saved a presentation with the Start Persuasion in slide show option checked, all you have to do is give instructions to the presenter to double-click the Persuasion presentation file icon and the show will start. If you want to change this option for future shows, stop the presentation (using *Command - .*), open the Slide show dialog box, and uncheck the Start Persuasion in the Slide show option. Then save the presentation file.

The *Slide advance* options let you choose between having Persuasion automatically advance slides, or letting the presenter do it with keyboard or mouse. An automatic slide advance makes it possible for you to set up a continuously running presentation that you can use in unattended situations such as a trade show or retail store.

When you select the *Automatic slide advance* option, you also have to decide how long of a delay you want between slides. You can enter a delay of up to 60 seconds in the *Delay between slides* text box. If you are using layers on slides (or slide builds) you also have to enter the delay between layers up to a 60-second maximum. Unfortunately, you cannot set delays for specific slides within a show because the settings you make in both of the delays text boxes will apply to every slide in the presentation.

For manual control over the pace of the presentation, choose the *Manual slide* advance option. The presenter can use the keyboard and mouse actions summarized in Table 19.2 to control the movements between slides and layers. Notice that for most actions there are several alternative keystrokes.

Table 19.2. Summary of keyboard and mouse techniques for controlling a presentation.

Action	Keystroke
Forward by a layer	Down arrow Right arrow N Command - 3 Click
Forward to end of slide	Shift - down arrow Shift - right arrow Shift - N Shift - Command - 3 Shift - click
Backward by a slide	Up arrow Left arrow P Delete Command - 2 Double-click
Backward by a layer	Shift - up arrow Shift - Left arrow Shift - P Shift - delete key Shift - Command + 2 Shift double-click
Last layer of first slide	Command - H Command - 1 Command - left arrow
First layer of first slide	Shift Command - H Shift Command - 1 Shift Command - left arrow
Last layer of last slide	Command - 4 Command - right arrow

(continued)

Table 19.2. *(continued)*

First layer of last slide	Shift Command - 4 Shift Command - right arrow
Last layer of selected slide	Slide number, then press Return or Enter
First layer of selected slide	Shift - slide number, then press Return or Enter
Back to slide on screen before the *Go to* command	` (accent grave key in upper left of keyboard)
Pause or continue the auto-advance feature. Any other slide command also continues after a pause	Space Triple-click
Toggle mouse cursor on and off	A
Toggle between automatic and manual slide advance	Shift =
Blank screen	B , (comma)
Set screen to black	. (period)
Exit from slide show	- (hyphen) Command + . (period) Command + Q

Running Multiple Presentations

With a little advance planning, Persuasion can also run several slide shows, one following the other. This feature is useful if you need to string several different presentations together for a single long run presentation. For example, let's say you need a self-running demonstration at a trade show. You have several different products to show off using Persuasion, and each product marketing director has developed their own separate presentation. (Incidentally, they each used a common AutoTemplate to maintain consistency between each presentation.)

The easiest and safest way to show multiple presentations is to name (or rename, as the case may be) each presentation file with names that are alphabetically in order. Place each file in the same folder and choose *View by name* from the View menu in the Finder.

When you are ready to show a presentation, open that window with the finder, click on any one of the show presentations, and, while still in the Finder, shift-click to select all the other show presentations.

Now double-click on any one of the selected presentations to begin the slide show. The fact that you used *View by name*, plus the fact that your presentation files are alphabetically in order, causes the show to be run in the correct order.

If you want the master slide show to open automatically as a slide show, check the *Start Persuasion in slide show* box in the first presentation file. All of the selected presentations will automatically open consecutively in the slide show. Also note that if the first presentation file has the *Continuous cycle* option checked, Persuasion will show each slide show and then repeat the last presentation file continuously.

Transition Effects

Persuasion's transition effects make a strong argument for using the on-screen slide show feature whenever appropriate. On-screen transition effects add motion to otherwise static slides. Not only can you apply any of 14 transition effects for moving between slides, you can apply transition effects to individual layers on individual slides, as well.

The transition effects are like those you see on television. There are no set rules for using transition effects, although the common rule about keeping it simple applies here, too. Transition effects are effective for maintaining visual interest in a presentation, but you don't want the effects to distract from the message of the show.

Setting Transition Effects

You can set transition effects in two ways. In the slide show dialog box, you can select a default transition effect for slides and layers in the Slide show dialog box. Persuasion uses this transition effect between every slide in your presentation. If you don't want a transition, you can choose *None* from the pop-up menu (see Figure 19.3).

If the transition between every slide were the same, your audience might become bored after a while. The second way to use transition effects is to assign them to individual slides. Transitions you set for individual slides override the default settings. The most efficient way to use transitions is to choose a default effect in the Slide show dialog box. This should be the effect that you want to use the most. Then, move to the Slide sorter or Outline view to apply different transitions to individual slides. Select the slide or outline heading and then use the rightmost pop-up menu at the bottom of the window to assign a transition to the selected slide.

To review what transition effect has been assigned to a particular slide, select the slide or outline heading and then look at the transition pop-up menu at the bottom of the window as in Figure 19.4. The visible part of the pop-up menu will say what effect is applied to the particular slide. If the pop-up menu just says "Transition," then the slide is using the default setting from Slide show dialog box.

If you can, set one transition effect for the first layer of a slide and other effects for the remaining layers. In Slide sorter or Outline view, choose *Layers* from the Transition pop-up menu and choose the effects for the first and/or subsequent layers.

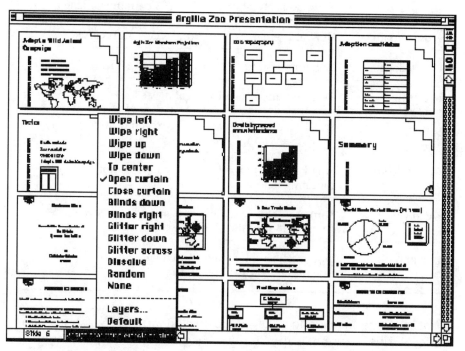

Figure 19.4   Both the slide sorter and outline views have a transition pop-up menu from which you can choose or review transitions.

Whether you are setting a default transition or a transition for a specific slide, Table 19.3 summarizes each of the effects available:

Table 19.3

Effect Name	Description of Effect
Wipe left	New slide enters from the right edge of the window, pushing the preceding slide off the screen.
Wipe right	New slide enters from the left edge of the window, pushing the preceding slide off the screen.
Wipe up	New slide enters from the bottom edge of the window, pushing the previous slide off the screen.
Wipe down	New slide enters from the top edge of the window, pushing the previous slide off the screen.
To center	New slide fills in the screen from the edges to the center.
Open curtain	New slide emerges from center as curtain is opened.
Close curtain	New slide emerges from sides as curtain is closed.
Blinds down	Horizontal blinds open to reveal new slide.
Blinds right	Vertical blinds open to reveal new slide.
Glitter right	Small squares glitter across the screen from left to right revealing new slide.
Glitter down	Small squares rain down from top to bottom to revealing new slide.
Dissolve	Similar to glitter, squares appear on entire screen that reveal new slide beneath.
Random	Not an effect, but when chosen will randomly select one of the 14 transition effects.

Note: When the caps lock key is down you will not get transition effects. This is a useful feature for quickly running through a presentation without taking the time to view the transition effects. However, for the presentation itself, make sure the caps lock is up!

Memory

The one limitation that you have to reckon with before assigning transition effects, is the memory required to use them. Persuasion needs to have extra memory so that it can bring the image of the next slide into your computer before showing it. For example, if you use the open curtain effect, Persuasion has to compose the slide "behind" the curtain while the current slide is in view so that when the curtain "opens," the next slide is already to be viewed.

If your Macintosh does not have sufficient memory to run transition effects, Persuasion will display slides one at a time. Table 19.4 lists the minimum memory requirements that Aldus recommends for running transition effects using a standard AppleColor RGB monitor. Larger monitors will require more available RAM, as will monitors with finer resolution than the Apple monitor's 72 dpi.

Table 19.4

Minimum RAM	Apple RGB Monitor mode
40 Kb	1-bit (black-and-white display)
155 Kb	4-bit color (16-color display)
310 Kb	8-bit color (256-color display)
1.2 Mb	24/32-bit color (19.7 million-color display)

Performance also increases with memory. For example, using a Macintosh II with 8 Mb of RAM, you will still notice a significant speed difference between having your display set at 1-bit (black and white) and 32-bit (full color). That's why its best to work in 1-bit mode as you create your presentation. You can take advantage of the speed since you don't need color for the entire creation process.

Screen Fonts

No discussion of on-screen presentations would be complete without a reference to the importance of screen font legibility. For your audience to see text in its best resolution, you need to either install the larger screen fonts that come with Persuasion or use a utility such as Adobe Type Manager that will render smooth characters from many fonts.

To have the widest choice of fonts and sizes, we recommend that you use a utility such as ATM. ATM gives you the freedom to choose practically any size (as long as the PostScript font you choose to use is an Adobe or other Type 1 font) and have it display smoothly on the screen. And, what's more, ATM opens the door to a vast library of fonts that you can use in presentations. You can purchase any Type 1 PostScript font and scale it to any size within your presentation using ATM.

You'll find a more detailed explanation of fonts and how to install different screen font solutions in Chapter 1, *Installing Persuasion*.

Running the On-Screen Slide Show

As important as rehearsing your show material itself, you should familiarize yourself with the various keyboard commands and mouse actions you need need to run the show, since in full screen view you will not have the advantage of pull-down menus. We can't stress the importance of memorizing the handful of commands that you will need for the presentation. You might even want to photocopy Table 19.3 and then highlight those commands that you use often or label your keyboard with the indispensable keyboard controls you need to keep your presentation going smoothly. That way if you get flustered during the presentation, you will still be able to keep in control of how the slides are displayed.

If you are simply using your Macintosh monitor as a presentation device, then you don't have any added considerations for preparing your show other than the items we've already discussed. However, for larger audiences, you will need a larger on-screen device, usually a video projector or an LCD projection panel.

Video Projectors

Video projectors are best suited for presentations to a larger audience where a monitor is too small. Video projectors share many of the benefits of monitors but the technology itself has some major drawbacks in installation and in the quality of the projected image.

The Technology

Video monitors are similar to standard monitors. However, instead of the single picture tube found in a monitor, a video projector uses three external picture tubes: red, green, and blue. Each one of these tubes is focused through its own lens and projected onto a screen. Like a slide projector, when using a video projector, the room must be dimmed for the best viewing conditions. Some video projectors incorporate audio circuits that can amplify Macintosh audio or accept audio from other sources.

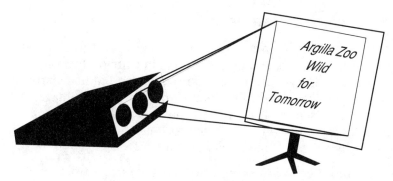

Figure 19.5   The video monitor works much like a standard television screen, only instead of displaying onto the back of a phosphorous tube, a video projector projects its image onto a screen.

Installation

To be Macintosh compatible, a video projector must accept an RGB analog signal (the video signal a color Macintosh puts out). It must also be able to accommodate the Macintosh's horizontal scanning rate. To work with a Mac Plus or a monochrome Mac SE, the projector must have a horizontal scan rate of at least 22.7 KHz. To work with a Macintosh II with an Apple video card, the projector must have a horizontal scanning rate of at least 35 KHz. If you have a SuperMac, Radius, or RasterOps video card, you require an even higher rate. The higher the scan rate, the higher the cost.

One of the problems in using some video projectors is keeping the three color guns properly aligned, or converged, so viewers don't see ghost images on the screen. The convergence adjustment depends on the unit's distance from and angle to the screen, so whenever the unit is moved, the convergence must be readjusted.

Making convergence and other adjustments to a video projector is downright difficult. Unless you are trained in how to make the adjustments you should be prepared to hire a technician to set up and maintain the projector. Otherwise, you risk putting the projector out of alignment just before your show, and having to put up with a technically inferior presentation.

In addition to difficulties with adjusting a projector, video projectors are not very portable. They are bulky and can weight well over 100 pounds.

Video projectors are good for trade shows, and for semipermanent installations for training sessions. To reduce glare, the room must be darkened somewhat.

Overhead Projection Panels

For more than 40 years, the overhead projector has been the dominant visual aid in business meetings and presentations, in spite of its limitation of projecting only static images printed on transparencies. But in a marriage of old and new technologies, overhead projectors can display images directly from a Macintosh screen. These panels enable overhead projectors to project both stationary and animated Macintosh-generated images on a screen for viewing by a small to medium-sized audience.

Compared to a monitor or video projector, an LCD projection panel is portable. In fact, most of them come in their own carrying cases. The one major sacrifice, however, is color. While color panel technology is just starting to emerge, it will be a few years before the cost of a high quality projection panel is low enough for many users, just as prices of monochrome LCD panels have been coming down as competition has increased. Plan to spend about $1,000 for a monochrome LCD panel.

The cost of a projection panel can be more easily justified if it can serve duty on more than one type of computer. For example, the nView II+2 panel comes with cables for connecting to a Macintosh II, IBM PS/2 (with CGA, EGA, or VGA graphics), or a PC with a Hercules monochrome card. Otherwise, look to the Kodak Datashow panel as one of the better panels in terms of projection quality.

The Technology

The technology of the projection panel is complex, but the concept is simple. The panel resembles a picture frame, with a transparent row and column matrix of liquid crystals in the center. When activated by the computer, pixels in the LCD panel turn on or off, duplicating the pixels on the Macintosh display. The light from the overhead projector passes through the panel, which sits where a transparency would, projecting the contents onto the presentation screen.

The Macintosh Plus and SE displays have a resolution of 512×342 pixels. All projections panels share this size as their minimum standard size. In addition, some brands of projection panels can project the Macintosh II monitor's standard 640×480 pixel resolution. Some panels also allow a

Macintosh Plus or SE to project a Macintosh II-size 640 × 480 pixel resolution, showing more pixels than are viewable on the compact Macintosh's built-in 9-inch screen.

Screen refresh rate is an important consideration. Some panels cannot display rapid mouse movements, or they leave ghost images of the pointer as it moves. This problem makes units unsuitable for animation or other types of presentations that involve frequent or rapid mouse movements.

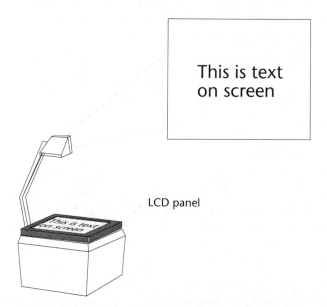

Figure 19.6   The LCD panel operates by switching tiny liquid-crystals on and off allowing light to pass through the off crystals and onto the screen.

When you are designing a presentation for use on an overhead projection panel, you don't have to be as concerned with gradations in shading, or colors. In fact, fine details will not show up on the screen at all. If your presentation is in color, but will be projected in monochrome, switch your Macintosh to monochrome to be sure that you have good contrast between shades of gray. Good color contrast is no guarantee of good monochrome contrast.

Installation

It is relatively easy to connect a projection panel device to one of the modular Macintosh II models. Most projection panels equipped for connecting to a modular Macintosh connect directly to the video output plug on the back of the computer. Some products, such as the Kodak Datashow, require that a separate interface card be plugged into an open slot in the computer.

If you want to use projection panel with one of the compact Macintoshes, such as the Macintosh Plus, SE, or SE/30, interfacing is a complicated proposition, just as it is for connecting a video projector. For any of the compact Macintosh models, you must have a dealer install an interface card inside the sealed Macintosh case, or risk voiding your Macintosh's warranty if you install a card yourself. Once the interface card is installed, the projection panel plugs into a newly added port on the back of the Macintosh.

While the projection panel itself is very portable, you will have to make arrangements to have a Macintosh with the appropriate interface card at your presentation site, or you will have to tote your Macintosh along with you as well.

Setting Up the Overhead Projector

Once the projection panel connections are all set, what you have to do at the presentation site is hook up the projection panel to the Macintosh and then place the LCD projection panel on the overhead projector where you would normally place overhead transparency film. Be sure to take along a supply of extension cords and ground-plug adaptors as part of your standard gear, as well as a spare projector bulb.

Older overhead projectors are designed with the projection bulb directly beneath the glass transparency holder. After the first few minutes, the heat generated by the projector bulb heats the liquid crystals and can change the contrast of the projection panel, making it necessary for you to repeatedly readjust the panel for about the first 20 minutes of your presentation. The way to minimize the readjust problem is to turn the overhead projector and LCD panel on about half an hour before the presentation to stabilize the LCD panel.

Projectors with high wattage bulbs (particularly older overhead projectors) can overheat the projection panel making it completely unusable after the first 20 minutes or so. Whenever possible, try to use one of the new style overhead projectors that have the projection bulb mounted on the side, such as the Elmo HP-series projectors. These projectors run cooler and minimize having to readjust the contrast of the LCD panel as the panel heats up.

Note: LCD projection panels do not work with "reflection style" portable overhead projectors that are designed with the light assembly in the head next to the lens rather than the light being under the projection panel.

Tip: **Never, never** leave an overhead projector turned on without also leaving on the projection panel. Most projection panels have built-in fans that protect the panel from excessive heat. If you turn the panel off without turning off the projector, you can destroy your projection panel.

Remote Control Accessory

If you are using a monitor, video projector, or LCD projection panel, you can free yourself from having to remain next to your Macintosh during your presentation with the addition of a remote control device. Similar to a television remote control, a presentation remote control allows you to run your slide show from a lectern or across the room.

An example of a basic remote control device is the Kodak Datashow Presentation Remote. With the Presentation Remote connected to a Macintosh, you can run Persuasion from as far away as 35 feet. Installing and using the Kodak Presentation Remote is generally the same for other brands of remote controls. You connect a small receiver to a vacant ADB receptacle on the back of your Macintosh or on either side of your keyboard.

Once the receiver is connected to the Macintosh, you have to aim it toward the person who holds the remote control. When it is ready to start the show, choose *Slide show* (or use one of the automatic slide show techniques discussed above). Click the *Manual Slide advance* option. Use the Presentation Remote to control the presentation from across the room. Unfortunately, the Kodak Presentation Remote can only move back and forth through a presentation. It cannot control any other aspects of the show, such as manually moving between layers in a slide or jumping to particular slides. However, other models and brands of remote controls are more versatile and let you control most functions from afar.

With its slide show feature, especially its transition effects, Persuasion makes a powerful argument for using a Macintosh as an active partner in not just creating a presentation, but showing it as well.

Part V ◆ Appendices

Appendix A

Menu Glossary

Persuasion provides eleven pull-down menus along the title bar at the top of the presentation window and six pop-up menus along the bottom of the window. Not all of them are available in all views. Their purpose is summarized here, along with some of the more common keyboard shortcuts.

Apple menu (all views)

Command	What it does
About Persuasion...	Shows the version, release date, and copyright notices for your copy of Persuasion, as well as the program's serial number and your user name
Help...	Opens Persuasion's on-line help system
Windows	Lets you move among open Persuasion documents

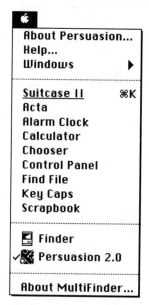

File menu (all views)

Command	What it does	Keyboard shortcut
New	Opens a new presentation using settings stored in *Persuasion prefs*	Command+N
Open...	Opens an existing Persuasion presentation or AutoTemplate	Command+O
Close	Closes the current presentation	
Data sheet	Opens Persuasion's own data sheet or an external text or WKS file from which you can import data	
Save	Saves any changes you've made since you last saved	Command+S
Save as...	Lets you save a presentation under a new name, in a new location, or as an AutoTemplate	
Revert	Reverts to the last-saved version of the file	
Import...	Copies text, graphics, spreadsheet data, or an entire presentation from another application	

(continued)

File menu (all views)

Command	What it does	Keyboard shortcut
AutoTemplates...	Imports slide masters, background masters, the notes master, defined text formats, colors, and chart formats from an existing AutoTemplate or other Persuasion presentation	
Export...	Saves your outline, slides,or data sheet in a file format that other applications can use	
Page setup...	Specifies the size and shape of slides, and sets page and print specifications for your presentation	
Print...	Prints all or part of your presentation as specified in the Print dialog box	Command+P
Slide show...	Sets options, including default transition effects, for viewing an on-screen version of your presentation, and runs the slide show	
Preferences...	Sets options specific to a presentation, including default slide master, drawing options, and shadow offset	

(continued)

File menu (all views)

Command	What it does	Keyboard shortcut
Quit	Ends your Persuasion session and returns you to the Macintosh desktop	Command+Q

File	
New	⌘N
Open...	⌘O
Close	
Data sheet	▶
Save	⌘S
Save as...	
Revert	
Import...	
AutoTemplates...	
Export...	
Page setup...	
Print...	⌘P
Slide show...	
Preferences...	
Quit	⌘Q

Edit menu (all views)

Command	What it does	Keyboard shortcut
Undo	Reverses the last action, including the last Undo	Command+Z
Cut	Deletes selected items and moves them to the Clipboard	Command+X
Copy	Copies selected items to the Clipboard, leaving the originals in the document	Command+C
Paste	Places a copy of the Clipboard contents into a document	Command+V
Clear	Deletes selected items from the document without moving them to the Clipboard	Delete/Backspace
Select all	Selects all objects on the current slide, master, or notes page if the pointer tool is selected, or selects the objects created with the selected tool	Command+A
Duplicate	Copies selected items and pastes them slightly offset from the originals; contents in the Clipboard are not affected	Command+D

(continued)

Edit menu (all views)

Command	What it does	Keyboard shortcut
Find/Change...	Locates specified text in your outline, slides, and notes, to replace it with other text you specify	Command+5
Find again	Searches for the next occurrence of the text most recently entered in the Find/Change dialog box	Command+6
Change	Replaces selected text with the text most recently entered in the Change to box in the Find/Change dialog box	Command+7
Change then find	Replaces selected text with the most recently entered text in the Change to box in the Find/Change dialog box and continues the search	Command+8
Spelling	Compares words in all or part of a presentation to words in Persuasion's main dictionary or supplementary dictionary	Command+9
Insert	Creates a new row or column next to the selected row or column in the data sheet	Command+I

(continued)

Edit menu (all views)

Command	What it does	Keyboard shortcut
Delete	Removes the contents of a selected row or column from the data sheet	Command+K

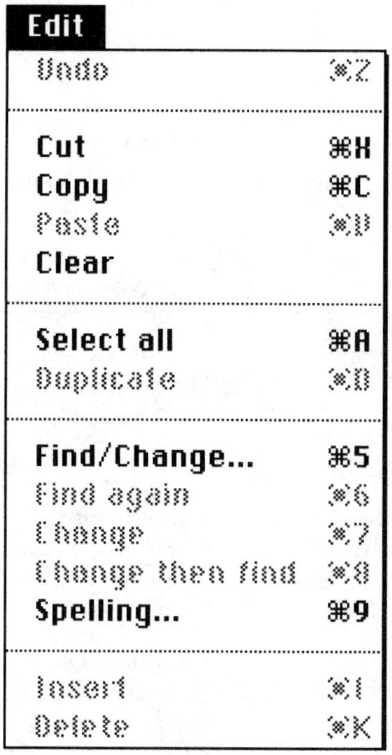

Edit

Undo	⌘Z
Cut	⌘H
Copy	⌘C
Paste	⌘P
Clear	
Select all	⌘A
Duplicate	⌘D
Find/Change...	⌘5
Find again	⌘6
Change	⌘7
Change then find	⌘8
Spelling...	⌘9
Insert	⌘I
Delete	⌘K

View menu (all views)

Command	Takes you to	Keyboard shortcut
Outline	The Outline view of your presentation	Click Outline icon
Slide #	The slide you selected	In Outline view, click slide number
		In master views, click Slide icon
Notes #	The notes page you selected	In Outline view, option+click slide number
		In master views, click Notes icon
Slide sorter	The Slide sorter view	In Outline and Slide views, Option+click Outline icon
Slide master	The slide master or background master assigned to the selected slide	In Slide view, to go to slide master, Option+click Slide icon
		In Slide view, to go to background master, Option+ Command+ click Slide icon
Notes master	The Notes master view	In Outline, Slide and Notes views, Option+click Notes icon

(continued)

View menu (all views)

Command	Takes you to	Keyboard shortcut
Handout master	The Handout master view	
Go to slide	An existing slide, or creates a new one	
Go to master	An existing slide master or background master, or creates a new one	

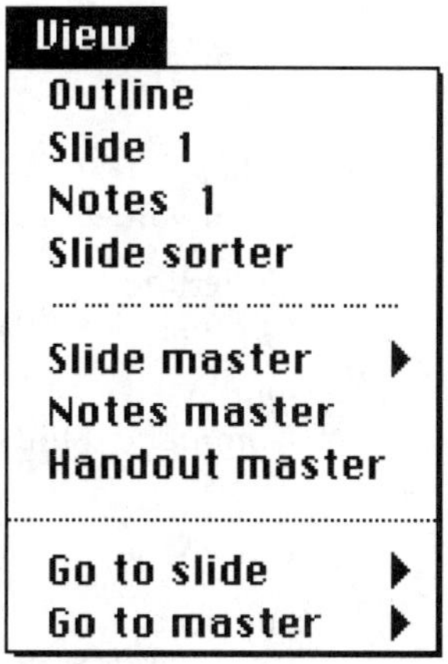

View

Outline
Slide 1
Notes 1
Slide sorter

Slide master   ▶
Notes master
Handout master

Go to slide   ▶
Go to master   ▶

Text menu (all views)

Command	What it does	Keyboard shortcut
Font	Changes the font of selected text	
Size	Changes the size of selected text	
Style	Changes the type style of selected text	Plain: Command+ Shift+Spacebar
		Bold: Command+ Shift+B
		Italic: Command+Shift+I
		Underline: Command+Shift+U
		Outline: Command+Shift+O
		Shadow: Command+Shift+S
		Superscript: Command+Shift+H
		Subscript: Command+Shift+L
Color	Changes the color of selected text	
Alignment	Applies one of four text alignments to paragraphs	
Apply format	Applies a named set of text attributes to selected text, as defined with the Define formats command	

(continued)

Text menu (all views)

Command	What it does	Keyboard shortcut
Text format...	Creates and names a set of text attributes which you can apply to text	Command+T
Line spacing...	Specifies the amount of space between lines of text and paragraphs	
Bullet marks	Displays typographic characters as specified with the Define bullet marks command in front of the first line of each paragraph of a selected text block	
Show text ruler	Displays a ruler that shows tabs and indents for selected text blocks	
Reapply style	Applies the text style defined with the Outline styles command to the selected headings	Command+0 (zero)
Move left	Raises the heading level of selected text in Outline or Slide view	Command+]
Move right	Lowers the heading level of selected text in Outline or Slide view	Command+[
Outline styles...	Creates and edits text styles for outline headings	

(continued)

Text menu (all views)

Command	What it does	Keyboard shortcut
Define formats...	Renames, creates, edits, and removes named text formats for slides, notes, and handouts	

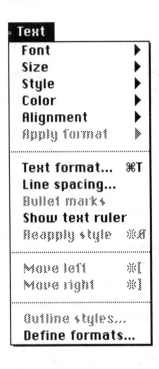

Outline menu (Outline view)

Command	What it does	Keyboard shortcut
Set heading as	Makes the selected heading a holder of slides, a subtitle, body text, or a slide title	Command+1 (Slide title) Command+2 (Subtitle) Command+3 (Body text)
Promote subheads	Moves all headings subordinate to the select heading one level up (left)	
New heading	Inserts a new heading at the same level as the currently selected heading in the outline	Command+H
New heading left	Inserts a new heading one level higher than the currently selected heading in the outline	Command+L
New heading right	Inserts a new heading one level lower than the currently selected heading in the outline	Command+R
Add notes	Adds a main note icon and a notes text icon immediately subordinate to the selected slide title	
Remove notes	Removes all notes headings from the selected slide title(s)	
Hide body text	Turns off the display of all body text headings in the entire outline	Command+B

(continued)

Outline menu (Outline view)

Command	What it does	Keyboard shortcut
Hide notes	Turns off the display of all notes text headings in the entire outline	Command+F
Auto subtitles	If the slide master has a subtitle placeholder, automatically makes any headings created immediately below the slide title heading (or its notes icons, if it has notes) into a subtitle	
Expand all	Displays all subordinate headings in the entire outline at every level	Option+ double-click topmost heading in the outline
Expand subs	For the selected heading(s), displays all subordinate headings at every level	Option+ double-click the icon for a heading
Expand selection	Displays all immediately subordinate headings of the selected slide(s), leaving all deeper levels of subhead collapsed or displayed as they were when the selected heading was collapsed	Double-click the icon for the heading
Collapse all	Hides all subheadings in the outline, displaying only first-level headings	Command+ double-click topmost heading in the outline
Show subs only	Displays only the immediately subordinate headings of the selected heading(s), hiding all deeper levels of subhead.	Command+ double-click the icon for a heading

(continued)

Outline menu (Outline view)

Command	What it does	Keyboard shortcut
Collapse selection	Hides the subheading(s) of the selected heading(s)	Double-click the icon for the heading

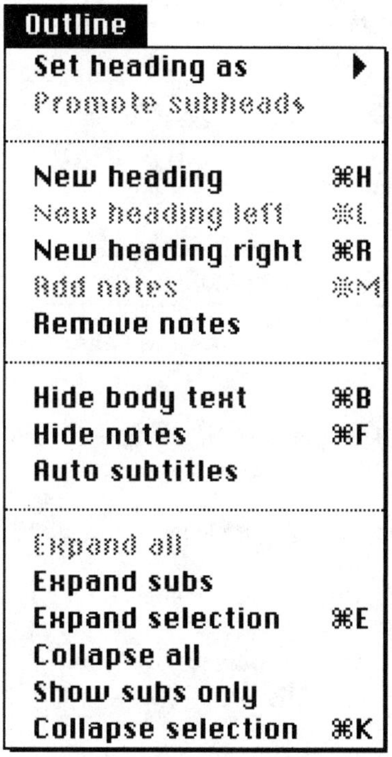

Outline

Set heading as	▶
Promote subheads	
New heading	⌘H
New heading left	⌘L
New heading right	⌘R
Add notes	⌘M
Remove notes	
Hide body text	⌘B
Hide notes	⌘F
Auto subtitles	
Expand all	
Expand subs	
Expand selection	⌘E
Collapse all	
Show subs only	
Collapse selection	⌘K

Chart menu (Slide view, Slide master view)

Command	What it does
Chart format	Specifies the format of a chart or table, chosen from a submenu
Overlay format...	Specifies the number of data series to plot on the overlay chart, and specifies the format for the overlay chart or table, chosen from a submenu
Axes	Changes the format of chart axes
Numbers	Changes the numbers format for charts
Symbols	Changes the marker symbol used to plot data on line, scatter, and high-low charts
Show depth	When checked, displays charts and tables with a three-dimensions effect
Show plot frame	When checked, displays lines marking the top and right boundaries of a chart's plot range
Show legend	When checked, displays the legend for a chart
Show value labels	When checked, displays value labels on a chart
Get data	Opens the data sheet and selects the data plotted in the selected chart or table
Get external data	Opens the external text or WKS file that contains the data you used to plot the selected chart or table
Redraw chart	Fine-tunes a resized chart by drawing it again, or regroups a chart without saving changes made to the chart while it was ungrouped

(continued)

Chart menu (Slide view, Slide master view)

Command	What it does
Define formats...	Saves the formatting of an enhanced chart or table so you can apply the format to other charts

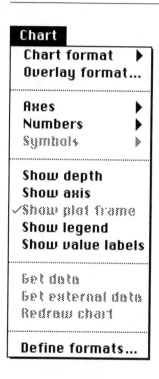

Draw menu (Slide view, Notes view, all Master views)

Command	What it does	Keyboard shortcut
Actual size	Shows objects at the size they will print	Command+1
Fit in window	Shows the entire slide or slide master on the screen	Command+W
Send	Moves selected objects forward or background in a stack of overlapping objects on the same layer	To front: Command+F Forward: Command+= To back: Command+B Backward: Command+-
Rotate/Flip	Moves objects clockwise or counterclockwise in 90-degree increments, and inverts objects vertically or horizontally	
Center on slide	Positions selected parts at the vertical or horizontal center of the slide	
Group	Joins selected objects so they are treated as one unit	Command+G
Ungroup	Selects the individual objects of a chart, PICT graphic, or grouped selected	Command+U

(continued)

Draw menu (Slide view, Notes view, all Master views)

Command	What it does	Keyboard shortcut
Regroup	Undoes the most recent Ungroup command	Command+U
Align objects...	Lines up selected objects in relation to each other, either vertically, horizontally, or both	Command+L
Align to grid	Lines up selected objects with the horizontal and vertical lines of the invisible grid	Command+H
Grid snap on	When checked, aligns newly drawn objects with the invisible grid created by the minor divisions of the rulers	Command+Y
Reshape arc/poly	If an arc is selected, lets you change the angle of the arc by moving handles on either end of the line	
	If a polygon is selected, lets you reshape the polygon by moving handles or lines and adding or removing points	

(continued)

Draw menu (Slide view, Notes view, all Master views)

Command	What it does	Keyboard shortcut
Round corners...	Lets you control the width and height of corners on objects drawn with the square-corner, round-corner, and ellipse tools	

```
┌─────────────────────────────┐
│ Draw                        │
├─────────────────────────────┤
│  Actual size         ⌘1     │
│ ✓Fit in window       ⌘W     │
│ ............................│
│  Send              ▶        │
│  Rotate/Flip       ▶        │
│  Center on slide   ▶        │
│ ............................│
│  Group               ⌘G     │
│  Ungroup             ⌘U     │
│  Regroup             ⌘R     │
│ ............................│
│  Align objects...  ⌘L       │
│  Align to grid     ⌘H       │
│  Grid snap on      ⌘Y       │
│ ............................│
│  Reshape arc                │
│  Round corners...           │
└─────────────────────────────┘
```

Effect menu (Slide view, Notes view, all Master views)

Command	Specifies
Line style	The thickness and type of horizontal and vertical lines or borders
Line pattern	The pattern used in a line or border
Fill pattern	The pattern used to fill an object
Shadow	The pattern used to fill shadows
Line color	The color of a line or border
Fill color	The color used to fill a object
Shadow color	The color used to fill shadows
Line background	The color of a line's background
Fill background	The color of the fill background
Set colors...	The color of text and of graphic attributes
Define colors...	Colors you want to add, rename, or remove from the color palette, or colors you want to edit on the color grid

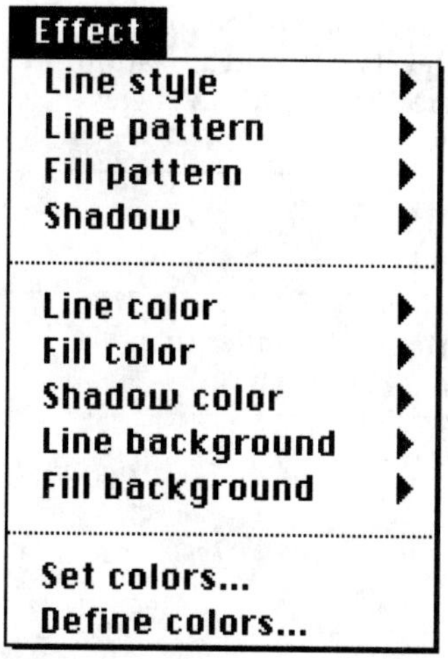

Effect

Line style   ▶
Line pattern   ▶
Fill pattern   ▶
Shadow   ▶

Line color   ▶
Fill color   ▶
Shadow color   ▶
Line background   ▶
Fill background   ▶

Set colors...
Define colors...

Master menu (Slide master view, Notes master view)

Command	What it does
Add title...	Adds a slide title placeholder to a slide master
Add subtitle...	Adds a subtitle placeholder to a slide master
Add body text...	Adds a text placeholder to a slide master
Add chart...	Adds a chart placeholder to a slide master
Add table...	Adds a table placeholder to a slide master
Add org. chart...	Adds an organization chart placeholder to a slide master
Add page number...	Adds a page number placeholder to a slide master
Add slide copy	Adds a placeholder for miniatures of slide to the Notes slide master
Adds notes text	Adds a placeholder for notes text to the Notes slide master
Anchor placeholder...	Specifies the direction in which titles, body text, and organization charts flow into their placeholders
Build layers...	Specifies whether levels of outline text, data on charts, or levels of an organization chart are displayed all at once or in stages during a slide show
Slide background fill...	Adds a pattern, color, or blend of colors to fill the slide master
Tall orientation	Sets up a slide master that is taller than it is wide

(continued)

Master menu (Slide master view, Notes master view)

Command	What it does
Re-create from slide...	Re-creates an existing slide master using elements from a slide as a model
Define bullet marks...	Specifies the typographic characters that introduce each heading level of slide text
Define masters...	Lets you name or rename an existing slide maser or create a new slide master

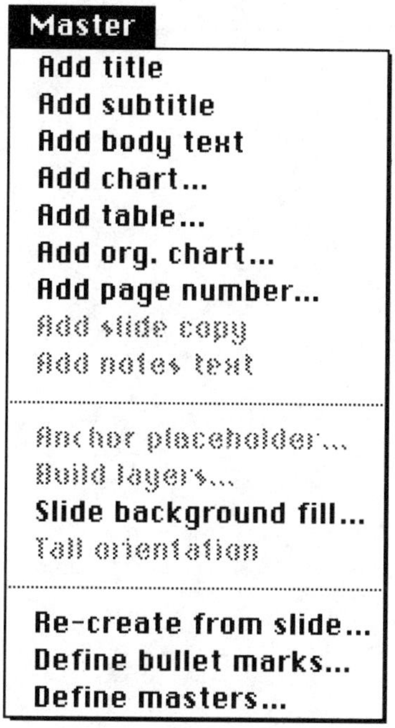

Master

Add title
Add subtitle
Add body text
Add chart...
Add table...
Add org. chart...
Add page number...
Add slide copy
Add notes text

Anchor placeholder...
Build layers...
Slide background fill...
Tall orientation

Re-create from slide...
Define bullet marks...
Define masters...

Sorter menu (Slide sorter view)

Command	Displays the slide miniatures
Normal size	In the standard Slide sorter size
66% normal	At 66% of their normal Slide sorter size
33% normal	At 33% of their normal Slide sorter size
20% normal	At 20% of their normal Slide sorter size
Black & white	In black and white so you can more quickly sort slide or reassign masters

```
┌─────────────────┐
│ Sorter          │
├─────────────────┤
│ ✓Normal size    │
│  66% normal     │
│  33% normal     │
│  20% normal     │
│·················│
│  Black & white  │
└─────────────────┘
```

Pop-up menus (lower menu bar)
Slide menu (Outline view, Slide view, Slide sorter view)

Command	What it does
New	Creates a slide based on the default slide master
Slide #	Displays that slide

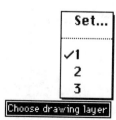

Layer menu (Slide view)

Command	What it does
Set...	Lets you specify the current drawing layer, and specify which layers are active and visible
Layer #	Specifies the current drawing layer, or assigns selected objects to that layer

Go to Master menu (Master view)

Command	What it does
New...	Creates a slide master
New background...	Creates a background master
Master X	Displays that slide master
Background X	Displays that background master

```
┌─────────────────────────┐
│ New...                   │
│ New background...        │
│·························│
│ Background               │
│ Title background         │
│ Title                    │
│ Text 1                   │
│ Text 2                   │
│ Graphic 1                │
│ Org Chart                │
│ Graphic 2                │
│ Table                    │
└─────────────────────────┘
│Go to slide master│
```

Assign Master to Slide menu (Outline view, Slide view, Slide sorter view)

Command	What it does
None	Leaves the selected slide(s) without a master assigned to them
Gallery...	Lets you view a miniature of each slide master and apply one to the selected slide(s)
Master X	Assigns that master to the selected slide(s)
Background X	Replaces the current master with Background X

```
┌─────────────────────────┐
│ Gallery...              │
├ ─ ─ ─ ─ ─ ─ ─ ─ ─ ─ ─ ─ ┤
│ None                    │
│ Background              │
│ Title background        │
│ ✓Title                  │
│ Text 1                  │
│ Text 2                  │
│ Graphic 1               │
│ Org Chart               │
│ Graphic 2               │
│ Table                   │
└─────────────────────────┘
 │Assign master to slide│
```

Background menu (Master view)

Command	What it does
None	Leaves the selected master without a background master assigned to it
Background X	Replaces the current master with Background X

```
 None
 Background
✓Title background
Assign background master to slide master
```

Transition menu (Slide sorter view, Outline view)

Command	What it does
Transition X	Assigns that transition effect to the selected slide(s)
Layers...	Assigns one transition effect to the first layer and a second transition effect to subsequent layers of the selected slide
Default	Assigns an effect of Default to the selected slide(s), which causes Persuasion to apply the global effect specified in the Slide show dialog box to the slide(s)

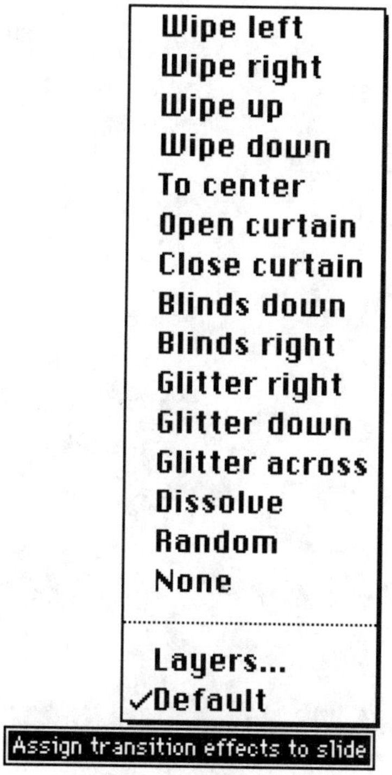

Wipe left
Wipe right
Wipe up
Wipe down
To center
Open curtain
Close curtain
Blinds down
Blinds right
Glitter right
Glitter down
Glitter across
Dissolve
Random
None

Layers...
✓Default

Assign transition effects to slide

Notes menu (Notes view)

Command	What it does
Notes X	Displays that note

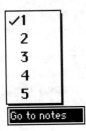

Appendix B

Keyboard Shortcuts and Mouse Techniques

Table B-1.   Command Key Shortcuts

To choose	Press
New	Command + N
Open	Command + O
Print	Command + P
Quit	Command + Q
Save	Command + S
Select all	Command + A (except Outline view)
Actual size	Command + 1 (except Outline and Slide sorter views)
Duplicate	Command + D (except Outline and Slide sorter views)
Fit in window	Command + W (except Outline and Slide sorter views)
Change	Command + 7 (except Slide sorter view)
Change then find	Command + 8 (except Slide sorter view)
Copy	Command + C (except Slide sorter view)

(continued)

Table B-1. Command Key Shortcuts *(continued)*

To choose	Press
Cut	Command + X (except Slide sorter view)
Find/Change	Command + 5 (except Slide sorter view)
Find next	Command + 6 (except Slide sorter view)
Paste	Command + V (except Slide sorter view)
Spelling	Command + 9 (except Slide sorter view)
Text format	Command + T (except Slide sorter view)
Undo	Command + Z (except Slide sorter view)

Table B-2. Formatting Text

To make selected text	Press
Plain	Command + Shift + Spacebar
Bold	Command + Shift + B
Italic	Command + Shift + I
Underline	Command + Shift + U
Outline	Command + Shift + O
Shadow	Command + Shift + S
Superscript	Command + Shift + H
Subscript	Command + Shift + L
Reapply the outline style	Command + 0 (zero)
Delete selected text without copying it to the Clipboard	Delete/Backspace key

Table B-3.   Text Navigation Techniques

To do this	Choose *Persuasion 1.0* in Preferences dialog box Press	Choose *Word processing* in Preferences dialog box Press
Move insertion point one character forward	Right arrow	Right arrow
Move insertion point one character back	Left arrow	Left arrow
Move insertion point one word forward	-	Option + right arrow
Move insertion point one word backward	-	Option + left arrow
Move insertion point to end of paragraph	Option + right arrow	Command + right arrow
Move insertion point to beginning of paragraph	Option + left arrow	Command + left arrow
Toggle from Outline view to Slide view to Notes view	Command + left arrow Command + right arrow	Command + > Command + <

Table B-4 Moving Around

To go to	Do this
Slide view	Click Slide icon
Outline view	Click Outline icon
Notes view	Click Notes icon
Slide master view	Press Option + click Slide icon
Background master	Press Option + Command + click Slide icon
Notes master view	Press Option + click Outline icon
Slide view from Slide sorter view	Double-click a slide miniature
Slide sorter view from Outline view	Press Option + click Outline icon
Slide view of a particular slide from Outline view	Click slide number
Notes view of a particular slide from Outline view	Press Option + click slide number
To move between slides in a given view	Press Command + up arrow or Command + down arrow
To move between the Outline, Slide, and Notes views of a particular slide	Press Command + left arrow or Command + right arrow

Table B-5.   Outline View

To do this	Do this
Collapse subheads	Press Command + K
Demote headings	Press Command + Tab
Expand subheads	Press Command + E
Move left	Press Command + [
Move right	Press Command +]
New heading	Press Command + H
New heading left	Press Command + L
New heading right	Press Command + R
Collapse subheads	Double-click the higher-level icon
Partially expand a collapsed heading	Double-click the collapsed level icon
Compress subheads	Press Command + double-click the higher-level icon
Move cursor to top of outline	Click the outline icon
Fully expand a collapsed heading	Press Option + double-click the higher level icon

Table B-6.   Running a Slide Show

To do this	Press
Forward by a layer	Down arrow, or Right arrow, or N, or Command + 3, or Click
Forward to end of slide	Shift + down arrow, or Shift + right arrow, or Shift + N, or Shift + Command + 3, or Shift + click
Backward by a slide	Up arrow, or Left arrow, or P, or Delete/Backspace, or Command + 2, or Double-click
Backward by a layer	Shift + up arrow, or Shift + left arrow, or Shift + P, or Shift + Delete/Backspace, or Shift + Command + 2, or Shift + double-click
Last layer of first slide	Command + H, or Command + 1, or Command + left arrow
First layer of first slide	Shift + Command + H, or Shift + Command + 1, or Shift + Command + left arrow
Last layer of last slide	Command + 4, or Command + right arrow
First layer of last slide	Shift + Command + 4, or Shift + Command + right arrow
Last layer of selected slide	Type slide number, then press Return or Enter

(continued)

Table B-6. Running a Slide Show *(continued)*

To do this	Press
First layer of selected slide	Press Shift, type slide number, then press Return or Enter
Back to slide on screen before the "Go to" command	` (accent grave key in upper right of keyboard)
Pause or continue the auto-advance feature. Any other slide command also continues after a pause	Spacebar + triple-click
Toggle mouse cursor on and off	A
Toggle between automatic and manual slide advance	Shift + =
Blank screen	B, or , (comma)
Set screen to black	. (period)
Exit from slide show	- (hyphen), or Command + . (period), or Command + Q

Table B-7.   Drawing and Working with Graphics

To do this	Press
Align objects	Command + L
Align to grid	Command + H
Grid snap on	Command + Y
Group	Command + G
Ungroup	Command + U
Regroup	Command + R
Send backward	Command + -
Send forward	Command + =
Send to back	Command + B
Send to front	Command + F
To resize text block	Drag
To resize object from center	Option + drag
To select and resize object quickly	Command + drag
To resize object proportionally	Shift + drag
To resize object from center proportionally	Shift + Option + drag
Select pointer tool	Command + Spacebar
To fit a text block within a graphic	Double-click the graphic with the text tool
To resize a text block	Press Command + drag the text block with the text tool

Table B-8.   Working in the Data Sheet

To do this	Do this
To establish the nearest plotted data set as the target chart; then move between manual selection and target area	Click toggle box icon in the menu bar
To move to the next column within the selected area	Press Tab
To move to the next row within the selected area	Press Return
To move between the currently plotted and the last manually selected value sets	Click the toggle box icon in the menu bar
To move through plotted value sets	Click the up or down arrow icon in the menu bar
To move through columns	Press the left or right arrow key
To move through rows	Press the up or down arrow key

Table B-9.   Working with Charts and Tables

To do this	Do this
Resize a table or chart	Drag any handle
Select a subset of a selected area	Double-click
Select a subset of a subselection	Triple-click (if you haven't selected a subset) or double-click (if you have already selected a subset)
Select another set at the same level as the current selection	Press Option + click

Table B-10. Running a Slide Show (Manual)

To do this	Do this
Move forward to the next slide	Click, or press down arrow key
Move forward one or more slides	Press the down arrow key one or more times
Back up to the previous slide	Double-click, or press the up arrow key
Back up one or more slides	Press the up arrow key one or more times
Cancel the slide show	Command + . (period), or Press any letter or number, or Press the left or right arrow key

Table B-11. Running a Slide Show (Automatic)

To do this	Do this
Override the user-defined delay and move immediately to the next slide	Click, or Press the down arrow key
Move ahead more than one slide	Press the down arrow key more than once
Pause on the current slide, then resume	Press the Spacebar, then press it again, or press and hold down the mouse button, then release it
Back up one slide and pause, then resume	Double-click, then click again, or Press the up arrow key, then press the down arrow key to resume
Back up any number of slides and pause, then resume	Press the up arrow key any number of times, then press the down arrow key once to resume
Cancel the slide show	Press Command + . (period), or Press any letter or number, or Press the left or right arrow key

Index

About the Authors

Kate Hatsy Thompson is a writer, consultant, trainer, and graphic design-er specializing in electronic publishing and desktop presentations. She also conducts workshops on graphic design for desktop publishing, and on writing, designing, and editing newsletters. Her articles have appeared in *Publish* magazine, and she is the co-author of several computer books published by Brady Books.

Keith J. Thompson is a freelance writer for several magazines including *MacWeek* and *MacWorld* as well as the author of two other books on the Macintosh. He is president of Datalex Corporation in Amherst, NH, a training and consulting company for Macintosh and DOS-based personal computers.